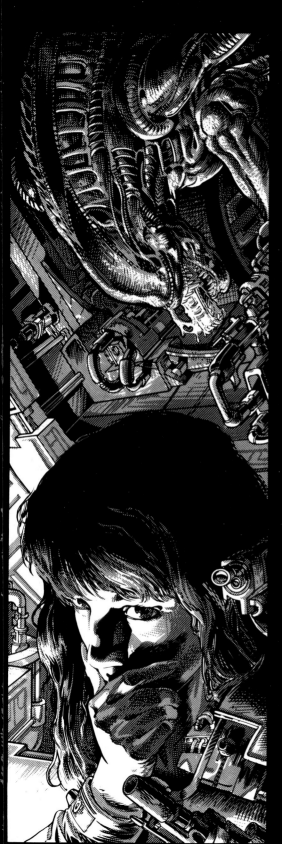

Ten years later...

A L I E N S ™

written by
MARK VERHEIDEN

illustrated by
MARK A. NELSON

lettered by
WILLIE SCHUBERT

INSPIRED BY THE DESIGNS AND CREATIONS OF H.R. GIGER
Based on the characters and events in theTwentieth Century Fox film

special thanks to:
Kathleen Aiken   Tom Baxa   Jeff Butler   Bob Dvorak   Jeff Easley   Scott Hill
Laurie Jenkins   Anitia Nelson   Pam North   Ron Randall   Gil Rocha   Mike Schneider

publisher
MIKE RICHARDSON

editor
RANDY STRADLEY

operations director
NEIL HANKERSON

production manager
CHRIS CHALENOR

production
JIM BRADRICK   JIM SPIVEY   JACK POLLOCK

controller
BRAD HORN

administrative assistants
DEBBIE BYRD   JERRY PROSSER

ALIENS BOOK ONE
ISBN 1 85286 276 9

Published by Titan Books Ltd,
42 - 44 Dolben Street,
London SE1 0UP
Copyright © 1994 Twentieth Century Fox Film Corporation

5 7 9 10 8 6 4

Printed and bound by Hartnolls Ltd, Bodmin, Cornwall.

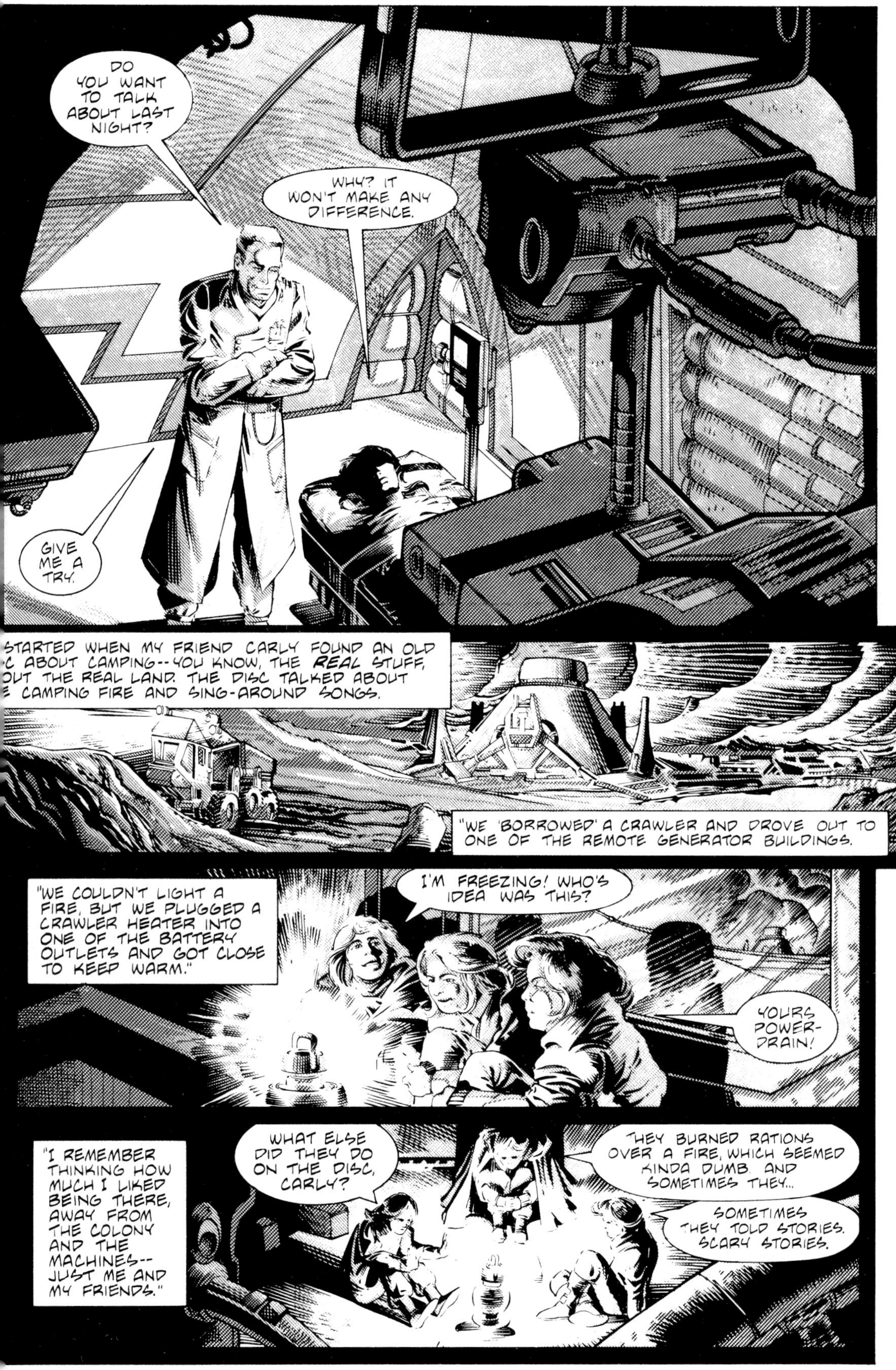
DO YOU WANT TO TALK ABOUT LAST NIGHT?
WHY? IT WON'T MAKE ANY DIFFERENCE.
GIVE ME A TRY.
STARTED WHEN MY FRIEND CARLY FOUND AN OLD C ABOUT CAMPING--YOU KNOW, THE REAL STUFF, OUT THE REAL LAND. THE DISC TALKED ABOUT E CAMPING FIRE AND SING-AROUND SONGS.
"WE 'BORROWED' A CRAWLER AND DROVE OUT TO ONE OF THE REMOTE GENERATOR BUILDINGS.
"WE COULDN'T LIGHT A FIRE, BUT WE PLUGGED A CRAWLER HEATER INTO ONE OF THE BATTERY OUTLETS AND GOT CLOSE TO KEEP WARM."
I'M FREEZING! WHO'S IDEA WAS THIS?
YOURS POWER-DRAIN!
"I REMEMBER THINKING HOW MUCH I LIKED BEING THERE, AWAY FROM THE COLONY AND THE MACHINES--JUST ME AND MY FRIENDS."
WHAT ELSE DID THEY DO ON THE DISC, CARLY?
THEY BURNED RATIONS OVER A FIRE, WHICH SEEMED KINDA DUMB. AND SOMETIMES THEY...
SOMETIMES THEY TOLD STORIES. SCARY STORIES.

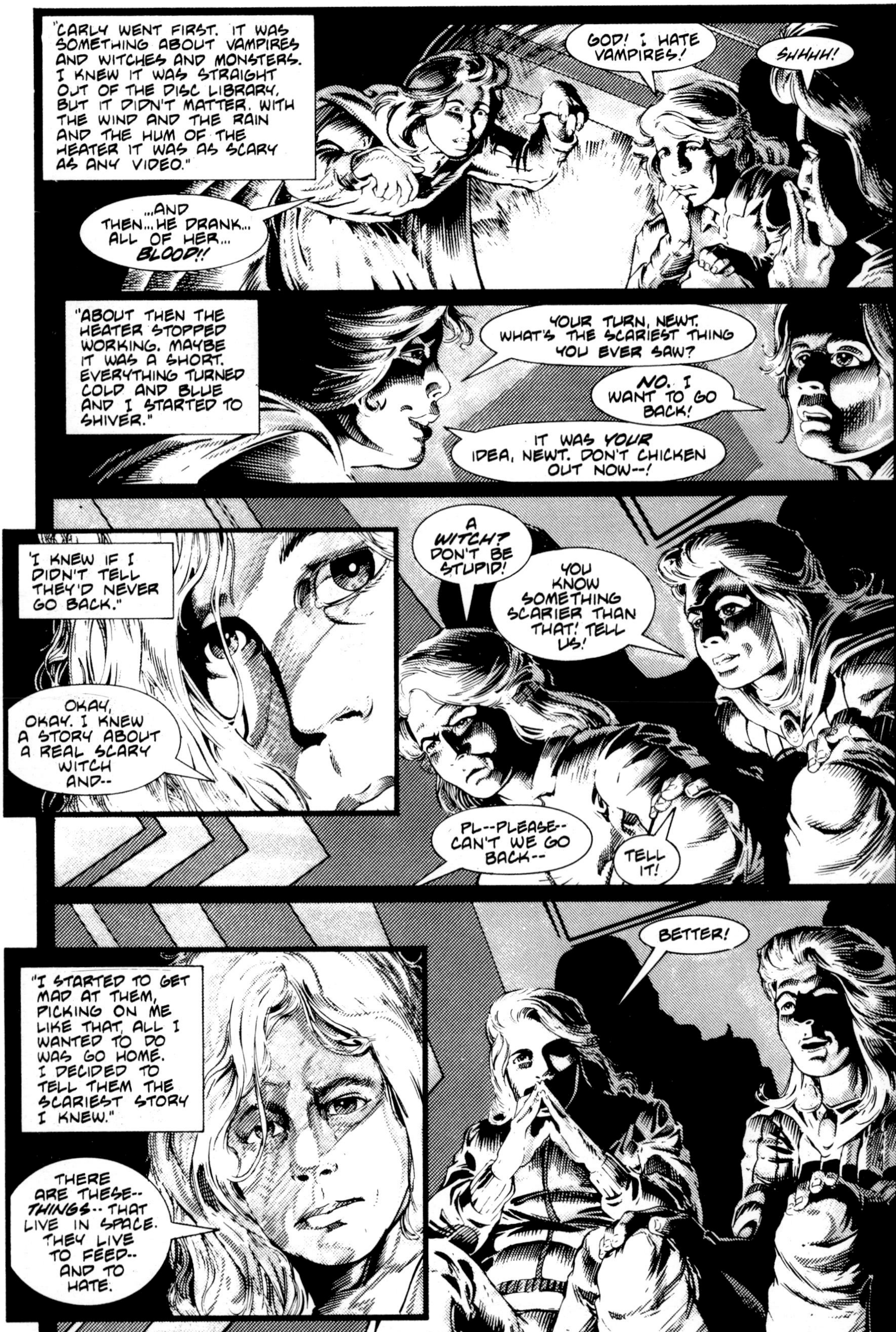
"CARLY WENT FIRST. IT WAS SOMETHING ABOUT VAMPIRES AND WITCHES AND MONSTERS. I KNEW IT WAS STRAIGHT OUT OF THE DISC LIBRARY, BUT IT DIDN'T MATTER. WITH THE WIND AND THE RAIN AND THE HUM OF THE HEATER IT WAS AS SCARY AS ANY VIDEO."
GOD! I HATE VAMPIRES!
SHHHH!
...AND THEN...HE DRANK... ALL OF HER... BLOOD!!
"ABOUT THEN THE HEATER STOPPED WORKING. MAYBE IT WAS A SHORT. EVERYTHING TURNED COLD AND BLUE AND I STARTED TO SHIVER."
YOUR TURN, NEWT. WHAT'S THE SCARIEST THING YOU EVER SAW?
NO. I WANT TO GO BACK!
IT WAS YOUR IDEA, NEWT. DON'T CHICKEN OUT NOW--!
"I KNEW IF I DIDN'T TELL THEY'D NEVER GO BACK."
OKAY, OKAY. I KNEW A STORY ABOUT A REAL SCARY WITCH AND--
A WITCH? DON'T BE STUPID!
YOU KNOW SOMETHING SCARIER THAN THAT! TELL US!
PL--PLEASE-- CAN'T WE GO BACK--
TELL IT!
"I STARTED TO GET MAD AT THEM, PICKING ON ME LIKE THAT. ALL I WANTED TO DO WAS GO HOME. I DECIDED TO TELL THEM THE SCARIEST STORY I KNEW."
THERE ARE THESE-- THINGS-- THAT LIVE IN SPACE. THEY LIVE TO FEED-- AND TO HATE.
BETTER!

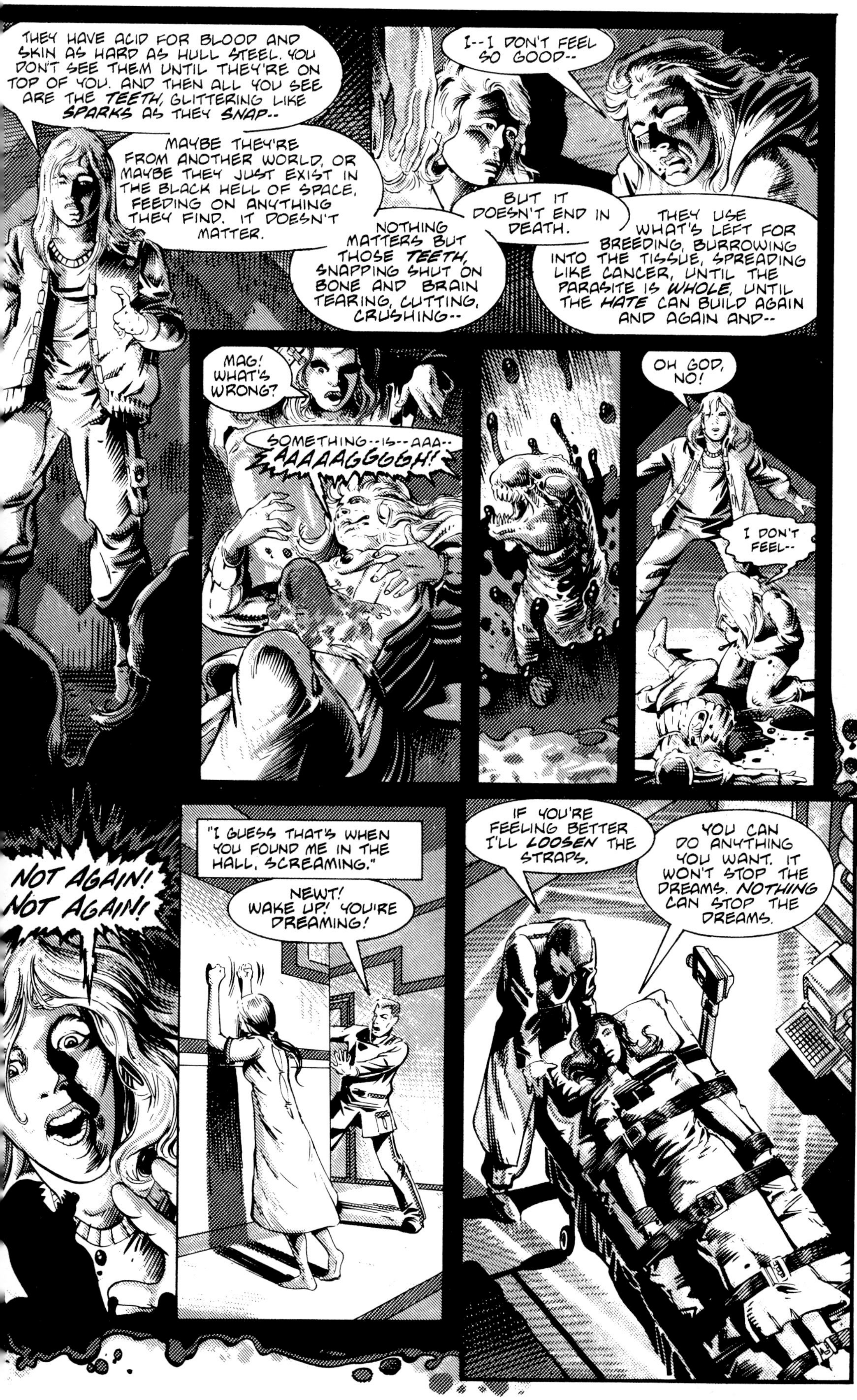
THEY HAVE ACID FOR BLOOD AND SKIN AS HARD AS HULL STEEL. YOU DON'T SEE THEM UNTIL THEY'RE ON TOP OF YOU. AND THEN ALL YOU SEE ARE THE TEETH, GLITTERING LIKE SPARKS AS THEY SNAP--
MAYBE THEY'RE FROM ANOTHER WORLD, OR MAYBE THEY JUST EXIST IN THE BLACK HELL OF SPACE, FEEDING ON ANYTHING THEY FIND. IT DOESN'T MATTER.
NOTHING MATTERS BUT THOSE TEETH, SNAPPING SHUT ON BONE AND BRAIN TEARING, CUTTING, CRUSHING--
I--I DON'T FEEL SO GOOD--
BUT IT DOESN'T END IN DEATH.
THEY USE WHAT'S LEFT FOR BREEDING, BURROWING INTO THE TISSUE, SPREADING LIKE CANCER, UNTIL THE PARASITE IS WHOLE, UNTIL THE HATE CAN BUILD AGAIN AND AGAIN AND--
MAG! WHAT'S WRONG?
SOMETHING--IS--AAA--
EAAAAAGGGGH!
OH GOD, NO!
I DON'T FEEL--
NOT AGAIN! NOT AGAIN!
"I GUESS THAT'S WHEN YOU FOUND ME IN THE HALL, SCREAMING."
NEWT! WAKE UP! YOU'RE DREAMING!
IF YOU'RE FEELING BETTER I'LL LOOSEN THE STRAPS.
YOU CAN DO ANYTHING YOU WANT. IT WON'T STOP THE DREAMS. NOTHING CAN STOP THE DREAMS.

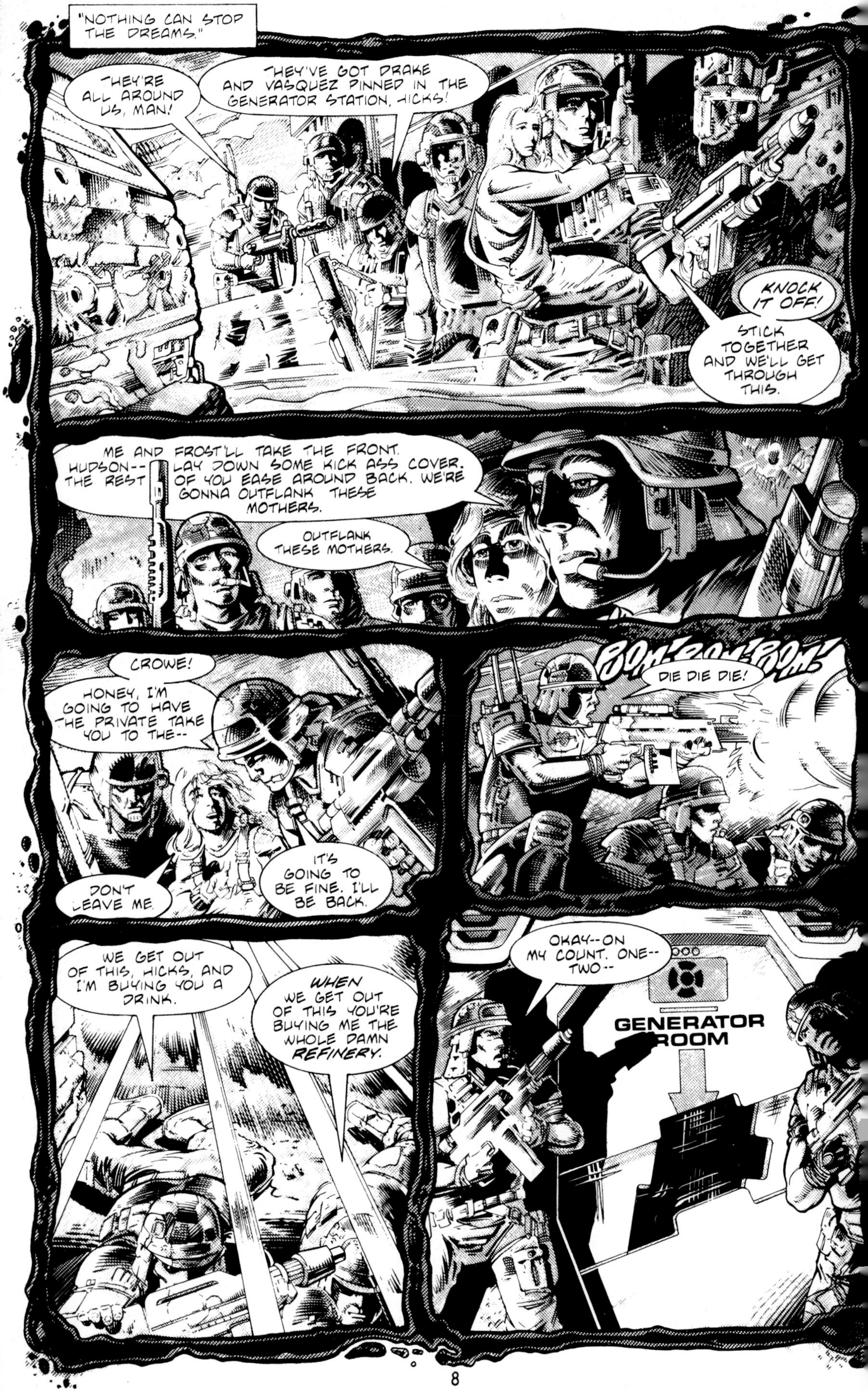
"NOTHING CAN STOP THE DREAMS."
THEY'RE ALL AROUND US, MAN!
THEY'VE GOT DRAKE AND VASQUEZ PINNED IN THE GENERATOR STATION, HICKS!
KNOCK IT OFF!
STICK TOGETHER AND WE'LL GET THROUGH THIS.
ME AND FROST'LL TAKE THE FRONT. HUDSON-- LAY DOWN SOME KICK ASS COVER. THE REST OF YOU EASE AROUND BACK. WE'RE GONNA OUTFLANK THESE MOTHERS.
OUTFLANK THESE MOTHERS.
CROWE!
HONEY, I'M GOING TO HAVE THE PRIVATE TAKE YOU TO THE--
DON'T LEAVE ME.
IT'S GOING TO BE FINE. I'LL BE BACK.
BOOM! BOOM! BOOM!
DIE DIE DIE!
WE GET OUT OF THIS, HICKS, AND I'M BUYING YOU A DRINK.
WHEN WE GET OUT OF THIS YOU'RE BUYING ME THE WHOLE DAMN REFINERY.
OKAY--ON MY COUNT. ONE-- TWO--
GENERATOR ROOM

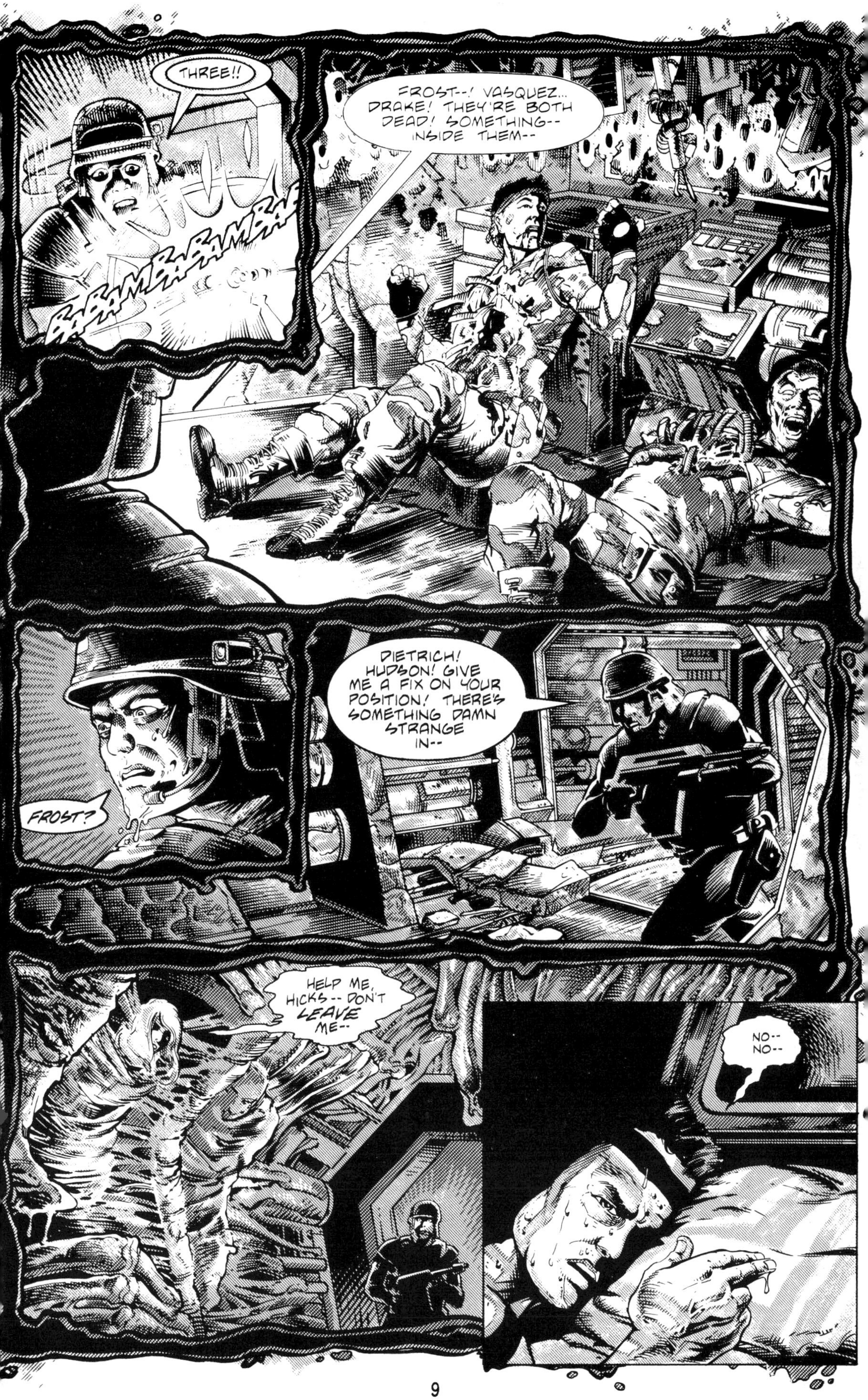
THREE!!
BRAMBRAMBRAM
FROST--! VASQUEZ... DRAKE! THEY'RE BOTH DEAD! SOMETHING-- INSIDE THEM--
FROST?
DIETRICH! HUDSON! GIVE ME A FIX ON YOUR POSITION! THERE'S SOMETHING DAMN STRANGE IN--
HELP ME, HICKS -- DON'T LEAVE ME--
NO-- NO--

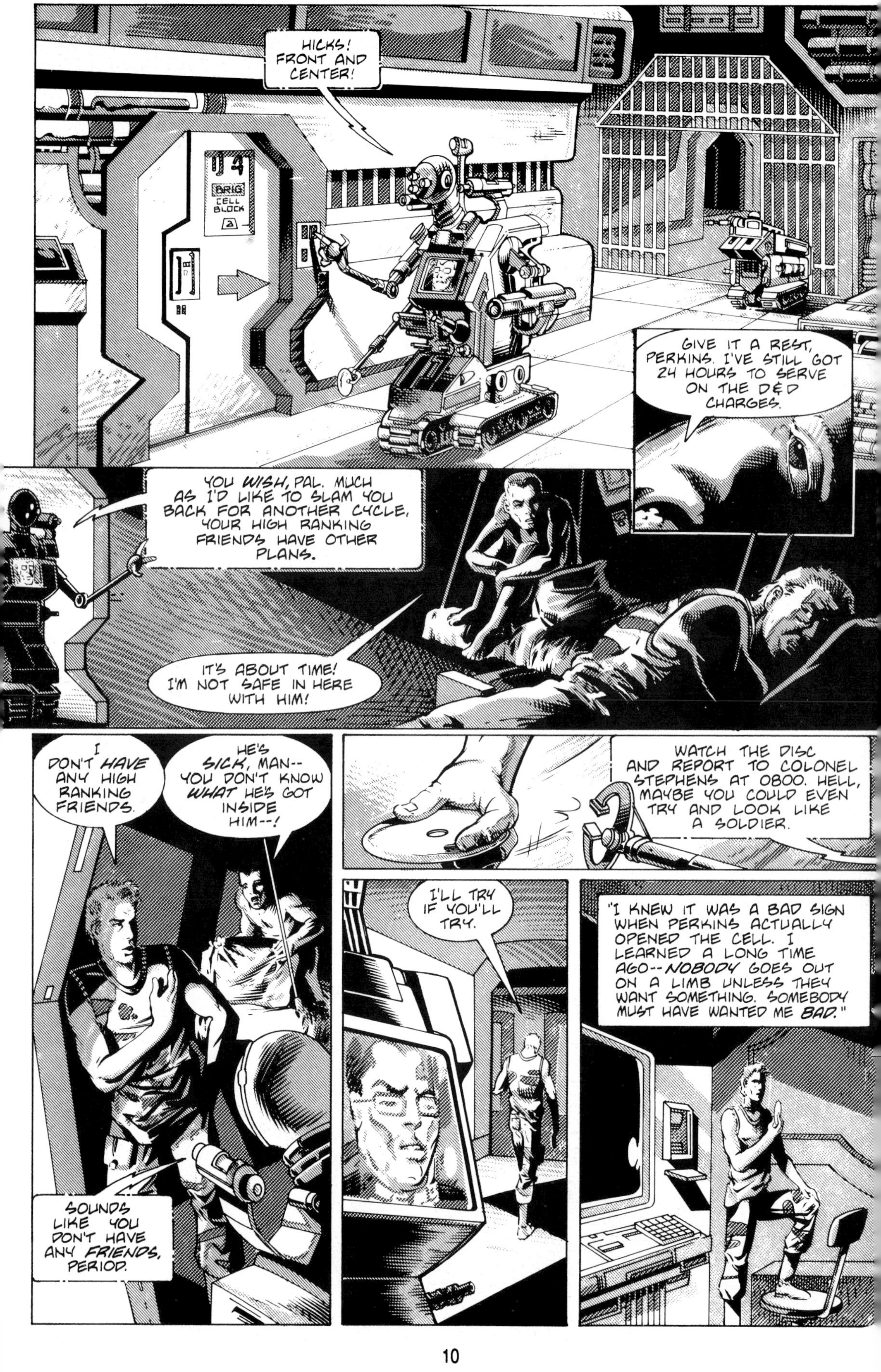

BRIG
CELL BLOCK
HICKS! FRONT AND CENTER!
GIVE IT A REST, PERKINS. I'VE STILL GOT 24 HOURS TO SERVE ON THE D&D CHARGES.
YOU WISH, PAL. MUCH AS I'D LIKE TO SLAM YOU BACK FOR ANOTHER CYCLE, YOUR HIGH RANKING FRIENDS HAVE OTHER PLANS.
IT'S ABOUT TIME! I'M NOT SAFE IN HERE WITH HIM!
I DON'T HAVE ANY HIGH RANKING FRIENDS.
HE'S SICK, MAN-- YOU DON'T KNOW WHAT HE'S GOT INSIDE HIM--!
SOUNDS LIKE YOU DON'T HAVE ANY FRIENDS, PERIOD.
WATCH THE DISC AND REPORT TO COLONEL STEPHENS AT 0800. HELL, MAYBE YOU COULD EVEN TRY AND LOOK LIKE A SOLDIER.
I'LL TRY IF YOU'LL TRY.
"I KNEW IT WAS A BAD SIGN WHEN PERKINS ACTUALLY OPENED THE CELL. I LEARNED A LONG TIME AGO--NOBODY GOES OUT ON A LIMB UNLESS THEY WANT SOMETHING. SOMEBODY MUST HAVE WANTED ME BAD."

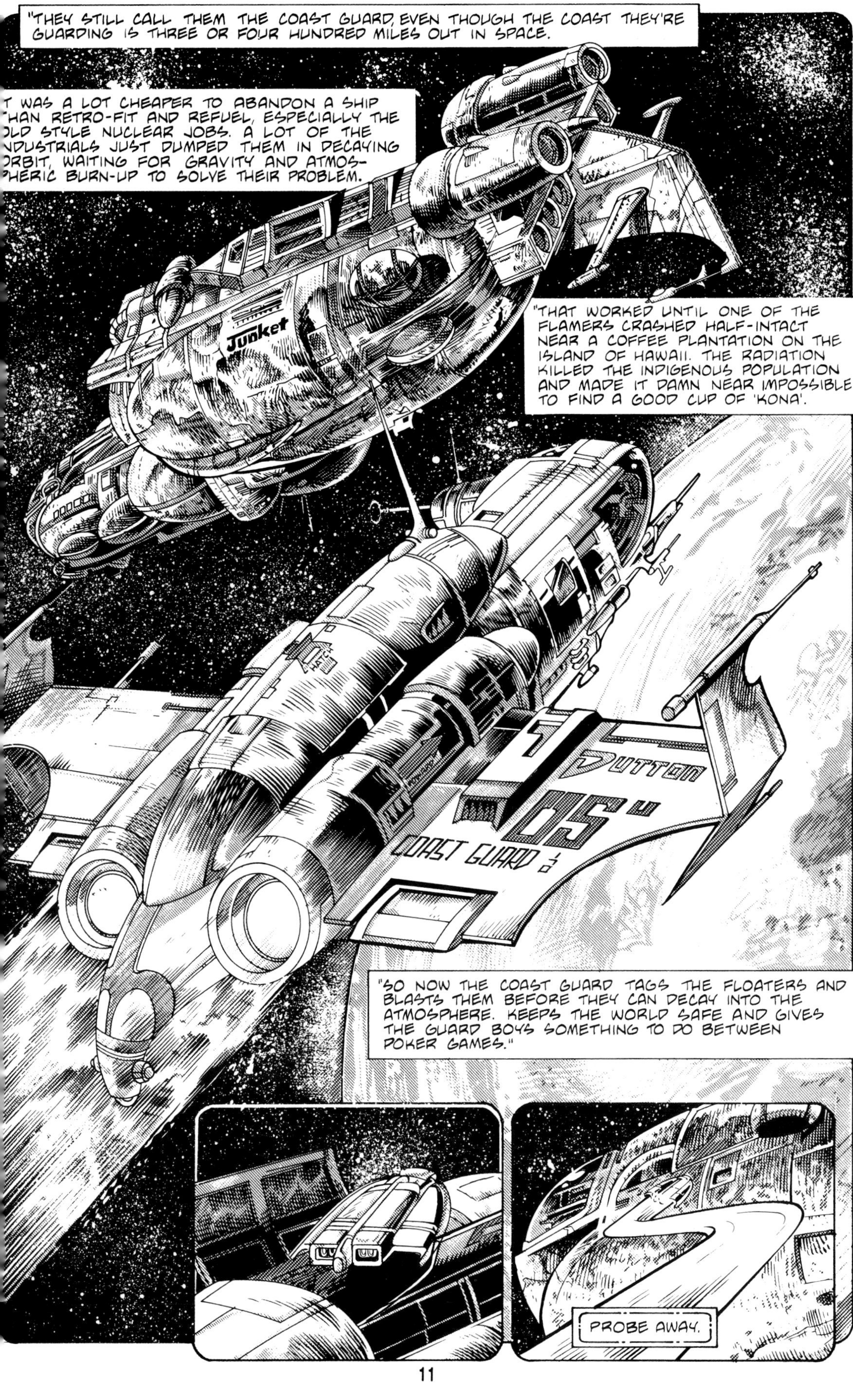
"THEY STILL CALL THEM THE COAST GUARD, EVEN THOUGH THE COAST THEY'RE GUARDING IS THREE OR FOUR HUNDRED MILES OUT IN SPACE.
T WAS A LOT CHEAPER TO ABANDON A SHIP HAN RETRO-FIT AND REFUEL, ESPECIALLY THE LD STYLE NUCLEAR JOBS. A LOT OF THE NDUSTRIALS JUST DUMPED THEM IN DECAYING RBIT, WAITING FOR GRAVITY AND ATMOS-PHERIC BURN-UP TO SOLVE THEIR PROBLEM.
Junket
"THAT WORKED UNTIL ONE OF THE FLAMERS CRASHED HALF-INTACT NEAR A COFFEE PLANTATION ON THE ISLAND OF HAWAII. THE RADIATION KILLED THE INDIGENOUS POPULATION AND MADE IT DAMN NEAR IMPOSSIBLE TO FIND A GOOD CUP OF 'KONA'.
DUTTON
05
COAST GUARD
"SO NOW THE COAST GUARD TAGS THE FLOATERS AND BLASTS THEM BEFORE THEY CAN DECAY INTO THE ATMOSPHERE. KEEPS THE WORLD SAFE AND GIVES THE GUARD BOYS SOMETHING TO DO BETWEEN POKER GAMES."
PROBE AWAY.

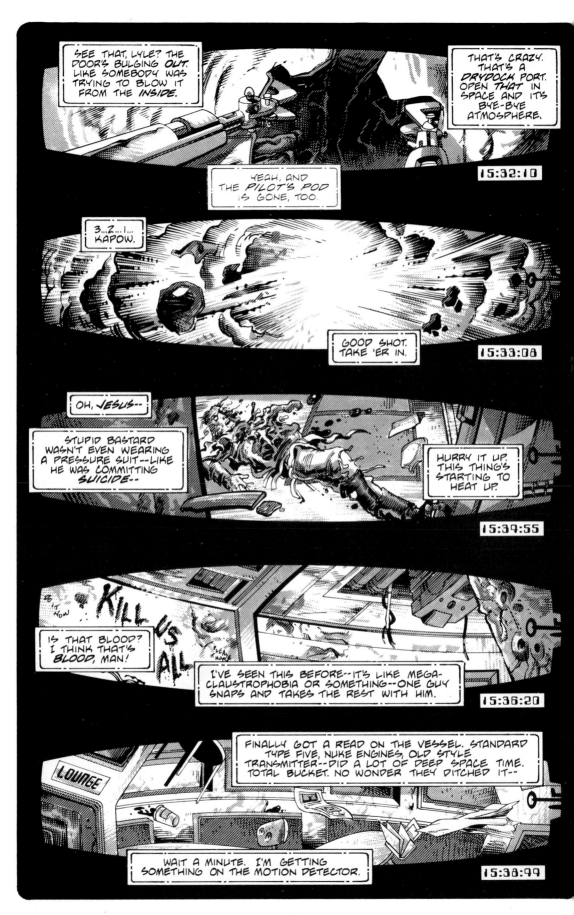

SEE THAT, LYLE? THE DOOR'S BULGING *OUT.* LIKE SOMEBODY WAS TRYING TO BLOW IT FROM THE *INSIDE.*

THAT'S CRAZY. THAT'S A *DRYDOCK* PORT. OPEN *THAT* IN SPACE AND IT'S BYE-BYE ATMOSPHERE.

15:32:10

YEAH, AND THE *PILOT'S POD* IS GONE, TOO.

3...2...1... KAPOW.

GOOD SHOT. TAKE 'ER IN.

15:33:08

OH, *JESUS*--

STUPID BASTARD WASN'T EVEN WEARING A PRESSURE SUIT--LIKE HE WAS COMMITTING *SUICIDE*--

HURRY IT UP. THIS THING'S STARTING TO HEAT UP.

15:34:55

IS THAT BLOOD? I THINK THAT'S *BLOOD,* MAN!

I'VE SEEN THIS BEFORE--IT'S LIKE MEGA-CLAUSTROPHOBIA OR SOMETHING--ONE GUY SNAPS AND TAKES THE REST WITH HIM.

15:36:20

FINALLY GOT A READ ON THE VESSEL. STANDARD TYPE FIVE, NUKE ENGINES, OLD STYLE TRANSMITTER--DID A LOT OF DEEP SPACE TIME. TOTAL BUCKET. NO WONDER THEY DITCHED IT--

WAIT A MINUTE. I'M GETTING SOMETHING ON THE MOTION DETECTOR.

15:38:99

12

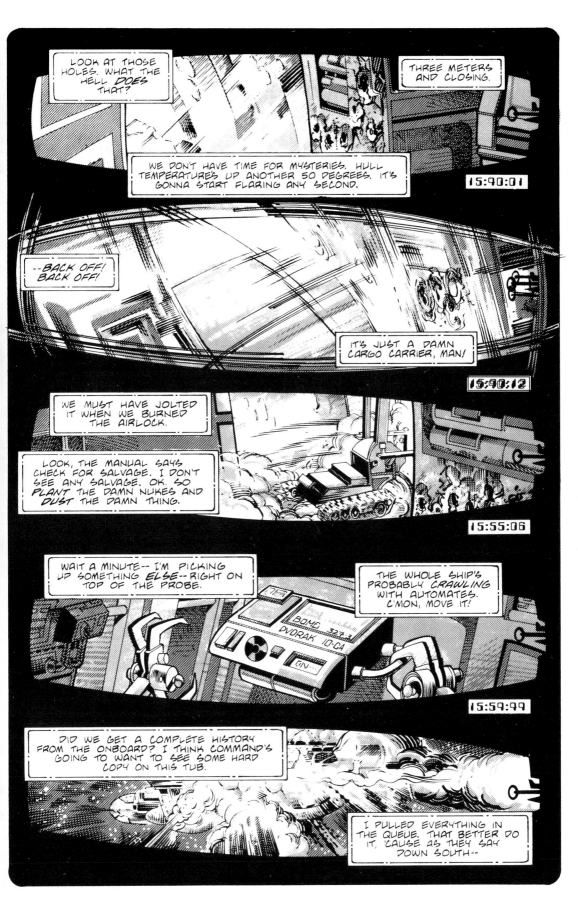

LOOK AT THOSE HOLES. WHAT THE HELL *DOES* THAT?

THREE METERS AND CLOSING.

WE DON'T HAVE TIME FOR MYSTERIES. HULL TEMPERATURE'S UP ANOTHER 50 DEGREES. IT'S GONNA START FLARING ANY SECOND.

15:40:01

--BACK OFF! BACK OFF!

IT'S JUST A DAMN CARGO CARRIER, MAN!

15:40:12

WE MUST HAVE JOLTED IT WHEN WE BURNED THE AIRLOCK.

LOOK, THE MANUAL SAYS CHECK FOR SALVAGE. I DON'T SEE ANY SALVAGE. OK. SO *PLANT* THE DAMN NUKES AND *DUST* THE DAMN THING.

15:55:06

WAIT A MINUTE-- I'M PICKING UP SOMETHING *ELSE*-- RIGHT ON TOP OF THE PROBE.

THE WHOLE SHIP'S PROBABLY *CRAWLING* WITH AUTOMATES. C'MON, MOVE IT!

BOMB 327.3 DVORAK 10-CA

ON

15:59:49

DID WE GET A COMPLETE HISTORY FROM THE ONBOARD? I THINK COMMAND'S GOING TO WANT TO SEE SOME HARD COPY ON THIS TUB.

I PULLED EVERYTHING IN THE QUEUE. THAT BETTER DO IT, 'CAUSE AS THEY SAY DOWN SOUTH--

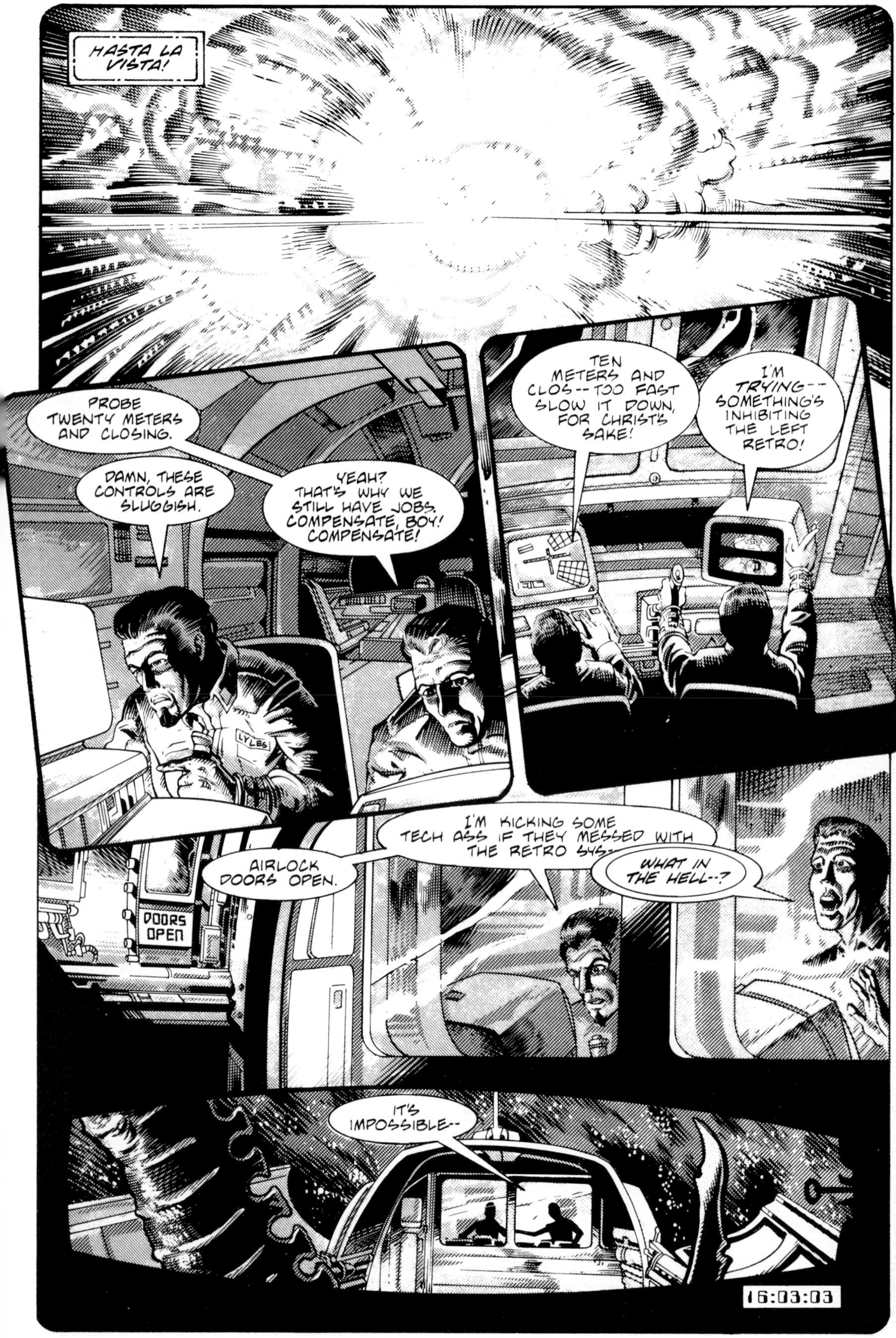
HASTA LA VISTA!
PROBE TWENTY METERS AND CLOSING.
DAMN, THESE CONTROLS ARE SLUGGISH.
YEAH? THAT'S WHY WE STILL HAVE JOBS. COMPENSATE, BOY! COMPENSATE!
LYLES
TEN METERS AND CLOS--TOO FAST SLOW IT DOWN, FOR CHRIST'S SAKE!
I'M TRYING--SOMETHING'S INHIBITING THE LEFT RETRO!
AIRLOCK DOORS OPEN.
DOORS OPEN
I'M KICKING SOME TECH ASS IF THEY MESSED WITH THE RETRO SYS--
WHAT IN THE HELL--?
IT'S IMPOSSIBLE--
16:03:03

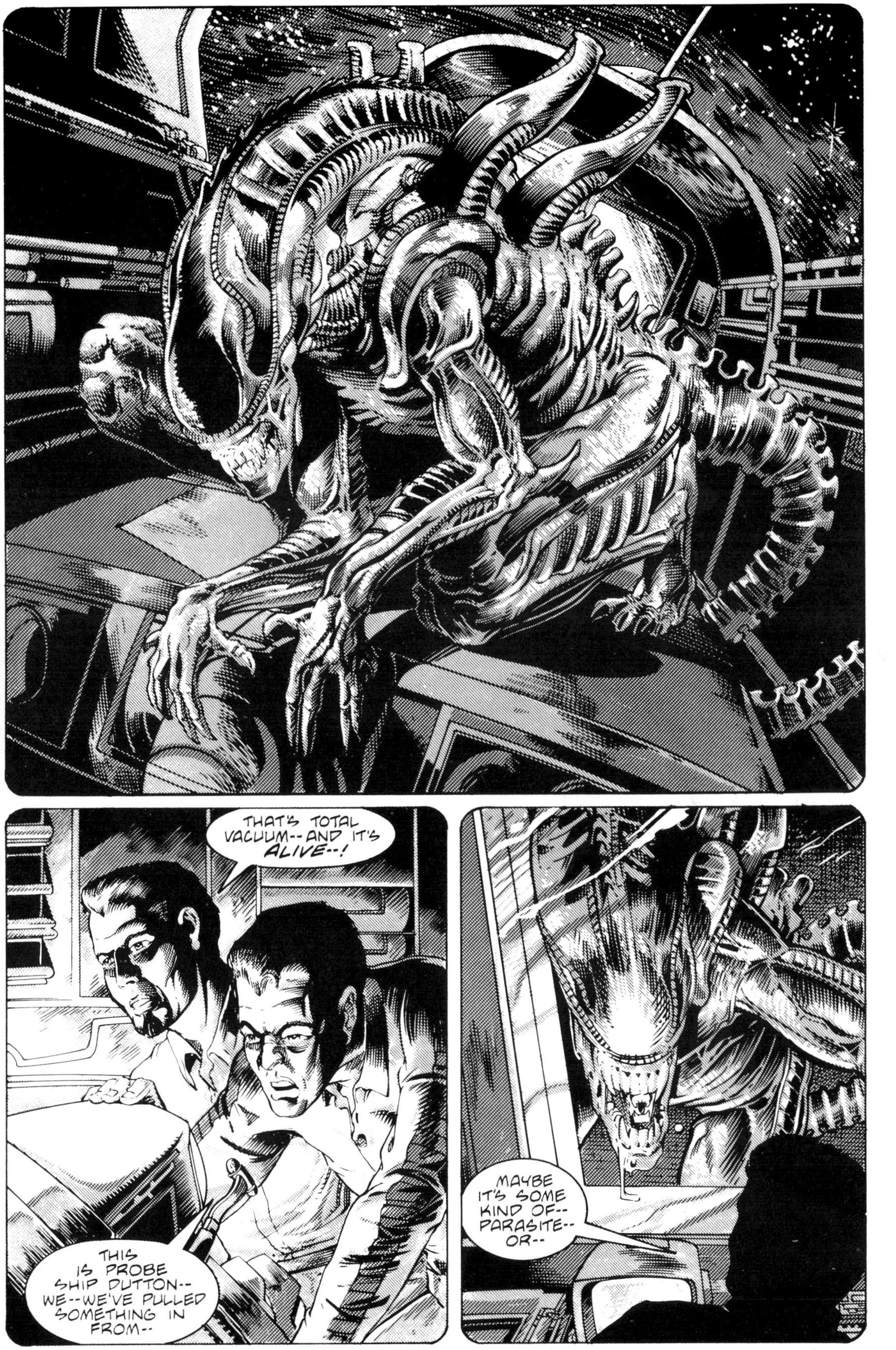
THAT'S TOTAL VACUUM--AND IT'S ALIVE--!
THIS IS PROBE SHIP DUTTON--WE--WE'VE PULLED SOMETHING IN FROM--
MAYBE IT'S SOME KIND OF--PARASITE--OR--

THAT'S NO PARASITE--

--OH MY GOD!

IT'S GOING TO--

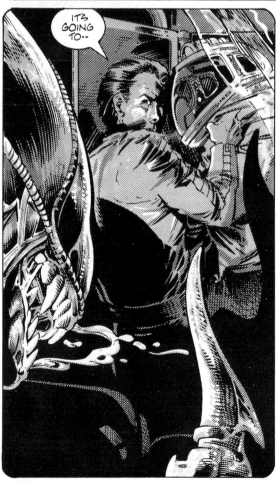

GAHHHHYYYY--*

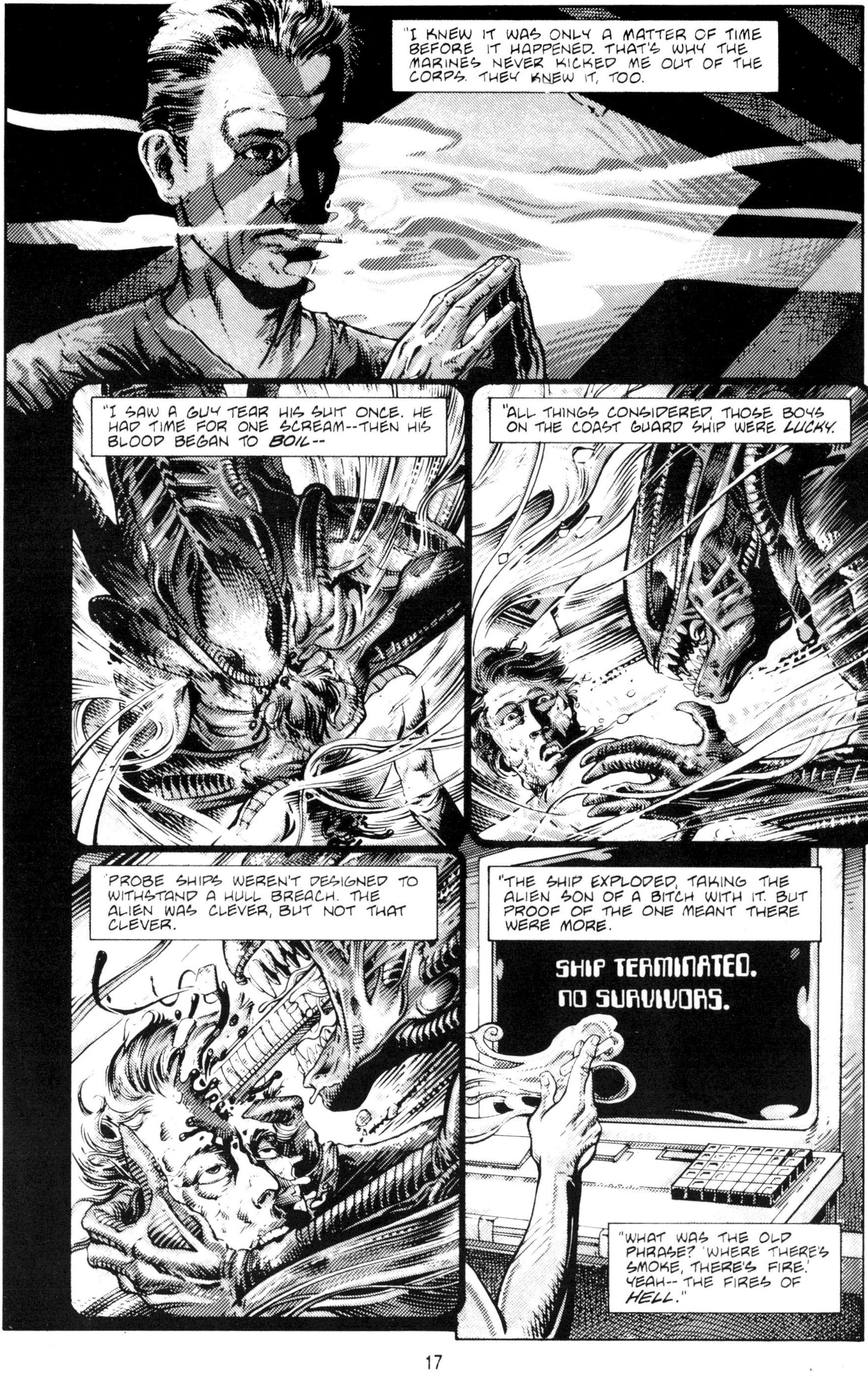

"I KNEW IT WAS ONLY A MATTER OF TIME BEFORE IT HAPPENED. THAT'S WHY THE MARINES NEVER KICKED ME OUT OF THE CORPS. THEY KNEW IT, TOO.
"I SAW A GUY TEAR HIS SUIT ONCE. HE HAD TIME FOR ONE SCREAM--THEN HIS BLOOD BEGAN TO BOIL--
"ALL THINGS CONSIDERED, THOSE BOYS ON THE COAST GUARD SHIP WERE LUCKY.
"PROBE SHIPS WEREN'T DESIGNED TO WITHSTAND A HULL BREACH. THE ALIEN WAS CLEVER, BUT NOT THAT CLEVER.
"THE SHIP EXPLODED, TAKING THE ALIEN SON OF A BITCH WITH IT. BUT PROOF OF THE ONE MEANT THERE WERE MORE.
SHIP TERMINATED.
NO SURVIVORS.
"WHAT WAS THE OLD PHRASE? 'WHERE THERE'S SMOKE, THERE'S FIRE.' YEAH-- THE FIRES OF HELL."

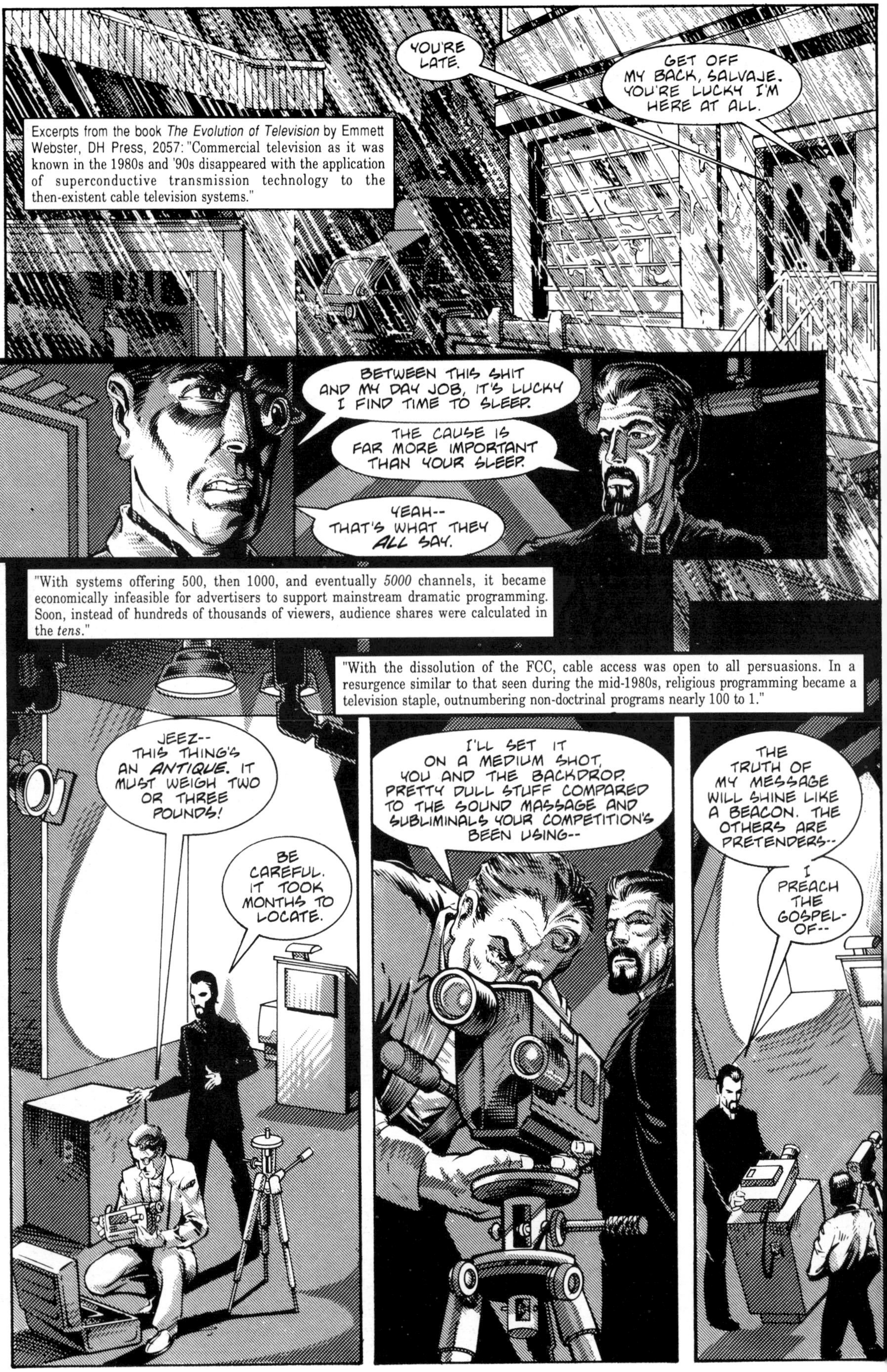
Excerpts from the book *The Evolution of Television* by Emmett Webster, DH Press, 2057: "Commercial television as it was known in the 1980s and '90s disappeared with the application of superconductive transmission technology to the then-existent cable television systems."
YOU'RE LATE.
GET OFF MY BACK, SALVAJE. YOU'RE LUCKY I'M HERE AT ALL.
BETWEEN THIS SHIT AND MY DAY JOB, IT'S LUCKY I FIND TIME TO SLEEP.
THE CAUSE IS FAR MORE IMPORTANT THAN YOUR SLEEP.
YEAH-- THAT'S WHAT THEY *ALL* SAY.
"With systems offering 500, then 1000, and eventually *5000* channels, it became economically infeasible for advertisers to support mainstream dramatic programming. Soon, instead of hundreds of thousands of viewers, audience shares were calculated in the *tens*."
"With the dissolution of the FCC, cable access was open to all persuasions. In a resurgence similar to that seen during the mid-1980s, religious programming became a television staple, outnumbering non-doctrinal programs nearly 100 to 1."
JEEZ-- THIS THING'S AN *ANTIQUE*. IT MUST WEIGH TWO OR THREE POUNDS!
BE CAREFUL. IT TOOK MONTHS TO LOCATE.
I'LL SET IT ON A MEDIUM SHOT, YOU AND THE BACKDROP. PRETTY DULL STUFF COMPARED TO THE SOUND MASSAGE AND SUBLIMINALS YOUR COMPETITION'S BEEN USING--
THE TRUTH OF MY MESSAGE WILL SHINE LIKE A BEACON. THE OTHERS ARE PRETENDERS--
I PREACH THE GOSPEL OF--

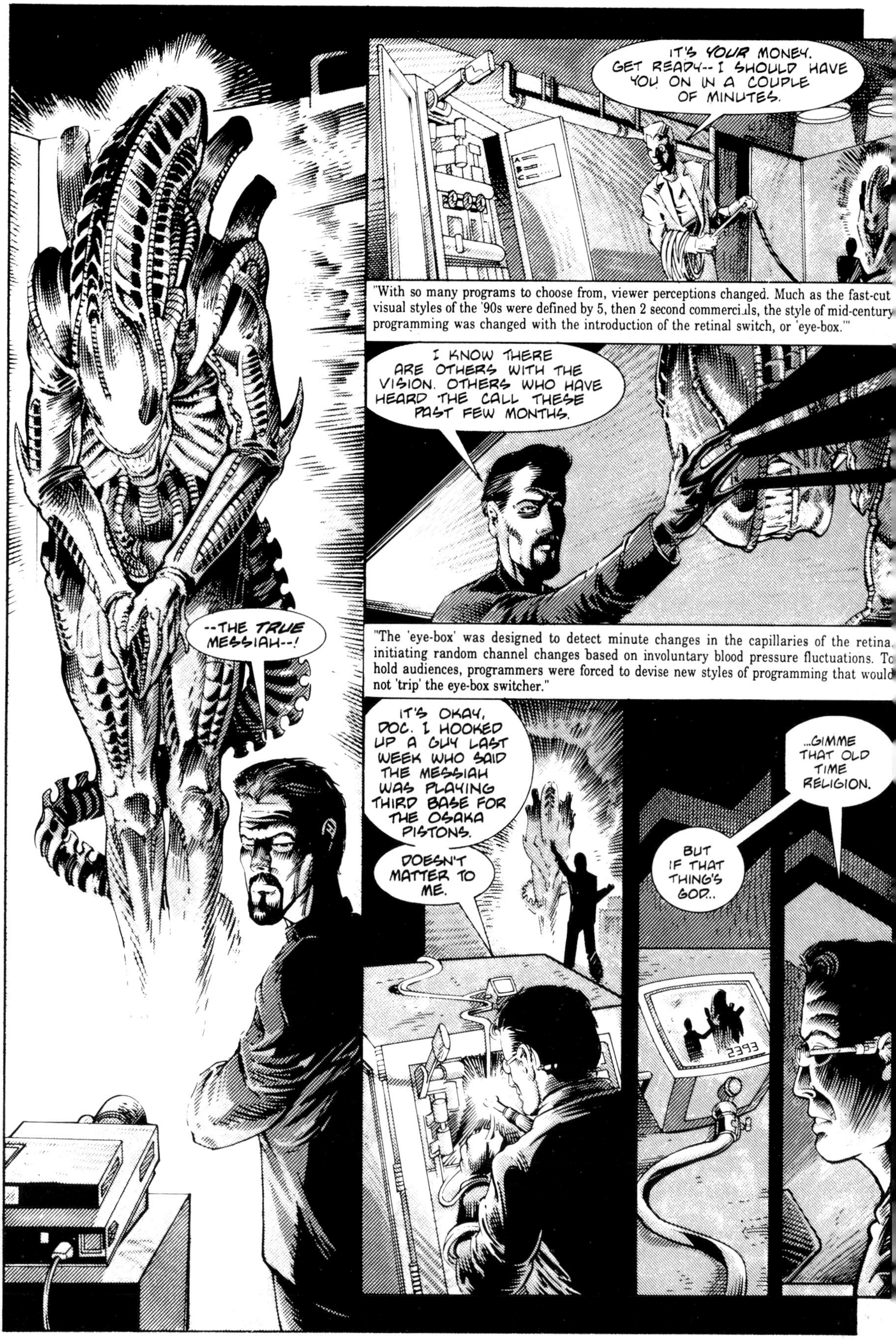
--THE TRUE MESSIAH--!
IT'S YOUR MONEY. GET READY-- I SHOULD HAVE YOU ON IN A COUPLE OF MINUTES.
"With so many programs to choose from, viewer perceptions changed. Much as the fast-cut visual styles of the '90s were defined by 5, then 2 second commercials, the style of mid-century programming was changed with the introduction of the retinal switch, or 'eye-box.'"
I KNOW THERE ARE OTHERS WITH THE VISION. OTHERS WHO HAVE HEARD THE CALL THESE PAST FEW MONTHS.
"The 'eye-box' was designed to detect minute changes in the capillaries of the retina, initiating random channel changes based on involuntary blood pressure fluctuations. To hold audiences, programmers were forced to devise new styles of programming that would not 'trip' the eye-box switcher."
IT'S OKAY, DOC. I HOOKED UP A GUY LAST WEEK WHO SAID THE MESSIAH WAS PLAYING THIRD BASE FOR THE OSAKA PISTONS.
DOESN'T MATTER TO ME.
BUT IF THAT THING'S GOD...
...GIMME THAT OLD TIME RELIGION.

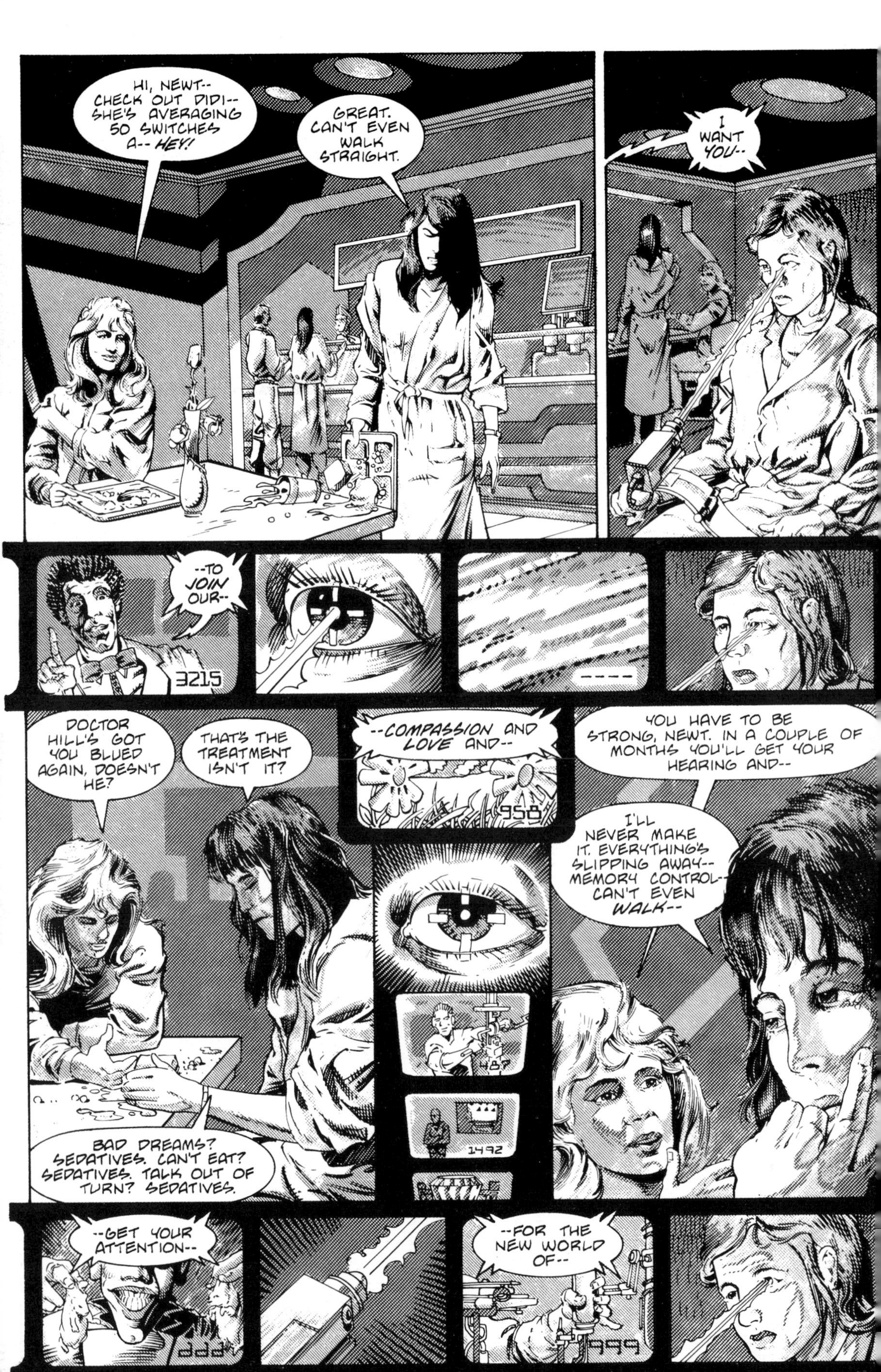

HI, NEWT-- CHECK OUT DIDI-- SHE'S AVERAGING 50 SWITCHES A-- HEY!
GREAT. CAN'T EVEN WALK STRAIGHT.
I WANT YOU--
--TO JOIN OUR--
3215

DOCTOR HILL'S GOT YOU BLUED AGAIN, DOESN'T HE?
THAT'S THE TREATMENT ISN'T IT?
BAD DREAMS? SEDATIVES. CAN'T EAT? SEDATIVES. TALK OUT OF TURN? SEDATIVES.
--COMPASSION AND LOVE AND--
958
487
1492
YOU HAVE TO BE STRONG, NEWT. IN A COUPLE OF MONTHS YOU'LL GET YOUR HEARING AND--
I'LL NEVER MAKE IT. EVERYTHING'S SLIPPING AWAY-- MEMORY CONTROL-- CAN'T EVEN WALK--
--GET YOUR ATTENTION--
ddd
--FOR THE NEW WORLD OF--
999

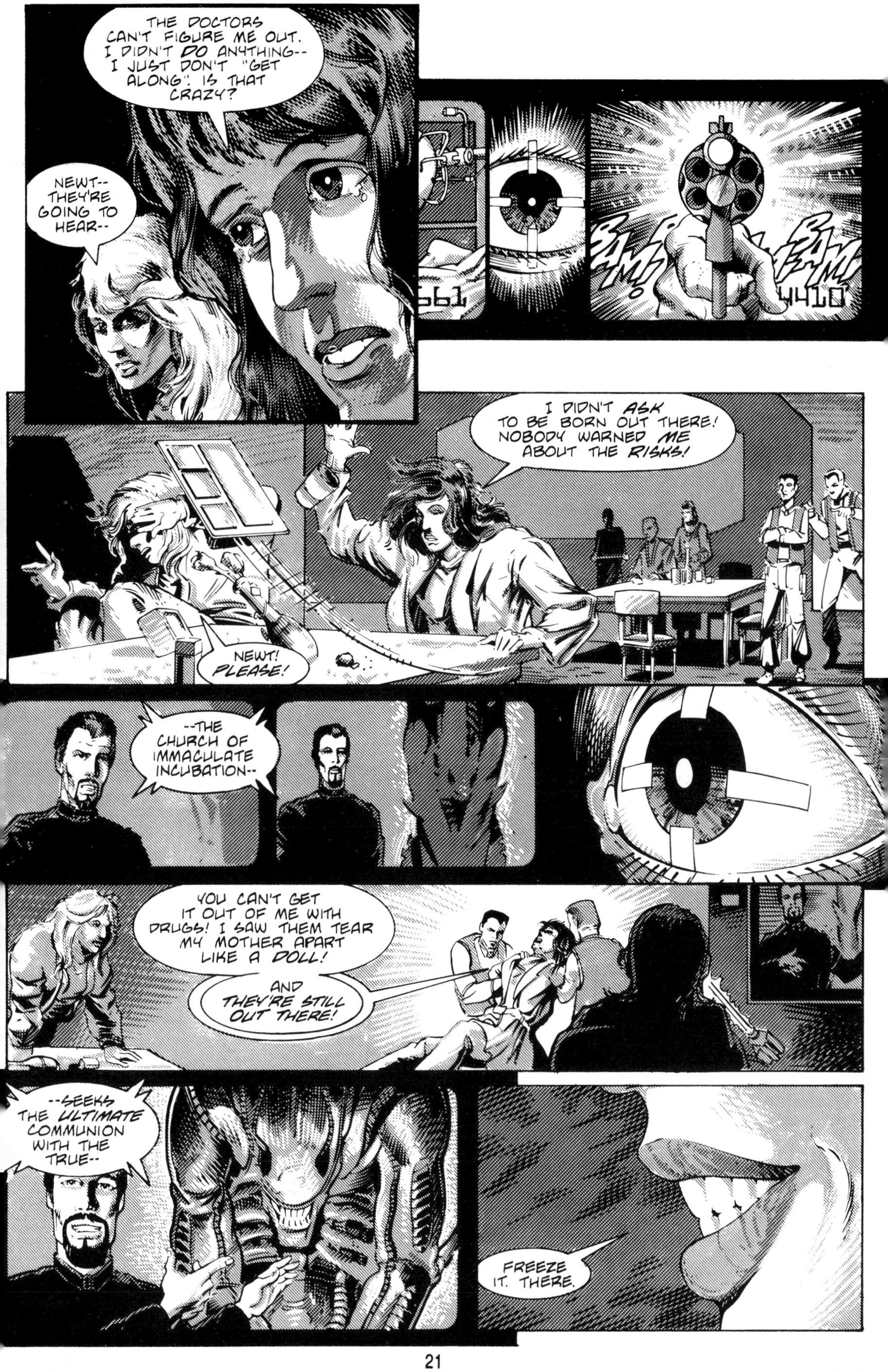
THE DOCTORS CAN'T FIGURE ME OUT. I DIDN'T DO ANYTHING-- I JUST DON'T "GET ALONG". IS THAT CRAZY?
NEWT-- THEY'RE GOING TO HEAR--
661
BAM! BAM!
4410
I DIDN'T ASK TO BE BORN OUT THERE! NOBODY WARNED ME ABOUT THE RISKS!
NEWT! PLEASE!
--THE CHURCH OF IMMACULATE INCUBATION--
YOU CAN'T GET IT OUT OF ME WITH DRUGS! I SAW THEM TEAR MY MOTHER APART LIKE A DOLL!
AND THEY'RE STILL OUT THERE!
--SEEKS THE ULTIMATE COMMUNION WITH THE TRUE--
FREEZE IT. THERE.

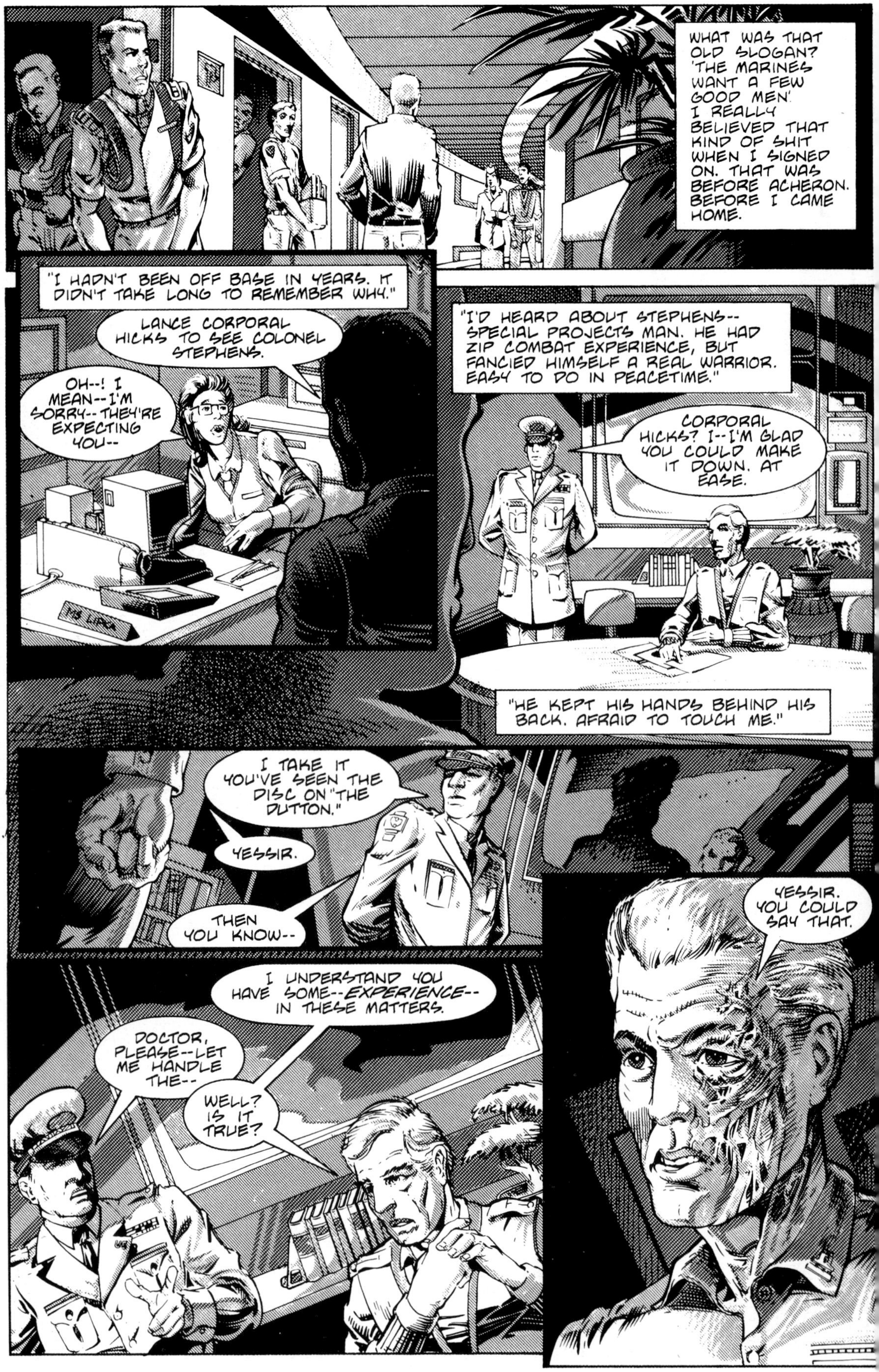
WHAT WAS THAT OLD SLOGAN? 'THE MARINES WANT A FEW GOOD MEN.' I REALLY BELIEVED THAT KIND OF SHIT WHEN I SIGNED ON. THAT WAS BEFORE ACHERON. BEFORE I CAME HOME.
"I HADN'T BEEN OFF BASE IN YEARS. IT DIDN'T TAKE LONG TO REMEMBER WHY."
LANCE CORPORAL HICKS TO SEE COLONEL STEPHENS.
OH--! I MEAN--I'M SORRY-- THEY'RE EXPECTING YOU--
"I'D HEARD ABOUT STEPHENS-- SPECIAL PROJECTS MAN. HE HAD ZIP COMBAT EXPERIENCE, BUT FANCIED HIMSELF A REAL WARRIOR. EASY TO DO IN PEACETIME."
CORPORAL HICKS? I--I'M GLAD YOU COULD MAKE IT DOWN. AT EASE.
"HE KEPT HIS HANDS BEHIND HIS BACK. AFRAID TO TOUCH ME."
I TAKE IT YOU'VE SEEN THE DISC ON "THE DUTTON."
YESSIR.
THEN YOU KNOW--
I UNDERSTAND YOU HAVE SOME--*EXPERIENCE*-- IN THESE MATTERS.
DOCTOR, PLEASE--LET ME HANDLE THE--
WELL? IS IT TRUE?
YESSIR. YOU COULD SAY THAT.

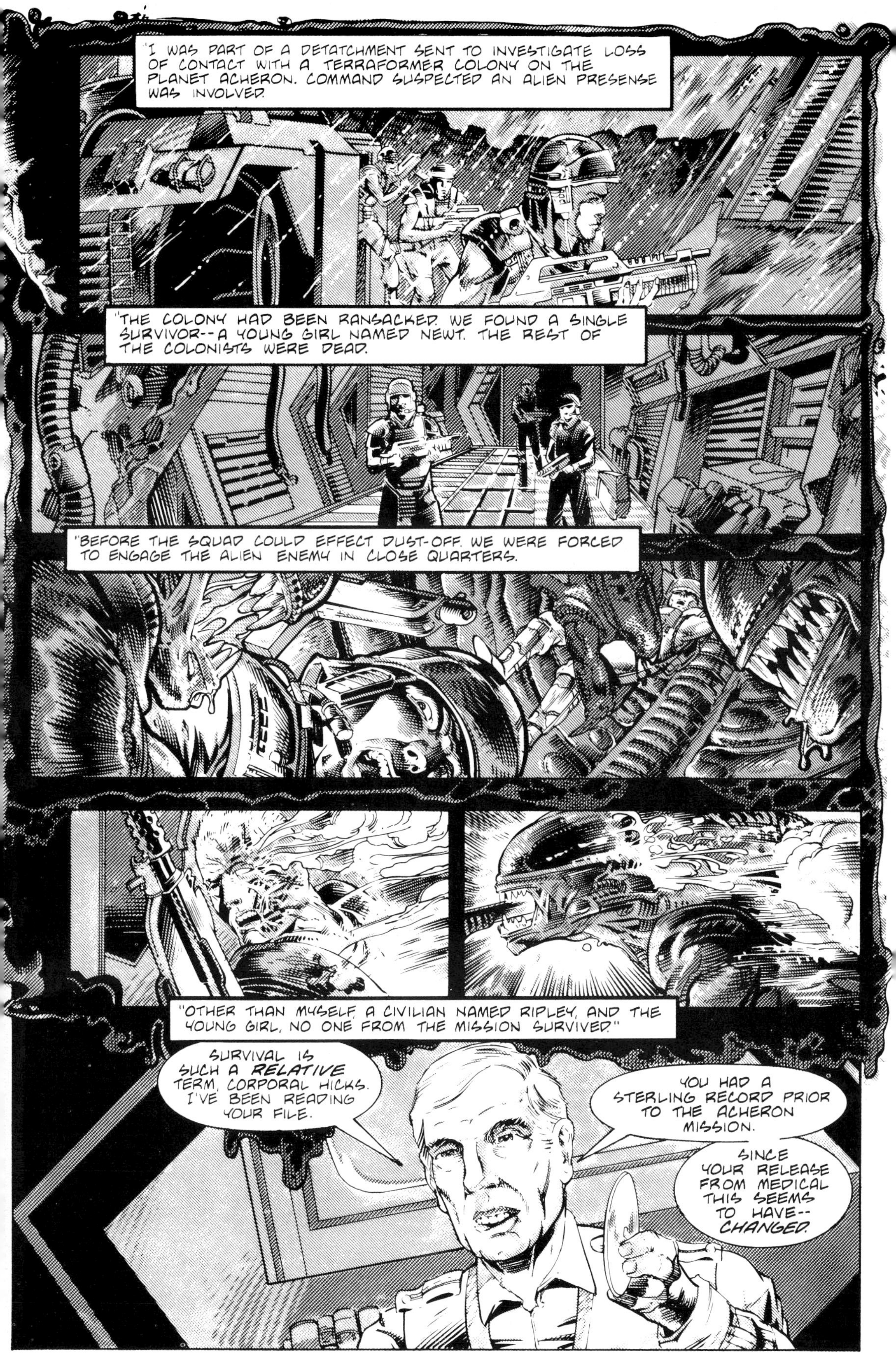
"I WAS PART OF A DETATCHMENT SENT TO INVESTIGATE LOSS OF CONTACT WITH A TERRAFORMER COLONY ON THE PLANET ACHERON. COMMAND SUSPECTED AN ALIEN PRESENSE WAS INVOLVED.
"THE COLONY HAD BEEN RANSACKED. WE FOUND A SINGLE SURVIVOR--A YOUNG GIRL NAMED NEWT. THE REST OF THE COLONISTS WERE DEAD.
"BEFORE THE SQUAD COULD EFFECT DUST-OFF, WE WERE FORCED TO ENGAGE THE ALIEN ENEMY IN CLOSE QUARTERS.
"OTHER THAN MYSELF, A CIVILIAN NAMED RIPLEY, AND THE YOUNG GIRL, NO ONE FROM THE MISSION SURVIVED."
SURVIVAL IS SUCH A *RELATIVE* TERM, CORPORAL HICKS. I'VE BEEN READING YOUR FILE.
YOU HAD A STERLING RECORD PRIOR TO THE ACHERON MISSION.
SINCE YOUR RELEASE FROM MEDICAL THIS SEEMS TO HAVE-- *CHANGED.*

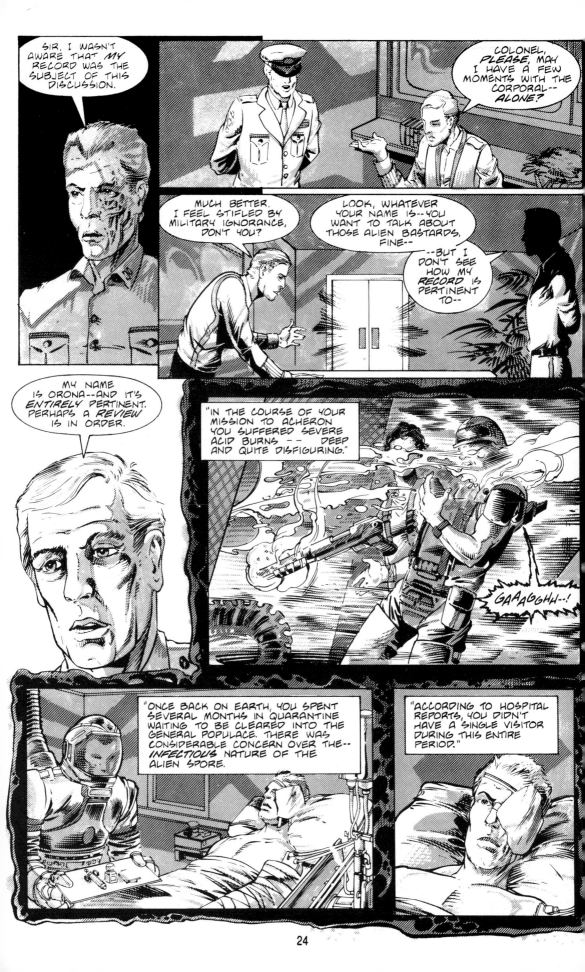

SIR, I WASN'T AWARE THAT *MY* RECORD WAS THE SUBJECT OF THIS DISCUSSION.

COLONEL, *PLEASE*, MAY I HAVE A FEW MOMENTS WITH THE CORPORAL-- *ALONE?*

MUCH BETTER. I FEEL STIFLED BY MILITARY IGNORANCE, DON'T YOU?

LOOK, WHATEVER YOUR NAME IS--YOU WANT TO TALK ABOUT THOSE ALIEN BASTARDS, FINE--

--BUT I DON'T SEE HOW MY *RECORD* IS PERTINENT TO--

MY NAME IS ORONA--AND IT'S *ENTIRELY* PERTINENT. PERHAPS A *REVIEW* IS IN ORDER.

"IN THE COURSE OF YOUR MISSION TO ACHERON YOU SUFFERED SEVERE ACID BURNS -- DEEP AND QUITE DISFIGURING."

GAAAGGHH--!

"ONCE BACK ON EARTH, YOU SPENT SEVERAL MONTHS IN QUARANTINE WAITING TO BE CLEARED INTO THE GENERAL POPULACE. THERE WAS CONSIDERABLE CONCERN OVER THE-- *INFECTIOUS* NATURE OF THE ALIEN SPORE.

"ACCORDING TO HOSPITAL REPORTS, YOU DIDN'T HAVE A SINGLE VISITOR DURING THIS ENTIRE PERIOD."

24

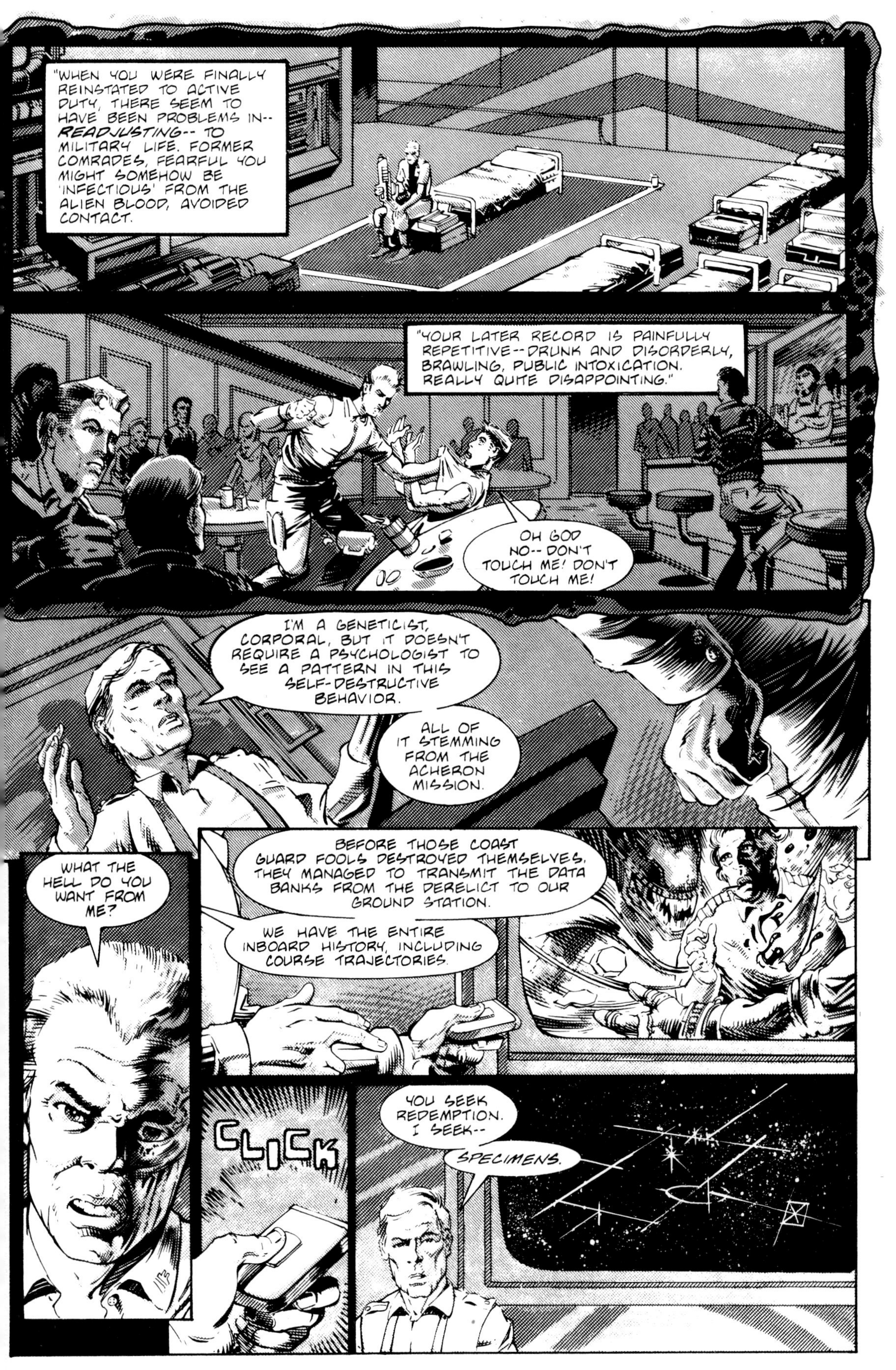
"WHEN YOU WERE FINALLY REINSTATED TO ACTIVE DUTY, THERE SEEM TO HAVE BEEN PROBLEMS IN-- READJUSTING-- TO MILITARY LIFE. FORMER COMRADES, FEARFUL YOU MIGHT SOMEHOW BE 'INFECTIOUS' FROM THE ALIEN BLOOD, AVOIDED CONTACT.
"YOUR LATER RECORD IS PAINFULLY REPETITIVE--DRUNK AND DISORDERLY, BRAWLING, PUBLIC INTOXICATION. REALLY QUITE DISAPPOINTING."
OH GOD NO-- DON'T TOUCH ME! DON'T TOUCH ME!
I'M A GENETICIST, CORPORAL, BUT IT DOESN'T REQUIRE A PSYCHOLOGIST TO SEE A PATTERN IN THIS SELF-DESTRUCTIVE BEHAVIOR.
ALL OF IT STEMMING FROM THE ACHERON MISSION.
WHAT THE HELL DO YOU WANT FROM ME?
BEFORE THOSE COAST GUARD FOOLS DESTROYED THEMSELVES, THEY MANAGED TO TRANSMIT THE DATA BANKS FROM THE DERELICT TO OUR GROUND STATION.
WE HAVE THE ENTIRE INBOARD HISTORY, INCLUDING COURSE TRAJECTORIES.
CLICK
YOU SEEK REDEMPTION. I SEEK--
SPECIMENS.

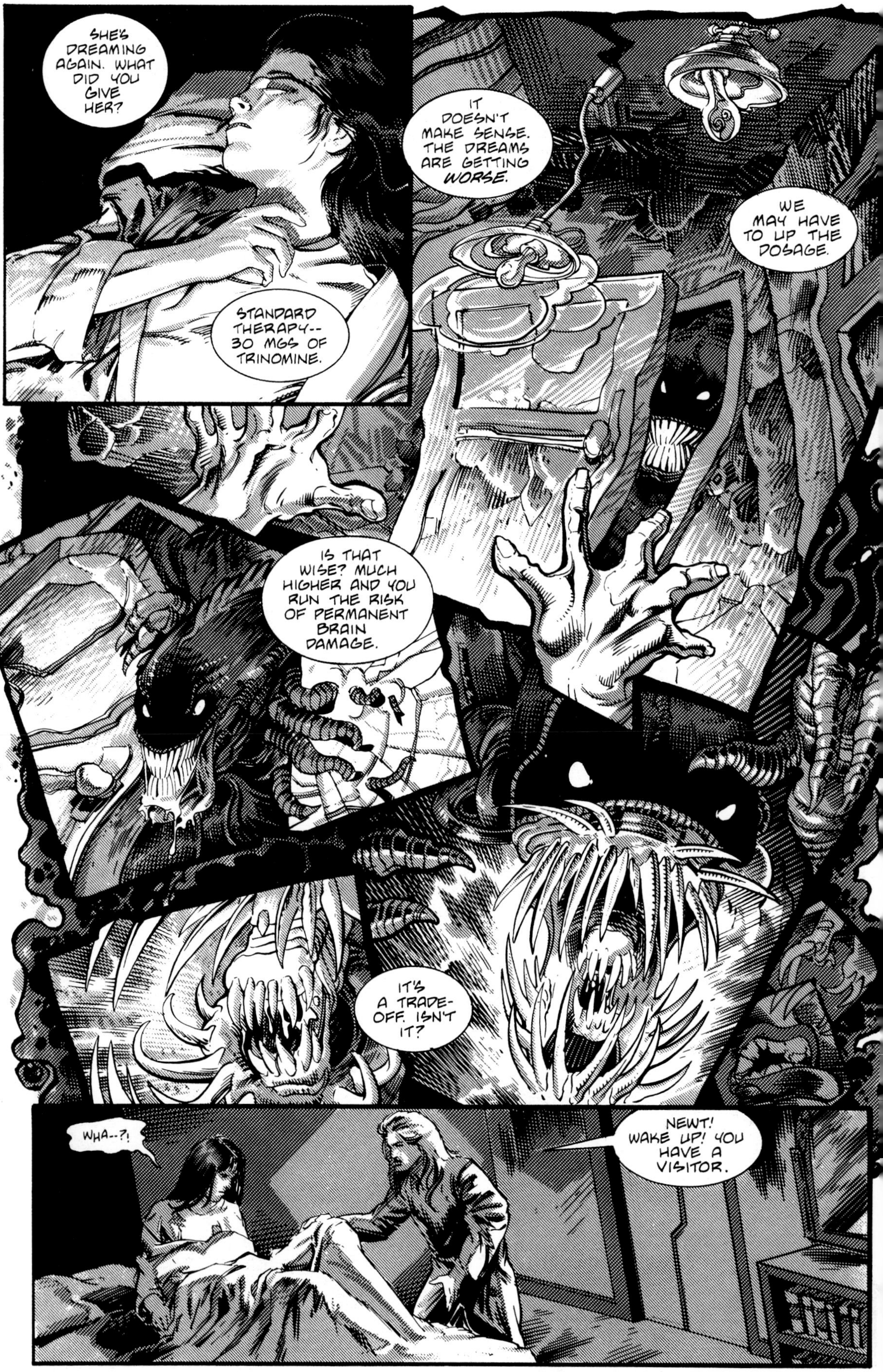

SHE'S DREAMING AGAIN. WHAT DID YOU GIVE HER?
STANDARD THERAPY-- 30 MGS OF TRINOMINE.
IT DOESN'T MAKE SENSE. THE DREAMS ARE GETTING *WORSE*.
WE MAY HAVE TO UP THE DOSAGE.
IS THAT WISE? MUCH HIGHER AND YOU RUN THE RISK OF PERMANENT BRAIN DAMAGE.
IT'S A TRADE-OFF. ISN'T IT?
WHA--?!
NEWT! WAKE UP! YOU HAVE A VISITOR.

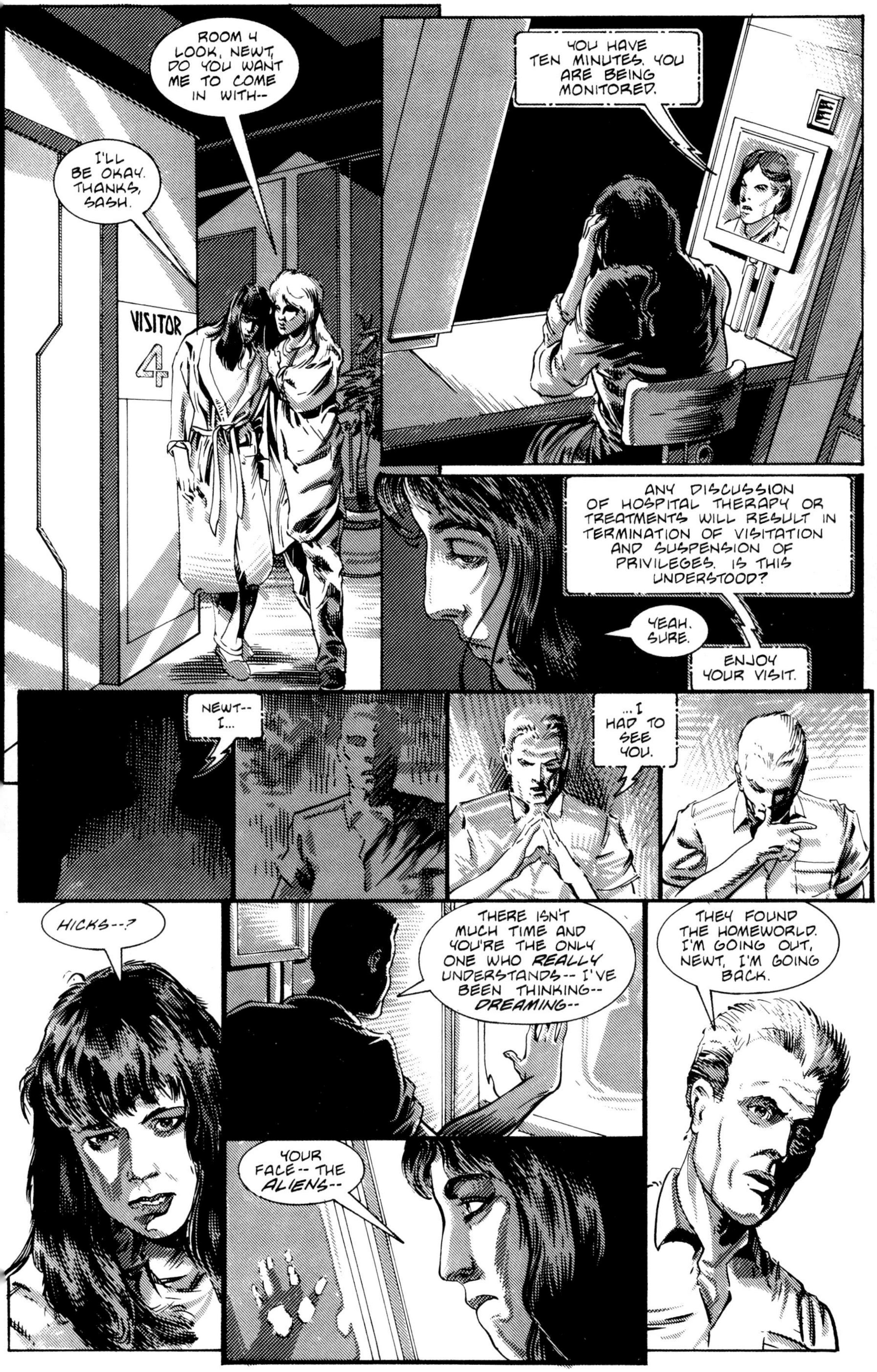
ROOM 4
LOOK, NEWT, DO YOU WANT ME TO COME IN WITH--
I'LL BE OKAY. THANKS, SASH.
VISITOR 4
YOU HAVE TEN MINUTES. YOU ARE BEING MONITORED.
ANY DISCUSSION OF HOSPITAL THERAPY OR TREATMENTS WILL RESULT IN TERMINATION OF VISITATION AND SUSPENSION OF PRIVILEGES. IS THIS UNDERSTOOD?
YEAH. SURE.
ENJOY YOUR VISIT.
NEWT-- I...
...I HAD TO SEE YOU.
HICKS--?
THERE ISN'T MUCH TIME AND YOU'RE THE ONLY ONE WHO REALLY UNDERSTANDS-- I'VE BEEN THINKING-- DREAMING--
YOUR FACE-- THE ALIENS--
THEY FOUND THE HOMEWORLD. I'M GOING OUT, NEWT, I'M GOING BACK.

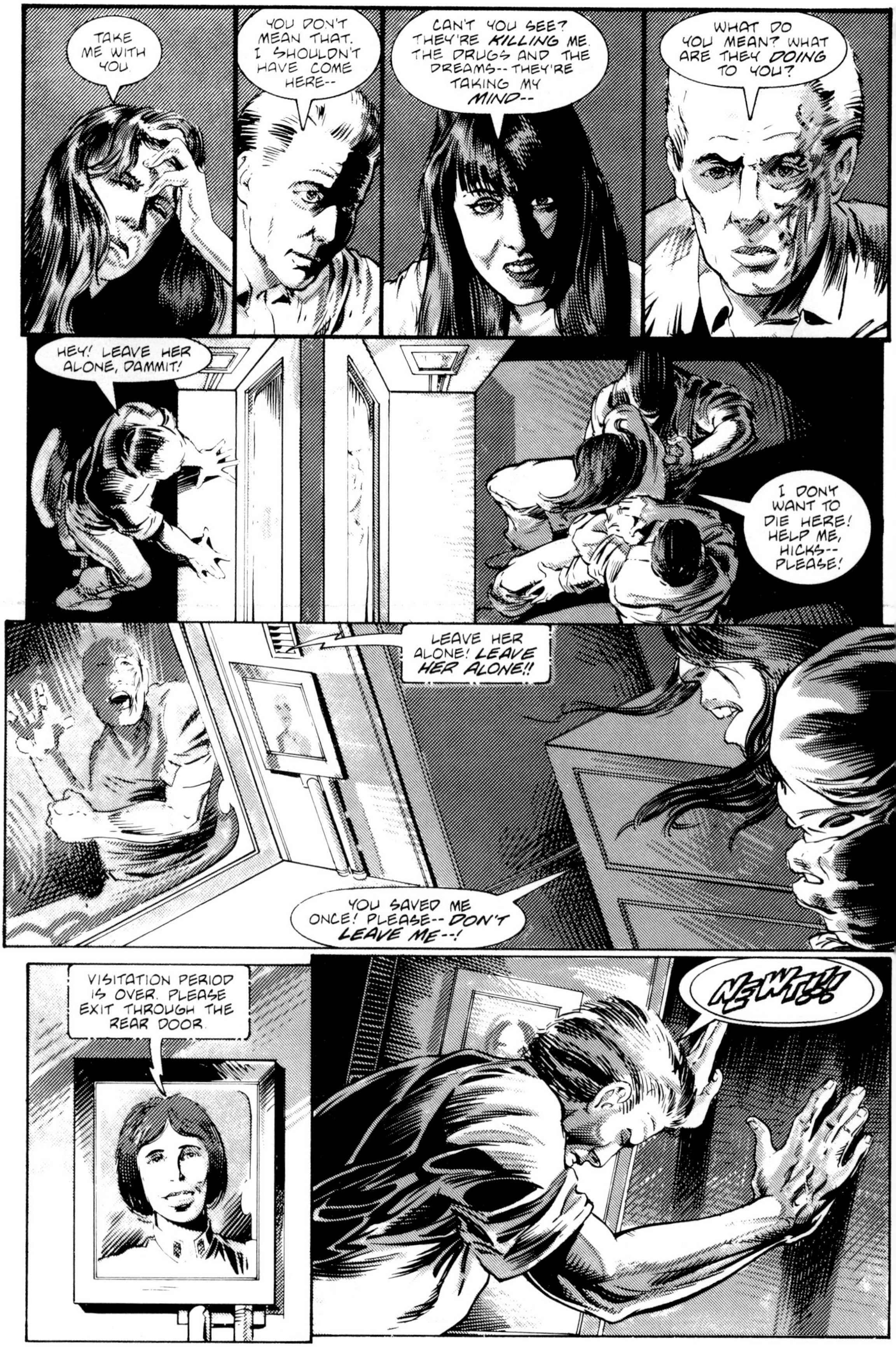
TAKE ME WITH YOU.
YOU DON'T MEAN THAT. I SHOULDN'T HAVE COME HERE--
CAN'T YOU SEE? THEY'RE KILLING ME. THE DRUGS AND THE DREAMS-- THEY'RE TAKING MY MIND--
WHAT DO YOU MEAN? WHAT ARE THEY DOING TO YOU?
HEY! LEAVE HER ALONE, DAMMIT!
I DONT WANT TO DIE HERE! HELP ME, HICKS-- PLEASE!
LEAVE HER ALONE! LEAVE HER ALONE!!
YOU SAVED ME ONCE! PLEASE-- DON'T LEAVE ME--!
VISITATION PERIOD IS OVER. PLEASE EXIT THROUGH THE REAR DOOR.
NEWT!!

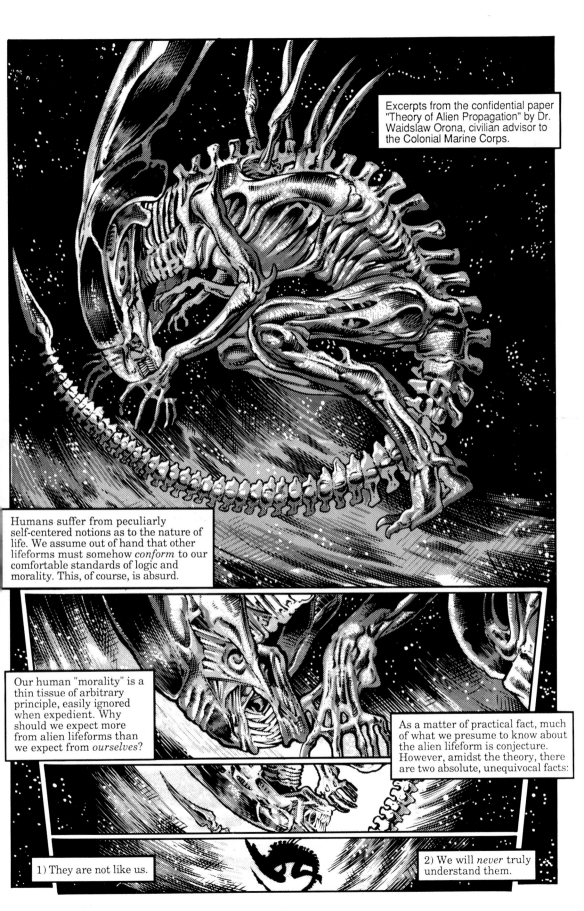

Excerpts from the confidential paper "Theory of Alien Propagation" by Dr. Waidslaw Orona, civilian advisor to the Colonial Marine Corps.

Humans suffer from peculiarly self-centered notions as to the nature of life. We assume out of hand that other lifeforms must somehow *conform* to our comfortable standards of logic and morality. This, of course, is absurd.

Our human "morality" is a thin tissue of arbitrary principle, easily ignored when expedient. Why should we expect more from alien lifeforms than we expect from *ourselves*?

As a matter of practical fact, much of what we presume to know about the alien lifeform is conjecture. However, amidst the theory, there are two absolute, unequivocal facts:

1) They are not like us.

2) We will *never* truly understand them.

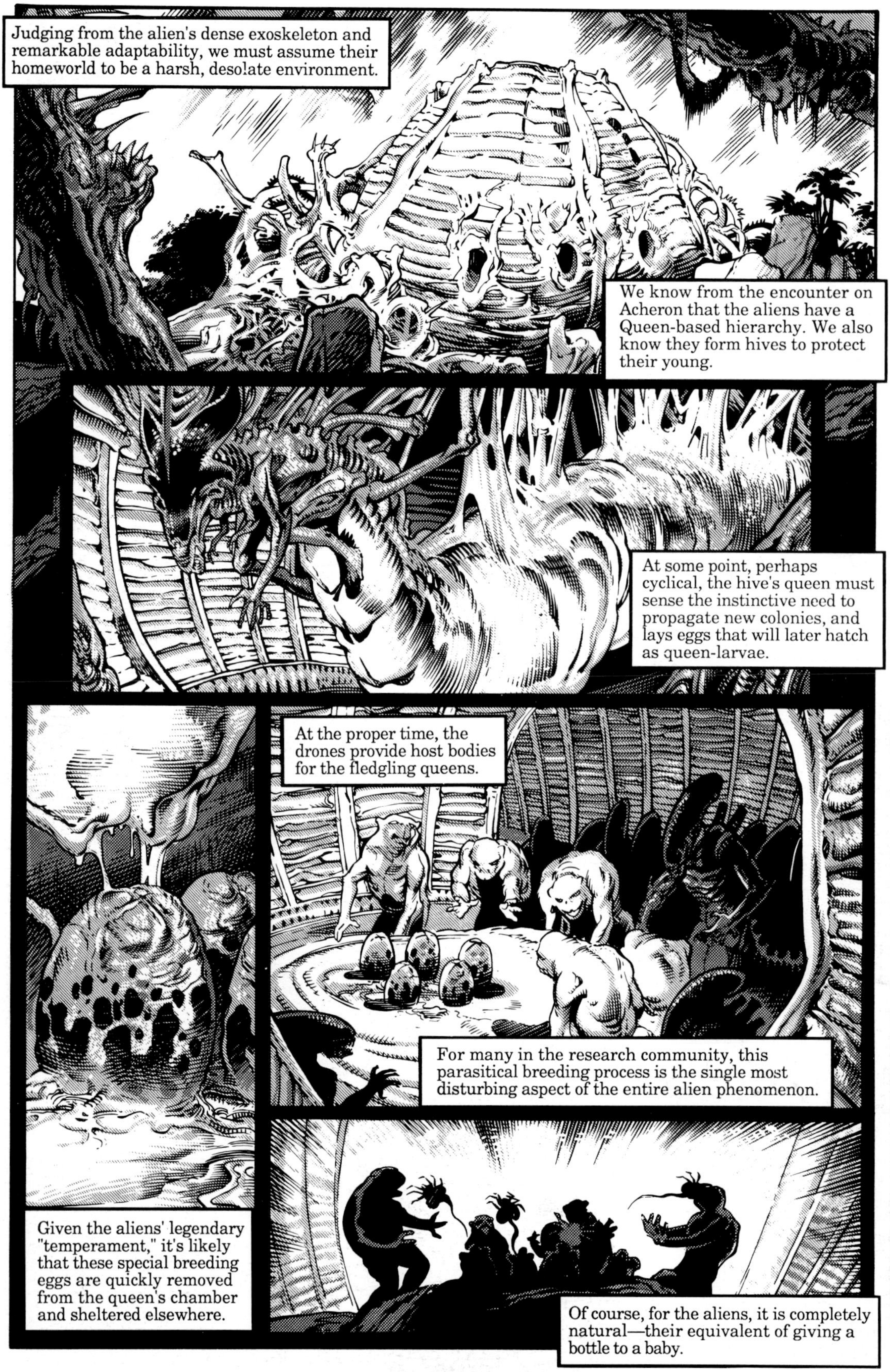

Judging from the alien's dense exoskeleton and remarkable adaptability, we must assume their homeworld to be a harsh, desolate environment.
We know from the encounter on Acheron that the aliens have a Queen-based hierarchy. We also know they form hives to protect their young.
At some point, perhaps cyclical, the hive's queen must sense the instinctive need to propagate new colonies, and lays eggs that will later hatch as queen-larvae.
Given the aliens' legendary "temperament," it's likely that these special breeding eggs are quickly removed from the queen's chamber and sheltered elsewhere.
At the proper time, the drones provide host bodies for the fledgling queens.
For many in the research community, this parasitical breeding process is the single most disturbing aspect of the entire alien phenomenon.
Of course, for the aliens, it is completely natural—their equivalent of giving a bottle to a baby.

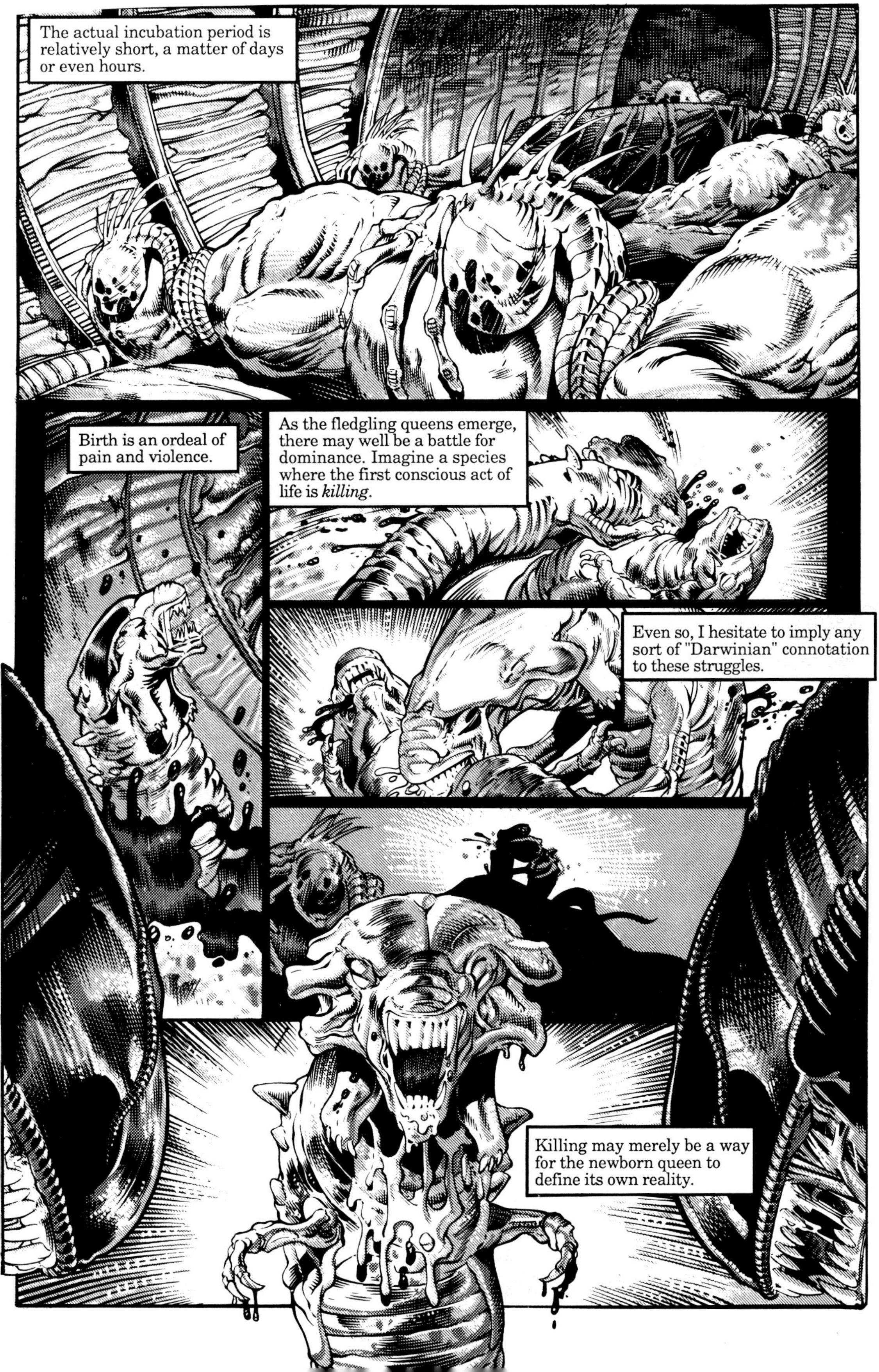
The actual incubation period is relatively short, a matter of days or even hours.
Birth is an ordeal of pain and violence.
As the fledgling queens emerge, there may well be a battle for dominance. Imagine a species where the first conscious act of life is *killing*.
Even so, I hesitate to imply any sort of "Darwinian" connotation to these struggles.
Killing may merely be a way for the newborn queen to define its own reality.

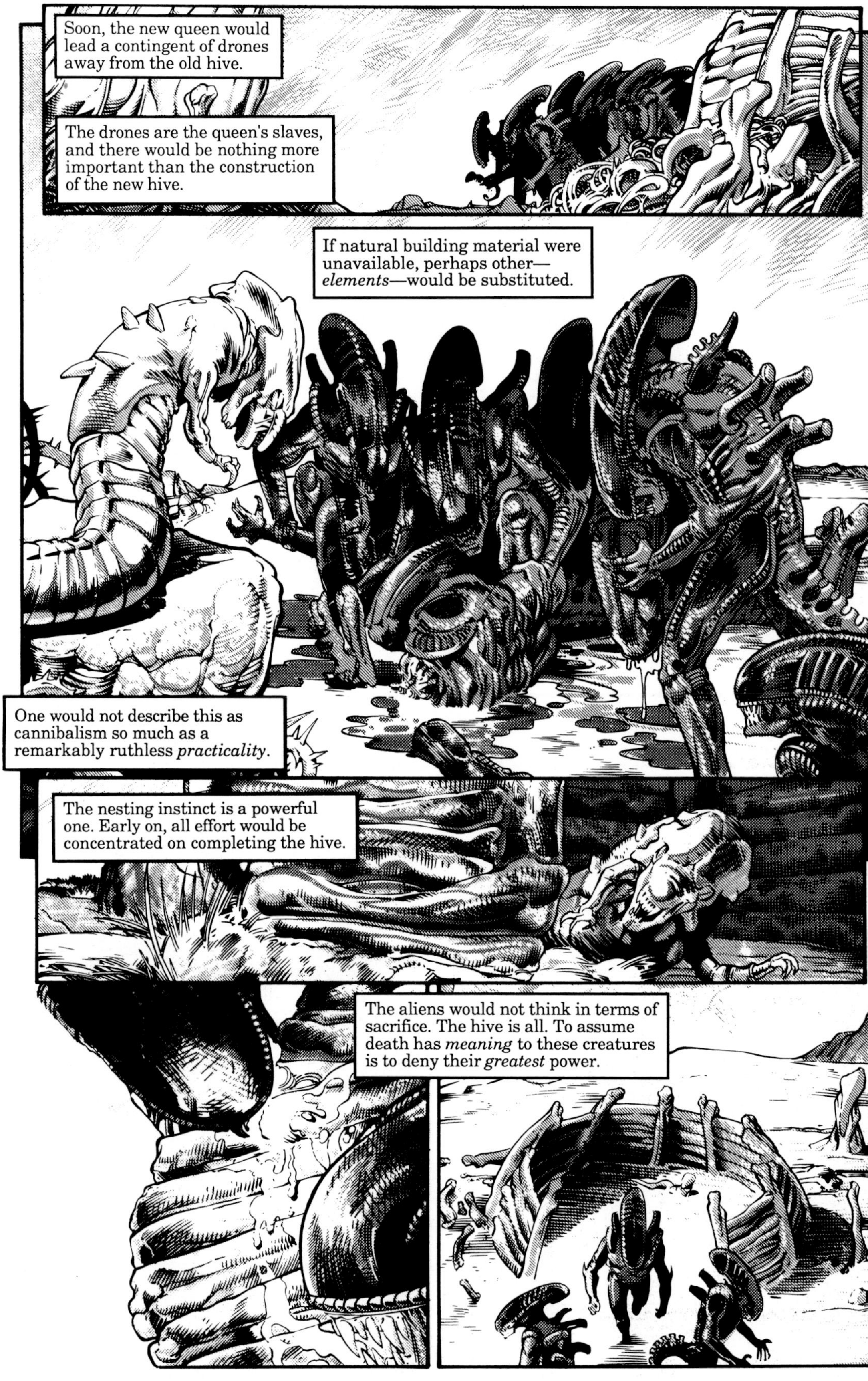

Soon, the new queen would lead a contingent of drones away from the old hive.
The drones are the queen's slaves, and there would be nothing more important than the construction of the new hive.
If natural building material were unavailable, perhaps other—*elements*—would be substituted.
One would not describe this as cannibalism so much as a remarkably ruthless *practicality*.
The nesting instinct is a powerful one. Early on, all effort would be concentrated on completing the hive.
The aliens would not think in terms of sacrifice. The hive is all. To assume death has *meaning* to these creatures is to deny their *greatest* power.

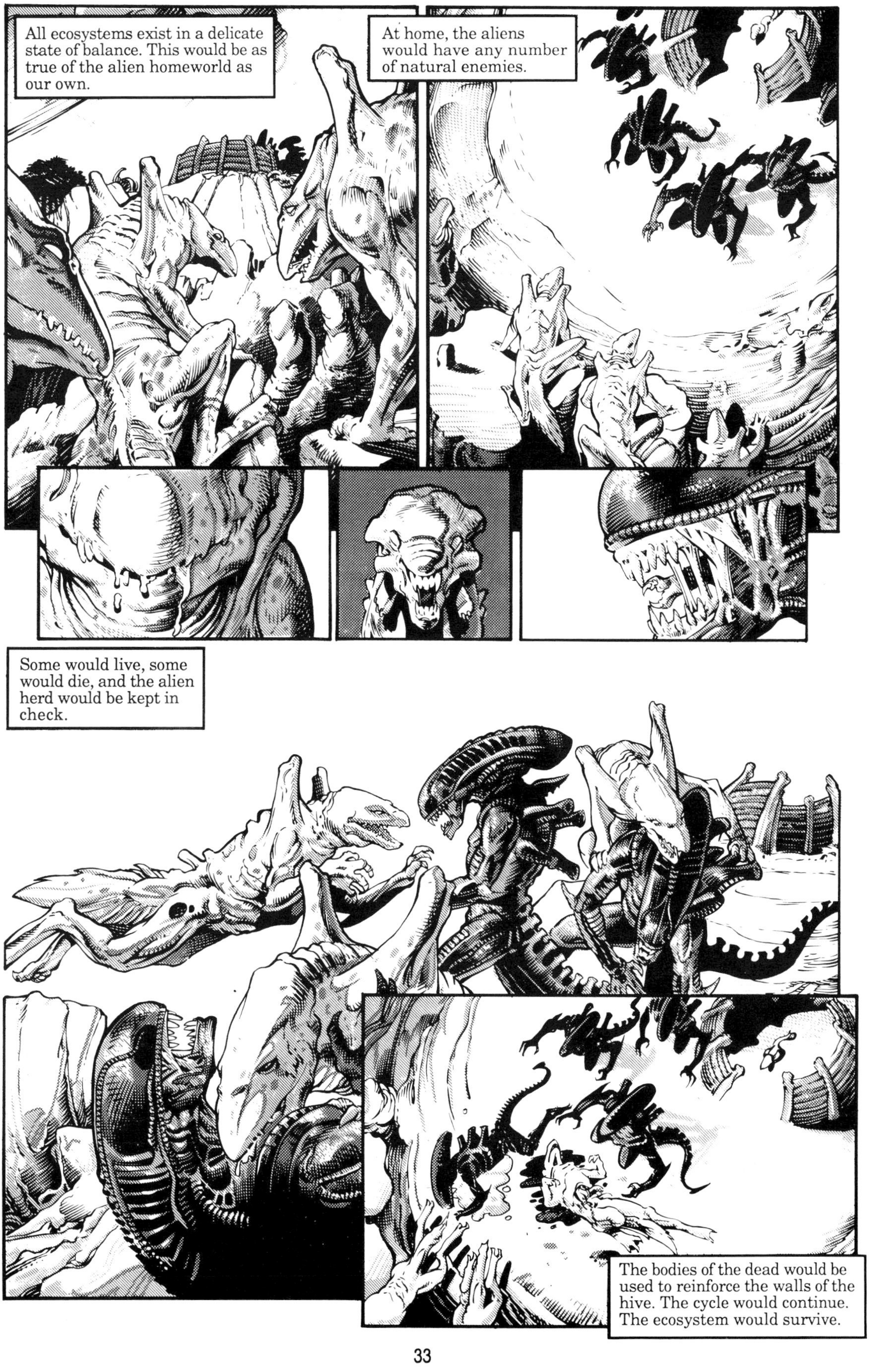
All ecosystems exist in a delicate state of balance. This would be as true of the alien homeworld as our own.
At home, the aliens would have any number of natural enemies.
Some would live, some would die, and the alien herd would be kept in check.
The bodies of the dead would be used to reinforce the walls of the hive. The cycle would continue. The ecosystem would survive.

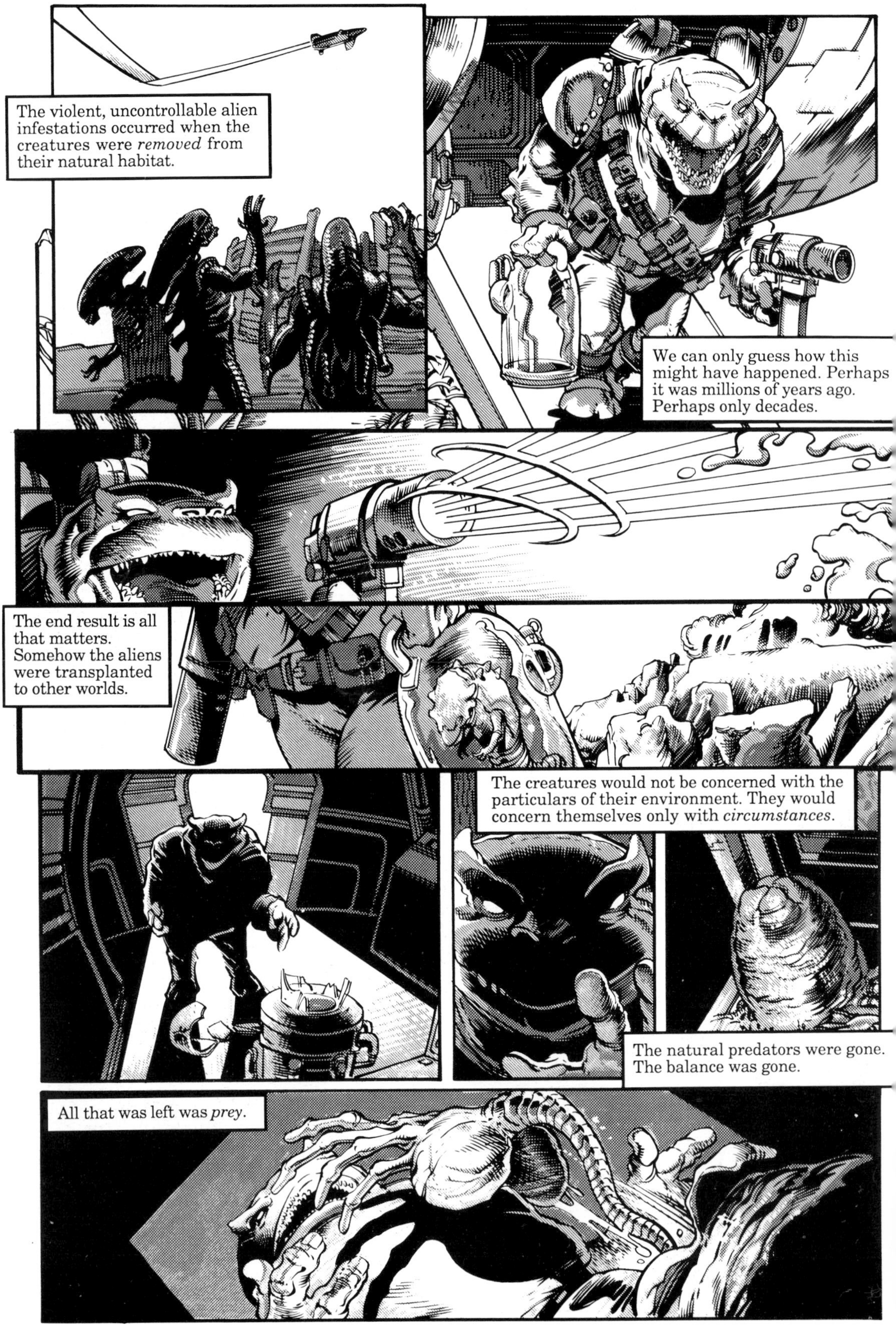

The violent, uncontrollable alien infestations occurred when the creatures were *removed* from their natural habitat.
We can only guess how this might have happened. Perhaps it was millions of years ago. Perhaps only decades.
The end result is all that matters. Somehow the aliens were transplanted to other worlds.
The creatures would not be concerned with the particulars of their environment. They would concern themselves only with *circumstances*.
The natural predators were gone. The balance was gone.
All that was left was *prey*.

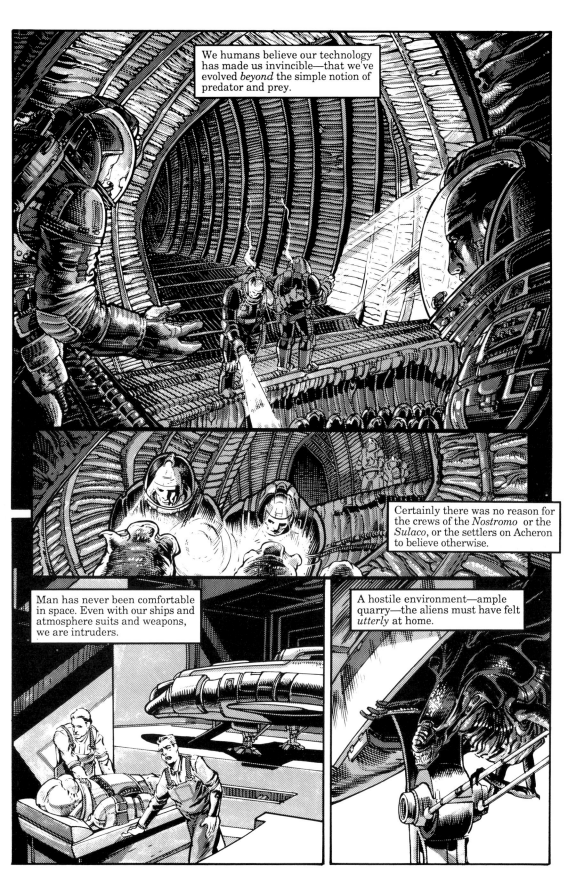

We humans believe our technology has made us invincible—that we've evolved *beyond* the simple notion of predator and prey.

Certainly there was no reason for the crews of the *Nostromo* or the *Sulaco*, or the settlers on Acheron to believe otherwise.

Man has never been comfortable in space. Even with our ships and atmosphere suits and weapons, we are intruders.

A hostile environment—ample quarry—the aliens must have felt *utterly* at home.

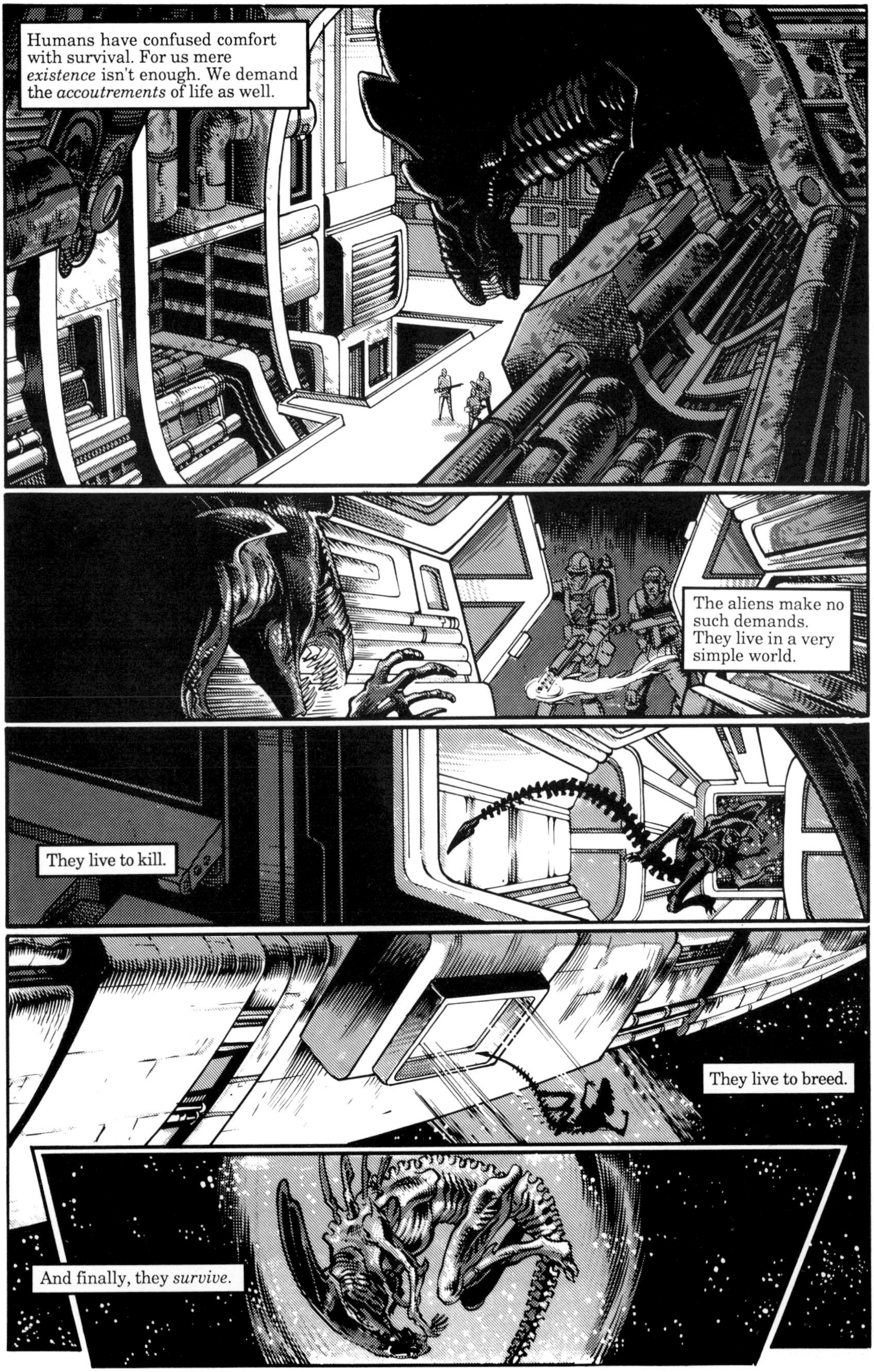
Humans have confused comfort with survival. For us mere *existence* isn't enough. We demand the *accoutrements* of life as well.
The aliens make no such demands. They live in a very simple world.
They live to kill.
They live to breed.
And finally, they *survive*.

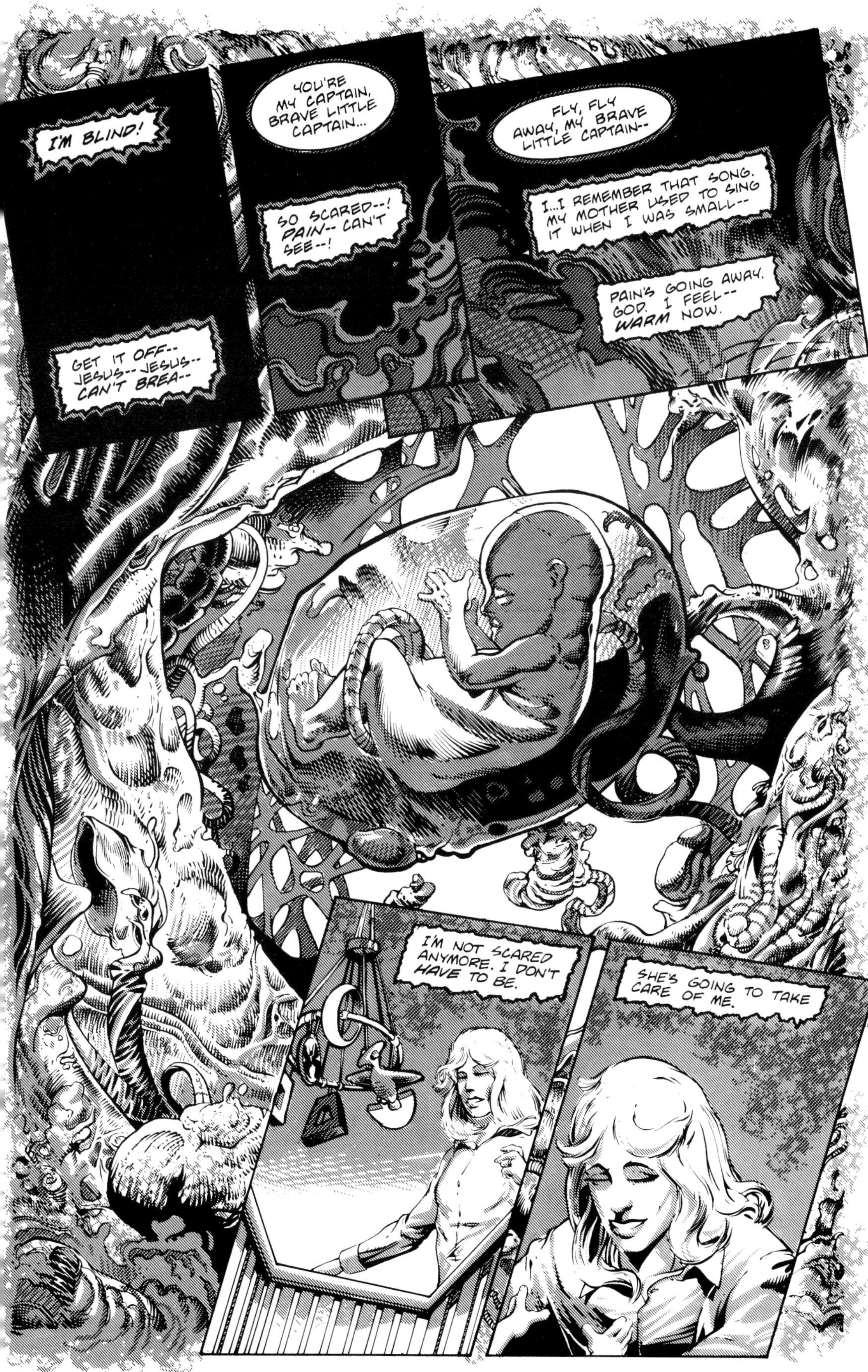
I'M BLIND!
GET IT OFF-- JESUS-- JESUS-- CAN'T BREA--
YOU'RE MY CAPTAIN, BRAVE LITTLE CAPTAIN...
SO SCARED--! PAIN-- CAN'T SEE--!
FLY, FLY AWAY, MY BRAVE LITTLE CAPTAIN--
I...I REMEMBER THAT SONG. MY MOTHER USED TO SING IT WHEN I WAS SMALL--
PAIN'S GOING AWAY. GOD. I FEEL-- WARM NOW.
I'M NOT SCARED ANYMORE. I DON'T HAVE TO BE.
SHE'S GOING TO TAKE CARE OF ME.

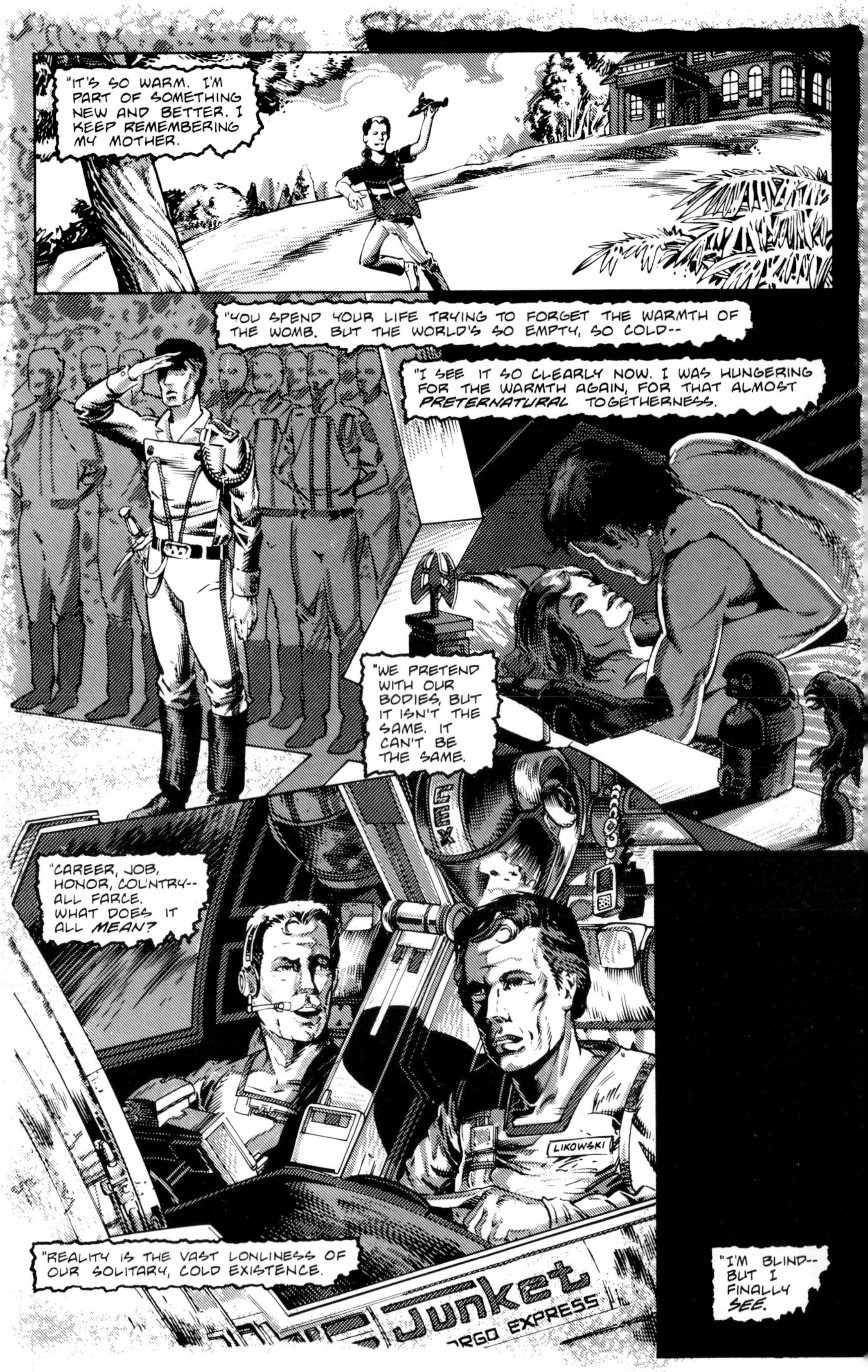
"IT'S SO WARM. I'M PART OF SOMETHING NEW AND BETTER. I KEEP REMEMBERING MY MOTHER.
"YOU SPEND YOUR LIFE TRYING TO FORGET THE WARMTH OF THE WOMB. BUT THE WORLD'S SO EMPTY, SO COLD--
"I SEE IT SO CLEARLY NOW. I WAS HUNGERING FOR THE WARMTH AGAIN, FOR THAT ALMOST *PRETERNATURAL* TOGETHERNESS.
"WE PRETEND WITH OUR BODIES, BUT IT ISN'T THE SAME. IT CAN'T BE THE SAME.
CEX
"CAREER, JOB, HONOR, COUNTRY-- ALL FARCE. WHAT DOES IT ALL *MEAN*?
LIKOWSKI
"REALITY IS THE VAST LONLINESS OF OUR SOLITARY, COLD EXISTENCE.
Junket
ORGO EXPRESS
"I'M BLIND-- BUT I FINALLY *SEE*.

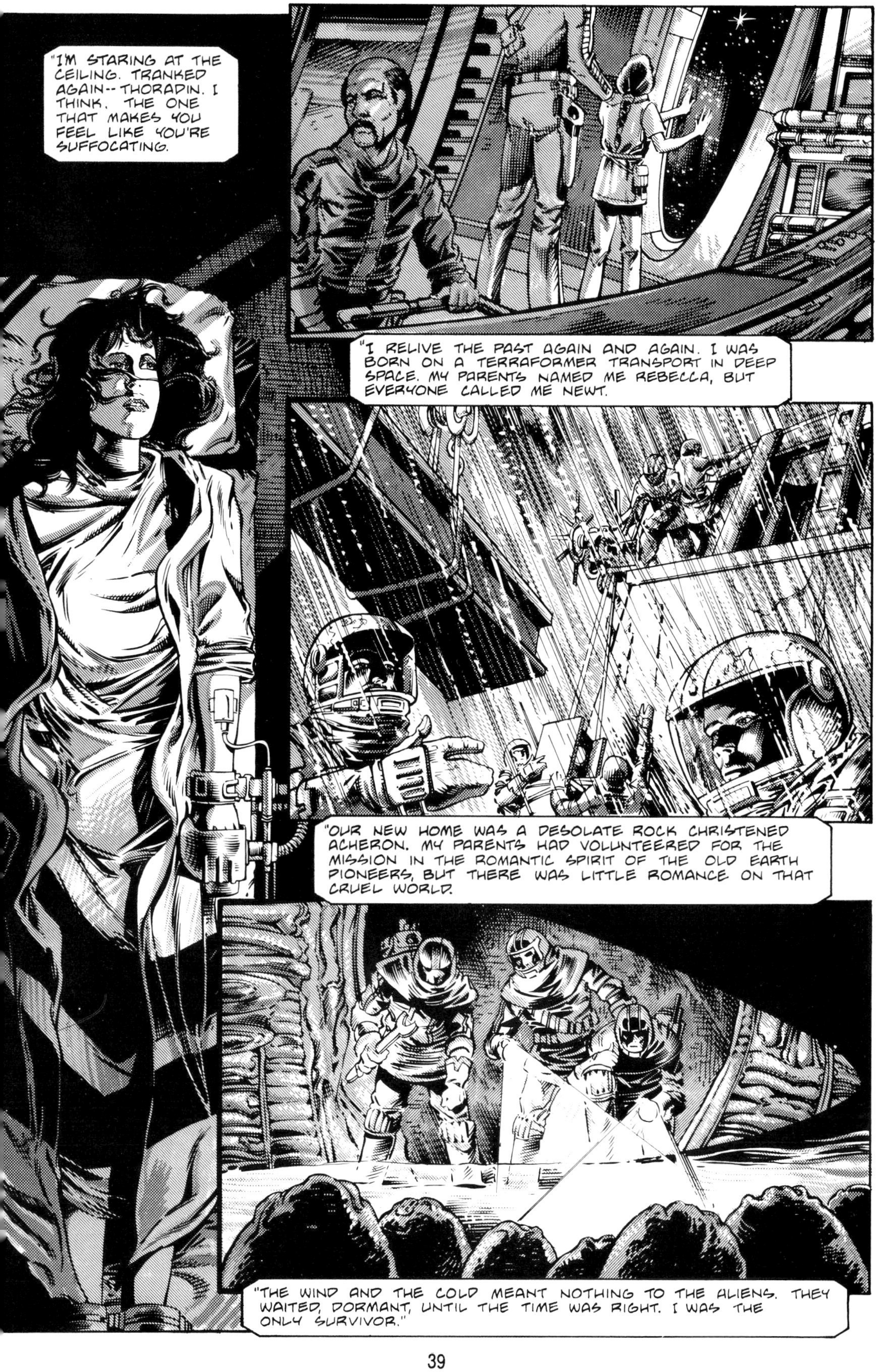
"I'M STARING AT THE CEILING. TRANKED AGAIN--THORADIN. I THINK. THE ONE THAT MAKES YOU FEEL LIKE YOU'RE SUFFOCATING.
"I RELIVE THE PAST AGAIN AND AGAIN. I WAS BORN ON A TERRAFORMER TRANSPORT IN DEEP SPACE. MY PARENTS NAMED ME REBECCA, BUT EVERYONE CALLED ME NEWT.
"OUR NEW HOME WAS A DESOLATE ROCK CHRISTENED ACHERON. MY PARENTS HAD VOLUNTEERED FOR THE MISSION IN THE ROMANTIC SPIRIT OF THE OLD EARTH PIONEERS, BUT THERE WAS LITTLE ROMANCE ON THAT CRUEL WORLD.
"THE WIND AND THE COLD MEANT NOTHING TO THE ALIENS. THEY WAITED, DORMANT, UNTIL THE TIME WAS RIGHT. I WAS THE ONLY SURVIVOR."

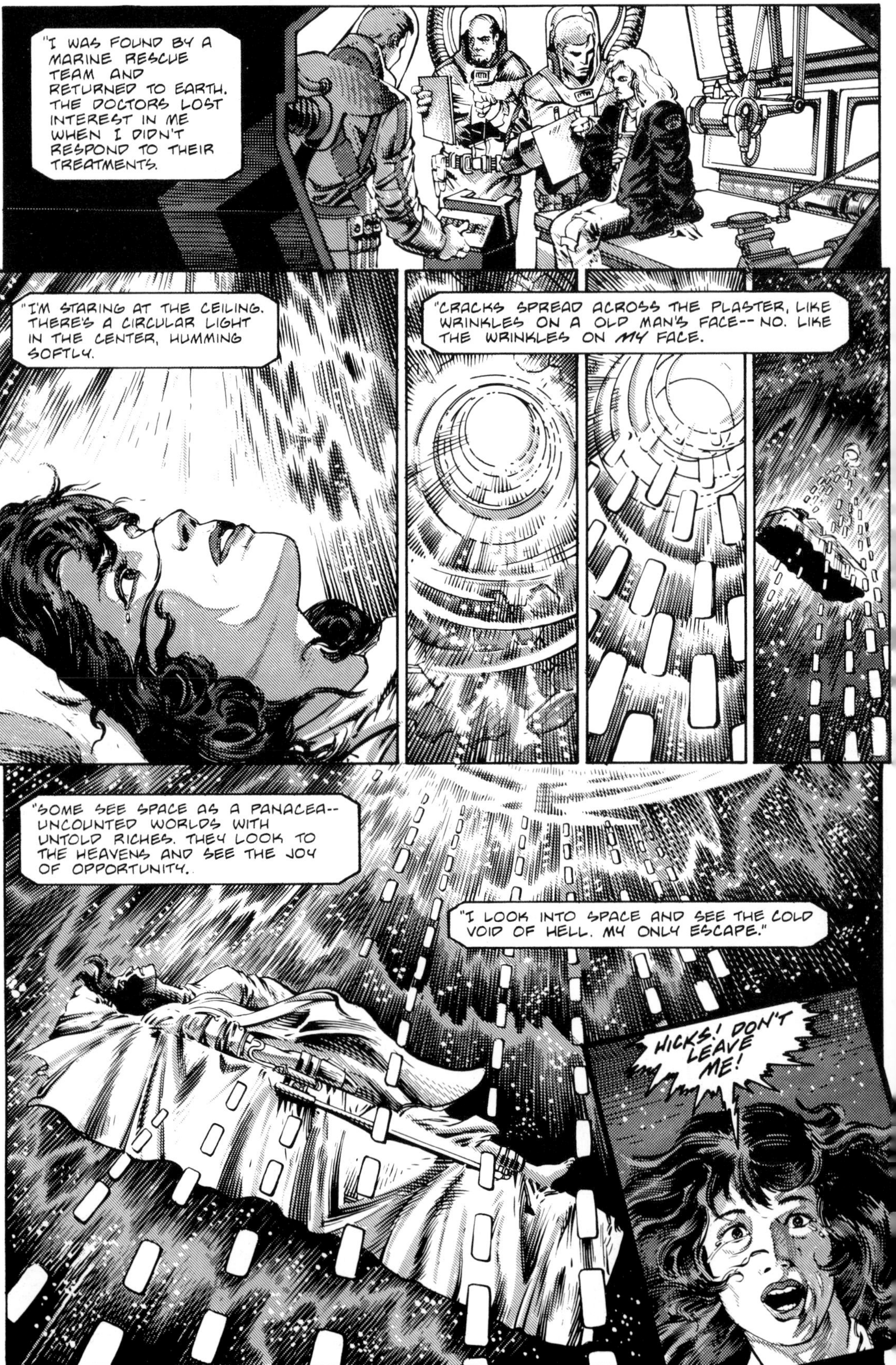

"I WAS FOUND BY A MARINE RESCUE TEAM AND RETURNED TO EARTH. THE DOCTORS LOST INTEREST IN ME WHEN I DIDN'T RESPOND TO THEIR TREATMENTS.
"I'M STARING AT THE CEILING. THERE'S A CIRCULAR LIGHT IN THE CENTER, HUMMING SOFTLY.
"CRACKS SPREAD ACROSS THE PLASTER, LIKE WRINKLES ON A OLD MAN'S FACE-- NO. LIKE THE WRINKLES ON MY FACE.
"SOME SEE SPACE AS A PANACEA-- UNCOUNTED WORLDS WITH UNTOLD RICHES. THEY LOOK TO THE HEAVENS AND SEE THE JOY OF OPPORTUNITY.
"I LOOK INTO SPACE AND SEE THE COLD VOID OF HELL. MY ONLY ESCAPE."
HICKS! DON'T LEAVE ME!

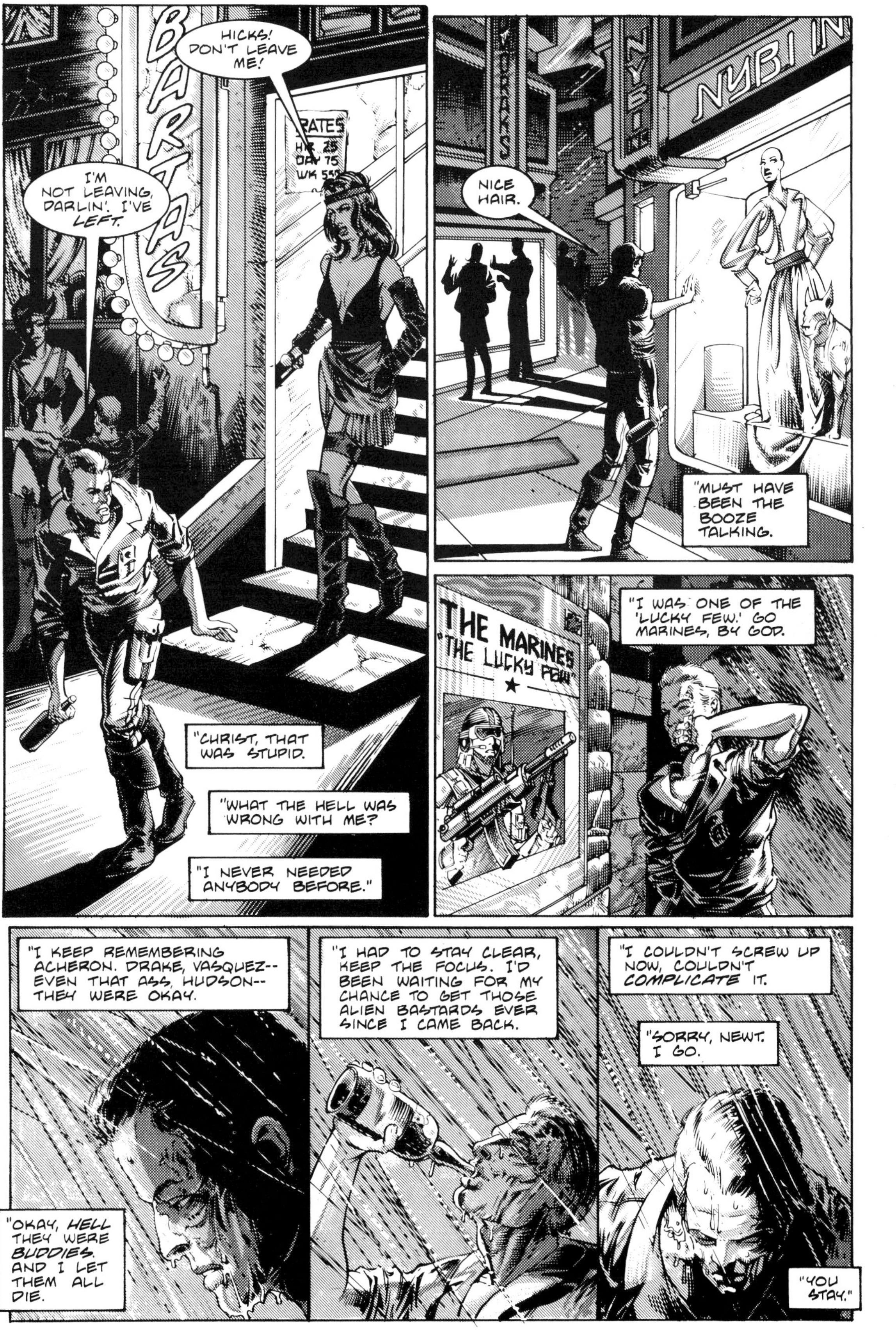
BARTAS
HICKS! DON'T LEAVE ME!
RATES HR 25 DAY 75 WK 55
I'M NOT LEAVING, DARLIN'. I'VE *LEFT*.
"CHRIST, THAT WAS STUPID.
"WHAT THE HELL WAS WRONG WITH ME?
"I NEVER NEEDED ANYBODY BEFORE."
NYBI IN
NICE HAIR.
"MUST HAVE BEEN THE BOOZE TALKING.
THE MARINES "THE LUCKY FEW"
"I WAS ONE OF THE 'LUCKY FEW.' GO MARINES, BY GOD.
"I KEEP REMEMBERING ACHERON. DRAKE, VASQUEZ-- EVEN THAT ASS, HUDSON-- THEY WERE OKAY.
"OKAY, *HELL* THEY WERE *BUDDIES*. AND I LET THEM ALL DIE.
"I HAD TO STAY CLEAR, KEEP THE FOCUS. I'D BEEN WAITING FOR MY CHANCE TO GET THOSE ALIEN BASTARDS EVER SINCE I CAME BACK.
"I COULDN'T SCREW UP NOW, COULDN'T *COMPLICATE* IT.
"SORRY, NEWT. I GO.
"YOU STAY."

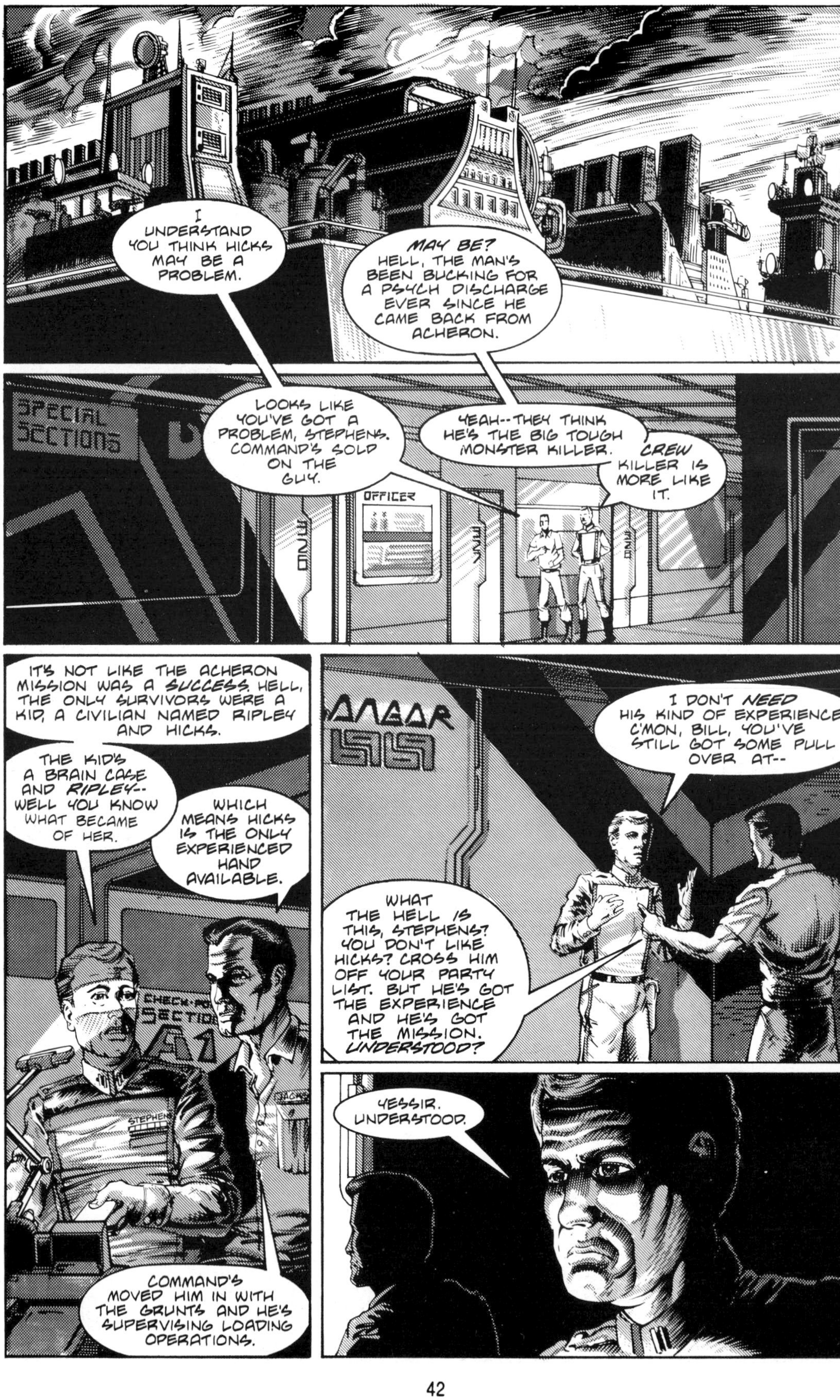
I UNDERSTAND YOU THINK HICKS MAY BE A PROBLEM.
MAY BE? HELL, THE MAN'S BEEN BUCKING FOR A PSYCH DISCHARGE EVER SINCE HE CAME BACK FROM ACHERON.
SPECIAL SECTIONS
LOOKS LIKE YOU'VE GOT A PROBLEM, STEPHENS. COMMAND'S SOLD ON THE GUY.
YEAH--THEY THINK HE'S THE BIG TOUGH MONSTER KILLER.
CREW KILLER IS MORE LIKE IT.
OFFICER
IT'S NOT LIKE THE ACHERON MISSION WAS A SUCCESS. HELL, THE ONLY SURVIVORS WERE A KID, A CIVILIAN NAMED RIPLEY AND HICKS.
THE KID'S A BRAIN CASE AND RIPLEY-- WELL YOU KNOW WHAT BECAME OF HER.
WHICH MEANS HICKS IS THE ONLY EXPERIENCED HAND AVAILABLE.
COMMAND'S MOVED HIM IN WITH THE GRUNTS AND HE'S SUPERVISING LOADING OPERATIONS.
I DON'T NEED HIS KIND OF EXPERIENCE. C'MON, BILL, YOU'VE STILL GOT SOME PULL OVER AT--
WHAT THE HELL IS THIS, STEPHENS? YOU DON'T LIKE HICKS? CROSS HIM OFF YOUR PARTY LIST. BUT HE'S GOT THE EXPERIENCE AND HE'S GOT THE MISSION. UNDERSTOOD?
YESSIR. UNDERSTOOD.

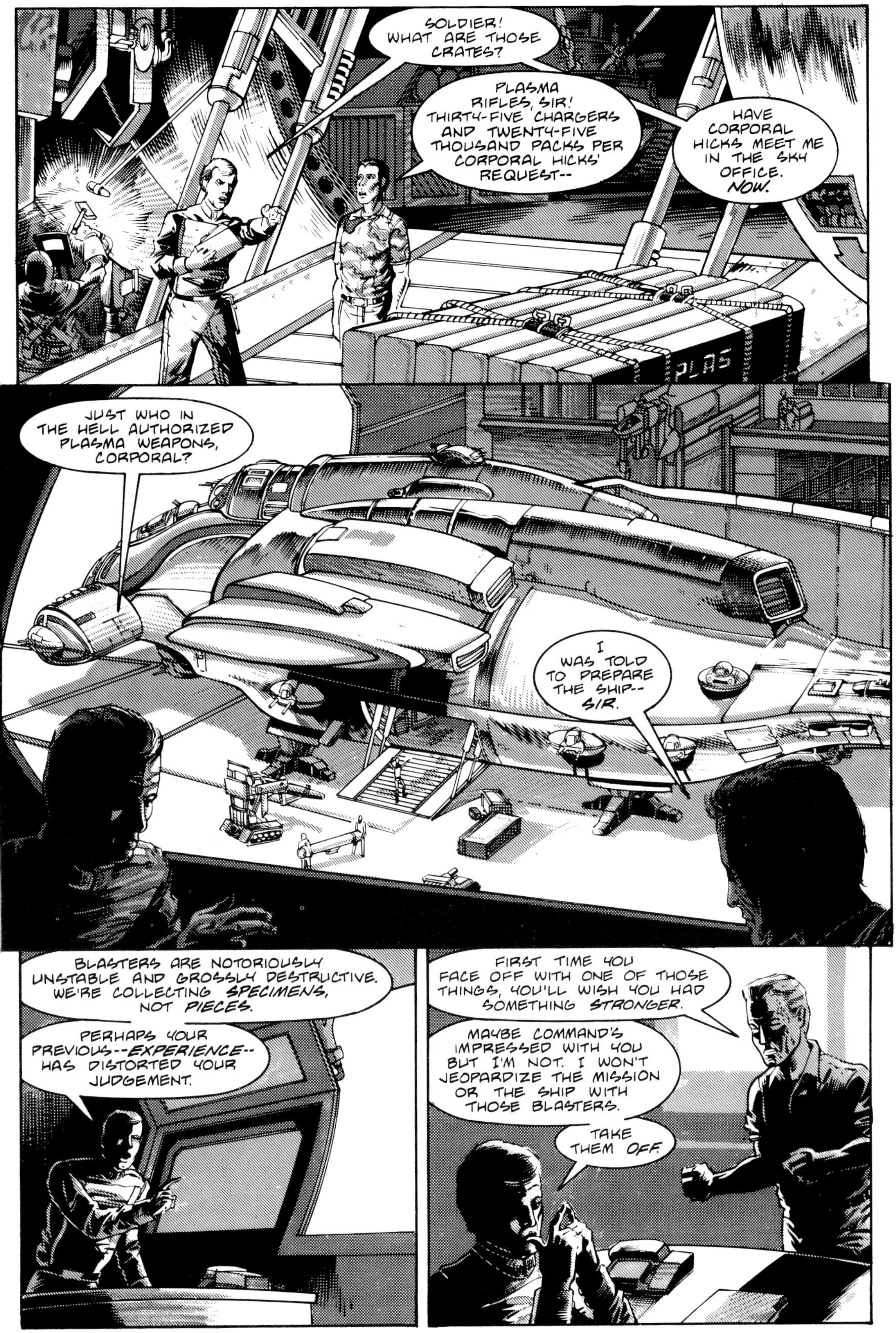
SOLDIER! WHAT ARE THOSE CRATES?
PLASMA RIFLES, SIR! THIRTY-FIVE CHARGERS AND TWENTY-FIVE THOUSAND PACKS PER CORPORAL HICKS' REQUEST--
HAVE CORPORAL HICKS MEET ME IN THE SKY OFFICE. NOW.
PLAS
JUST WHO IN THE HELL AUTHORIZED PLASMA WEAPONS, CORPORAL?
I WAS TOLD TO PREPARE THE SHIP-- SIR.
BLASTERS ARE NOTORIOUSLY UNSTABLE AND GROSSLY DESTRUCTIVE. WE'RE COLLECTING SPECIMENS, NOT PIECES.
PERHAPS YOUR PREVIOUS--EXPERIENCE-- HAS DISTORTED YOUR JUDGEMENT.
FIRST TIME YOU FACE OFF WITH ONE OF THOSE THINGS, YOU'LL WISH YOU HAD SOMETHING STRONGER.
MAYBE COMMAND'S IMPRESSED WITH YOU BUT I'M NOT. I WON'T JEOPARDIZE THE MISSION OR THE SHIP WITH THOSE BLASTERS.
TAKE THEM OFF.

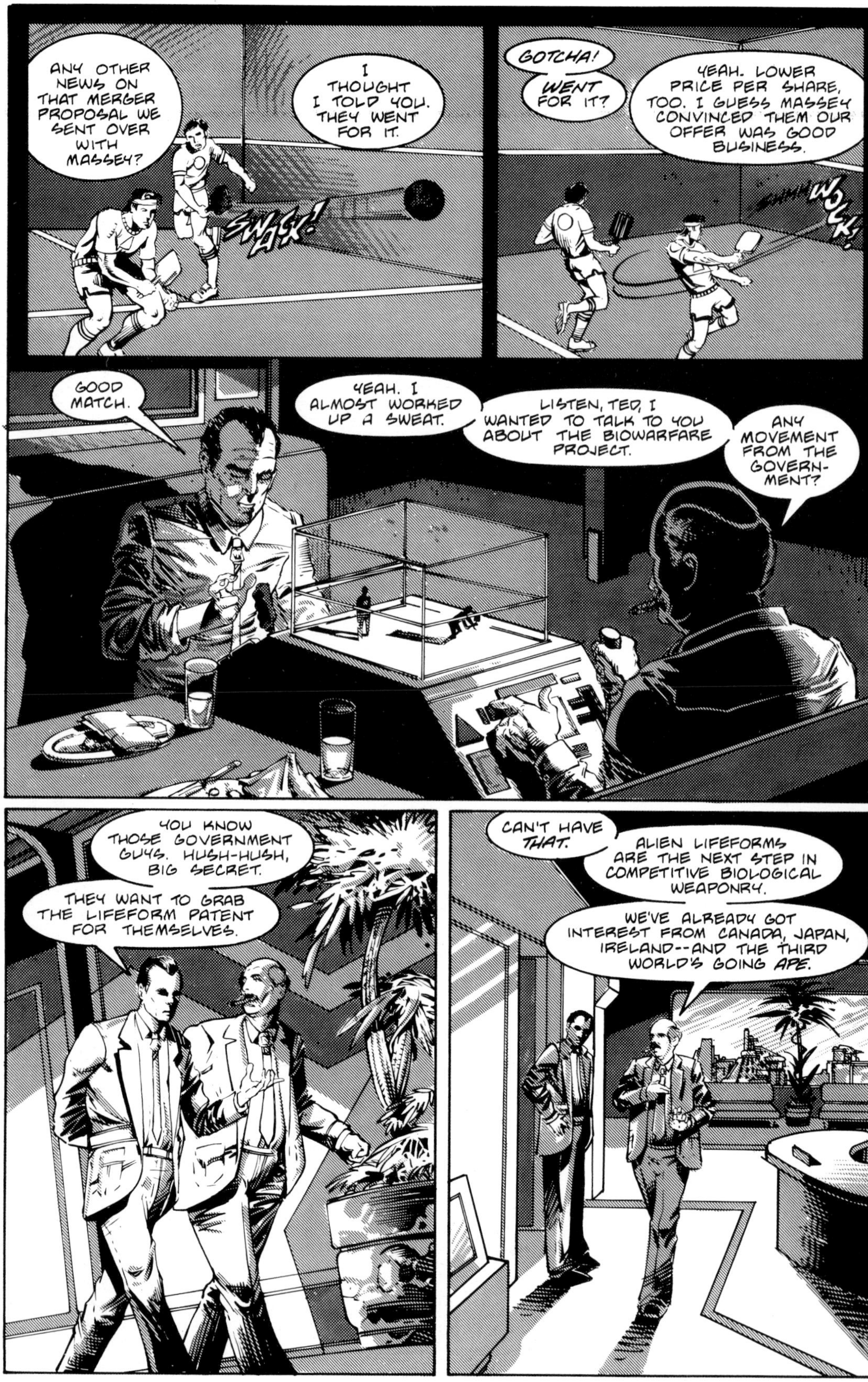
ANY OTHER NEWS ON THAT MERGER PROPOSAL WE SENT OVER WITH MASSEY?
I THOUGHT I TOLD YOU. THEY WENT FOR IT.
SWACK!
GOTCHA!
WENT FOR IT?
YEAH. LOWER PRICE PER SHARE, TOO. I GUESS MASSEY CONVINCED THEM OUR OFFER WAS GOOD BUSINESS.
SHHH WOCK!
GOOD MATCH.
YEAH. I ALMOST WORKED UP A SWEAT.
LISTEN, TED, I WANTED TO TALK TO YOU ABOUT THE BIOWARFARE PROJECT.
ANY MOVEMENT FROM THE GOVERN-MENT?
YOU KNOW THOSE GOVERNMENT GUYS. HUSH-HUSH, BIG SECRET.
THEY WANT TO GRAB THE LIFEFORM PATENT FOR THEMSELVES.
CAN'T HAVE THAT.
ALIEN LIFEFORMS ARE THE NEXT STEP IN COMPETITIVE BIOLOGICAL WEAPONRY.
WE'VE ALREADY GOT INTEREST FROM CANADA, JAPAN, IRELAND--AND THE THIRD WORLD'S GOING APE.

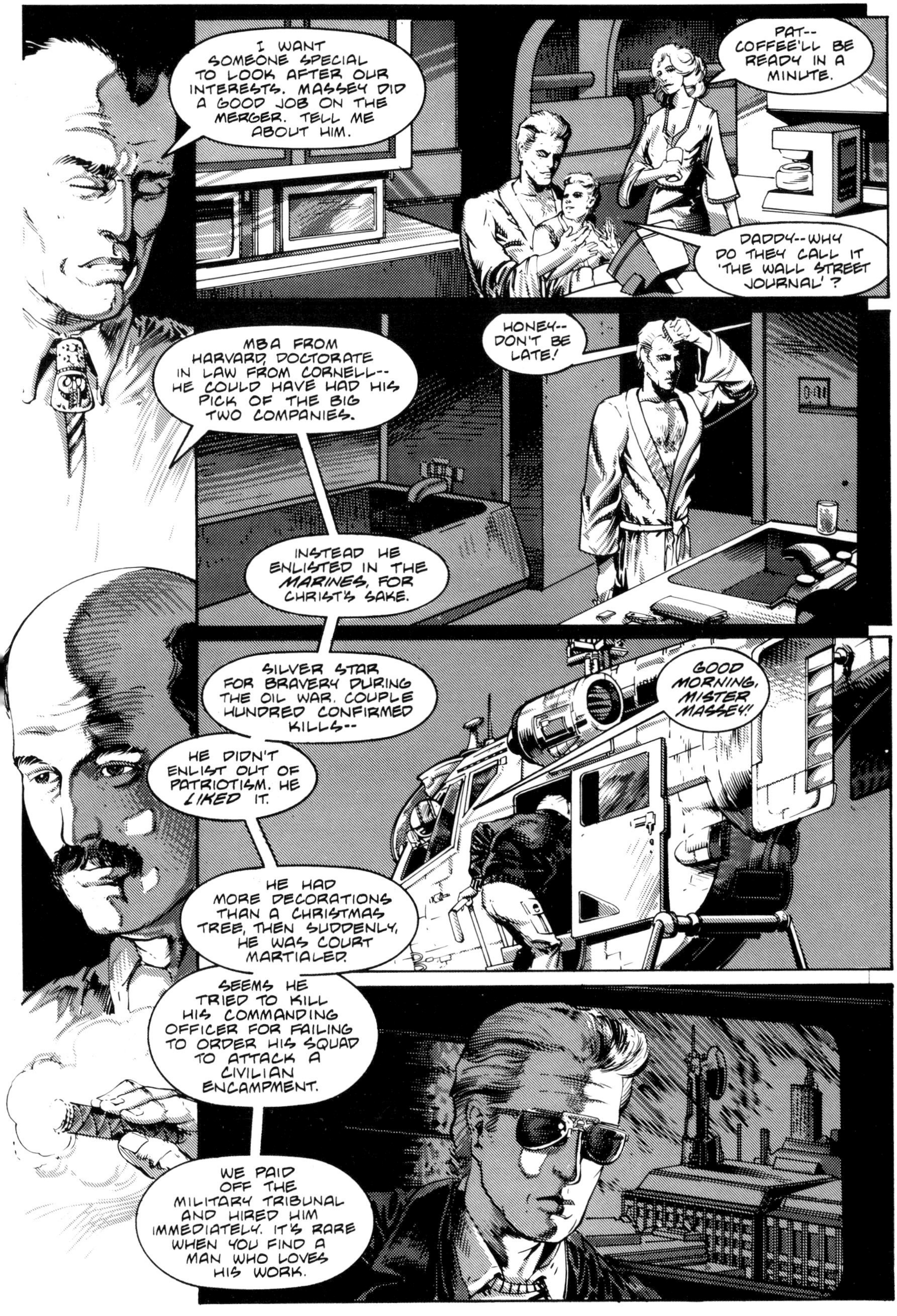
I WANT SOMEONE SPECIAL TO LOOK AFTER OUR INTERESTS. MASSEY DID A GOOD JOB ON THE MERGER. TELL ME ABOUT HIM.
PAT-- COFFEE'LL BE READY IN A MINUTE.
DADDY--WHY DO THEY CALL IT 'THE WALL STREET JOURNAL'?
MBA FROM HARVARD, DOCTORATE IN LAW FROM CORNELL-- HE COULD HAVE HAD HIS PICK OF THE BIG TWO COMPANIES.
HONEY-- DON'T BE LATE!
INSTEAD HE ENLISTED IN THE MARINES, FOR CHRIST'S SAKE.
SILVER STAR FOR BRAVERY DURING THE OIL WAR. COUPLE HUNDRED CONFIRMED KILLS--
GOOD MORNING, MISTER MASSEY!
HE DIDN'T ENLIST OUT OF PATRIOTISM. HE LIKED IT.
HE HAD MORE DECORATIONS THAN A CHRISTMAS TREE, THEN SUDDENLY, HE WAS COURT MARTIALED.
SEEMS HE TRIED TO KILL HIS COMMANDING OFFICER FOR FAILING TO ORDER HIS SQUAD TO ATTACK A CIVILIAN ENCAMPMENT.
WE PAID OFF THE MILITARY TRIBUNAL AND HIRED HIM IMMEDIATELY. IT'S RARE WHEN YOU FIND A MAN WHO LOVES HIS WORK.

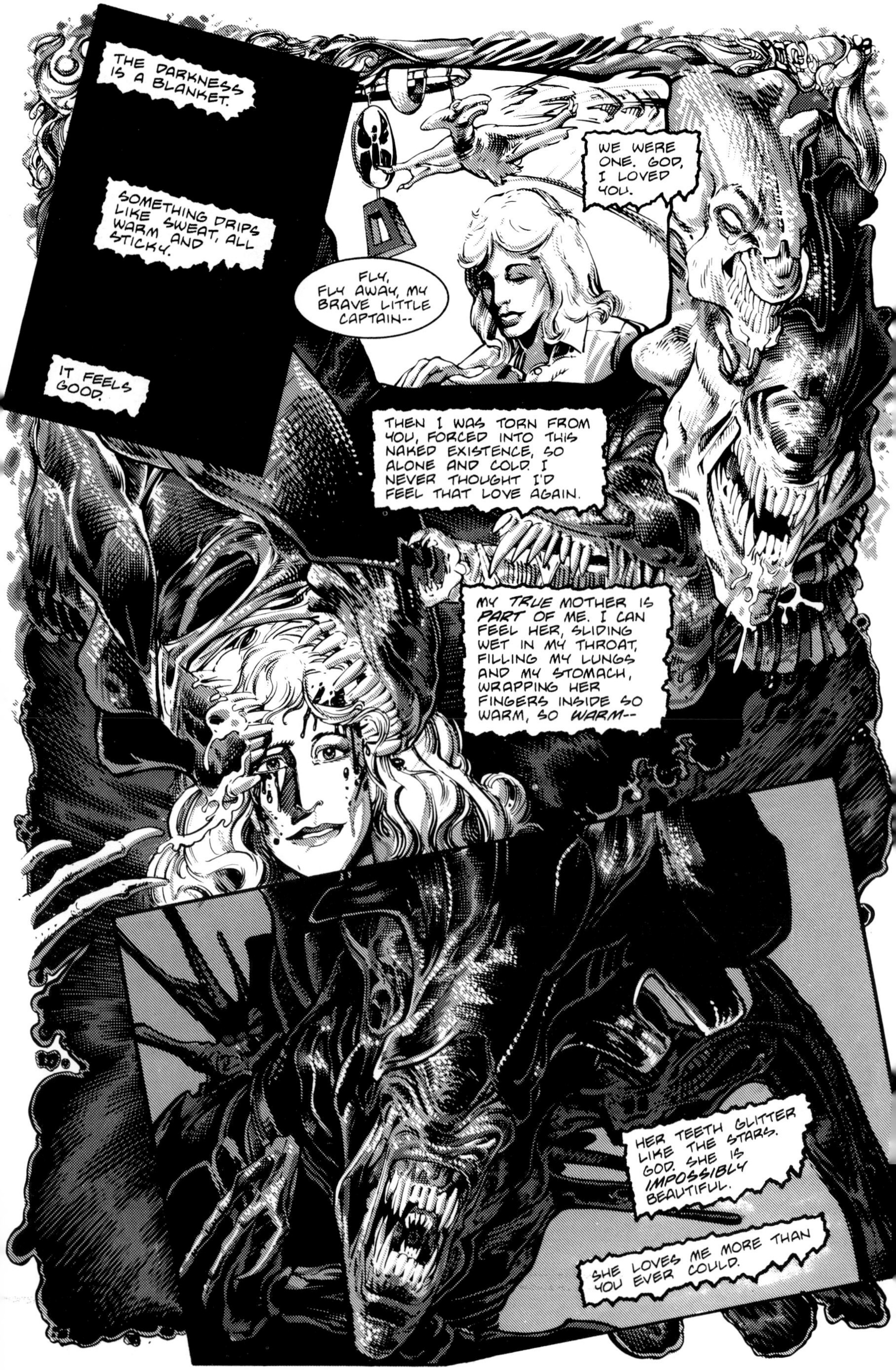
THE DARKNESS IS A BLANKET.
SOMETHING DRIPS LIKE SWEAT, ALL WARM AND STICKY.
IT FEELS GOOD.
FLY, FLY AWAY, MY BRAVE LITTLE CAPTAIN--
WE WERE ONE. GOD, I LOVED YOU.
THEN I WAS TORN FROM YOU, FORCED INTO THIS NAKED EXISTENCE, SO ALONE AND COLD. I NEVER THOUGHT I'D FEEL THAT LOVE AGAIN.
MY TRUE MOTHER IS PART OF ME. I CAN FEEL HER, SLIDING WET IN MY THROAT, FILLING MY LUNGS AND MY STOMACH, WRAPPING HER FINGERS INSIDE SO WARM, SO WARM--
HER TEETH GLITTER LIKE THE STARS. GOD, SHE IS IMPOSSIBLY BEAUTIFUL.
SHE LOVES ME MORE THAN YOU EVER COULD.

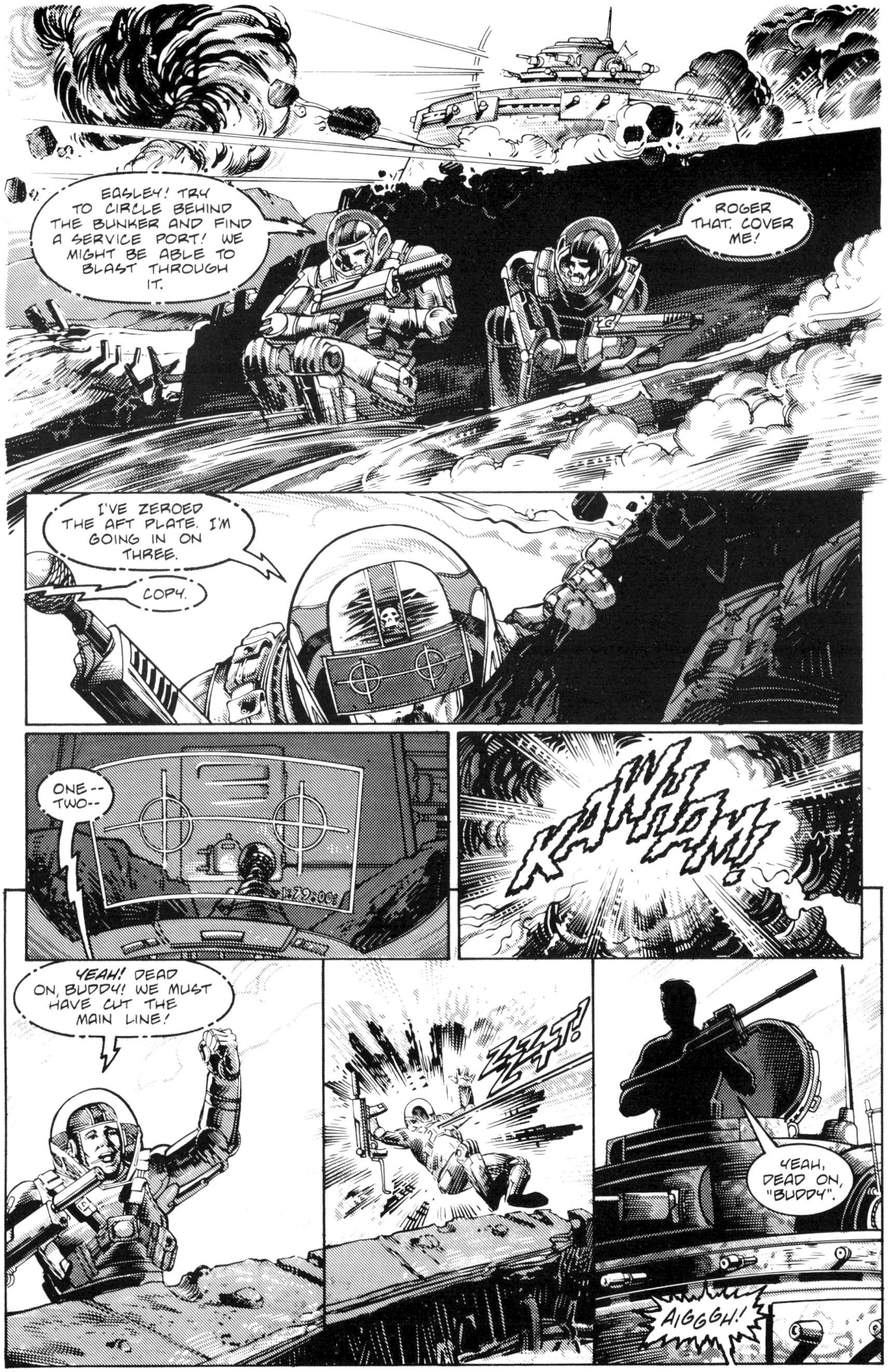
EASLEY! TRY TO CIRCLE BEHIND THE BUNKER AND FIND A SERVICE PORT! WE MIGHT BE ABLE TO BLAST THROUGH IT.
ROGER THAT. COVER ME!
I'VE ZEROED THE AFT PLATE. I'M GOING IN ON THREE.
COPY.
ONE-- TWO--
KAWHAM!
YEAH! DEAD ON, BUDDY! WE MUST HAVE CUT THE MAIN LINE!
ZZZT!
YEAH, DEAD ON, "BUDDY".
AIGGGH!

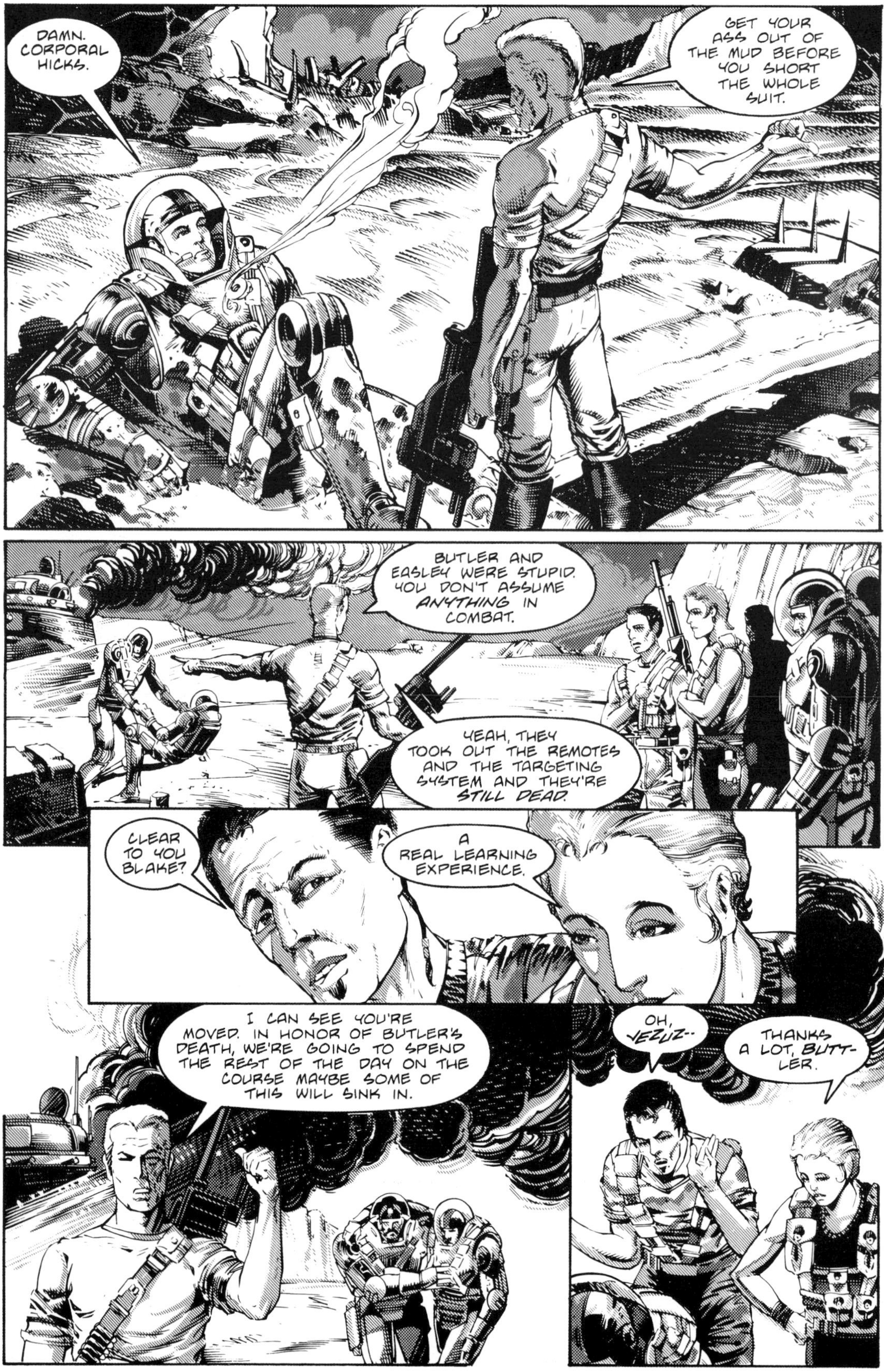

DAMN. CORPORAL HICKS.
GET YOUR ASS OUT OF THE MUD BEFORE YOU SHORT THE WHOLE SUIT.
BUTLER AND EASLEY WERE STUPID. YOU DON'T ASSUME ANYTHING IN COMBAT.
YEAH, THEY TOOK OUT THE REMOTES AND THE TARGETING SYSTEM AND THEY'RE STILL DEAD.
CLEAR TO YOU BLAKE?
A REAL LEARNING EXPERIENCE.
I CAN SEE YOU'RE MOVED. IN HONOR OF BUTLER'S DEATH, WE'RE GOING TO SPEND THE REST OF THE DAY ON THE COURSE MAYBE SOME OF THIS WILL SINK IN.
OH, JEZUZ--
THANKS A LOT, BUTT-LER.

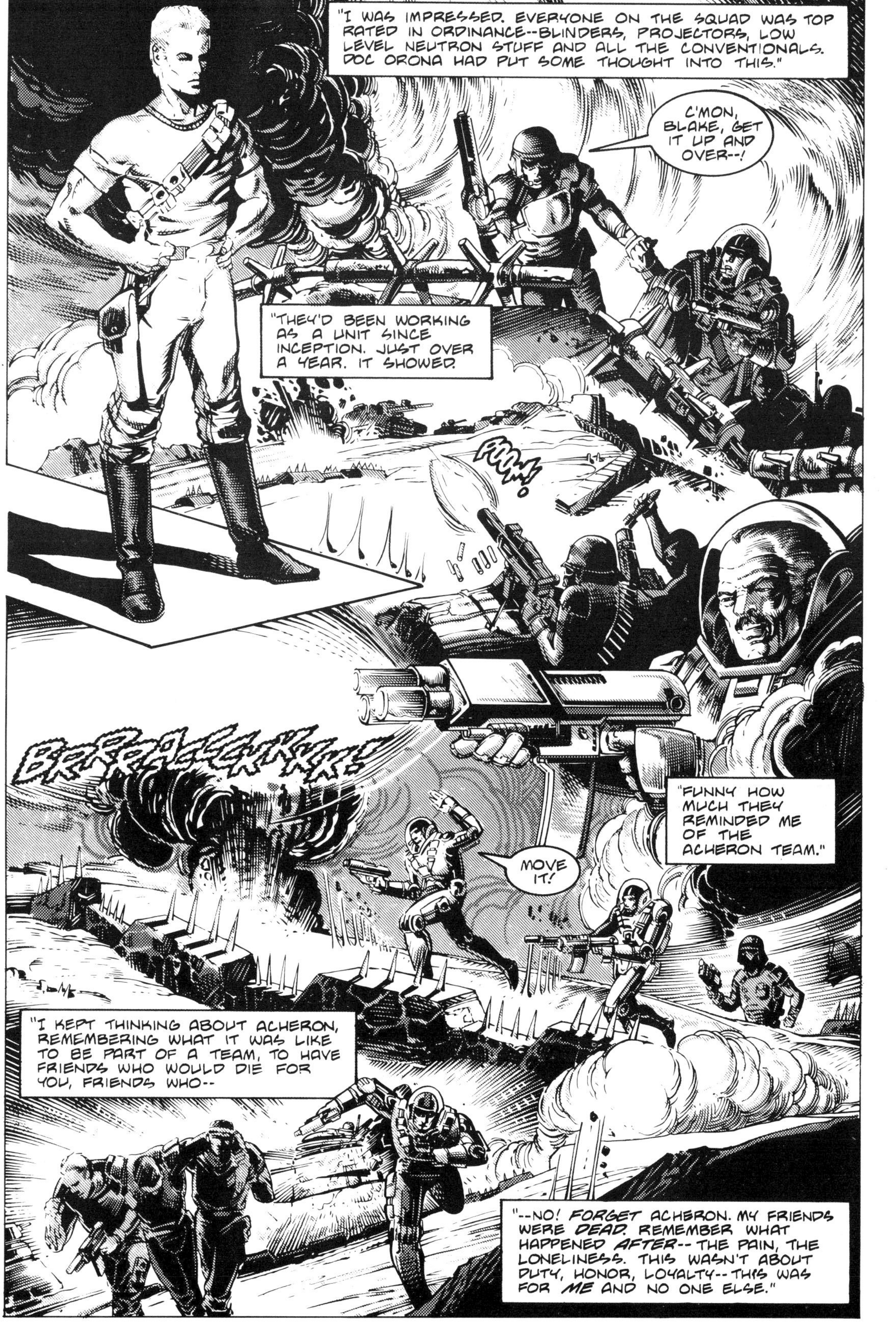
"I WAS IMPRESSED. EVERYONE ON THE SQUAD WAS TOP RATED IN ORDINANCE--BLINDERS, PROJECTORS, LOW LEVEL NEUTRON STUFF AND ALL THE CONVENTIONALS. DOC ORONA HAD PUT SOME THOUGHT INTO THIS."
C'MON, BLAKE, GET IT UP AND OVER--!
"THEY'D BEEN WORKING AS A UNIT SINCE INCEPTION. JUST OVER A YEAR. IT SHOWED.
"FUNNY HOW MUCH THEY REMINDED ME OF THE ACHERON TEAM."
MOVE IT!
"I KEPT THINKING ABOUT ACHERON, REMEMBERING WHAT IT WAS LIKE TO BE PART OF A TEAM, TO HAVE FRIENDS WHO WOULD DIE FOR YOU, FRIENDS WHO--
"--NO! FORGET ACHERON. MY FRIENDS WERE DEAD. REMEMBER WHAT HAPPENED AFTER-- THE PAIN, THE LONELINESS. THIS WASN'T ABOUT DUTY, HONOR, LOYALTY-- THIS WAS FOR ME AND NO ONE ELSE."

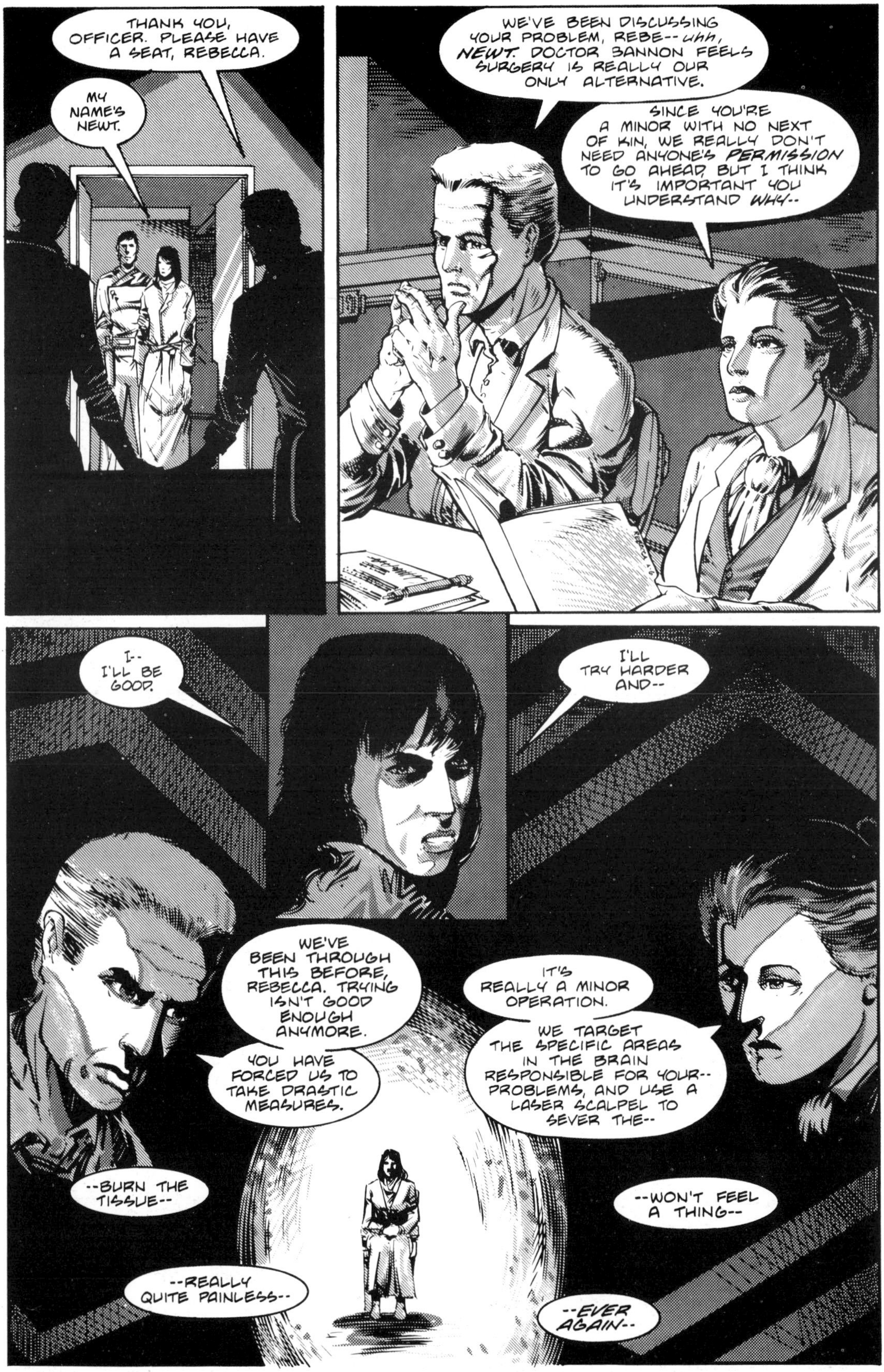
THANK YOU, OFFICER. PLEASE HAVE A SEAT, REBECCA.
MY NAME'S NEWT.
WE'VE BEEN DISCUSSING YOUR PROBLEM, REBE-- uhh, NEWT. DOCTOR BANNON FEELS SURGERY IS REALLY OUR ONLY ALTERNATIVE.
SINCE YOU'RE A MINOR WITH NO NEXT OF KIN, WE REALLY DON'T NEED ANYONE'S PERMISSION TO GO AHEAD, BUT I THINK IT'S IMPORTANT YOU UNDERSTAND WHY--
I-- I'LL BE GOOD.
I'LL TRY HARDER AND--
WE'VE BEEN THROUGH THIS BEFORE, REBECCA. TRYING ISN'T GOOD ENOUGH ANYMORE.
YOU HAVE FORCED US TO TAKE DRASTIC MEASURES.
IT'S REALLY A MINOR OPERATION.
WE TARGET THE SPECIFIC AREAS IN THE BRAIN RESPONSIBLE FOR YOUR-- PROBLEMS, AND USE A LASER SCALPEL TO SEVER THE--
--BURN THE TISSUE--
--WON'T FEEL A THING--
--REALLY QUITE PAINLESS--
--EVER AGAIN--

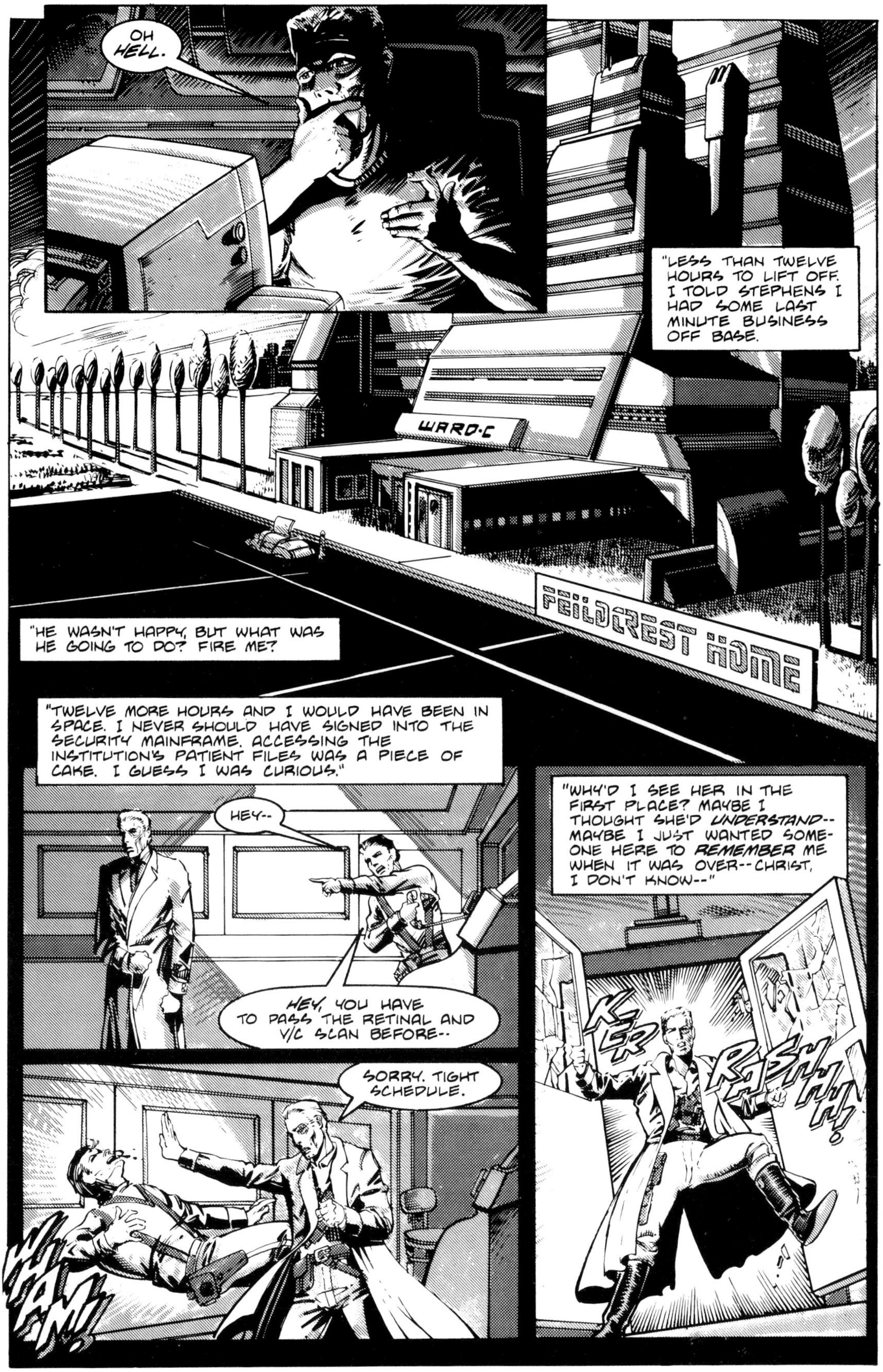

OH HELL.
"LESS THAN TWELVE HOURS TO LIFT OFF. I TOLD STEPHENS I HAD SOME LAST MINUTE BUSINESS OFF BASE.
WARD-C
FEILDCREST HOME
"HE WASN'T HAPPY, BUT WHAT WAS HE GOING TO DO? FIRE ME?
"TWELVE MORE HOURS AND I WOULD HAVE BEEN IN SPACE. I NEVER SHOULD HAVE SIGNED INTO THE SECURITY MAINFRAME. ACCESSING THE INSTITUTION'S PATIENT FILES WAS A PIECE OF CAKE. I GUESS I WAS CURIOUS."
HEY--
HEY, YOU HAVE TO PASS THE RETINAL AND V/C SCAN BEFORE--
SORRY. TIGHT SCHEDULE.
WHAM!
"WHY'D I SEE HER IN THE FIRST PLACE? MAYBE I THOUGHT SHE'D UNDERSTAND-- MAYBE I JUST WANTED SOMEONE HERE TO REMEMBER ME WHEN IT WAS OVER--CHRIST, I DON'T KNOW--"
KERRASHH!

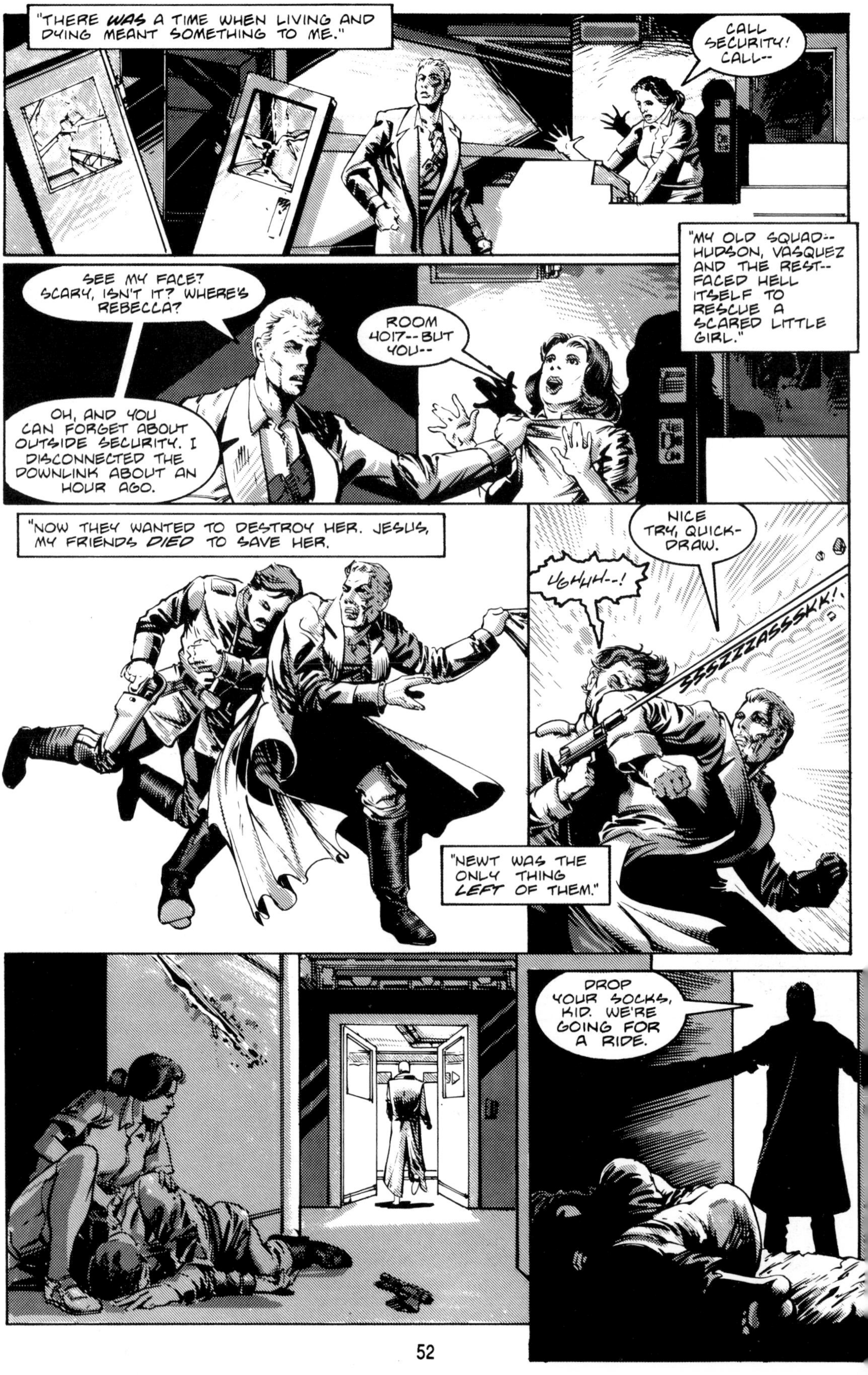
"THERE WAS A TIME WHEN LIVING AND DYING MEANT SOMETHING TO ME."
CALL SECURITY! CALL--
SEE MY FACE? SCARY, ISN'T IT? WHERE'S REBECCA?
ROOM 4017--BUT YOU--
OH, AND YOU CAN FORGET ABOUT OUTSIDE SECURITY. I DISCONNECTED THE DOWNLINK ABOUT AN HOUR AGO.
"MY OLD SQUAD--HUDSON, VASQUEZ AND THE REST--FACED HELL ITSELF TO RESCUE A SCARED LITTLE GIRL."
"NOW THEY WANTED TO DESTROY HER. JESUS, MY FRIENDS DIED TO SAVE HER.
UGHHH--!
NICE TRY, QUICK-DRAW.
SSSZZZZASSSSKK!
"NEWT WAS THE ONLY THING LEFT OF THEM."
DROP YOUR SOCKS, KID. WE'RE GOING FOR A RIDE.

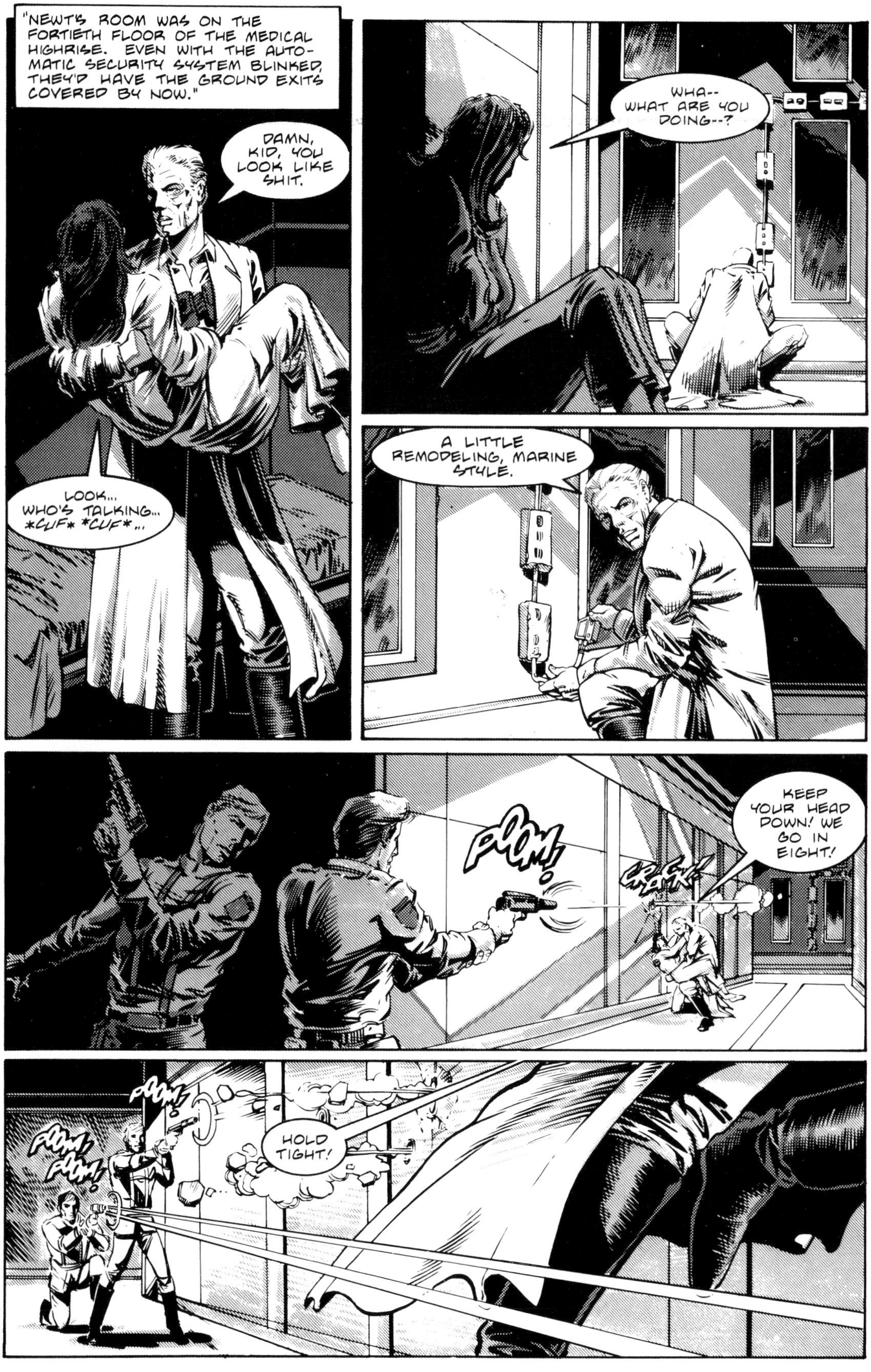

"NEWT'S ROOM WAS ON THE FORTIETH FLOOR OF THE MEDICAL HIGHRISE. EVEN WITH THE AUTOMATIC SECURITY SYSTEM BLINKED, THEY'D HAVE THE GROUND EXITS COVERED BY NOW."
DAMN, KID, YOU LOOK LIKE SHIT.
LOOK... WHO'S TALKING... *CUF* *CUF*...
WHA-- WHAT ARE YOU DOING--?
A LITTLE REMODELING, MARINE STYLE.
POOM!
CRACK!
KEEP YOUR HEAD DOWN! WE GO IN EIGHT!
POOM!
POOM! POOM!
HOLD TIGHT!

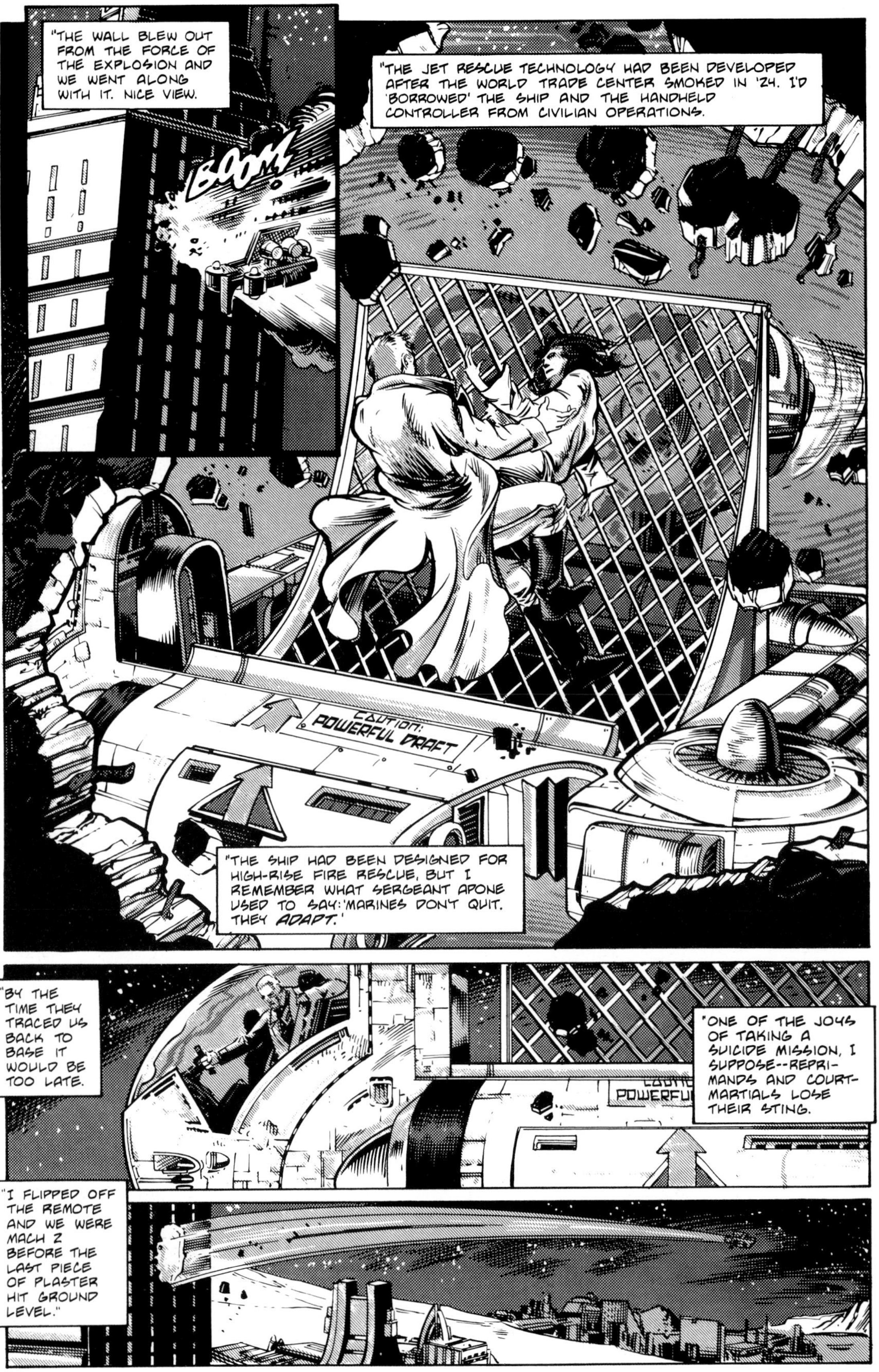
"THE WALL BLEW OUT FROM THE FORCE OF THE EXPLOSION AND WE WENT ALONG WITH IT. NICE VIEW.
BOOM
"THE JET RESCUE TECHNOLOGY HAD BEEN DEVELOPED AFTER THE WORLD TRADE CENTER SMOKED IN '24. I'D 'BORROWED' THE SHIP AND THE HANDHELD CONTROLLER FROM CIVILIAN OPERATIONS.
CAUTION: POWERFUL DRAFT
"THE SHIP HAD BEEN DESIGNED FOR HIGH-RISE FIRE RESCUE, BUT I REMEMBER WHAT SERGEANT APONE USED TO SAY: 'MARINES DON'T QUIT. THEY ADAPT.'
"BY THE TIME THEY TRACED US BACK TO BASE IT WOULD BE TOO LATE.
"ONE OF THE JOYS OF TAKING A SUICIDE MISSION, I SUPPOSE--REPRIMANDS AND COURT-MARTIALS LOSE THEIR STING.
"I FLIPPED OFF THE REMOTE AND WE WERE MACH 2 BEFORE THE LAST PIECE OF PLASTER HIT GROUND LEVEL."

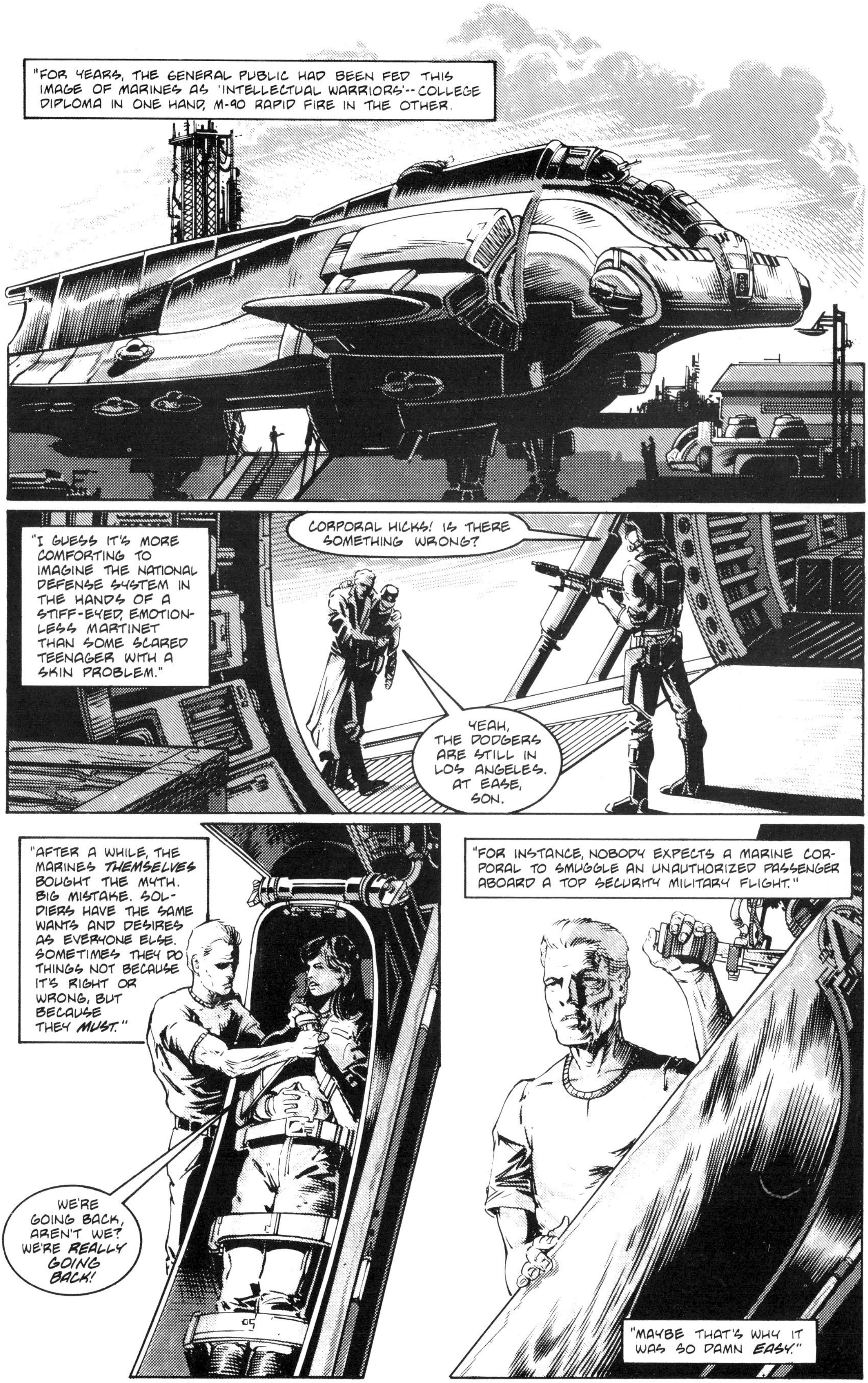
"FOR YEARS, THE GENERAL PUBLIC HAD BEEN FED THIS IMAGE OF MARINES AS 'INTELLECTUAL WARRIORS'--COLLEGE DIPLOMA IN ONE HAND, M-90 RAPID FIRE IN THE OTHER.
"I GUESS IT'S MORE COMFORTING TO IMAGINE THE NATIONAL DEFENSE SYSTEM IN THE HANDS OF A STIFF-EYED, EMOTIONLESS MARTINET THAN SOME SCARED TEENAGER WITH A SKIN PROBLEM."
CORPORAL HICKS! IS THERE SOMETHING WRONG?
YEAH, THE DODGERS ARE STILL IN LOS ANGELES. AT EASE, SON.
"AFTER A WHILE, THE MARINES THEMSELVES BOUGHT THE MYTH. BIG MISTAKE. SOLDIERS HAVE THE SAME WANTS AND DESIRES AS EVERYONE ELSE. SOMETIMES THEY DO THINGS NOT BECAUSE IT'S RIGHT OR WRONG, BUT BECAUSE THEY MUST."
WE'RE GOING BACK, AREN'T WE? WE'RE REALLY GOING BACK!
"FOR INSTANCE, NOBODY EXPECTS A MARINE CORPORAL TO SMUGGLE AN UNAUTHORIZED PASSENGER ABOARD A TOP SECURITY MILITARY FLIGHT."
"MAYBE THAT'S WHY IT WAS SO DAMN EASY."

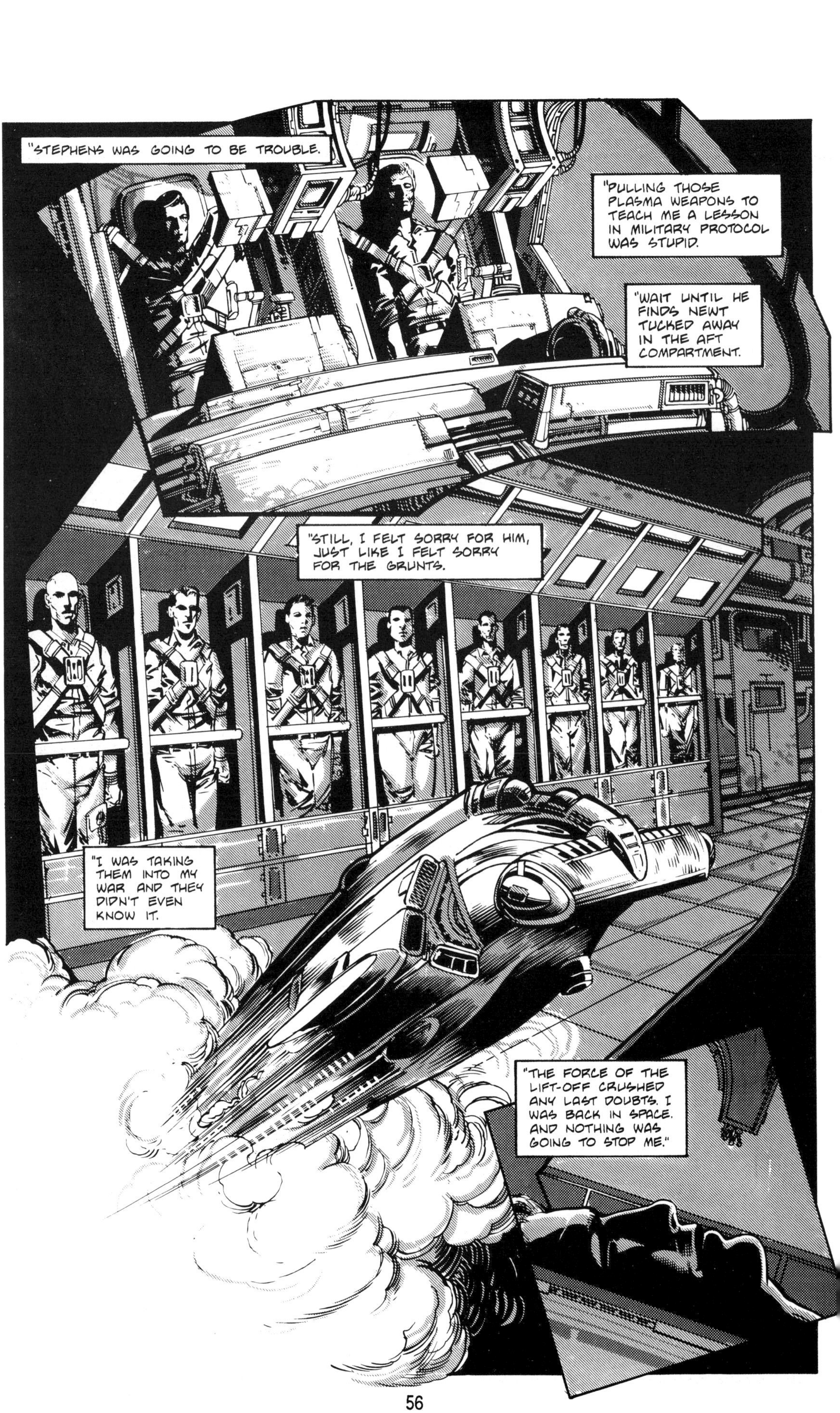
"STEPHENS WAS GOING TO BE TROUBLE.
"PULLING THOSE PLASMA WEAPONS TO TEACH ME A LESSON IN MILITARY PROTOCOL WAS STUPID.
"WAIT UNTIL HE FINDS NEWT TUCKED AWAY IN THE AFT COMPARTMENT.
"STILL, I FELT SORRY FOR HIM, JUST LIKE I FELT SORRY FOR THE GRUNTS.
"I WAS TAKING THEM INTO MY WAR AND THEY DIDN'T EVEN KNOW IT.
"THE FORCE OF THE LIFT-OFF CRUSHED ANY LAST DOUBTS. I WAS BACK IN SPACE. AND NOTHING WAS GOING TO STOP ME."

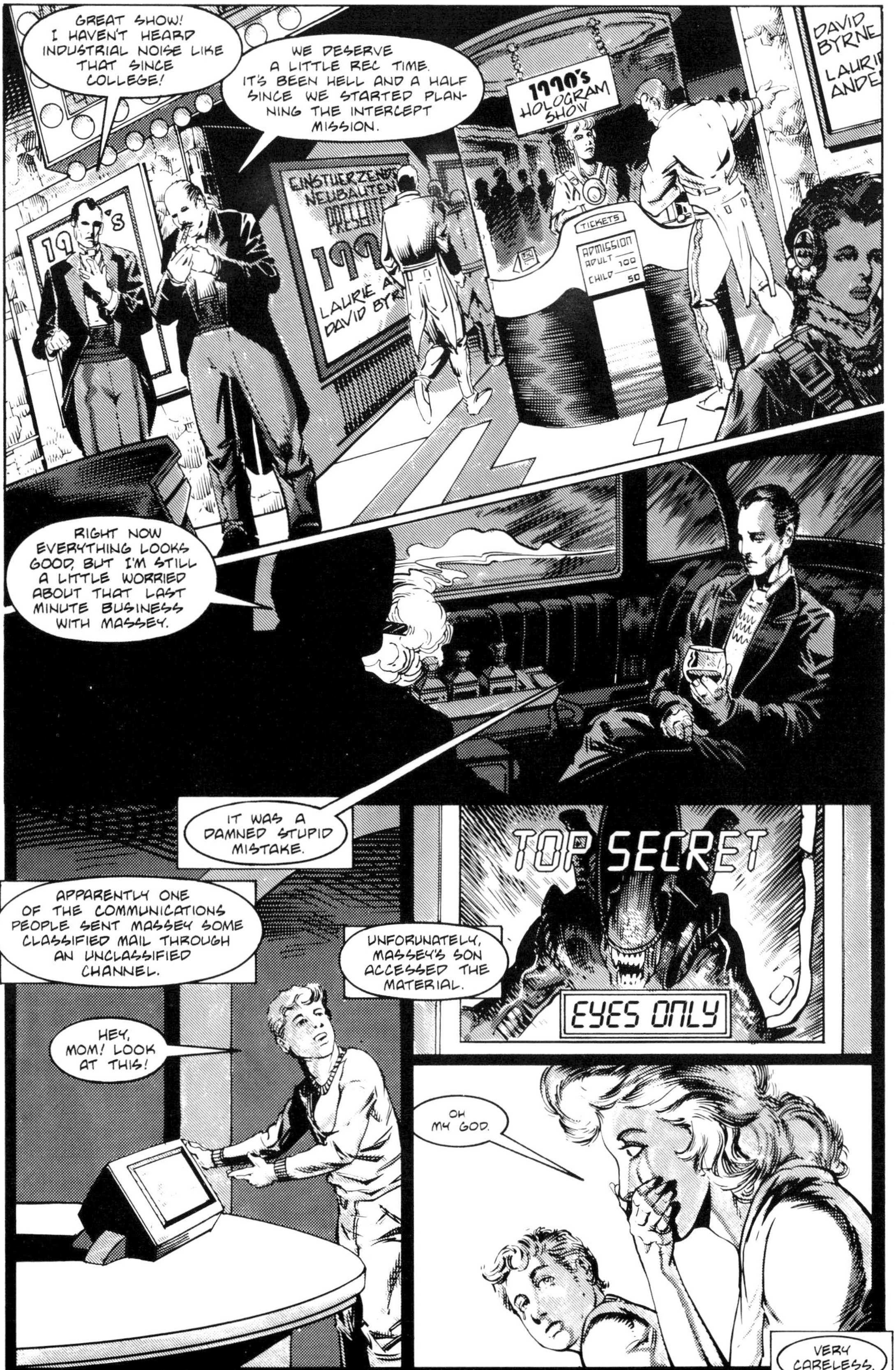
GREAT SHOW! I HAVEN'T HEARD INDUSTRIAL NOISE LIKE THAT SINCE COLLEGE!
WE DESERVE A LITTLE REC TIME. IT'S BEEN HELL AND A HALF SINCE WE STARTED PLANNING THE INTERCEPT MISSION.
1990's HOLOGRAM SHOW
DAVID BYRNE LAURIE ANDE
EINSTUERZENDE NEUBAUTEN
TICKETS
ADMISSION ADULT 100 CHILD 50
LAURIE A DAVID BYR
RIGHT NOW EVERYTHING LOOKS GOOD, BUT I'M STILL A LITTLE WORRIED ABOUT THAT LAST MINUTE BUSINESS WITH MASSEY.
IT WAS A DAMNED STUPID MISTAKE.
APPARENTLY ONE OF THE COMMUNICATIONS PEOPLE SENT MASSEY SOME CLASSIFIED MAIL THROUGH AN UNCLASSIFIED CHANNEL.
UNFORUNATELY, MASSEY'S SON ACCESSED THE MATERIAL.
TOP SECRET
EYES ONLY
HEY, MOM! LOOK AT THIS!
OH MY GOD.
VERY CARELESS.

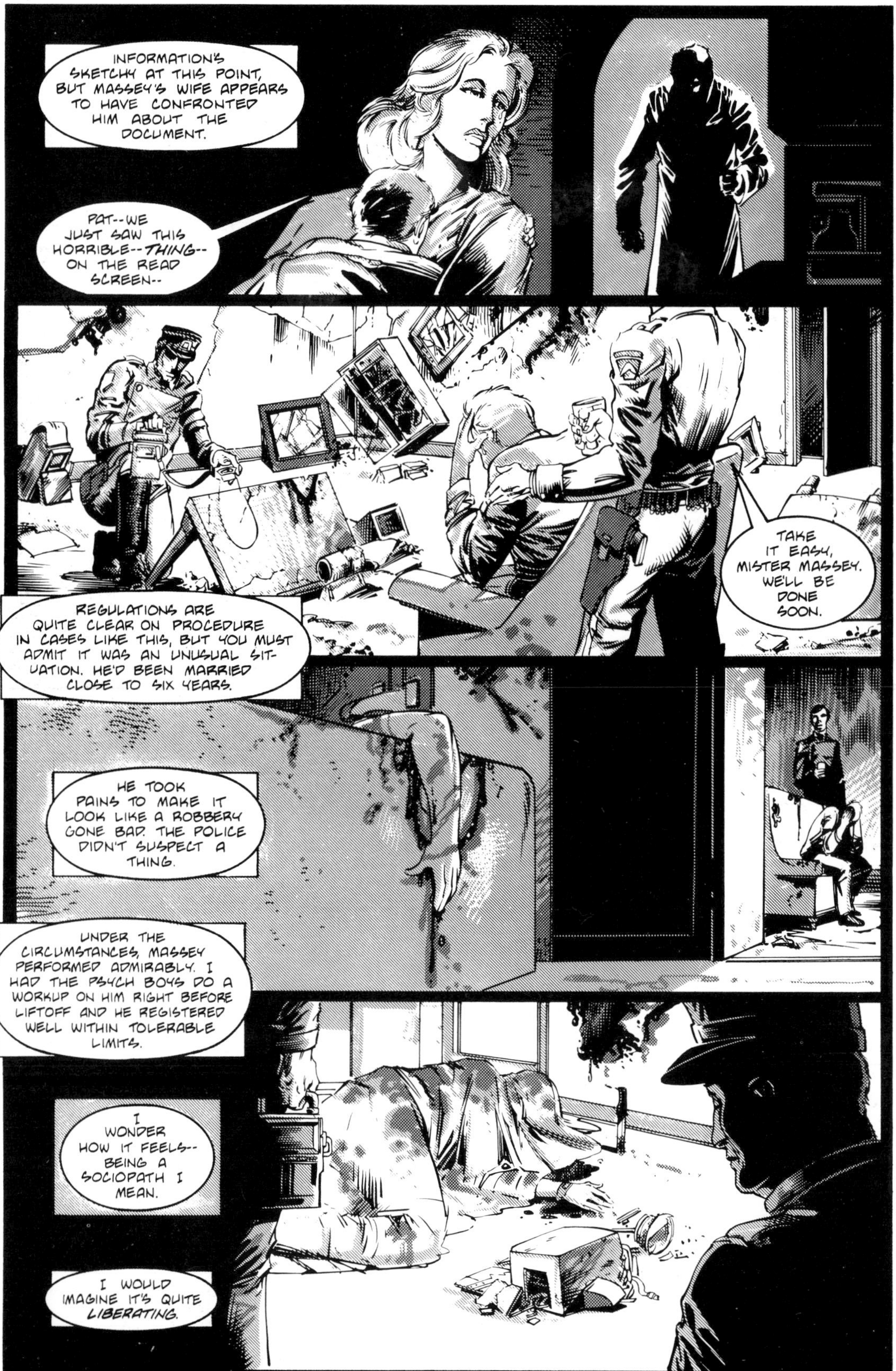
INFORMATION'S SKETCHY AT THIS POINT, BUT MASSEY'S WIFE APPEARS TO HAVE CONFRONTED HIM ABOUT THE DOCUMENT.
PAT--WE JUST SAW THIS HORRIBLE--*THING*--ON THE READ SCREEN--
TAKE IT EASY, MISTER MASSEY. WE'LL BE DONE SOON.
REGULATIONS ARE QUITE CLEAR ON PROCEDURE IN CASES LIKE THIS, BUT YOU MUST ADMIT IT WAS AN UNUSUAL SITUATION. HE'D BEEN MARRIED CLOSE TO SIX YEARS.
HE TOOK PAINS TO MAKE IT LOOK LIKE A ROBBERY GONE BAD. THE POLICE DIDN'T SUSPECT A THING.
UNDER THE CIRCUMSTANCES, MASSEY PERFORMED ADMIRABLY. I HAD THE PSYCH BOYS DO A WORKUP ON HIM RIGHT BEFORE LIFTOFF AND HE REGISTERED WELL WITHIN TOLERABLE LIMITS.
I WONDER HOW IT FEELS--BEING A SOCIOPATH I MEAN.
I WOULD IMAGINE IT'S QUITE *LIBERATING*.

EYES ONLY
DATA LOCK
BIONATIONAL INTERNAL MEMORANDUM
OPERATION: *OUTREACH*
Progress report. The Government vessel *Benedict* launched on schedule 4/5/54. First in command, Col. Stephens, second in command, Cpl. Hicks.
BIONATIONAL
Our chase ship *K-014* launched in pursuit immediately thereafter, captained by Bionational Executive Assistant Patrick Massey.
The government is seeking to retrieve specimens of an alien lifeform for its Weapons Development Program. If they are successful, this could seriously impact Bionational's claim of sole patent right on the new lifeform technology.
The *K-014*'s mission is twofold. First, to follow the *Benedict* to the alien homeworld and gather biological data on the lifeform.
Second, to inhibit the *Benedict*'s crew from retrieving a viable test subject. Captain Massey has been given *carte blanche* toward this end.

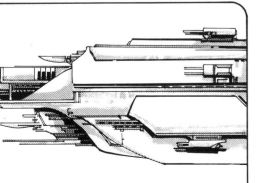

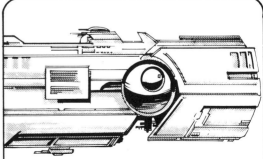

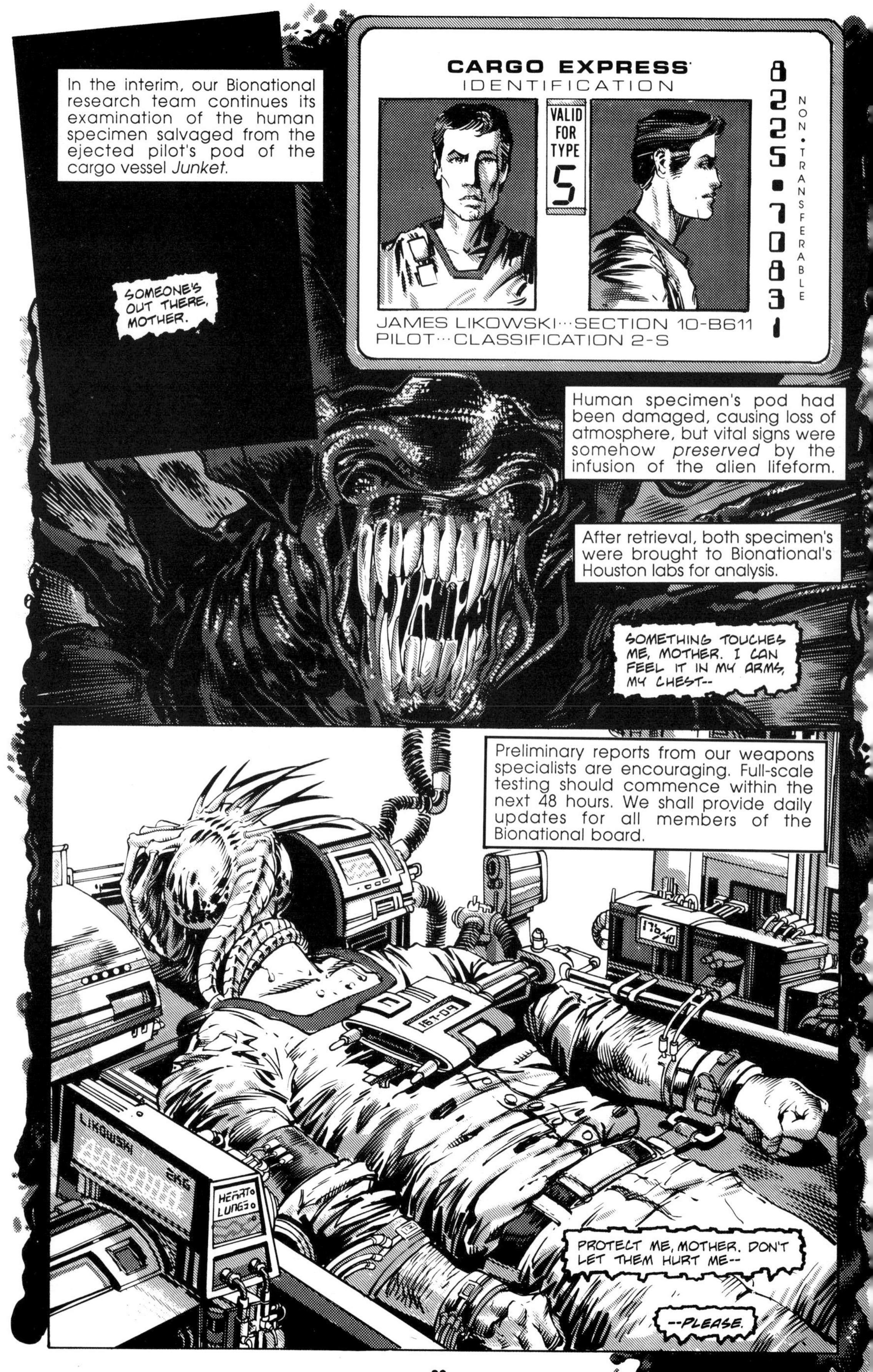

In the interim, our Bionational research team continues its examination of the human specimen salvaged from the ejected pilot's pod of the cargo vessel *Junket*.
CARGO EXPRESS
IDENTIFICATION
VALID FOR TYPE
5
8225•70831
NON•TRANSFERABLE
JAMES LIKOWSKI···SECTION 10-B611
PILOT···CLASSIFICATION 2-S
SOMEONE'S OUT THERE, MOTHER.
Human specimen's pod had been damaged, causing loss of atmosphere, but vital signs were somehow *preserved* by the infusion of the alien lifeform.
After retrieval, both specimen's were brought to Bionational's Houston labs for analysis.
SOMETHING TOUCHES ME, MOTHER. I CAN FEEL IT IN MY ARMS, MY CHEST--
Preliminary reports from our weapons specialists are encouraging. Full-scale testing should commence within the next 48 hours. We shall provide daily updates for all members of the Bionational board.
HEART
LUNGS
PROTECT ME, MOTHER. DON'T LET THEM HURT ME--
--PLEASE.

Dr. Ranier: Start wherever you'd like.

Patient Heerman: Okay. Okay. **(pause)** I'm with my mother. We're still in L.A. —

Dr. Ranier: Your mother died several years ago?

Patient Heerman: Cancer. **(pause)** We're taking the Wilshire tube into downtown L.A. Right then I knew I was dreaming...I've *never* seen an empty tube.

Patient Heerman: All of the sudden, we hear this loud—*scraping* sound —

Dr. Ranier: Scraping? How do you mean?

Patient Heerman: Like...like fingernails ripping fabric. **(pause)** Then, suddenly, the car *stops* —

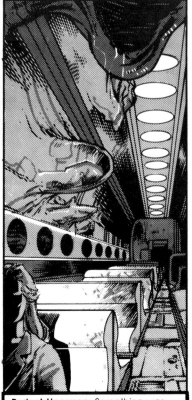

Patient Heerman: Something was trying to...*get in.* I pounded on the door, hoping someone would hear us—

Patient Heerman: Then these—*things* started to—*claw* into the car. I ran to my mother and she made this sick, *bubbling* sound, deep in her chest—

Patient Heerman: It was just a stupid nightmare, right? *Right?*

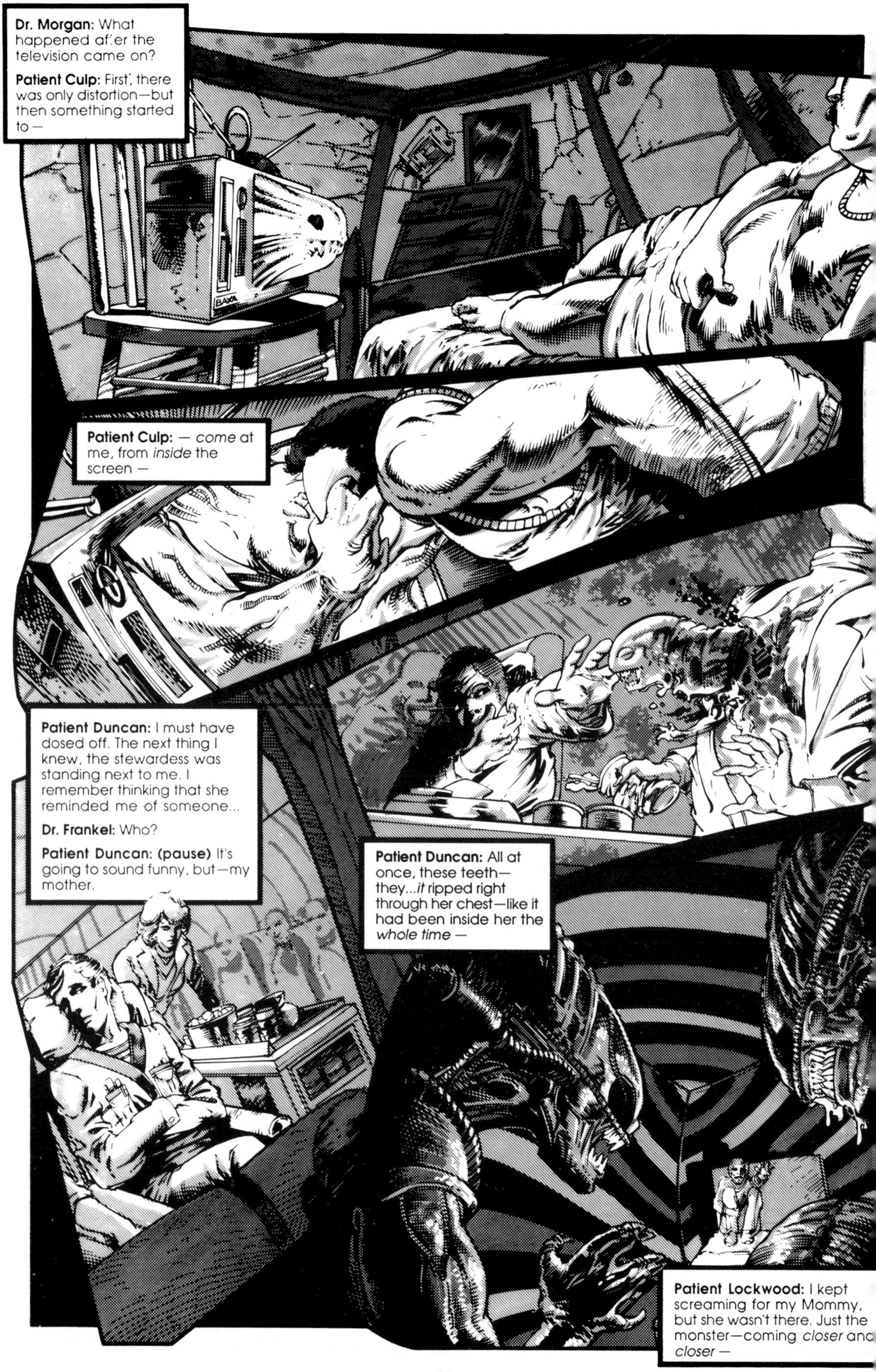
Dr. Morgan: What happened after the television came on?
Patient Culp: First, there was only distortion—but then something started to —
Patient Culp: — come at me, from inside the screen —
Patient Duncan: I must have dosed off. The next thing I knew, the stewardess was standing next to me. I remember thinking that she reminded me of someone...
Dr. Frankel: Who?
Patient Duncan: (pause) It's going to sound funny, but—my mother.
Patient Duncan: All at once, these teeth—they...it ripped right through her chest—like it had been inside her the whole time —
Patient Lockwood: I kept screaming for my Mommy, but she wasn't there. Just the monster—coming closer and closer —

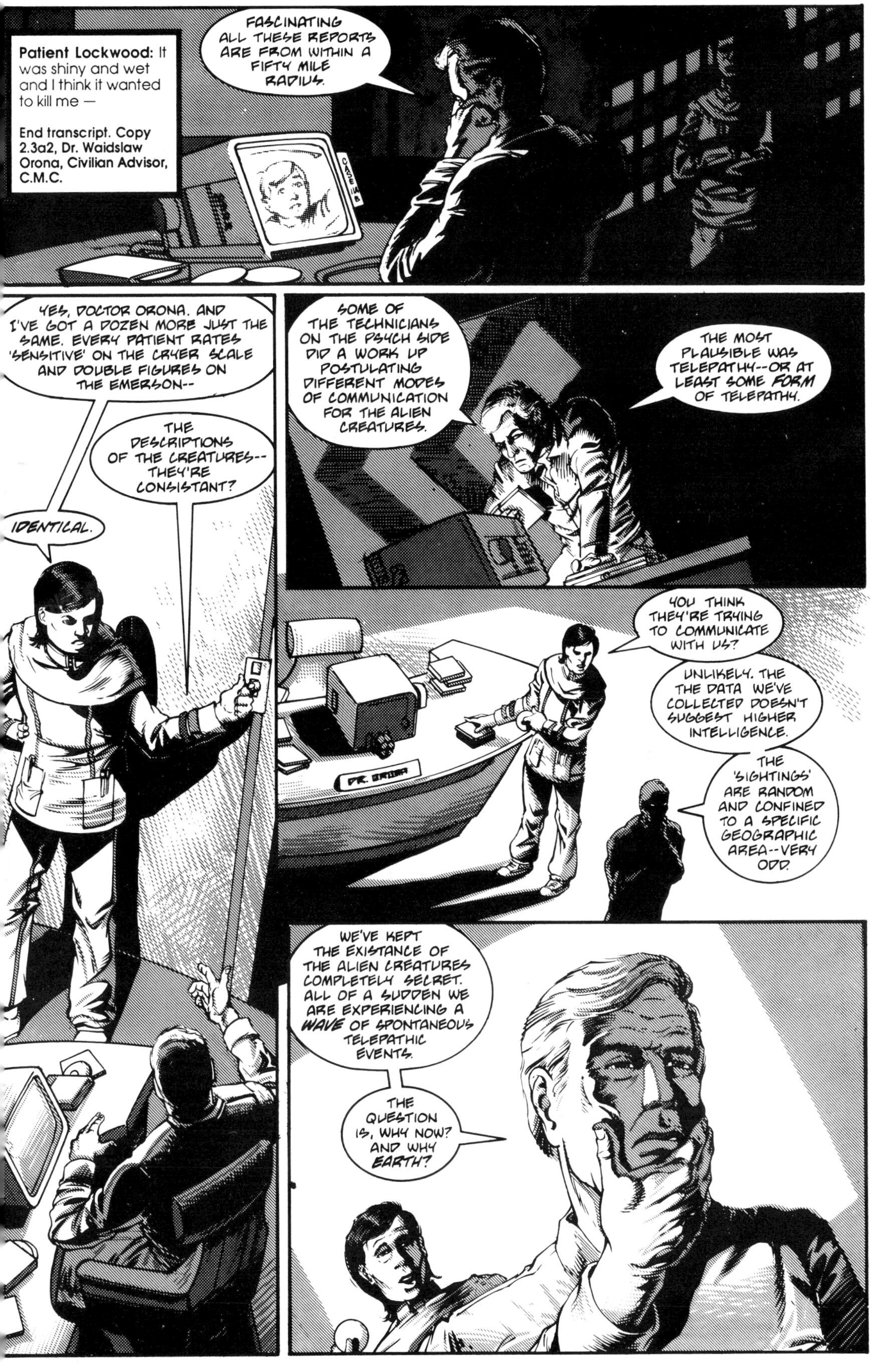
Patient Lockwood: It was shiny and wet and I think it wanted to kill me —
End transcript. Copy 2.3a2, Dr. Waidslaw Orona, Civilian Advisor, C.M.C.
FASCINATING ALL THESE REPORTS ARE FROM WITHIN A FIFTY MILE RADIUS.
CASE 14B
YES, DOCTOR ORONA. AND I'VE GOT A DOZEN MORE JUST THE SAME. EVERY PATIENT RATES 'SENSITIVE' ON THE CRYER SCALE AND DOUBLE FIGURES ON THE EMERSON--
THE DESCRIPTIONS OF THE CREATURES-- THEY'RE CONSISTANT?
IDENTICAL.
SOME OF THE TECHNICIANS ON THE PSYCH SIDE DID A WORK UP POSTULATING DIFFERENT MODES OF COMMUNICATION FOR THE ALIEN CREATURES.
THE MOST PLAUSIBLE WAS TELEPATHY--OR AT LEAST SOME FORM OF TELEPATHY.
YOU THINK THEY'RE TRYING TO COMMUNICATE WITH US?
UNLIKELY. THE THE DATA WE'VE COLLECTED DOESN'T SUGGEST HIGHER INTELLIGENCE.
THE 'SIGHTINGS' ARE RANDOM AND CONFINED TO A SPECIFIC GEOGRAPHIC AREA--VERY ODD.
WE'VE KEPT THE EXISTANCE OF THE ALIEN CREATURES COMPLETELY SECRET. ALL OF A SUDDEN WE ARE EXPERIENCING A WAVE OF SPONTANEOUS TELEPATHIC EVENTS.
THE QUESTION IS, WHY NOW? AND WHY EARTH?

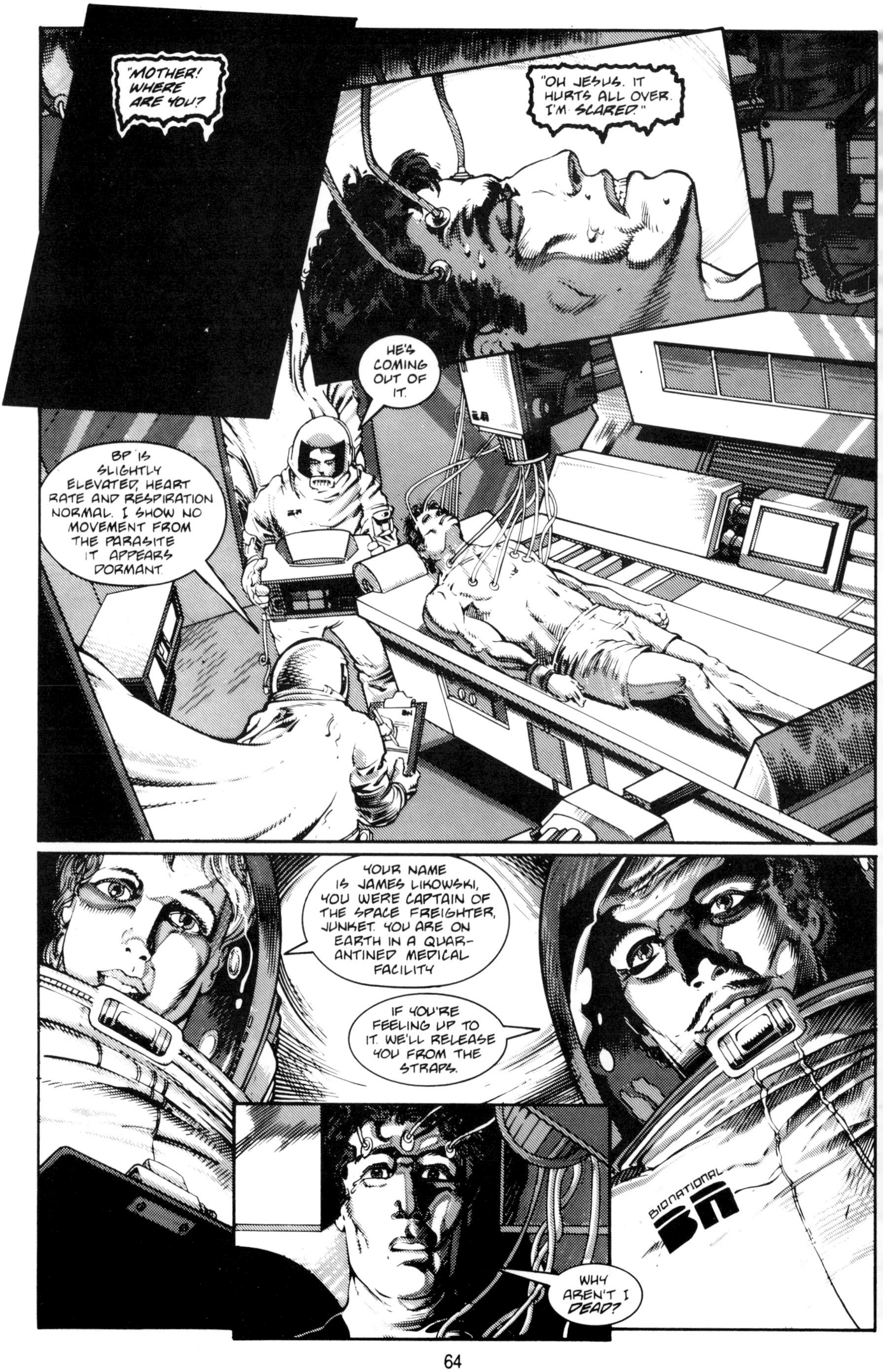
"MOTHER! WHERE ARE YOU?
"OH JESUS. IT HURTS ALL OVER. I'M SCARED."
HE'S COMING OUT OF IT.
BP IS SLIGHTLY ELEVATED, HEART RATE AND RESPIRATION NORMAL. I SHOW NO MOVEMENT FROM THE PARASITE IT APPEARS DORMANT.
YOUR NAME IS JAMES LIKOWSKI, YOU WERE CAPTAIN OF THE SPACE FREIGHTER, JUNKET. YOU ARE ON EARTH IN A QUAR-ANTINED MEDICAL FACILITY
IF YOU'RE FEELING UP TO IT. WE'LL RELEASE YOU FROM THE STRAPS.
BIONATIONAL BN
WHY AREN'T I DEAD?

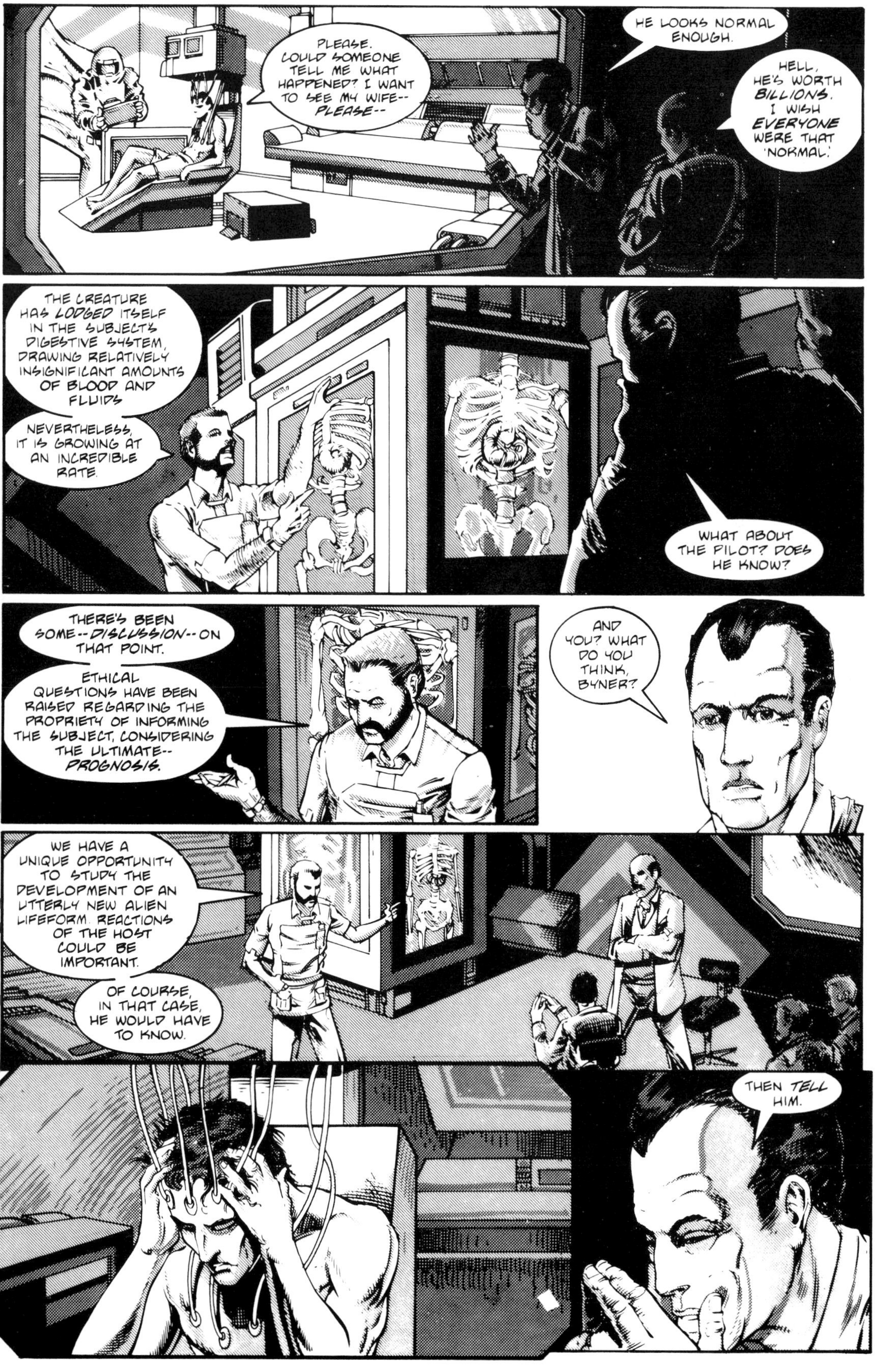
PLEASE. COULD SOMEONE TELL ME WHAT HAPPENED? I WANT TO SEE MY WIFE-- PLEASE--
HE LOOKS NORMAL ENOUGH.
HELL, HE'S WORTH BILLIONS. I WISH EVERYONE WERE THAT 'NORMAL.'
THE CREATURE HAS LODGED ITSELF IN THE SUBJECT'S DIGESTIVE SYSTEM, DRAWING RELATIVELY INSIGNIFICANT AMOUNTS OF BLOOD AND FLUIDS.
NEVERTHELESS, IT IS GROWING AT AN INCREDIBLE RATE.
WHAT ABOUT THE PILOT? DOES HE KNOW?
THERE'S BEEN SOME--DISCUSSION--ON THAT POINT.
ETHICAL QUESTIONS HAVE BEEN RAISED REGARDING THE PROPRIETY OF INFORMING THE SUBJECT, CONSIDERING THE ULTIMATE--PROGNOSIS.
AND YOU? WHAT DO YOU THINK, BYNER?
WE HAVE A UNIQUE OPPORTUNITY TO STUDY THE DEVELOPMENT OF AN UTTERLY NEW ALIEN LIFEFORM. REACTIONS OF THE HOST COULD BE IMPORTANT.
OF COURSE, IN THAT CASE, HE WOULD HAVE TO KNOW.
THEN TELL HIM.

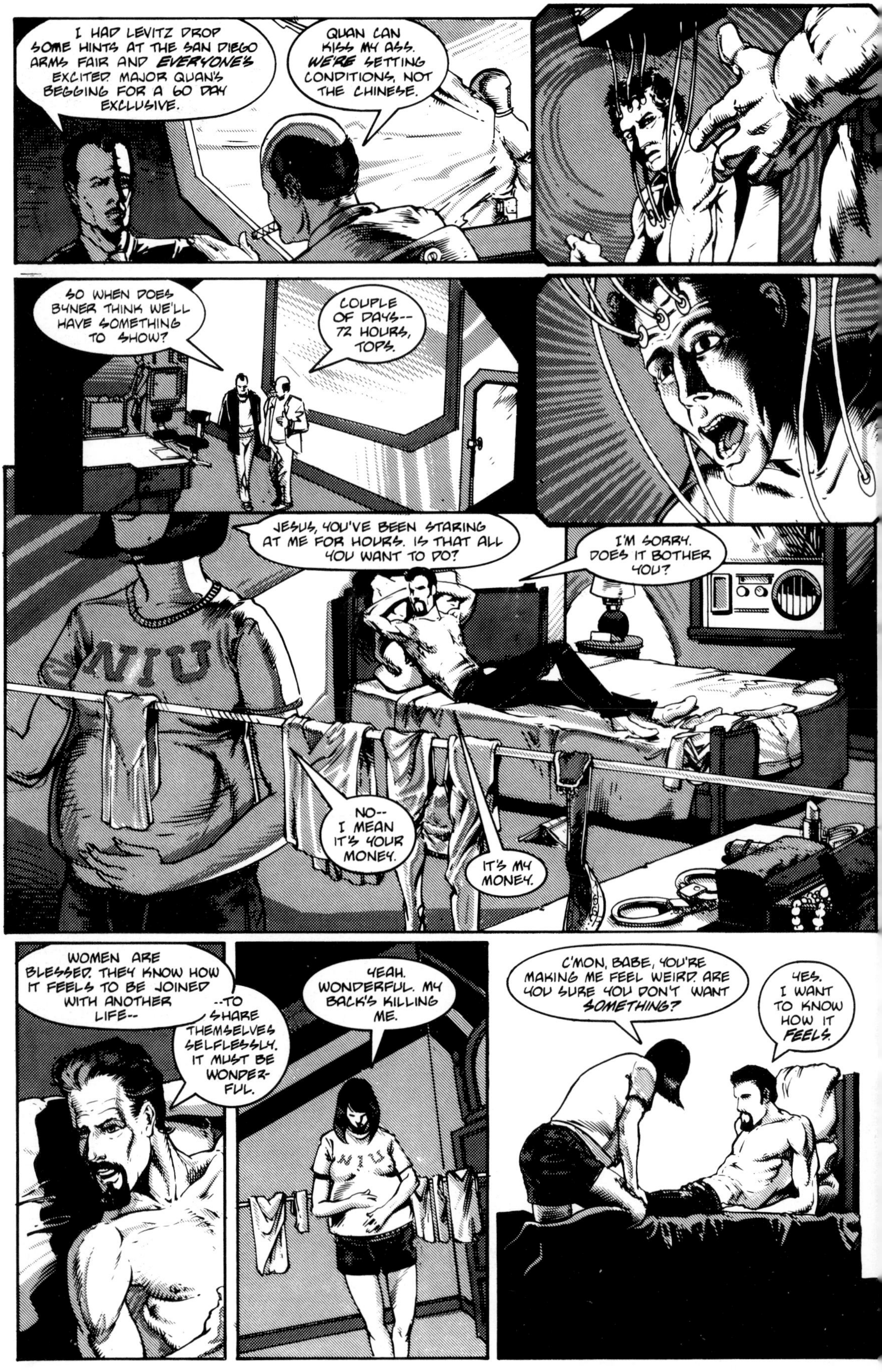
I HAD LEVITZ DROP SOME HINTS AT THE SAN DIEGO ARMS FAIR AND EVERYONE'S EXCITED. MAJOR QUAN'S BEGGING FOR A 60 DAY EXCLUSIVE.
QUAN CAN KISS MY ASS. WE'RE SETTING CONDITIONS, NOT THE CHINESE.
SO WHEN DOES BYNER THINK WE'LL HAVE SOMETHING TO SHOW?
COUPLE OF DAYS-- 72 HOURS, TOPS.
JESUS, YOU'VE BEEN STARING AT ME FOR HOURS. IS THAT ALL YOU WANT TO DO?
I'M SORRY. DOES IT BOTHER YOU?
NO-- I MEAN IT'S YOUR MONEY.
IT'S MY MONEY.
WOMEN ARE BLESSED. THEY KNOW HOW IT FEELS TO BE JOINED WITH ANOTHER LIFE--
--TO SHARE THEMSELVES SELFLESSLY. IT MUST BE WONDERFUL.
YEAH. WONDERFUL. MY BACK'S KILLING ME.
C'MON, BABE, YOU'RE MAKING ME FEEL WEIRD. ARE YOU SURE YOU DON'T WANT SOMETHING?
YES. I WANT TO KNOW HOW IT FEELS.

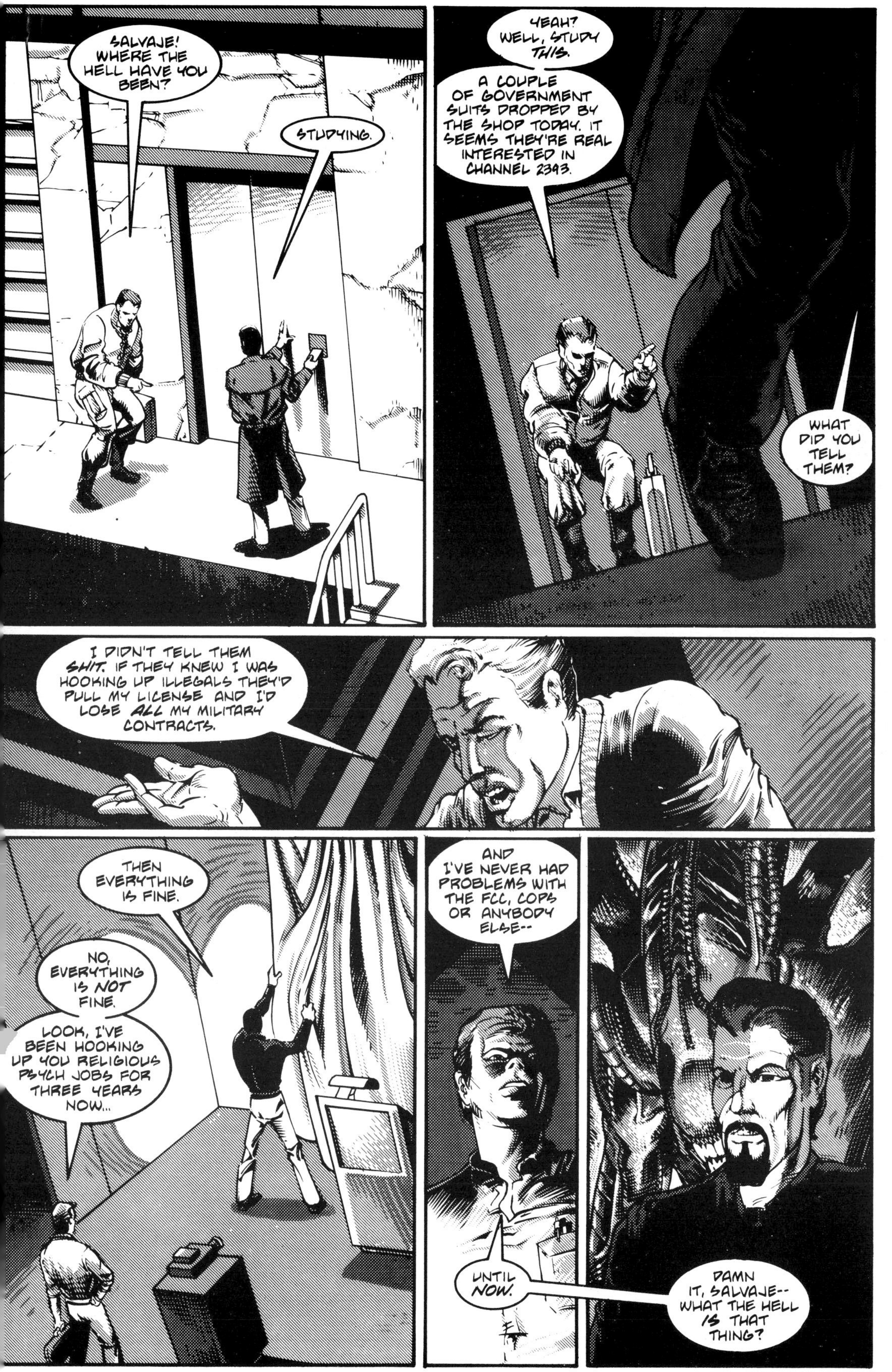
SALVAJE! WHERE THE HELL HAVE YOU BEEN?
STUDYING.
YEAH? WELL, STUDY THIS.
A COUPLE OF GOVERNMENT SUITS DROPPED BY THE SHOP TODAY. IT SEEMS THEY'RE REAL INTERESTED IN CHANNEL 2343.
WHAT DID YOU TELL THEM?
I DIDN'T TELL THEM SHIT. IF THEY KNEW I WAS HOOKING UP ILLEGALS THEY'D PULL MY LICENSE AND I'D LOSE ALL MY MILITARY CONTRACTS.
THEN EVERYTHING IS FINE.
NO, EVERYTHING IS NOT FINE.
LOOK, I'VE BEEN HOOKING UP YOU RELIGIOUS PSYCH JOBS FOR THREE YEARS NOW...
AND I'VE NEVER HAD PROBLEMS WITH THE FCC, COPS OR ANYBODY ELSE--
UNTIL NOW.
DAMN IT, SALVAJE-- WHAT THE HELL IS THAT THING?

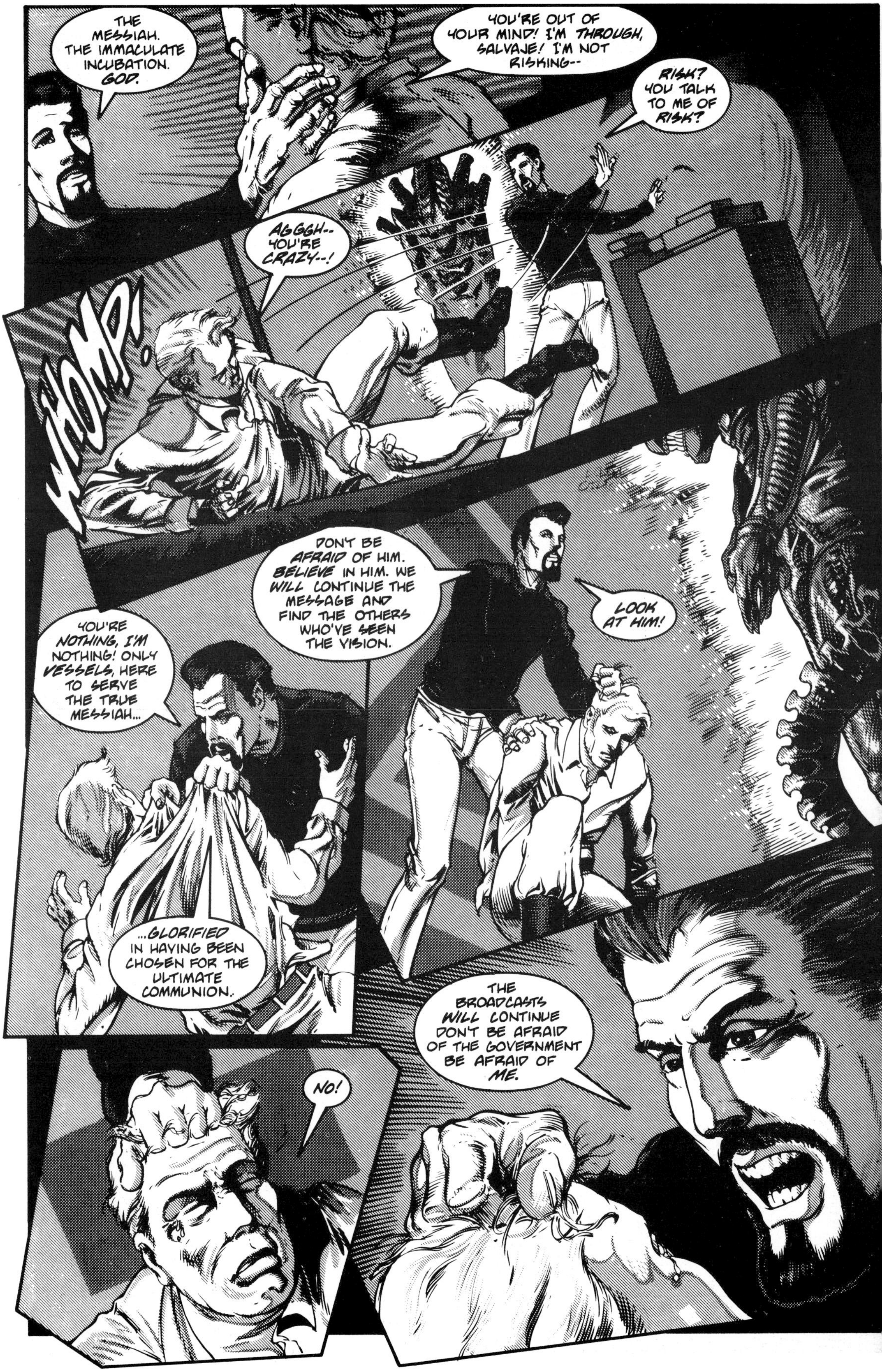
THE MESSIAH. THE IMMACULATE INCUBATION. GOD.
YOU'RE OUT OF YOUR MIND! I'M THROUGH, SALVAJE! I'M NOT RISKING--
RISK? YOU TALK TO ME OF RISK?
AGGGH-- YOU'RE CRAZY--!
WHOMP!
DON'T BE AFRAID OF HIM. BELIEVE IN HIM. WE WILL CONTINUE THE MESSAGE AND FIND THE OTHERS WHO'VE SEEN THE VISION.
LOOK AT HIM!
YOU'RE NOTHING, I'M NOTHING! ONLY VESSELS, HERE TO SERVE THE TRUE MESSIAH...
...GLORIFIED IN HAVING BEEN CHOSEN FOR THE ULTIMATE COMMUNION.
NO!
THE BROADCASTS WILL CONTINUE DON'T BE AFRAID OF THE GOVERNMENT BE AFRAID OF ME.

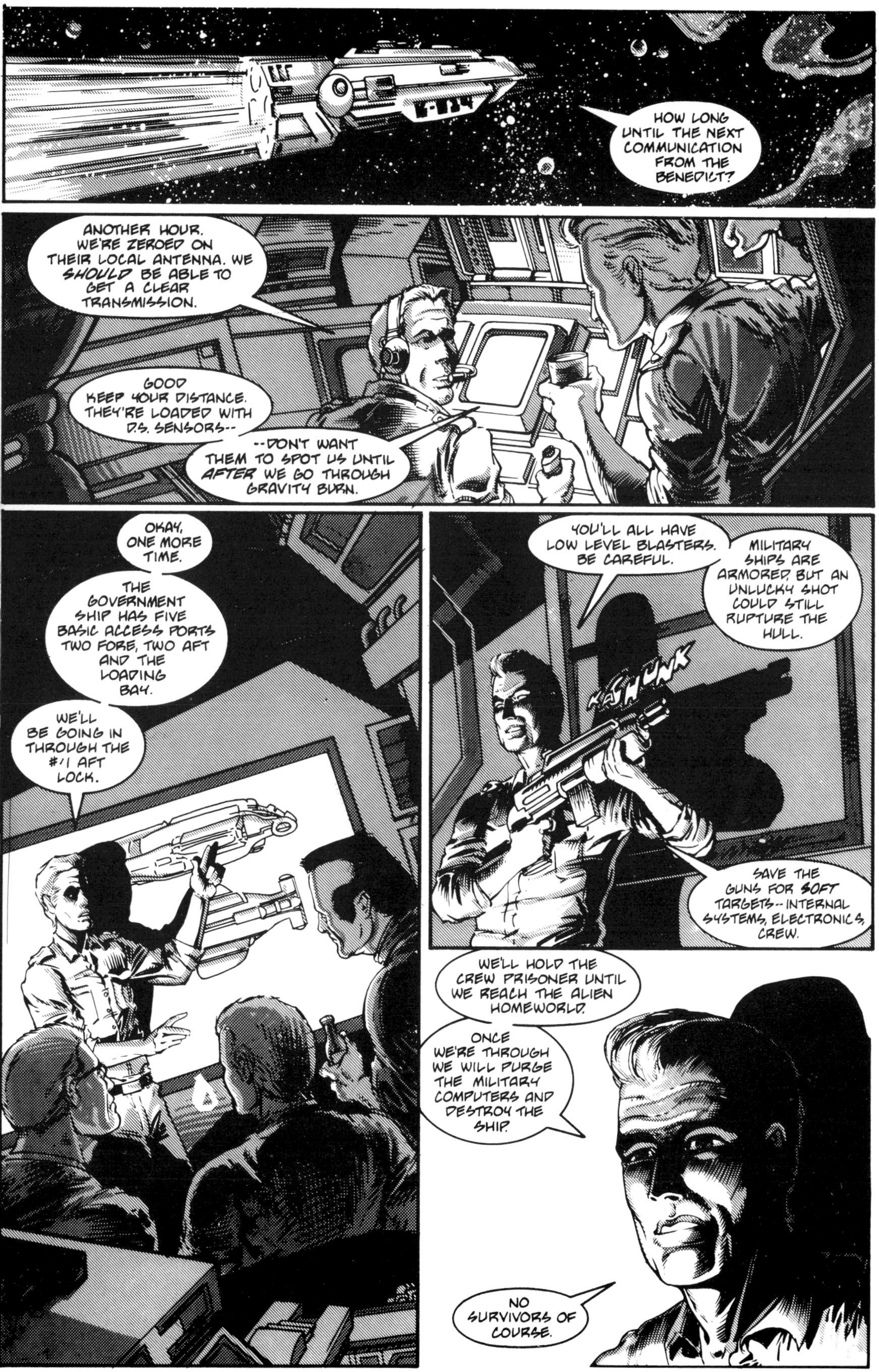

HOW LONG UNTIL THE NEXT COMMUNICATION FROM THE BENEDICT?
ANOTHER HOUR. WE'RE ZEROED ON THEIR LOCAL ANTENNA. WE *SHOULD* BE ABLE TO GET A CLEAR TRANSMISSION.
GOOD KEEP YOUR DISTANCE. THEY'RE LOADED WITH D.S. SENSORS--
--DON'T WANT THEM TO SPOT US UNTIL *AFTER* WE GO THROUGH GRAVITY BURN.
OKAY, ONE MORE TIME.
THE GOVERNMENT SHIP HAS FIVE BASIC ACCESS PORTS TWO FORE, TWO AFT AND THE LOADING BAY.
WE'LL BE GOING IN THROUGH THE #1 AFT LOCK.
YOU'LL ALL HAVE LOW LEVEL BLASTERS. BE CAREFUL.
MILITARY SHIPS ARE ARMORED, BUT AN UNLUCKY SHOT COULD STILL RUPTURE THE HULL.
KASHUNK
SAVE THE GUNS FOR *SOFT* TARGETS--INTERNAL SYSTEMS, ELECTRONICS, CREW.
WE'LL HOLD THE CREW PRISONER UNTIL WE REACH THE ALIEN HOMEWORLD.
ONCE WE'RE THROUGH WE WILL PURGE THE MILITARY COMPUTERS AND DESTROY THE SHIP.
NO SURVIVORS OF COURSE.

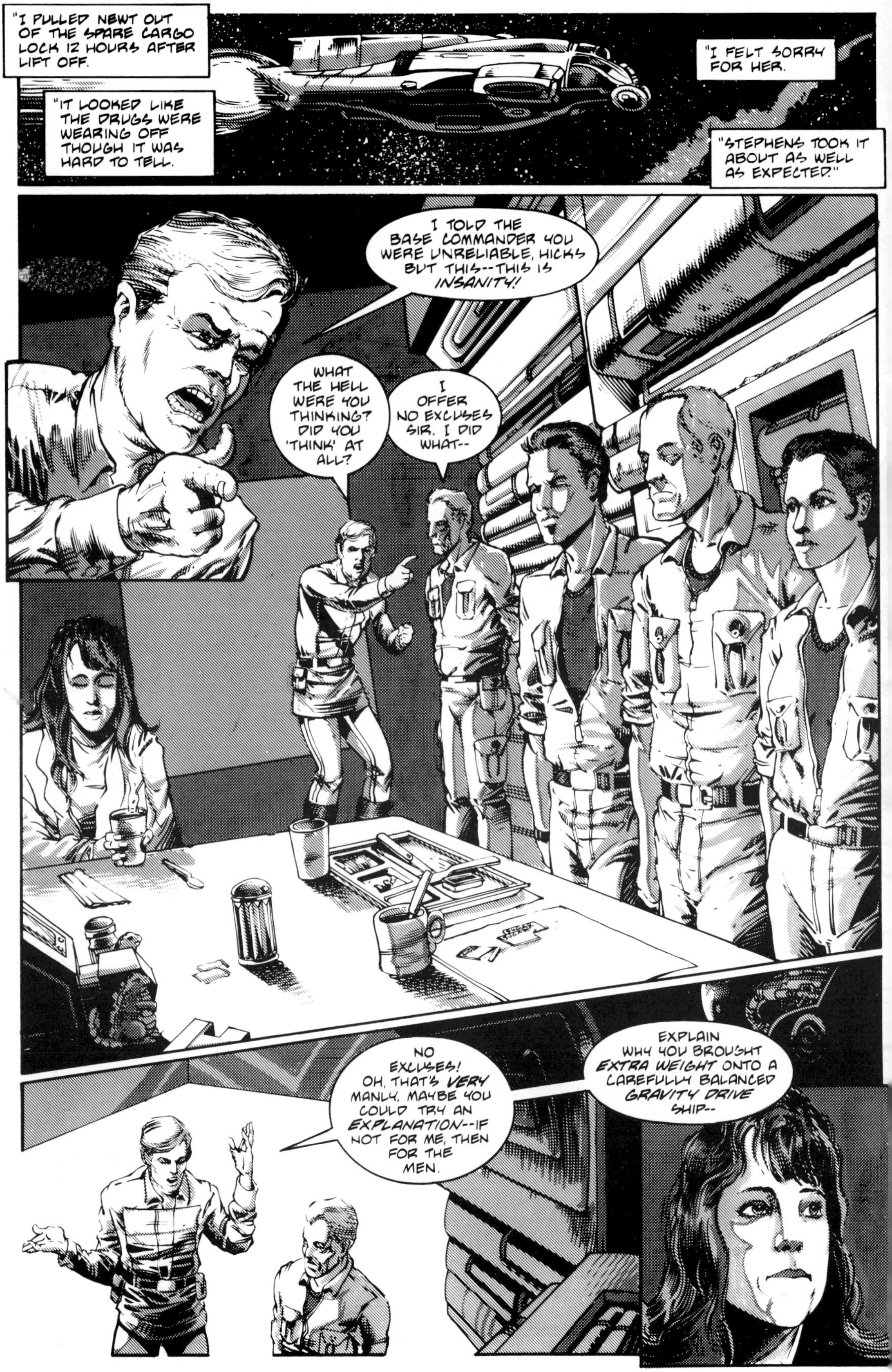
"I PULLED NEWT OUT OF THE SPARE CARGO LOCK 12 HOURS AFTER LIFT OFF.
"IT LOOKED LIKE THE DRUGS WERE WEARING OFF THOUGH IT WAS HARD TO TELL.
"I FELT SORRY FOR HER.
"STEPHENS TOOK IT ABOUT AS WELL AS EXPECTED."
I TOLD THE BASE COMMANDER YOU WERE UNRELIABLE, HICKS BUT THIS--THIS IS INSANITY!
WHAT THE HELL WERE YOU THINKING? DID YOU 'THINK' AT ALL?
I OFFER NO EXCUSES SIR. I DID WHAT--
NO EXCUSES! OH, THAT'S VERY MANLY. MAYBE YOU COULD TRY AN EXPLANATION--IF NOT FOR ME, THEN FOR THE MEN.
EXPLAIN WHY YOU BROUGHT EXTRA WEIGHT ONTO A CAREFULLY BALANCED GRAVITY DRIVE SHIP--

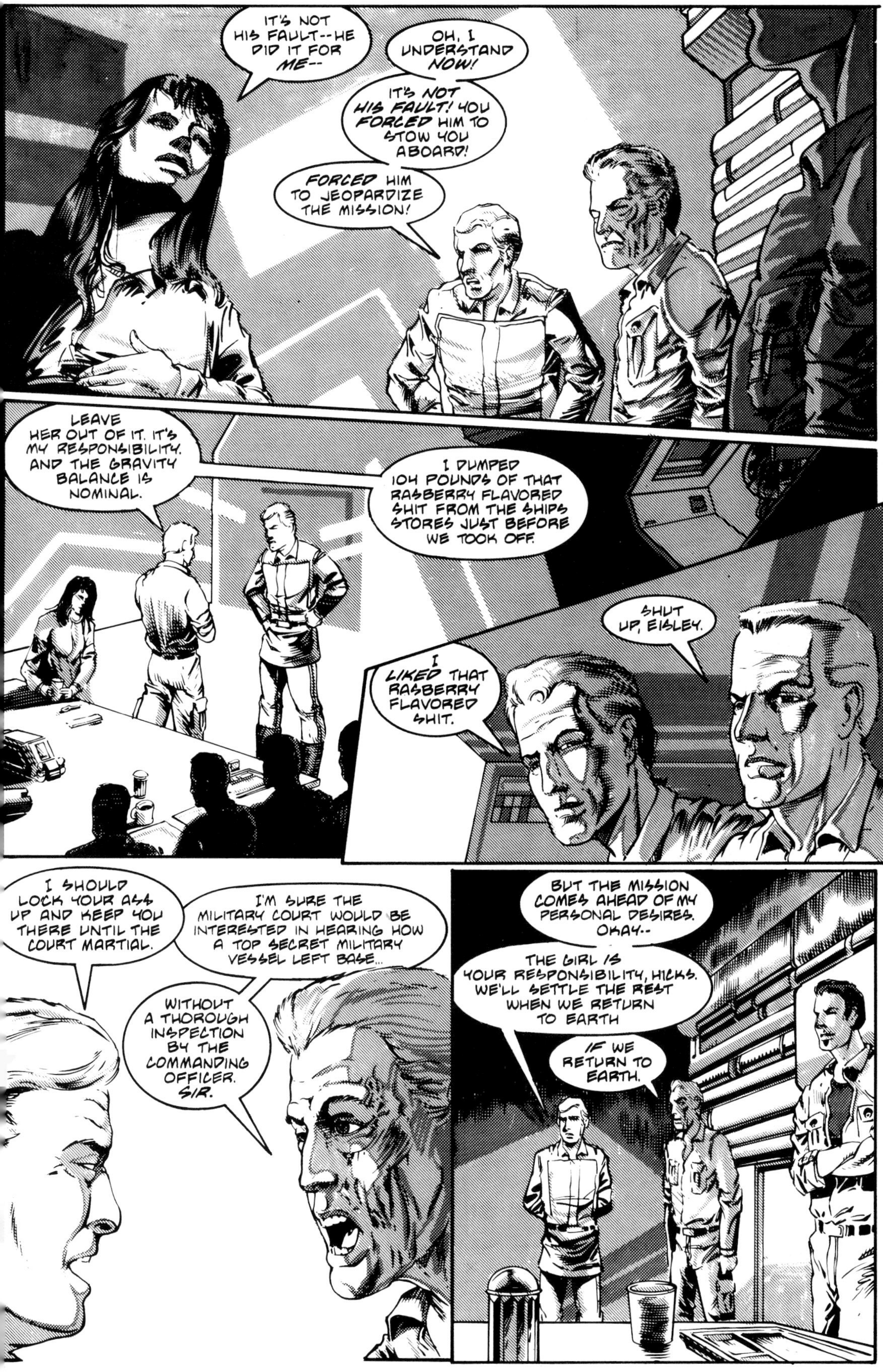
IT'S NOT HIS FAULT--HE DID IT FOR ME--
OH, I UNDERSTAND NOW!
IT'S NOT HIS FAULT! YOU FORCED HIM TO STOW YOU ABOARD!
FORCED HIM TO JEOPARDIZE THE MISSION!
LEAVE HER OUT OF IT. IT'S MY RESPONSIBILITY. AND THE GRAVITY BALANCE IS NOMINAL.
I DUMPED 104 POUNDS OF THAT RASBERRY FLAVORED SHIT FROM THE SHIPS STORES JUST BEFORE WE TOOK OFF.
SHUT UP, EISLEY.
I LIKED THAT RASBERRY FLAVORED SHIT.
I SHOULD LOCK YOUR ASS UP AND KEEP YOU THERE UNTIL THE COURT MARTIAL.
I'M SURE THE MILITARY COURT WOULD BE INTERESTED IN HEARING HOW A TOP SECRET MILITARY VESSEL LEFT BASE...
WITHOUT A THOROUGH INSPECTION BY THE COMMANDING OFFICER. SIR.
BUT THE MISSION COMES AHEAD OF MY PERSONAL DESIRES. OKAY.-
THE GIRL IS YOUR RESPONSIBILITY, HICKS. WE'LL SETTLE THE REST WHEN WE RETURN TO EARTH
IF WE RETURN TO EARTH.

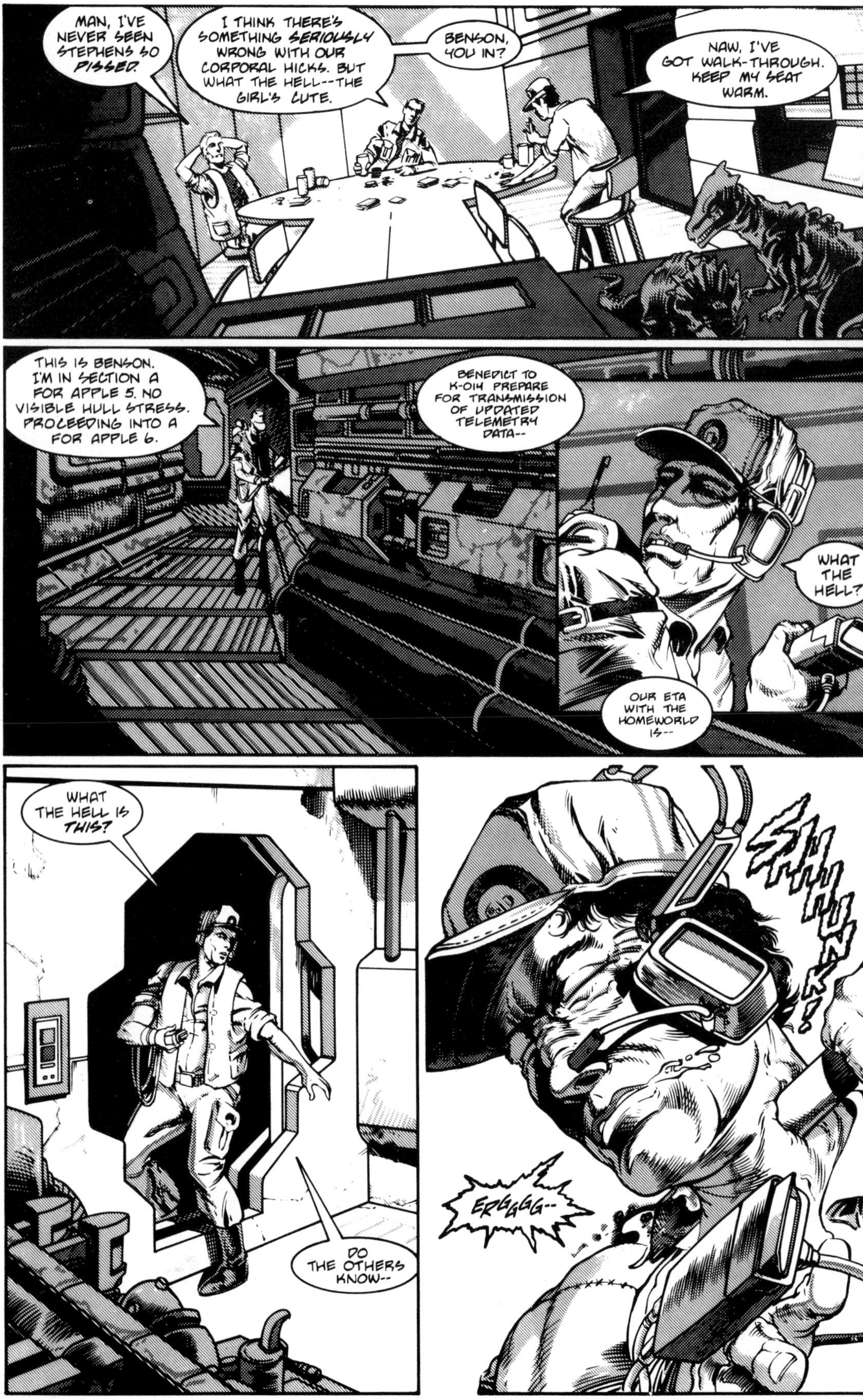
MAN, I'VE NEVER SEEN STEPHENS SO PISSED.
I THINK THERE'S SOMETHING SERIOUSLY WRONG WITH OUR CORPORAL HICKS. BUT WHAT THE HELL--THE GIRL'S CUTE.
BENSON, YOU IN?
NAW, I'VE GOT WALK-THROUGH. KEEP MY SEAT WARM.
THIS IS BENSON. I'M IN SECTION A FOR APPLE 5. NO VISIBLE HULL STRESS. PROCEEDING INTO A FOR APPLE 6.
BENEDICT TO K-014 PREPARE FOR TRANSMISSION OF UPDATED TELEMETRY DATA--
WHAT THE HELL?
OUR ETA WITH THE HOMEWORLD IS--
WHAT THE HELL IS THIS?
DO THE OTHERS KNOW--
SHHUNK!
ERGGGG--

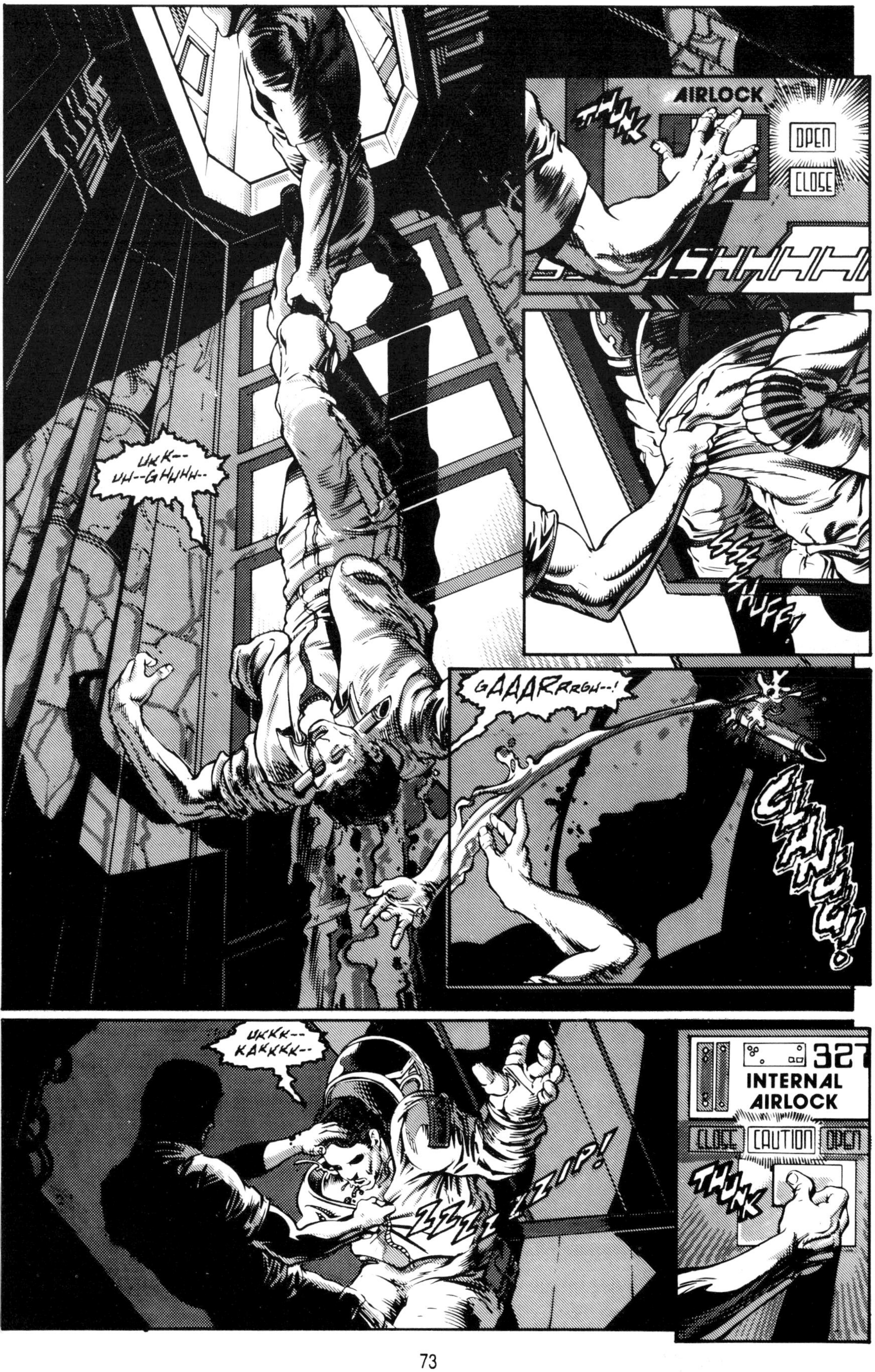

AIRLOCK
THUNK
OPEN
CLOSE
UKK--
UH--GHUHH--
SSSS
HUFF
GAAARRRGH--!
UKKK--
KAKKKK--
327
INTERNAL
AIRLOCK
CLOSE
CAUTION
OPEN
THUNK
ZIP!

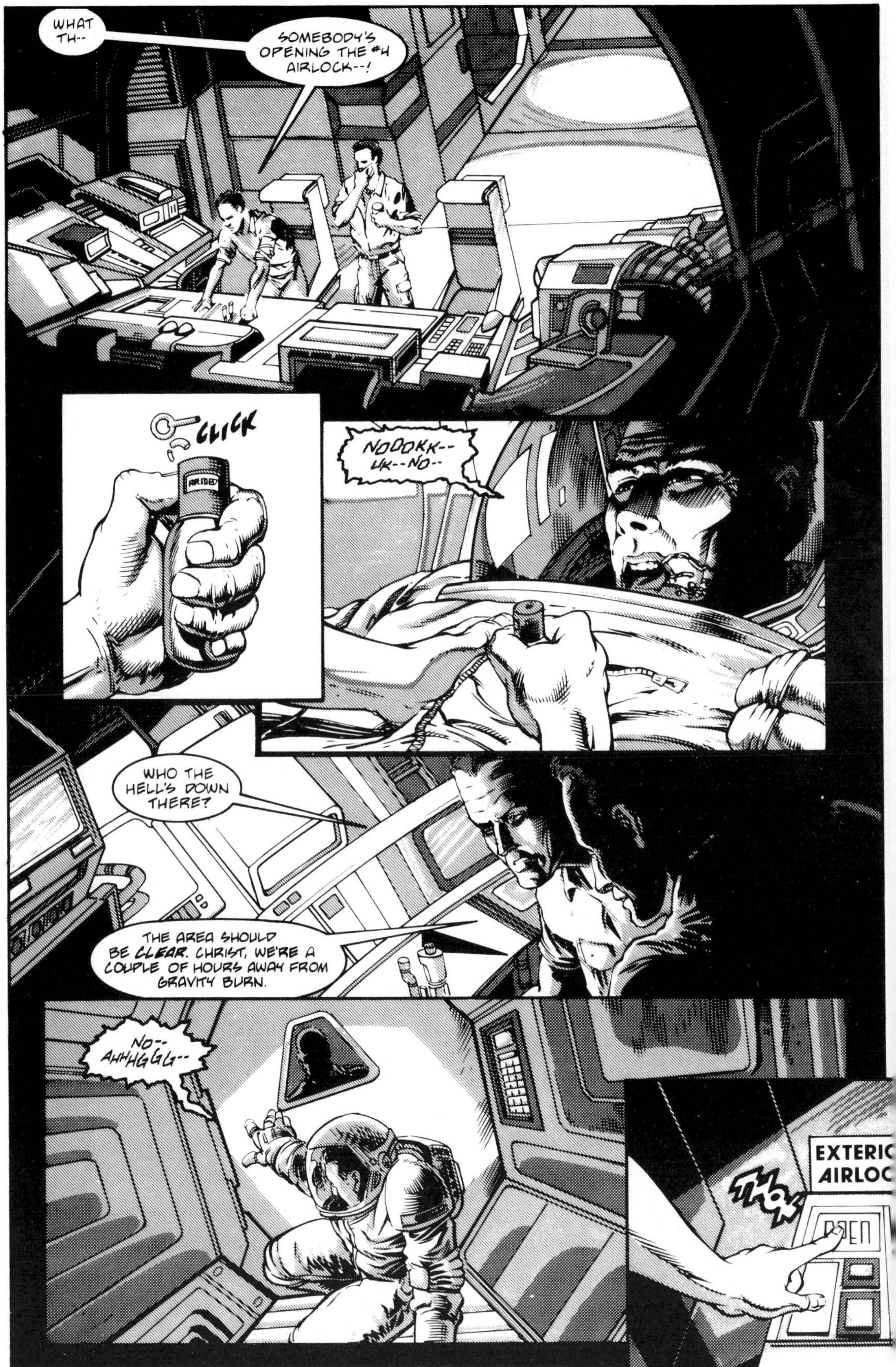

WHAT TH--
SOMEBODY'S OPENING THE #4 AIRLOCK--!
CLICK
NOOOKK-- UK--NO--
WHO THE HELL'S DOWN THERE?
THE AREA SHOULD BE CLEAR. CHRIST, WE'RE A COUPLE OF HOURS AWAY FROM GRAVITY BURN.
NO-- AHHHGGG--
EXTERIO AIRLOC
OPEN

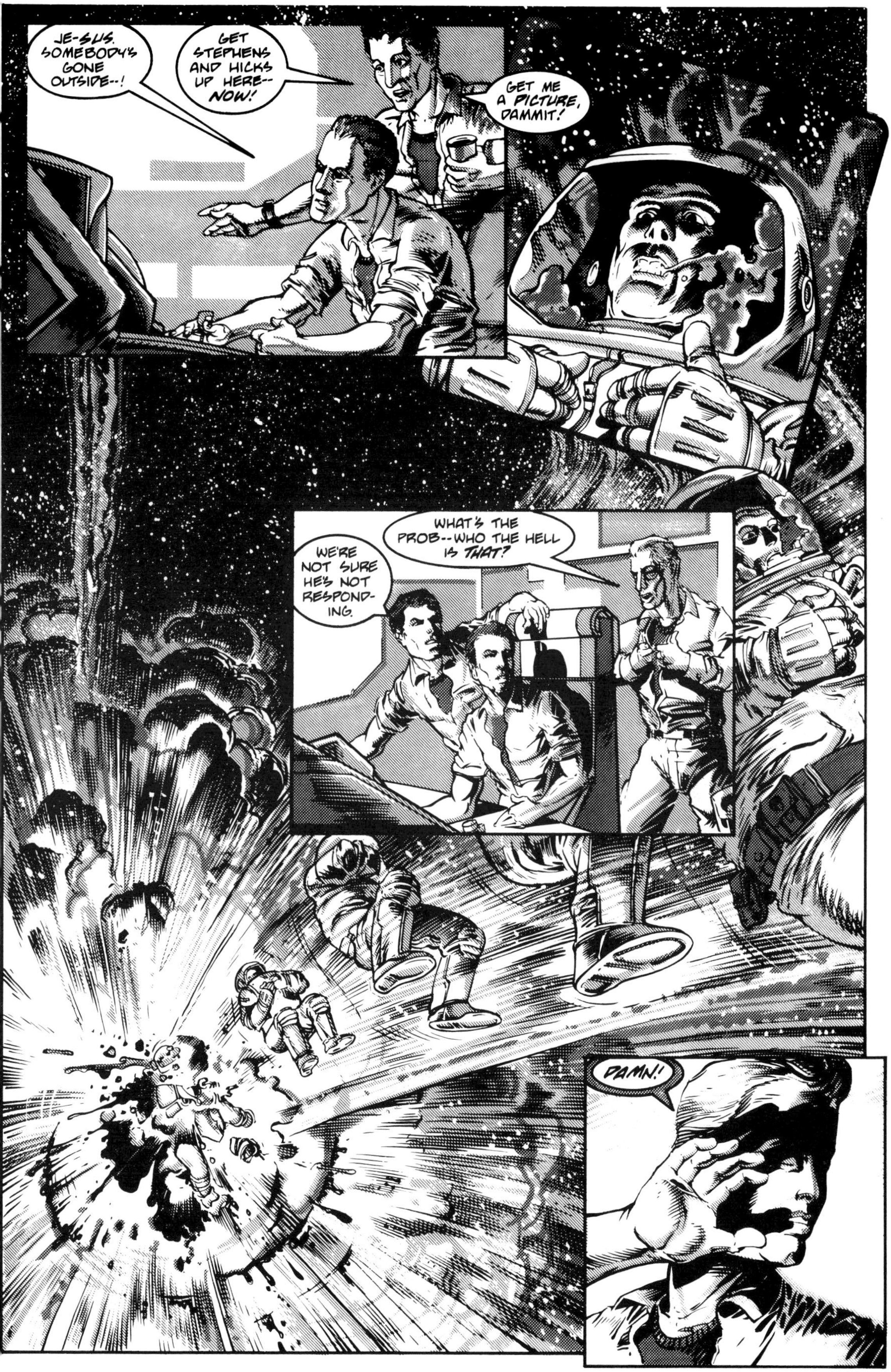
JE-SUS. SOMEBODY'S GONE OUTSIDE--!
GET STEPHENS AND HICKS UP HERE-- NOW!
GET ME A PICTURE, DAMMIT!
WE'RE NOT SURE HE'S NOT RESPONDING.
WHAT'S THE PROB--WHO THE HELL IS THAT?
DAMN!

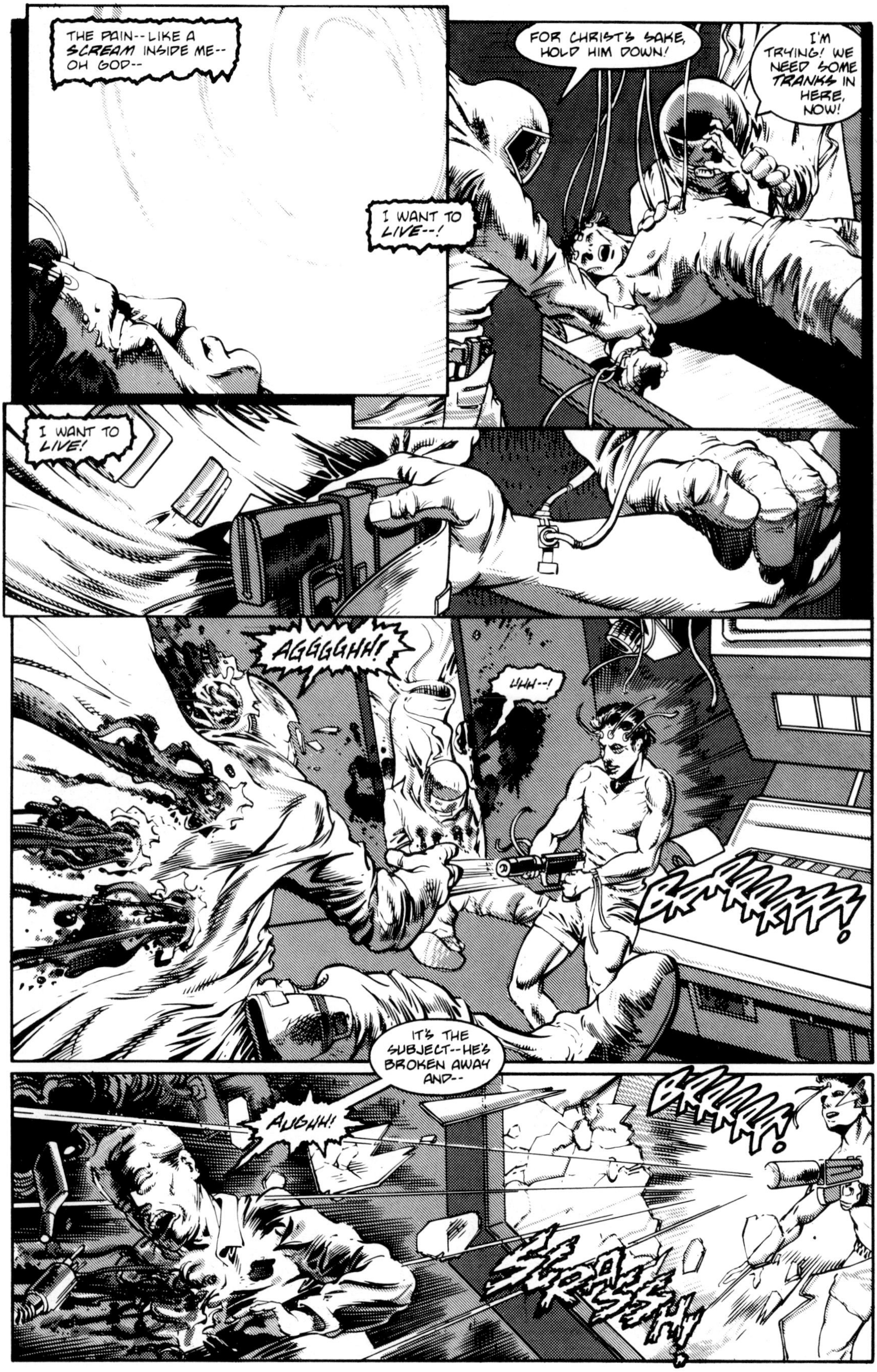
THE PAIN--LIKE A SCREAM INSIDE ME--OH GOD--
FOR CHRIST'S SAKE, HOLD HIM DOWN!
I'M TRYING! WE NEED SOME TRANKS IN HERE, NOW!
I WANT TO LIVE--!
I WANT TO LIVE!
AGGGGHH!
UHH--!
BRAAAAKT!
IT'S THE SUBJECT--HE'S BROKEN AWAY AND--
AUGHH!
BRAAAKT!
SKRASSH

THE GUARDS ARE DEAD. I WANT TO KILL *MORE* I CAN HEAR ALARMS. DON'T CARE.

FOOM!

BOOM!

BOOM!

CAN'T CARE.

GOT TO GET OUTSIDE. I WANT TO *FEEL* THE SUN.

POW! POW!

URGGHHH!

HOT OUTSIDE. WET WITH HUMIDITY.

GET OUT OF THE CAR!

MHZ UNLOADING ZONE

OH MY GOD--!

LEATHER SEATS--SMOOTH, SOFT-- I SMELL HOT OZONE AS I ACCELERATE.

SPAK

SPAK

SPAK

DEATH IS ALL AROUND ME.

KA THUMP

I FEEL UTTERLY *ALIVE.*

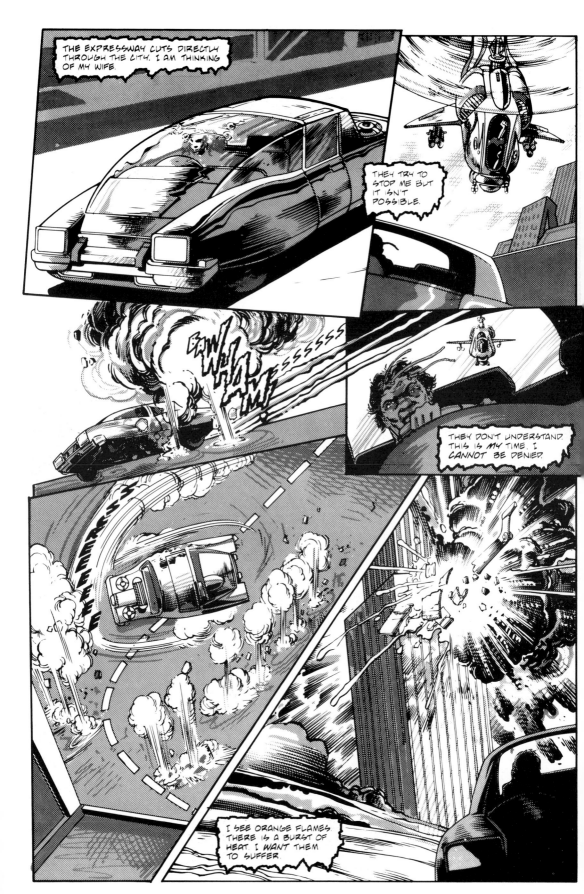

THE EXPRESSWAY CUTS DIRECTLY THROUGH THE CITY. I AM THINKING OF MY WIFE.

THEY TRY TO STOP ME BUT IT ISN'T POSSIBLE.

THEY DON'T UNDERSTAND. THIS IS MY TIME. I CANNOT BE DENIED.

I SEE ORANGE FLAMES. THERE IS A BURST OF HEAT. I WANT THEM TO SUFFER.

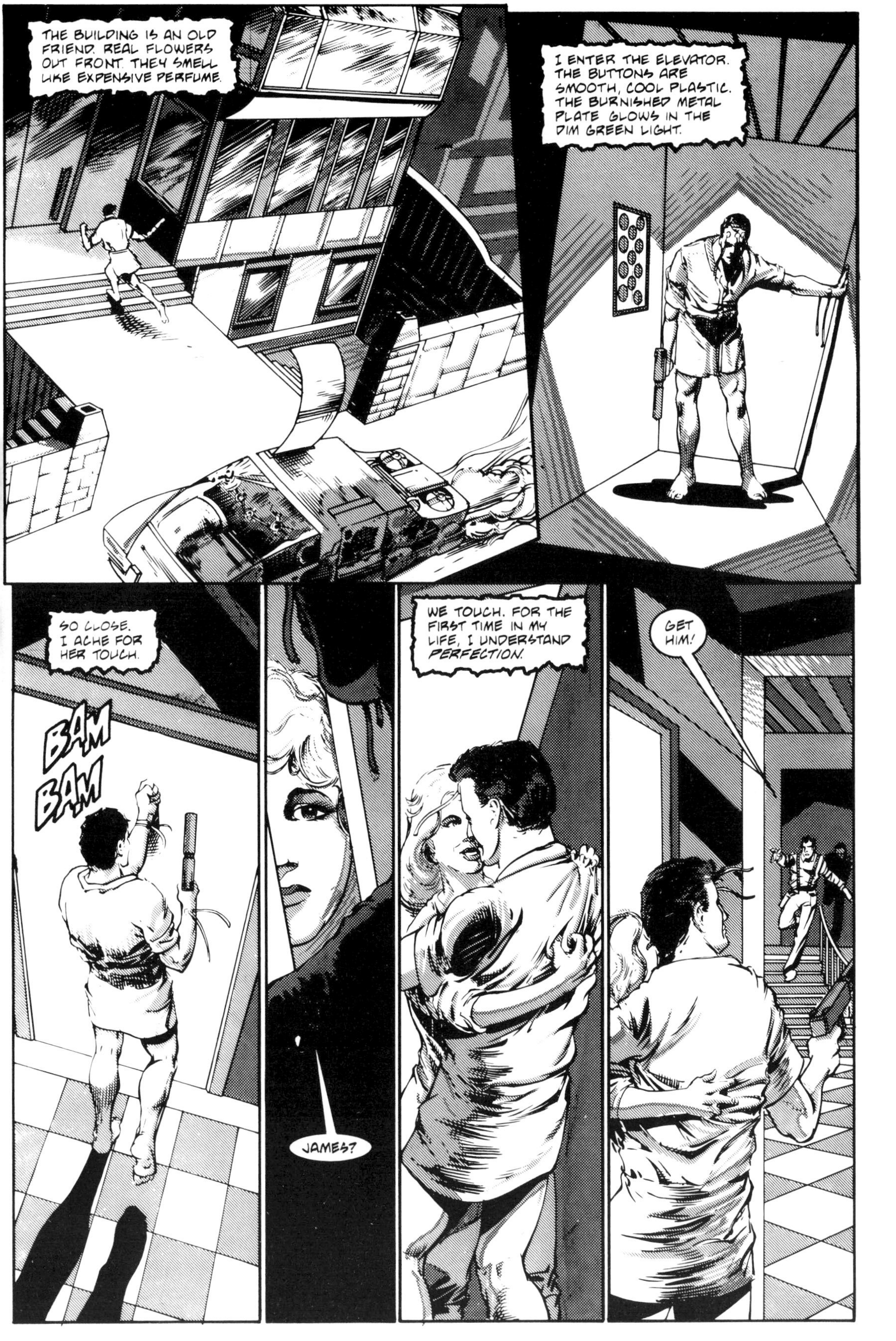
THE BUILDING IS AN OLD FRIEND. REAL FLOWERS OUT FRONT. THEY SMELL LIKE EXPENSIVE PERFUME.
I ENTER THE ELEVATOR. THE BUTTONS ARE SMOOTH, COOL PLASTIC. THE BURNISHED METAL PLATE GLOWS IN THE DIM GREEN LIGHT.
SO CLOSE. I ACHE FOR HER TOUCH.
BAM BAM
JAMES?
WE TOUCH. FOR THE FIRST TIME IN MY LIFE, I UNDERSTAND *PERFECTION.*
GET HIM!

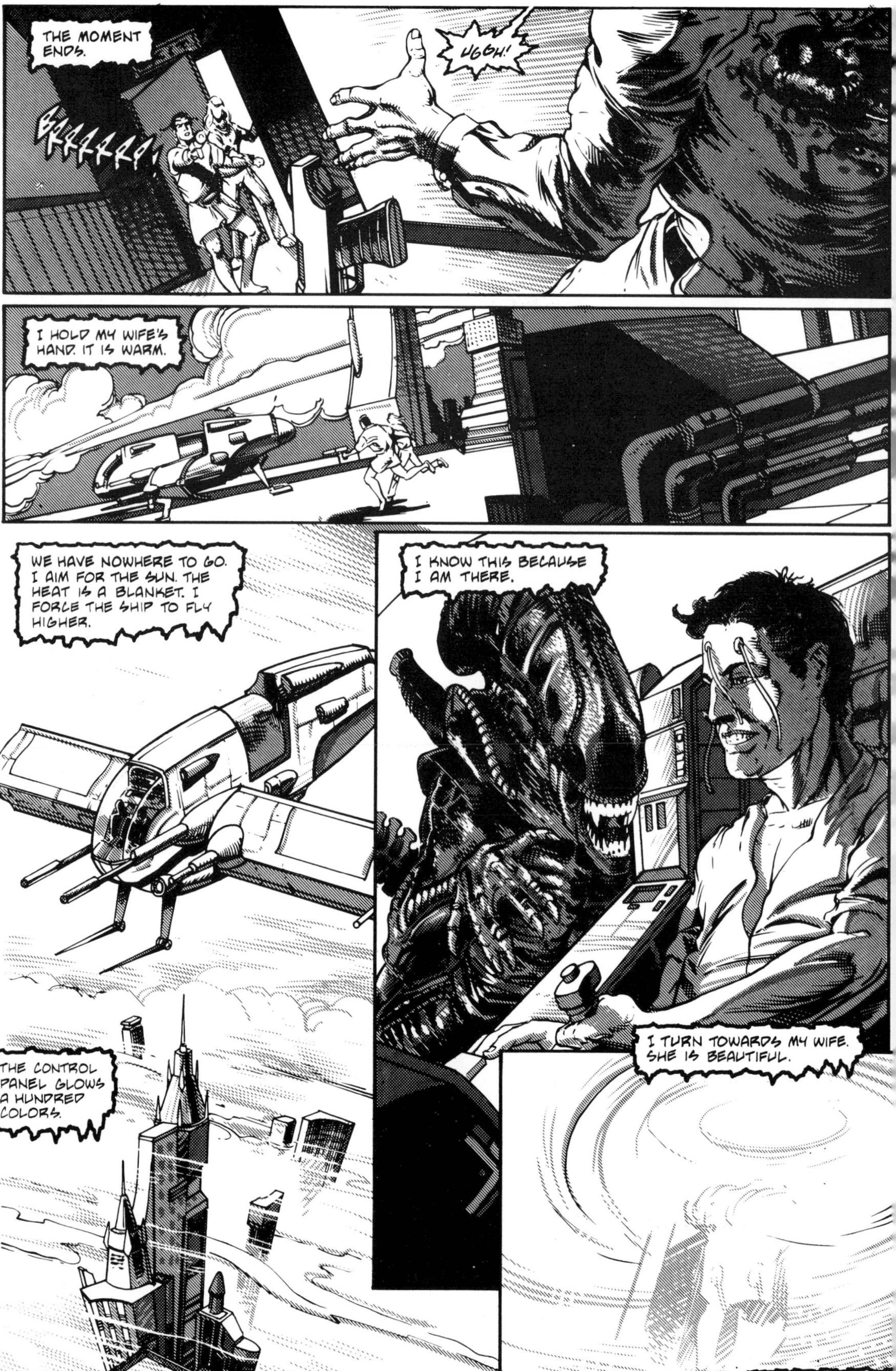
THE MOMENT ENDS.
BRRRRRRP.
UGGH!
I HOLD MY WIFE'S HAND. IT IS WARM.
WE HAVE NOWHERE TO GO. I AIM FOR THE SUN. THE HEAT IS A BLANKET. I FORCE THE SHIP TO FLY HIGHER.
THE CONTROL PANEL GLOWS A HUNDRED COLORS.
I KNOW THIS BECAUSE I AM THERE.
I TURN TOWARDS MY WIFE. SHE IS BEAUTIFUL.
MY GOD, THE SUN-IT'S SO BRIGHT.

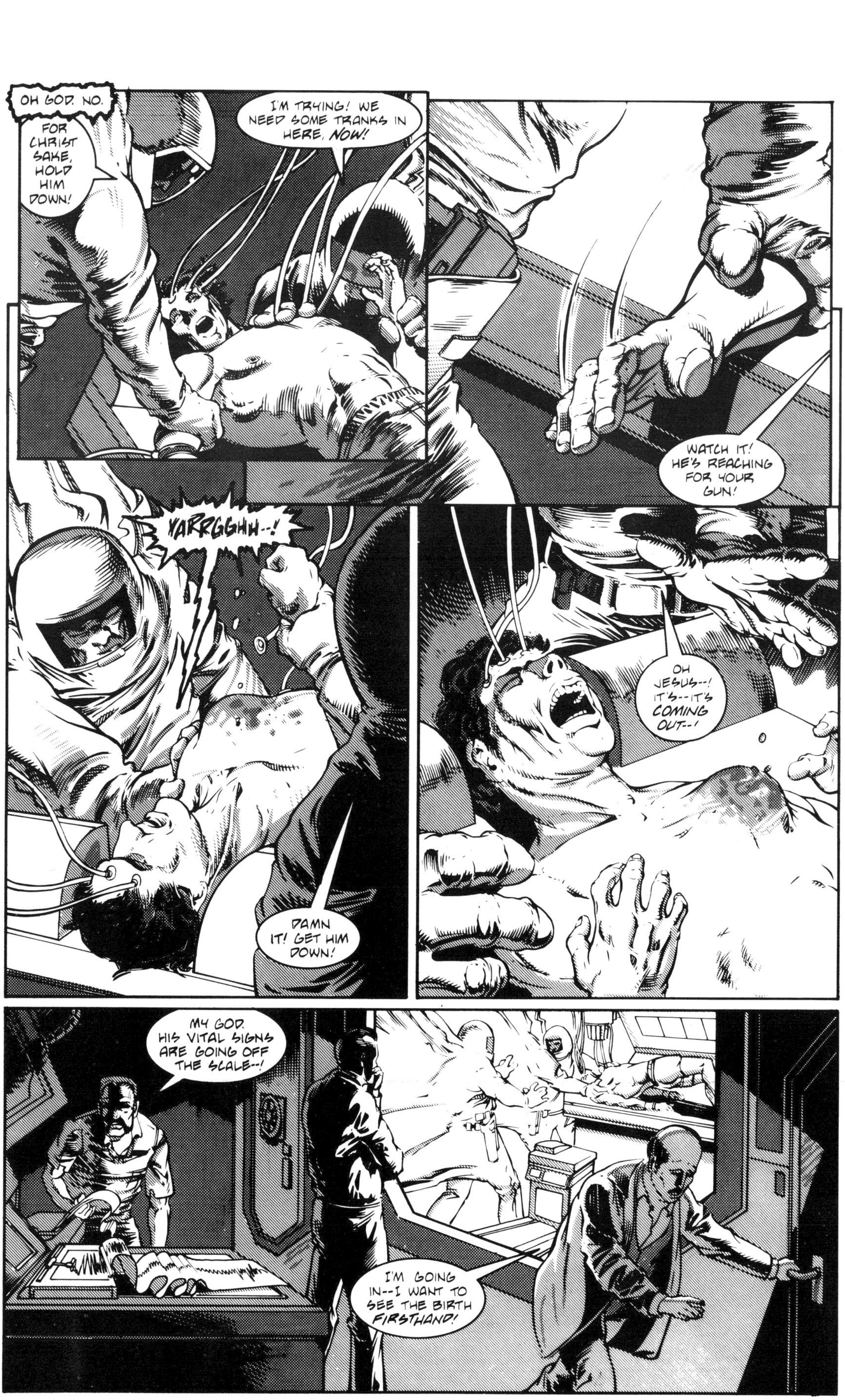

OH GOD. NO.
FOR CHRIST SAKE, HOLD HIM DOWN!
I'M TRYING! WE NEED SOME TRANKS IN HERE, NOW!
WATCH IT! HE'S REACHING FOR YOUR GUN!
YARRGGHH--!
DAMN IT! GET HIM DOWN!
OH JESUS--! IT'S--IT'S COMING OUT--!
MY GOD. HIS VITAL SIGNS ARE GOING OFF THE SCALE--!
I'M GOING IN--I WANT TO SEE THE BIRTH FIRSTHAND!

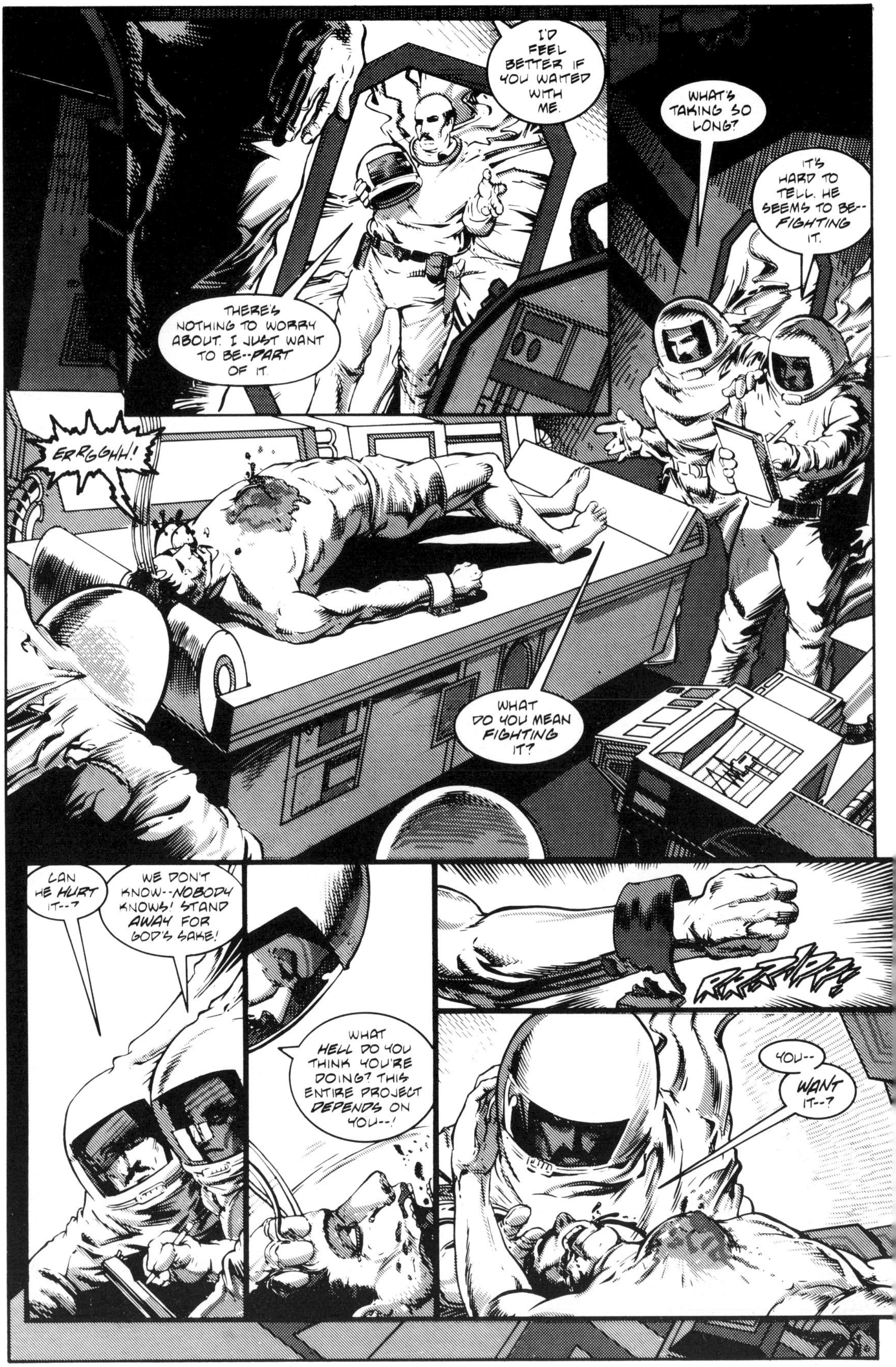
I'D FEEL BETTER IF YOU WAITED WITH ME.
THERE'S NOTHING TO WORRY ABOUT. I JUST WANT TO BE--PART OF IT.
WHAT'S TAKING SO LONG?
IT'S HARD TO TELL. HE SEEMS TO BE--FIGHTING IT.
ERRGGHH!
WHAT DO YOU MEAN FIGHTING IT?
CAN HE HURT IT--?
WE DON'T KNOW--NOBODY KNOWS! STAND AWAY FOR GOD'S SAKE!
WHAT HELL DO YOU THINK YOU'RE DOING? THIS ENTIRE PROJECT DEPENDS ON YOU--!
YOU--
WANT IT--?

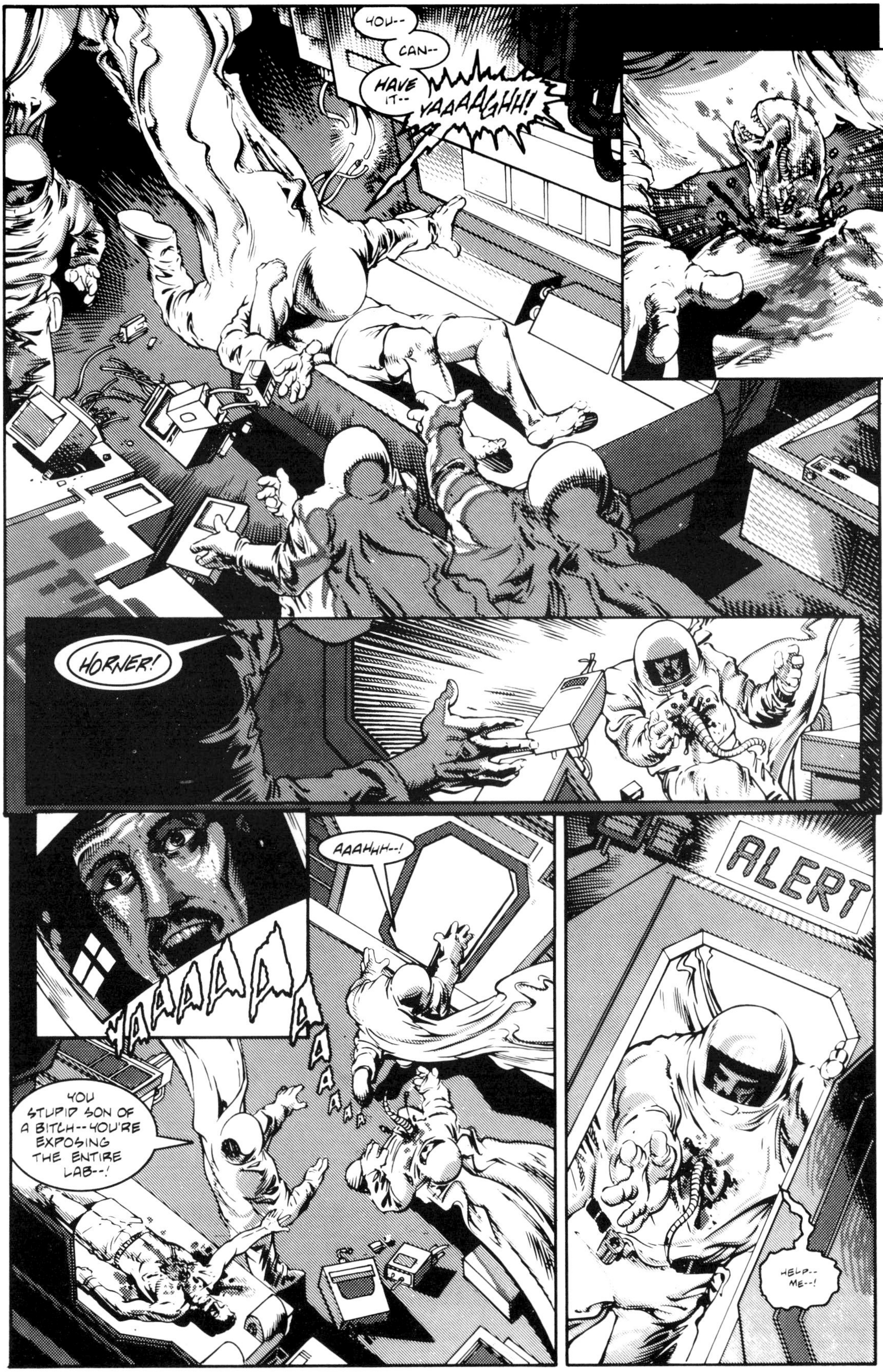

YOU--
CAN--
HAVE IT--
YAAAAGHH!
HORNER!
AAAHHH--!
YAAAAAAAAAAA
YOU STUPID SON OF A BITCH--YOU'RE EXPOSING THE ENTIRE LAB--!
ALERT
HELP-- ME--!

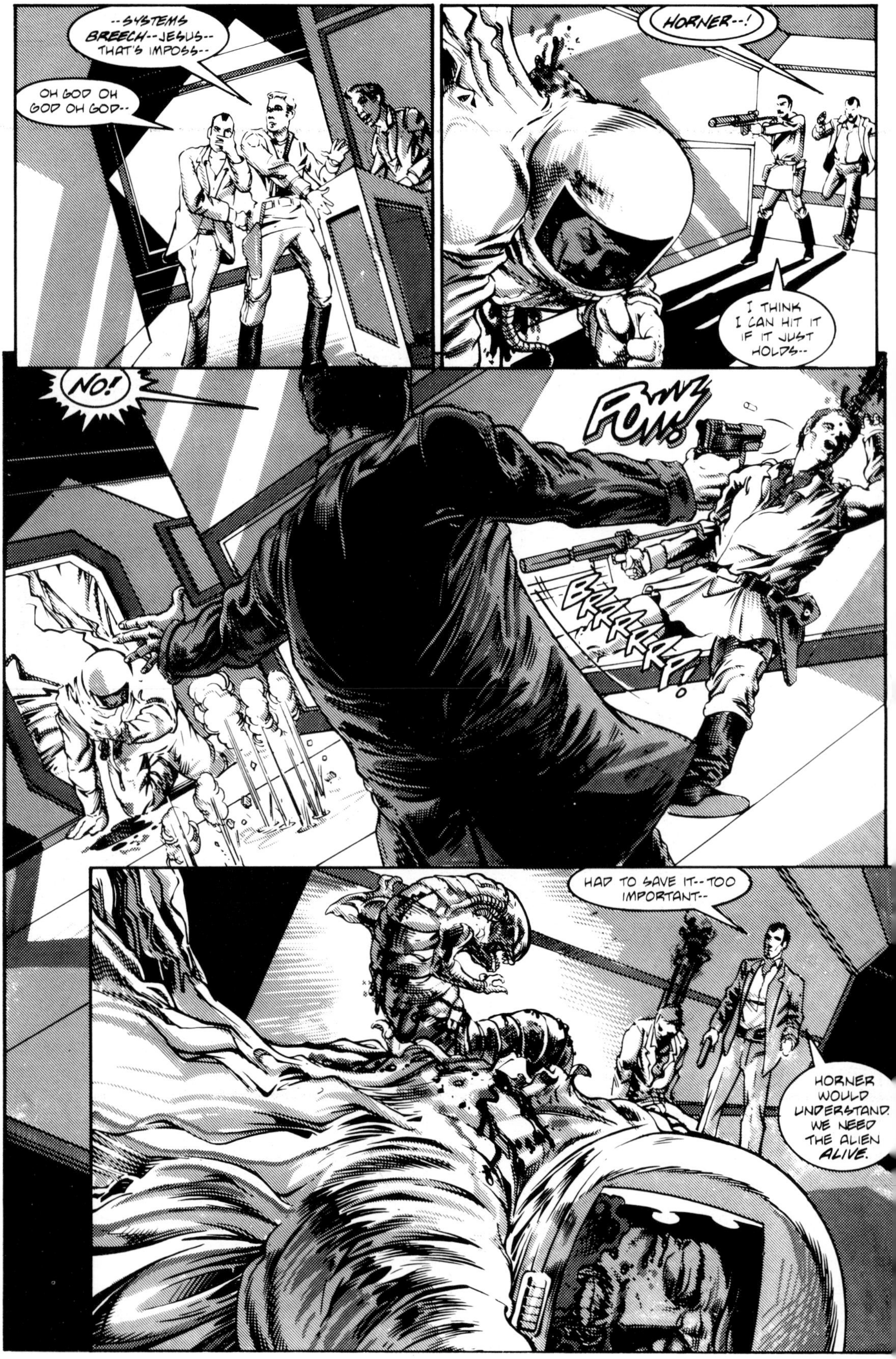

--SYSTEMS BREECH--JESUS--THAT'S IMPOSS--
OH GOD OH GOD OH GOD--
HORNER--!
I THINK I CAN HIT IT IF IT JUST HOLDS--
NO!
FOWN
BRRRRRP!
HAD TO SAVE IT--TOO IMPORTANT--
HORNER WOULD UNDERSTAND. WE NEED THE ALIEN ALIVE.

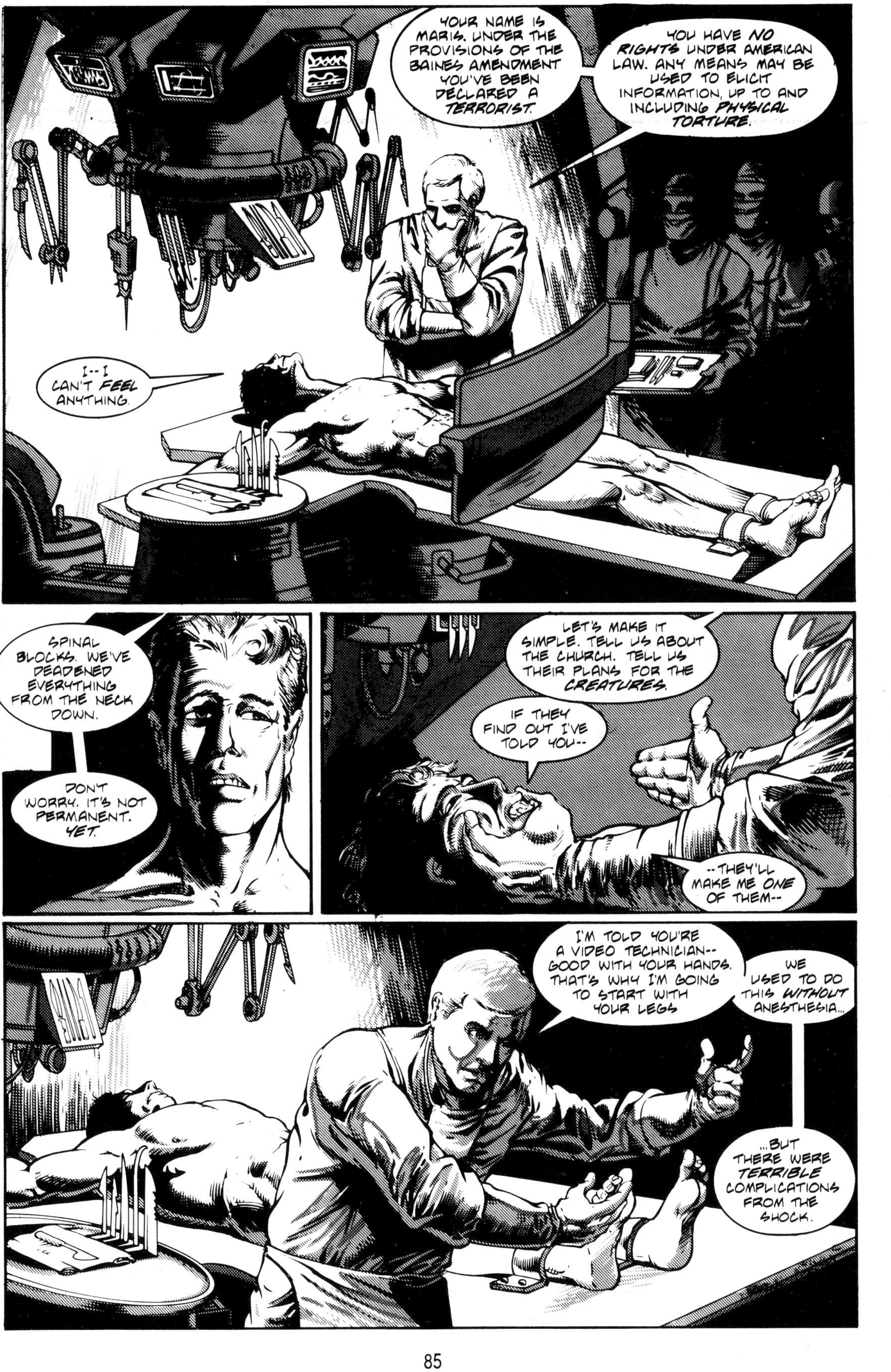
YOUR NAME IS MARIS. UNDER THE PROVISIONS OF THE BAINES AMENDMENT YOU'VE BEEN DECLARED A TERRORIST.
YOU HAVE NO RIGHTS UNDER AMERICAN LAW. ANY MEANS MAY BE USED TO ELICIT INFORMATION, UP TO AND INCLUDING PHYSICAL TORTURE.
I-- I CAN'T FEEL ANYTHING.
SPINAL BLOCKS. WE'VE DEADENED EVERYTHING FROM THE NECK DOWN.
DON'T WORRY. IT'S NOT PERMANENT. YET.
LET'S MAKE IT SIMPLE. TELL US ABOUT THE CHURCH. TELL US THEIR PLANS FOR THE CREATURES.
IF THEY FIND OUT I'VE TOLD YOU--
--THEY'LL MAKE ME ONE OF THEM--
I'M TOLD YOU'RE A VIDEO TECHNICIAN-- GOOD WITH YOUR HANDS. THAT'S WHY I'M GOING TO START WITH YOUR LEGS
WE USED TO DO THIS WITHOUT ANESTHESIA...
...BUT THERE WERE TERRIBLE COMPLICATIONS FROM THE SHOCK.

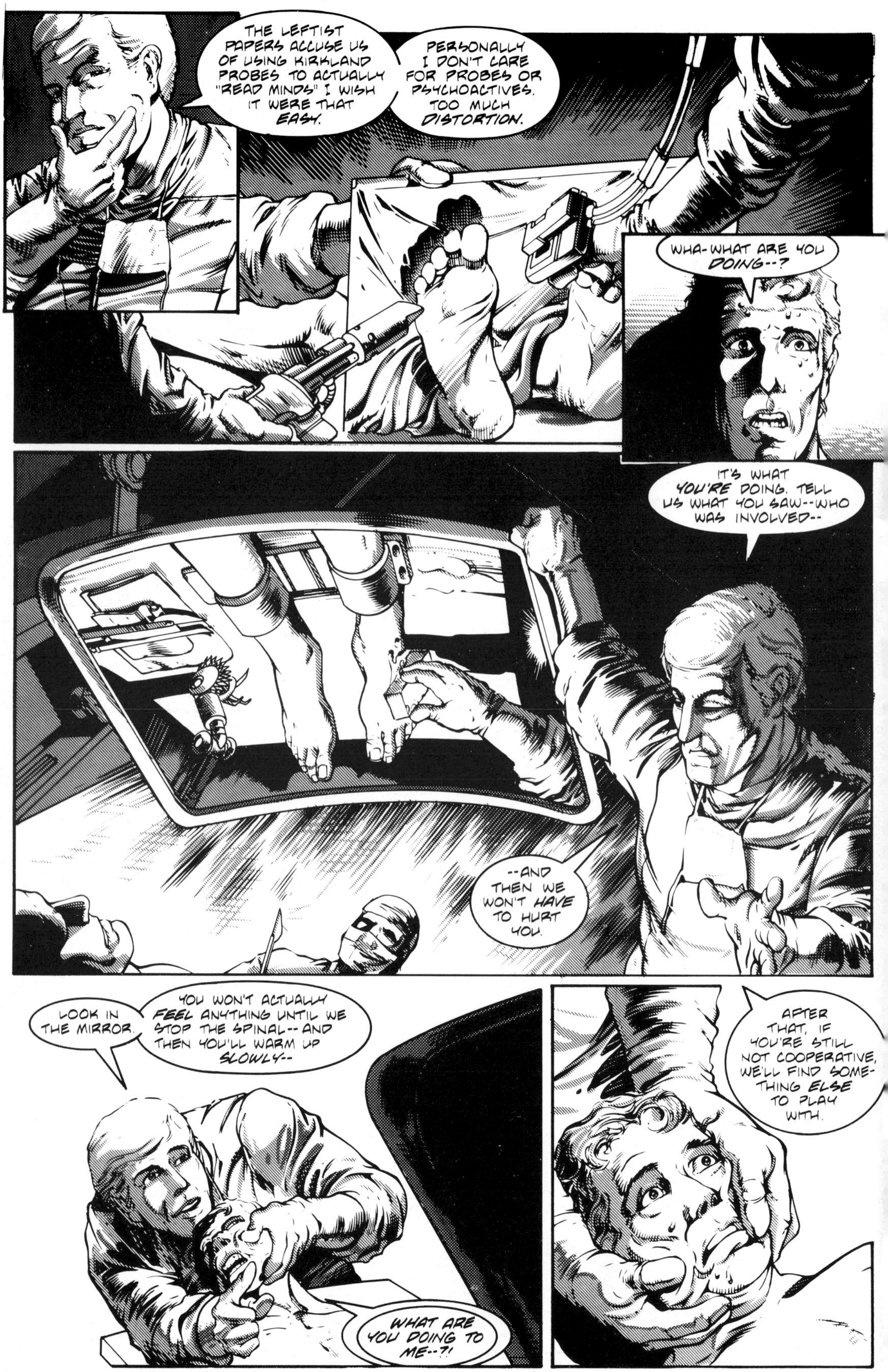

THE LEFTIST PAPERS ACCUSE US OF USING KIRKLAND PROBES TO ACTUALLY "READ MINDS" I WISH IT WERE THAT EASY.
PERSONALLY I DON'T CARE FOR PROBES OR PSYCHOACTIVES. TOO MUCH DISTORTION.
WHA-WHAT ARE YOU DOING--?
IT'S WHAT YOU'RE DOING. TELL US WHAT YOU SAW--WHO WAS INVOLVED--
--AND THEN WE WON'T HAVE TO HURT YOU.
LOOK IN THE MIRROR.
YOU WON'T ACTUALLY FEEL ANYTHING UNTIL WE STOP THE SPINAL--AND THEN YOU'LL WARM UP SLOWLY--
WHAT ARE YOU DOING TO ME--?!
AFTER THAT, IF YOU'RE STILL NOT COOPERATIVE, WE'LL FIND SOMETHING ELSE TO PLAY WITH.

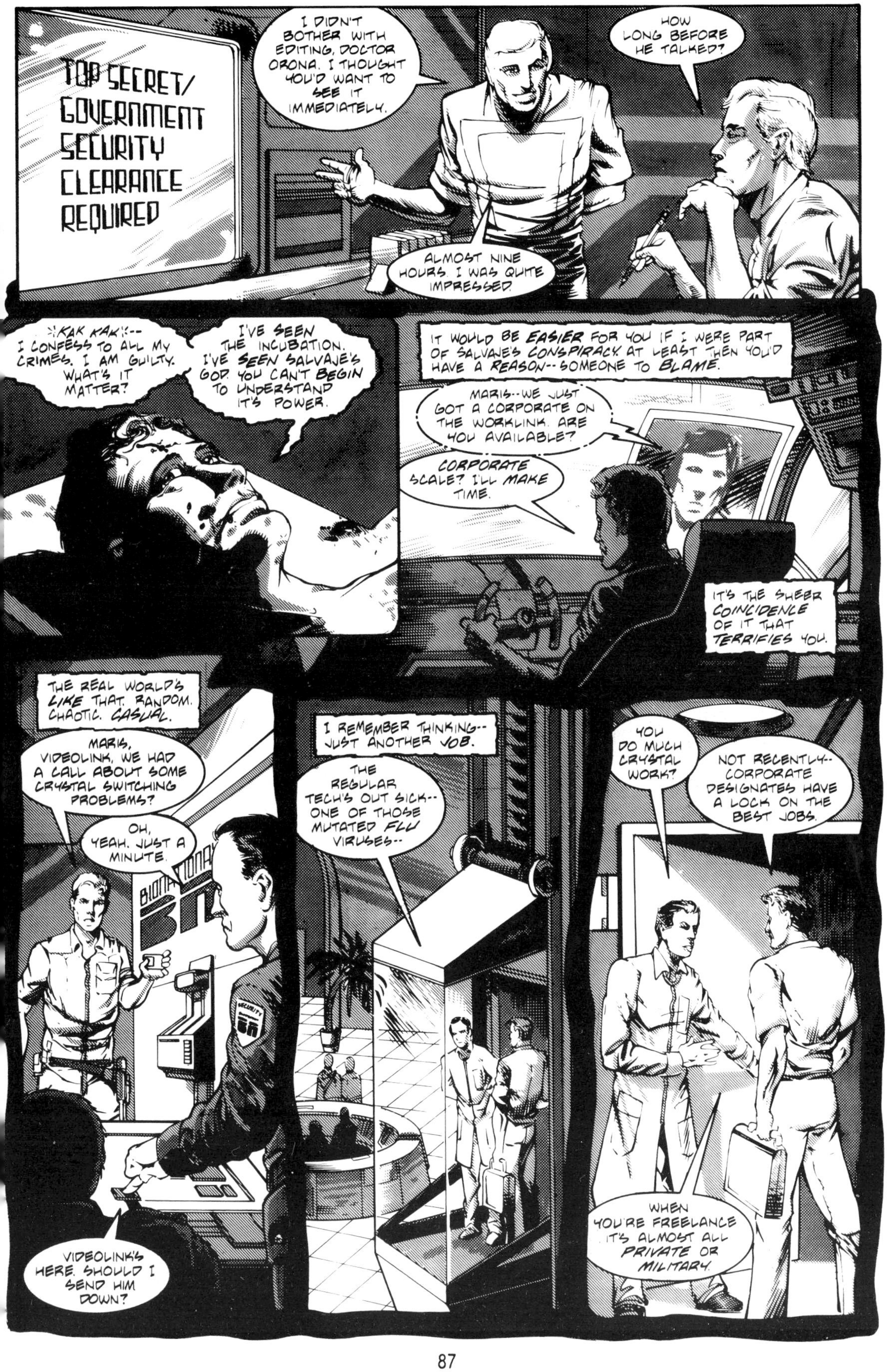
TOP SECRET/ GOVERNMENT SECURITY CLEARANCE REQUIRED
I DIDN'T BOTHER WITH EDITING, DOCTOR ORONA. I THOUGHT YOU'D WANT TO SEE IT IMMEDIATELY.
HOW LONG BEFORE HE TALKED?
ALMOST NINE HOURS. I WAS QUITE IMPRESSED.
KAK KAK-- I CONFESS TO ALL MY CRIMES. I AM GUILTY. WHAT'S IT MATTER?
I'VE SEEN THE INCUBATION. I'VE SEEN SALVAJE'S GOD. YOU CAN'T BEGIN TO UNDERSTAND IT'S POWER.
IT WOULD BE EASIER FOR YOU IF I WERE PART OF SALVAJE'S CONSPIRACY. AT LEAST THEN YOU'D HAVE A REASON--SOMEONE TO BLAME.
MARIS--WE JUST GOT A CORPORATE ON THE WORKLINK. ARE YOU AVAILABLE?
CORPORATE SCALE? I'LL MAKE TIME.
IT'S THE SHEER COINCIDENCE OF IT THAT TERRIFIES YOU.
THE REAL WORLD'S LIKE THAT. RANDOM. CHAOTIC. CASUAL.
MARIS, VIDEOLINK, WE HAD A CALL ABOUT SOME CRYSTAL SWITCHING PROBLEMS?
OH, YEAH. JUST A MINUTE.
VIDEOLINK'S HERE. SHOULD I SEND HIM DOWN?
I REMEMBER THINKING-- JUST ANOTHER JOB.
THE REGULAR TECH'S OUT SICK-- ONE OF THOSE MUTATED FLU VIRUSES--
YOU DO MUCH CRYSTAL WORK?
NOT RECENTLY-- CORPORATE DESIGNATES HAVE A LOCK ON THE BEST JOBS.
WHEN YOU'RE FREELANCE IT'S ALMOST ALL PRIVATE OR MILITARY.

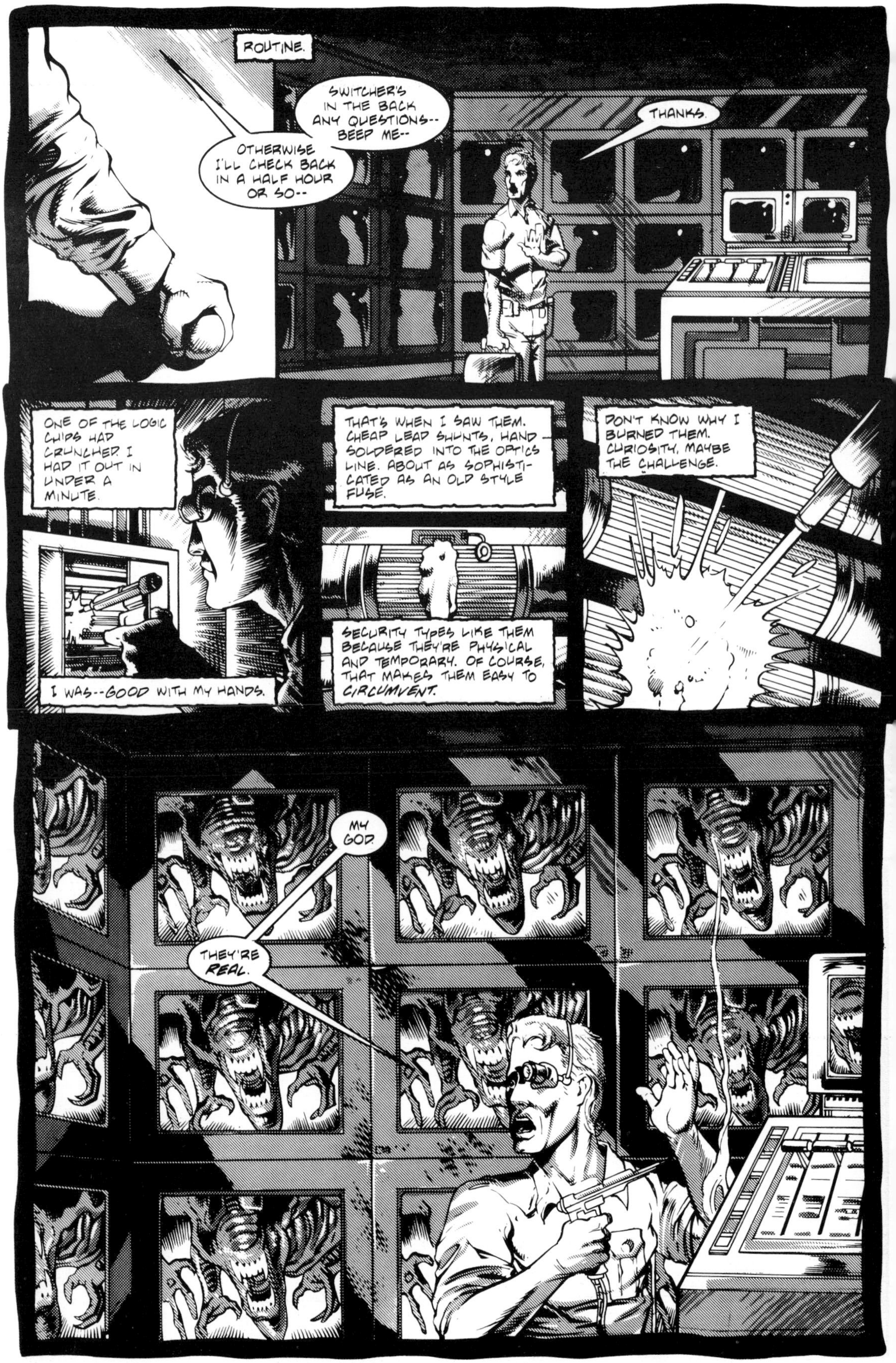
ROUTINE.
SWITCHER'S IN THE BACK ANY QUESTIONS-- BEEP ME--
OTHERWISE I'LL CHECK BACK IN A HALF HOUR OR SO--
THANKS.
ONE OF THE LOGIC CHIPS HAD CRUNCHED. I HAD IT OUT IN UNDER A MINUTE.
I WAS--GOOD WITH MY HANDS.
THAT'S WHEN I SAW THEM. CHEAP LEAD SHUNTS, HAND-SOLDERED INTO THE OPTICS LINE. ABOUT AS SOPHISTICATED AS AN OLD STYLE FUSE.
SECURITY TYPES LIKE THEM BECAUSE THEY'RE PHYSICAL AND TEMPORARY. OF COURSE, THAT MAKES THEM EASY TO CIRCUMVENT.
DON'T KNOW WHY I BURNED THEM. CURIOSITY, MAYBE THE CHALLENGE.
MY GOD.
THEY'RE REAL.

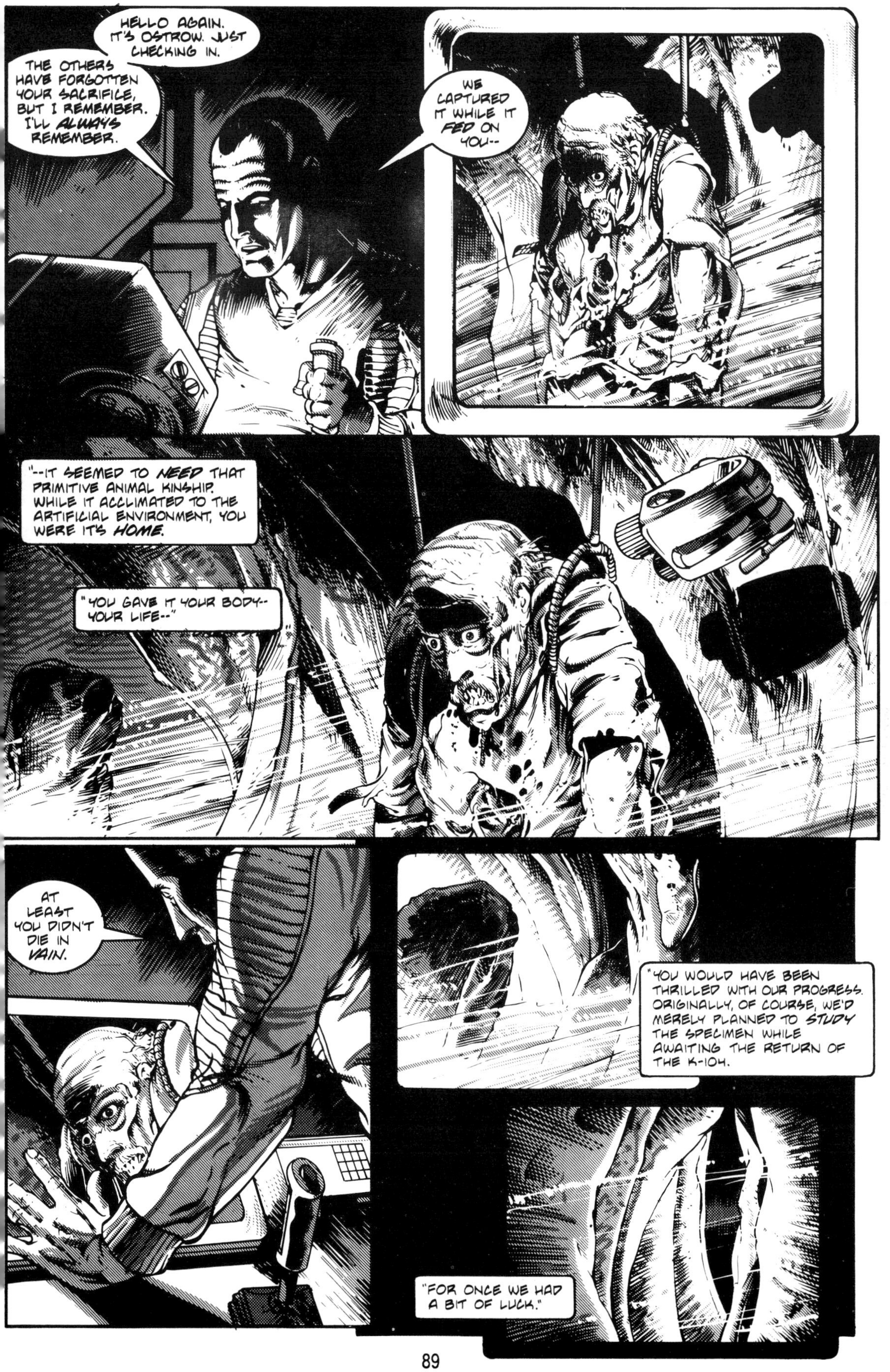
HELLO AGAIN. IT'S OSTROW. JUST CHECKING IN.
THE OTHERS HAVE FORGOTTEN YOUR SACRIFICE, BUT I REMEMBER. I'LL ALWAYS REMEMBER.
WE CAPTURED IT WHILE IT FED ON YOU--
"--IT SEEMED TO NEED THAT PRIMITIVE ANIMAL KINSHIP. WHILE IT ACCLIMATED TO THE ARTIFICIAL ENVIRONMENT, YOU WERE IT'S HOME.
"YOU GAVE IT YOUR BODY-- YOUR LIFE--"
AT LEAST YOU DIDN'T DIE IN VAIN.
"YOU WOULD HAVE BEEN THRILLED WITH OUR PROGRESS. ORIGINALLY, OF COURSE, WE'D MERELY PLANNED TO STUDY THE SPECIMEN WHILE AWAITING THE RETURN OF THE K-104.
"FOR ONCE WE HAD A BIT OF LUCK."

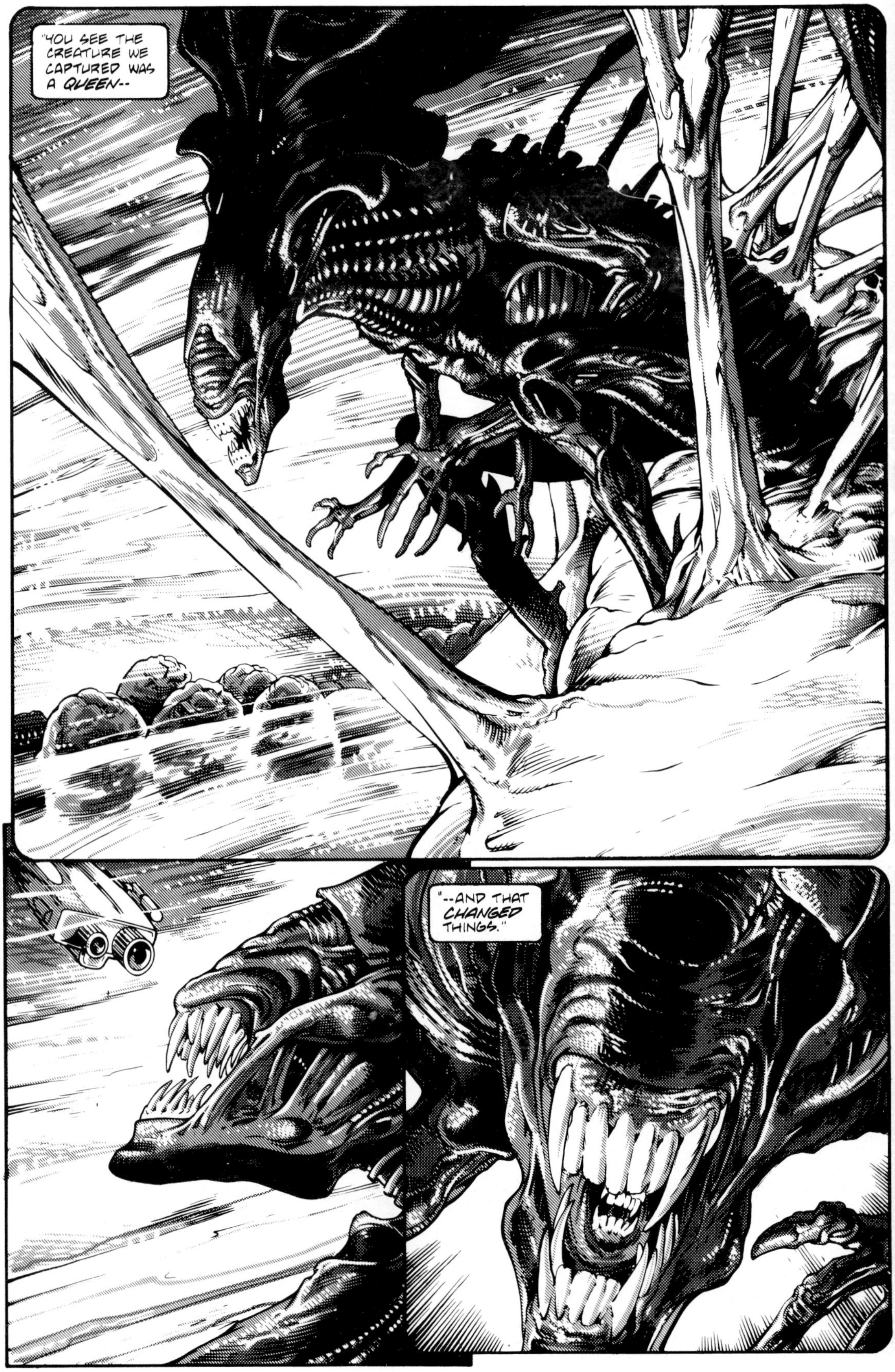
"YOU SEE THE CREATURE WE CAPTURED WAS A *QUEEN*--
"--AND THAT *CHANGED* THINGS."

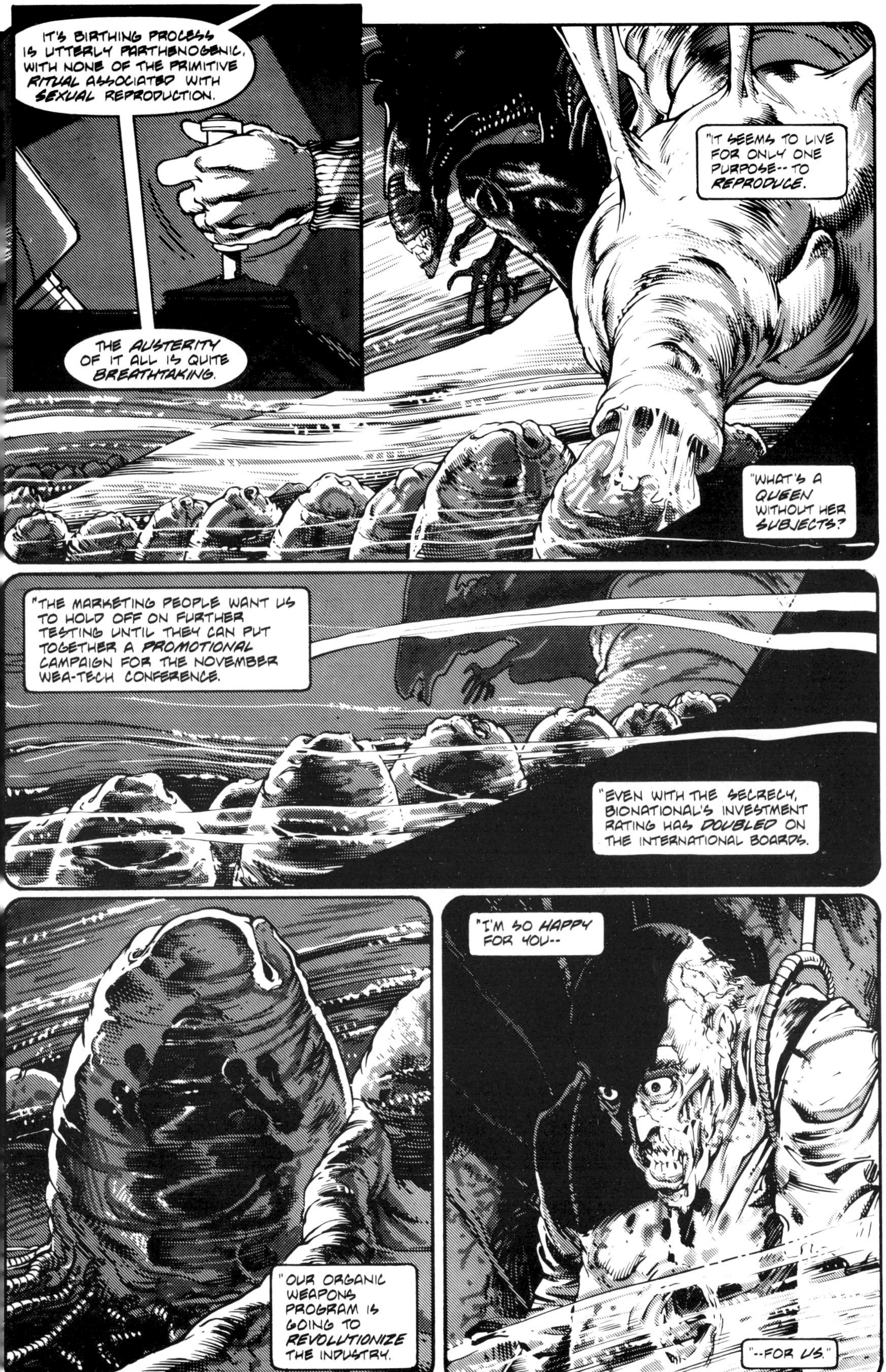
IT'S BIRTHING PROCESS IS UTTERLY PARTHENOGENIC, WITH NONE OF THE PRIMITIVE RITUAL ASSOCIATED WITH SEXUAL REPRODUCTION.
THE AUSTERITY OF IT ALL IS QUITE BREATHTAKING.
"IT SEEMS TO LIVE FOR ONLY ONE PURPOSE-- TO REPRODUCE.
"WHAT'S A QUEEN WITHOUT HER SUBJECTS?
"THE MARKETING PEOPLE WANT US TO HOLD OFF ON FURTHER TESTING UNTIL THEY CAN PUT TOGETHER A PROMOTIONAL CAMPAIGN FOR THE NOVEMBER WEA-TECH CONFERENCE.
"EVEN WITH THE SECRECY, BIONATIONAL'S INVESTMENT RATING HAS DOUBLED ON THE INTERNATIONAL BOARDS.
"OUR ORGANIC WEAPONS PROGRAM IS GOING TO REVOLUTIONIZE THE INDUSTRY.
"I'M SO HAPPY FOR YOU--
"--FOR US."

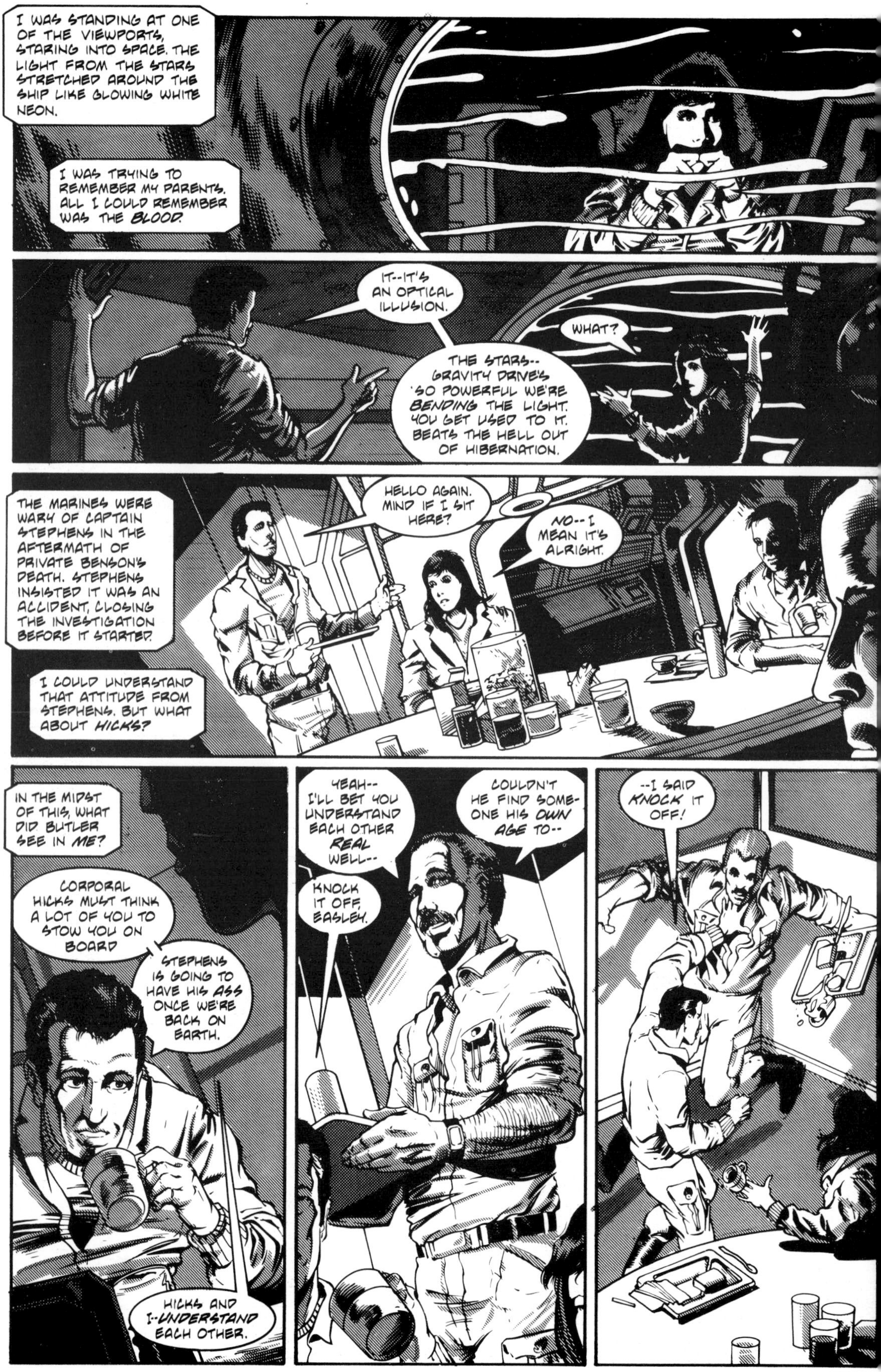
I WAS STANDING AT ONE OF THE VIEWPORTS, STARING INTO SPACE. THE LIGHT FROM THE STARS STRETCHED AROUND THE SHIP LIKE GLOWING WHITE NEON.
I WAS TRYING TO REMEMBER MY PARENTS. ALL I COULD REMEMBER WAS THE BLOOD.
IT--IT'S AN OPTICAL ILLUSION.
WHAT?
THE STARS--GRAVITY DRIVE'S SO POWERFUL WE'RE BENDING THE LIGHT. YOU GET USED TO IT. BEATS THE HELL OUT OF HIBERNATION.
THE MARINES WERE WARY OF CAPTAIN STEPHENS IN THE AFTERMATH OF PRIVATE BENSON'S DEATH. STEPHENS INSISTED IT WAS AN ACCIDENT, CLOSING THE INVESTIGATION BEFORE IT STARTED.
I COULD UNDERSTAND THAT ATTITUDE FROM STEPHENS. BUT WHAT ABOUT HICKS?
HELLO AGAIN. MIND IF I SIT HERE?
NO--I MEAN IT'S ALRIGHT.
IN THE MIDST OF THIS, WHAT DID BUTLER SEE IN ME?
CORPORAL HICKS MUST THINK A LOT OF YOU TO STOW YOU ON BOARD
STEPHENS IS GOING TO HAVE HIS ASS ONCE WE'RE BACK ON EARTH.
HICKS AND I--UNDERSTAND EACH OTHER.
YEAH--I'LL BET YOU UNDERSTAND EACH OTHER REAL WELL--
COULDN'T HE FIND SOME-ONE HIS OWN AGE TO--
KNOCK IT OFF EASLEY.
--I SAID KNOCK IT OFF!

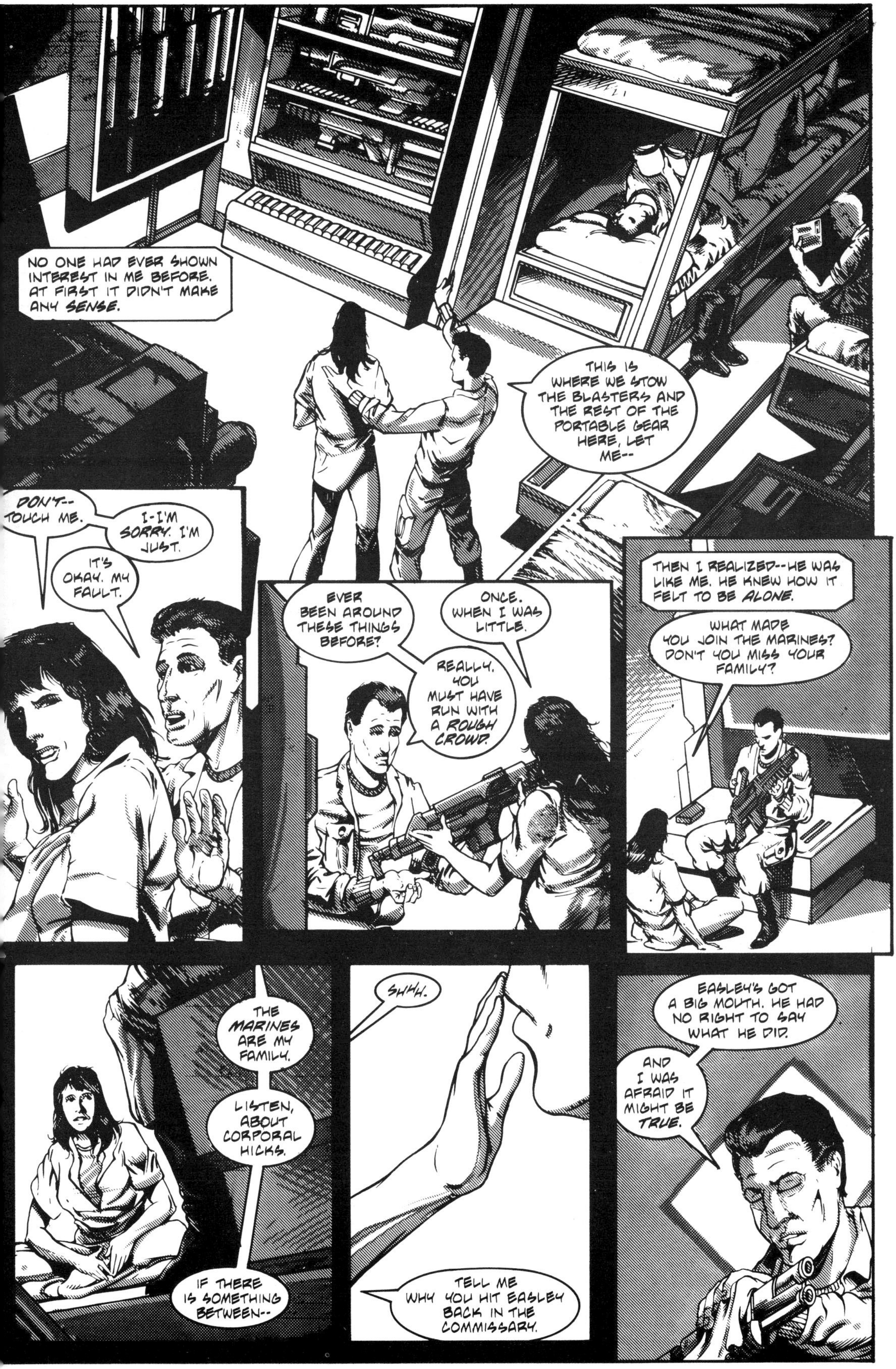
NO ONE HAD EVER SHOWN INTEREST IN ME BEFORE. AT FIRST IT DIDN'T MAKE ANY SENSE.
THIS IS WHERE WE STOW THE BLASTERS AND THE REST OF THE PORTABLE GEAR HERE, LET ME--
DON'T-- TOUCH ME.
I-I'M SORRY. I'M JUST.
IT'S OKAY. MY FAULT.
EVER BEEN AROUND THESE THINGS BEFORE?
ONCE. WHEN I WAS LITTLE.
REALLY. YOU MUST HAVE RUN WITH A ROUGH CROWD.
THEN I REALIZED--HE WAS LIKE ME. HE KNEW HOW IT FELT TO BE ALONE.
WHAT MADE YOU JOIN THE MARINES? DON'T YOU MISS YOUR FAMILY?
THE MARINES ARE MY FAMILY.
LISTEN, ABOUT CORPORAL HICKS.
IF THERE IS SOMETHING BETWEEN--
SHHH.
TELL ME WHY YOU HIT EASLEY BACK IN THE COMMISSARY.
EASLEY'S GOT A BIG MOUTH. HE HAD NO RIGHT TO SAY WHAT HE DID.
AND I WAS AFRAID IT MIGHT BE TRUE.

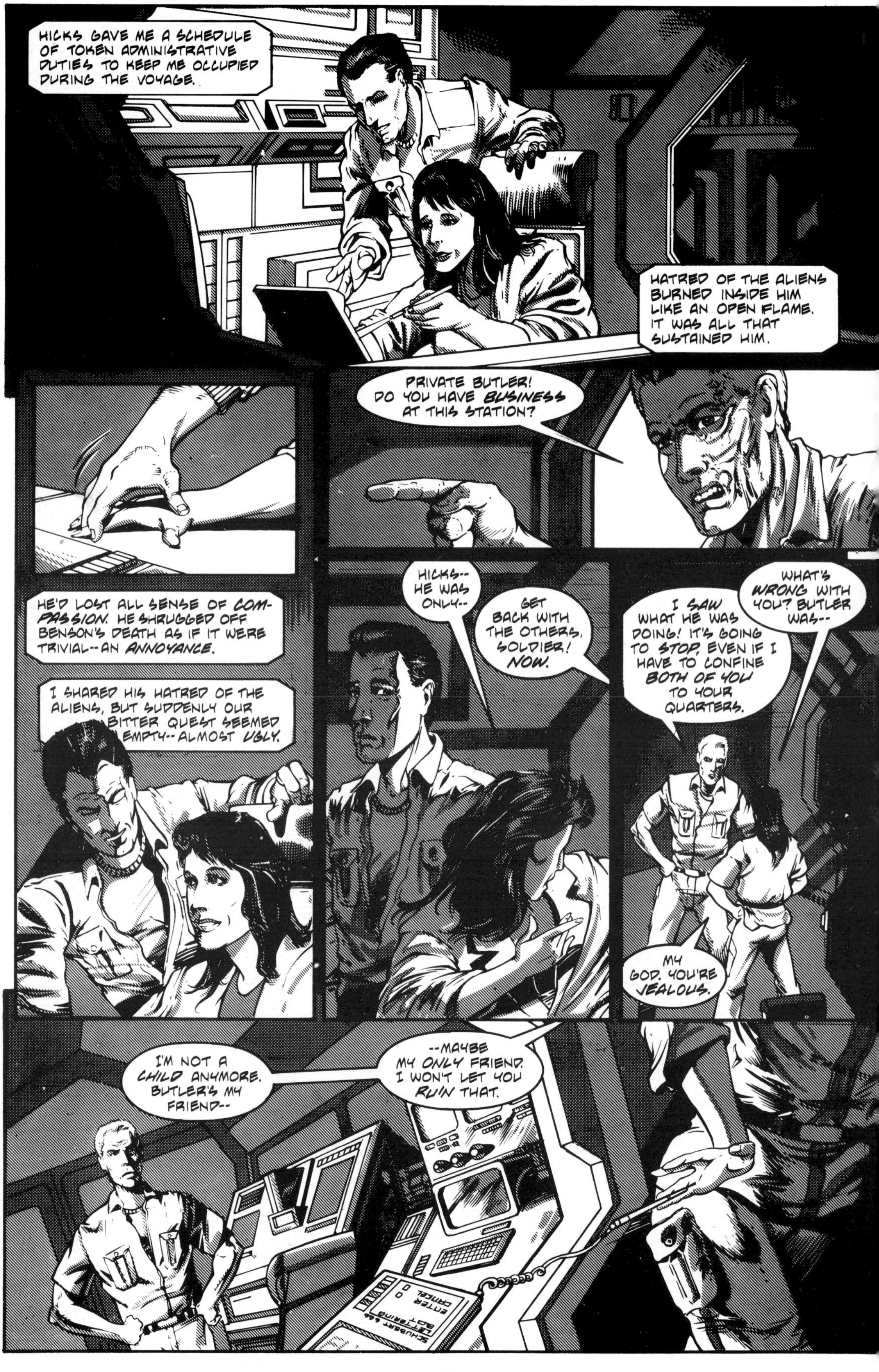
HICKS GAVE ME A SCHEDULE OF TOKEN ADMINISTRATIVE DUTIES TO KEEP ME OCCUPIED DURING THE VOYAGE.
HATRED OF THE ALIENS BURNED INSIDE HIM LIKE AN OPEN FLAME. IT WAS ALL THAT SUSTAINED HIM.
PRIVATE BUTLER! DO YOU HAVE BUSINESS AT THIS STATION?
HE'D LOST ALL SENSE OF COMPASSION. HE SHRUGGED OFF BENSON'S DEATH AS IF IT WERE TRIVIAL--AN ANNOYANCE.
I SHARED HIS HATRED OF THE ALIENS, BUT SUDDENLY OUR BITTER QUEST SEEMED EMPTY--ALMOST UGLY.
HICKS--HE WAS ONLY--
GET BACK WITH THE OTHERS, SOLDIER! NOW.
WHAT'S WRONG WITH YOU? BUTLER WAS--
I SAW WHAT HE WAS DOING! IT'S GOING TO STOP, EVEN IF I HAVE TO CONFINE BOTH OF YOU TO YOUR QUARTERS.
MY GOD. YOU'RE JEALOUS.
I'M NOT A CHILD ANYMORE. BUTLER'S MY FRIEND--
--MAYBE MY ONLY FRIEND. I WON'T LET YOU RUIN THAT.

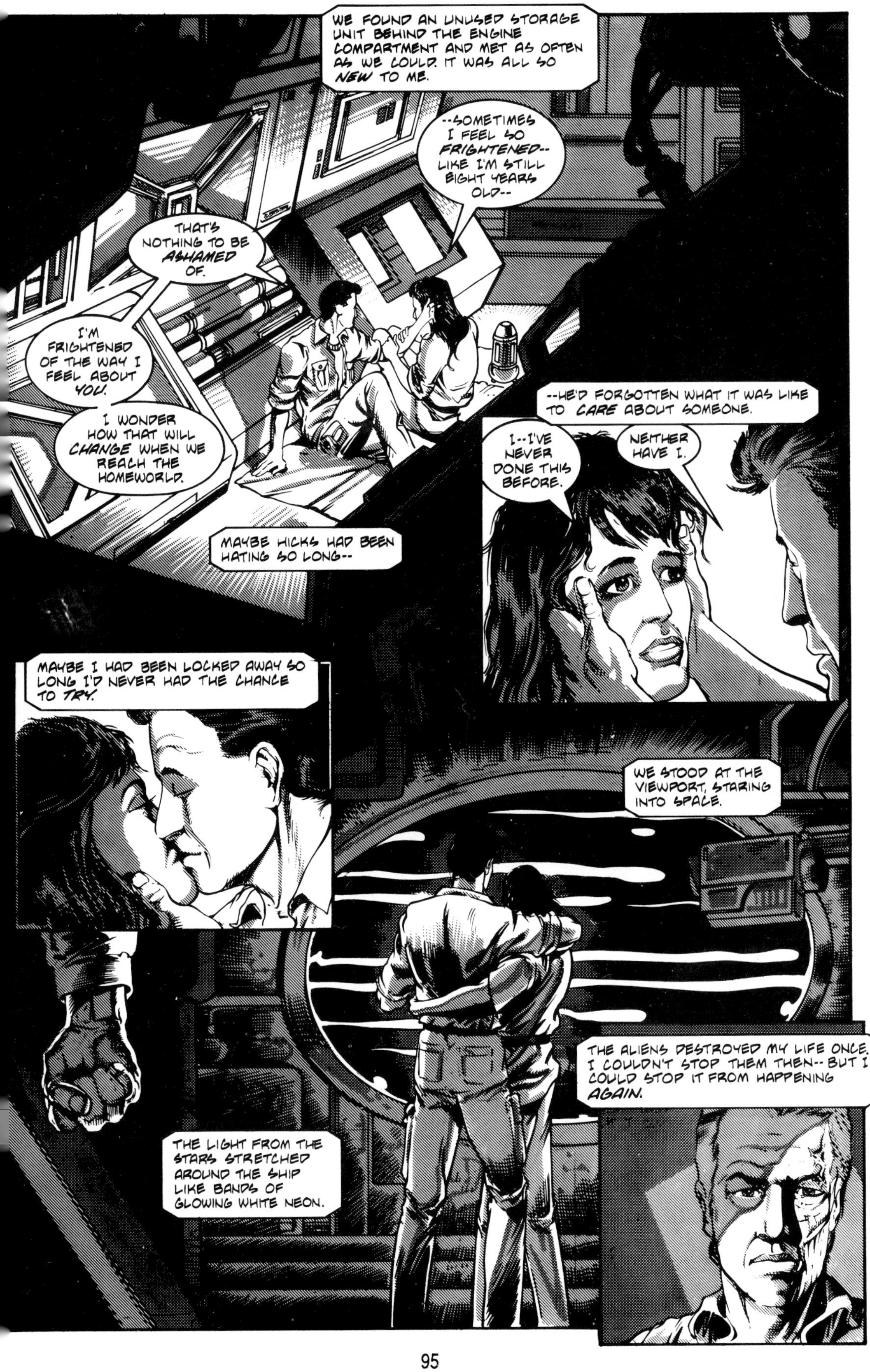

WE FOUND AN UNUSED STORAGE UNIT BEHIND THE ENGINE COMPARTMENT AND MET AS OFTEN AS WE COULD. IT WAS ALL SO NEW TO ME.
--SOMETIMES I FEEL SO FRIGHTENED-- LIKE I'M STILL EIGHT YEARS OLD--
THAT'S NOTHING TO BE ASHAMED OF.
I'M FRIGHTENED OF THE WAY I FEEL ABOUT YOU.
I WONDER HOW THAT WILL CHANGE WHEN WE REACH THE HOMEWORLD.
MAYBE HICKS HAD BEEN HATING SO LONG--
--HE'D FORGOTTEN WHAT IT WAS LIKE TO CARE ABOUT SOMEONE.
I--I'VE NEVER DONE THIS BEFORE.
NEITHER HAVE I.
MAYBE I HAD BEEN LOCKED AWAY SO LONG I'D NEVER HAD THE CHANCE TO TRY.
WE STOOD AT THE VIEWPORT, STARING INTO SPACE.
THE LIGHT FROM THE STARS STRETCHED AROUND THE SHIP LIKE BANDS OF GLOWING WHITE NEON.
THE ALIENS DESTROYED MY LIFE ONCE. I COULDN'T STOP THEM THEN-- BUT I COULD STOP IT FROM HAPPENING AGAIN.

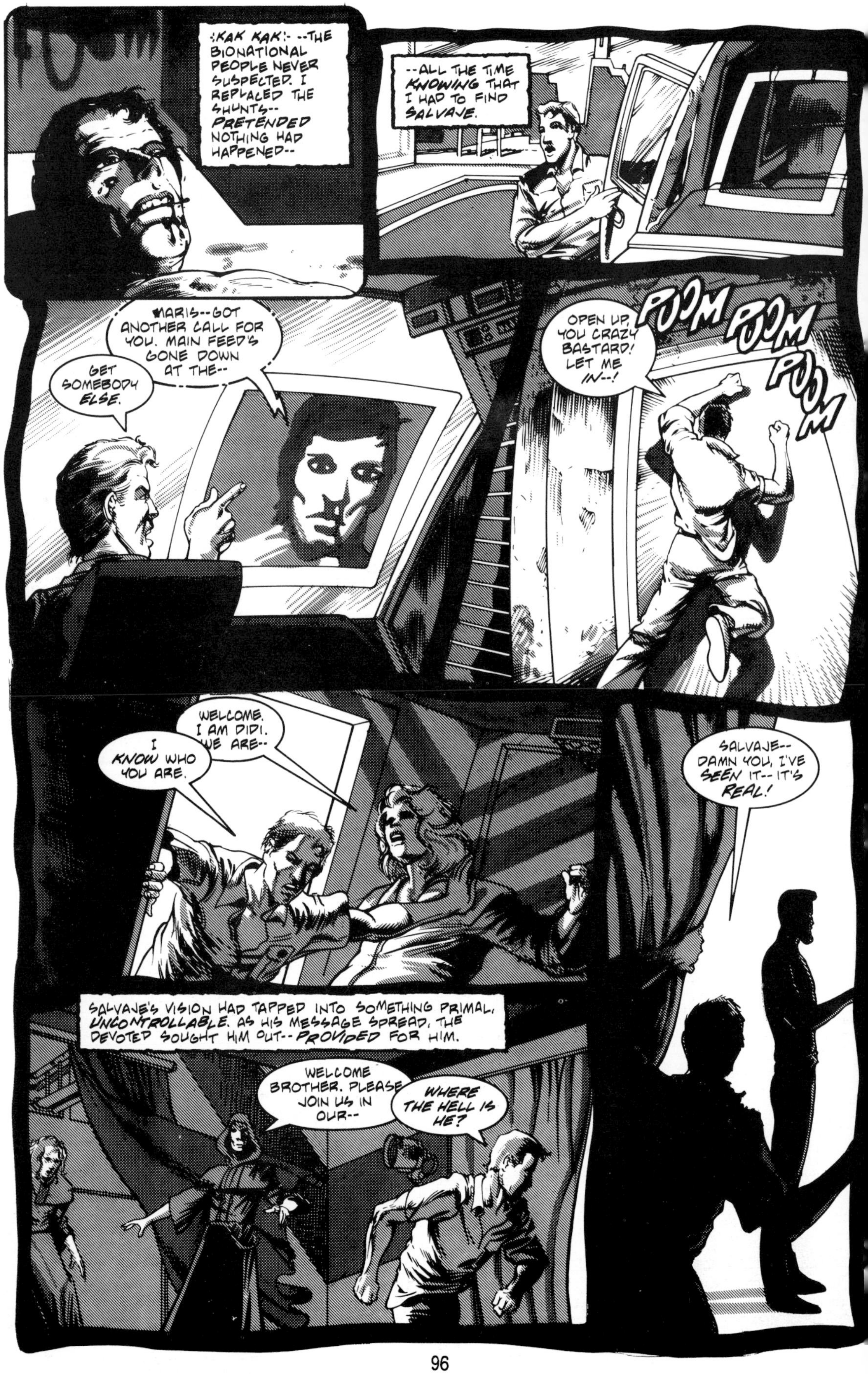
:KAK KAK:- --THE BIONATIONAL PEOPLE NEVER SUSPECTED. I REPLACED THE SHUNTS-- PRETENDED NOTHING HAD HAPPENED--
--ALL THE TIME KNOWING THAT I HAD TO FIND SALVAJE.
MARIS--GOT ANOTHER CALL FOR YOU. MAIN FEED'S GONE DOWN AT THE--
GET SOMEBODY ELSE.
OPEN UP, YOU CRAZY BASTARD! LET ME IN--!
POOM POOM POOM
WELCOME. I AM DIDI. WE ARE--
I KNOW WHO YOU ARE.
SALVAJE-- DAMN YOU, I'VE SEEN IT-- IT'S REAL!
SALVAJE'S VISION HAD TAPPED INTO SOMETHING PRIMAL, UNCONTROLLABLE. AS HIS MESSAGE SPREAD, THE DEVOTED SOUGHT HIM OUT--PROVIDED FOR HIM.
WELCOME BROTHER. PLEASE JOIN US IN OUR--
WHERE THE HELL IS HE?

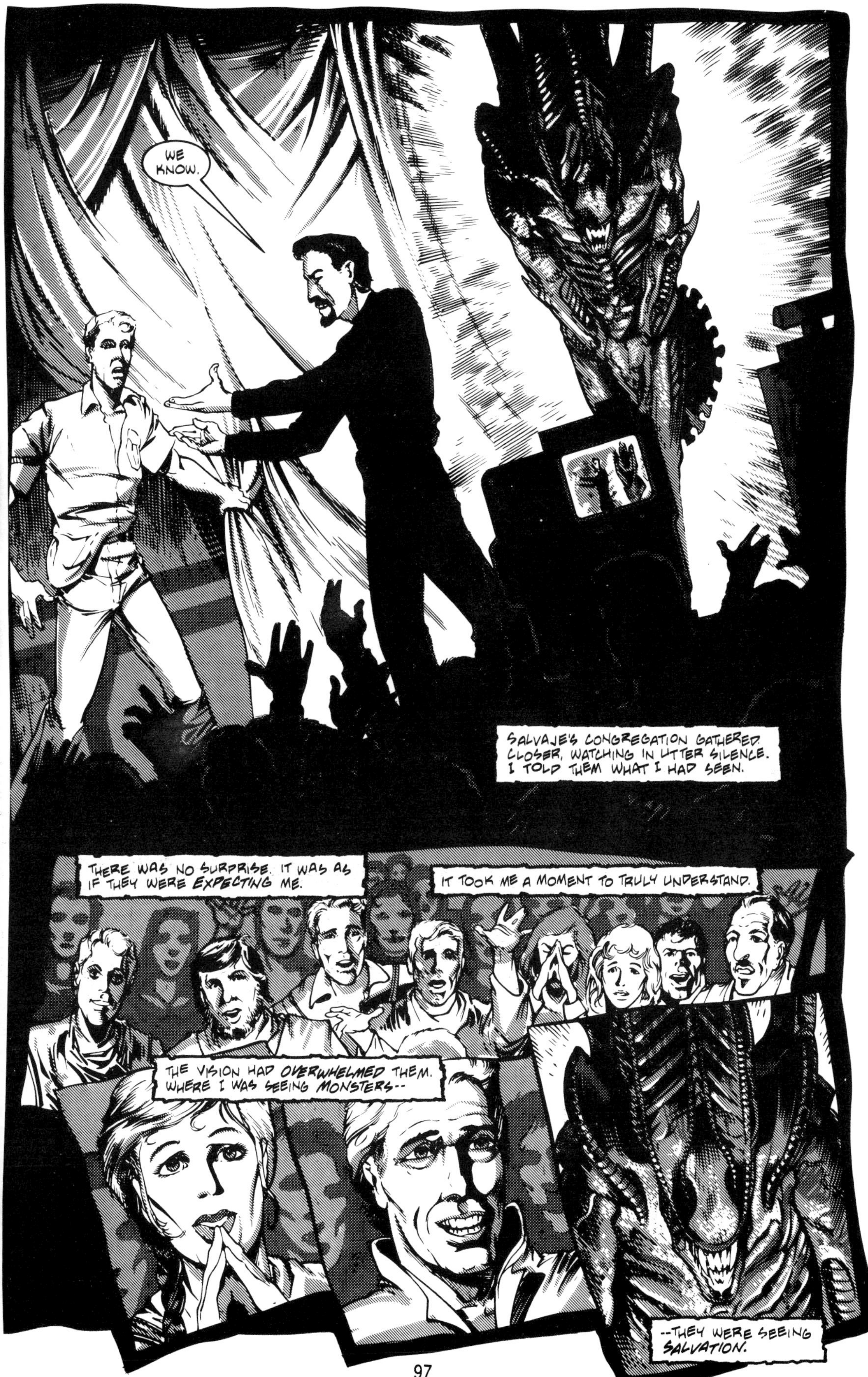
WE KNOW.
SALVAJE'S CONGREGATION GATHERED CLOSER, WATCHING IN UTTER SILENCE. I TOLD THEM WHAT I HAD SEEN.
THERE WAS NO SURPRISE. IT WAS AS IF THEY WERE EXPECTING ME.
IT TOOK ME A MOMENT TO TRULY UNDERSTAND.
THE VISION HAD OVERWHELMED THEM. WHERE I WAS SEEING MONSTERS--
--THEY WERE SEEING SALVATION.

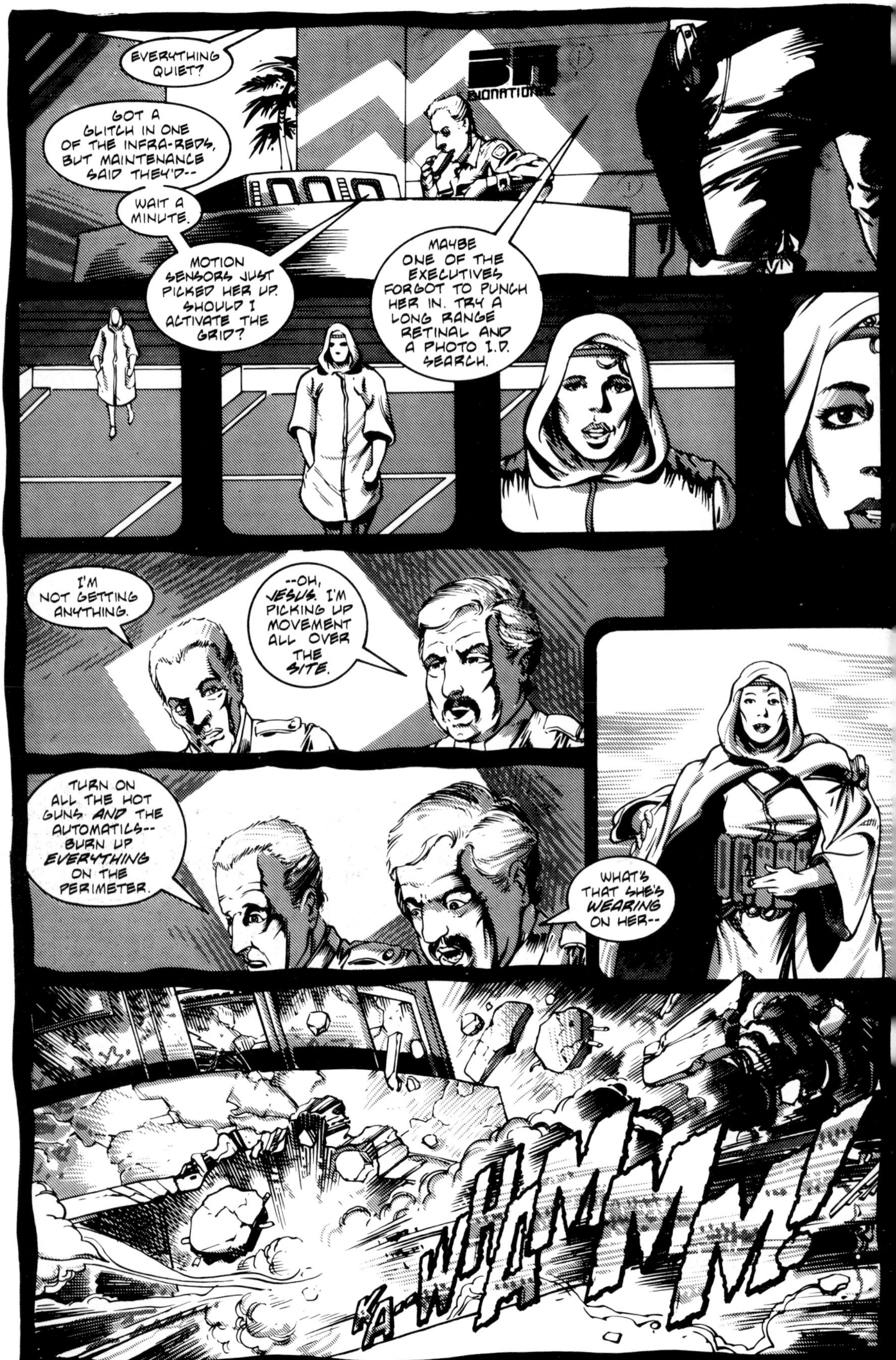
EVERYTHING QUIET?
GOT A GLITCH IN ONE OF THE INFRA-REDS, BUT MAINTENANCE SAID THEY'D--
WAIT A MINUTE.
MOTION SENSORS JUST PICKED HER UP. SHOULD I ACTIVATE THE GRID?
MAYBE ONE OF THE EXECUTIVES FORGOT TO PUNCH HER IN. TRY A LONG RANGE RETINAL AND A PHOTO I.D. SEARCH.
I'M NOT GETTING ANYTHING.
--OH, JESUS. I'M PICKING UP MOVEMENT ALL OVER THE SITE.
TURN ON ALL THE HOT GUNS AND THE AUTOMATICS-- BURN UP EVERYTHING ON THE PERIMETER.
WHAT'S THAT SHE'S WEARING ON HER--
KA-WHAMMM!

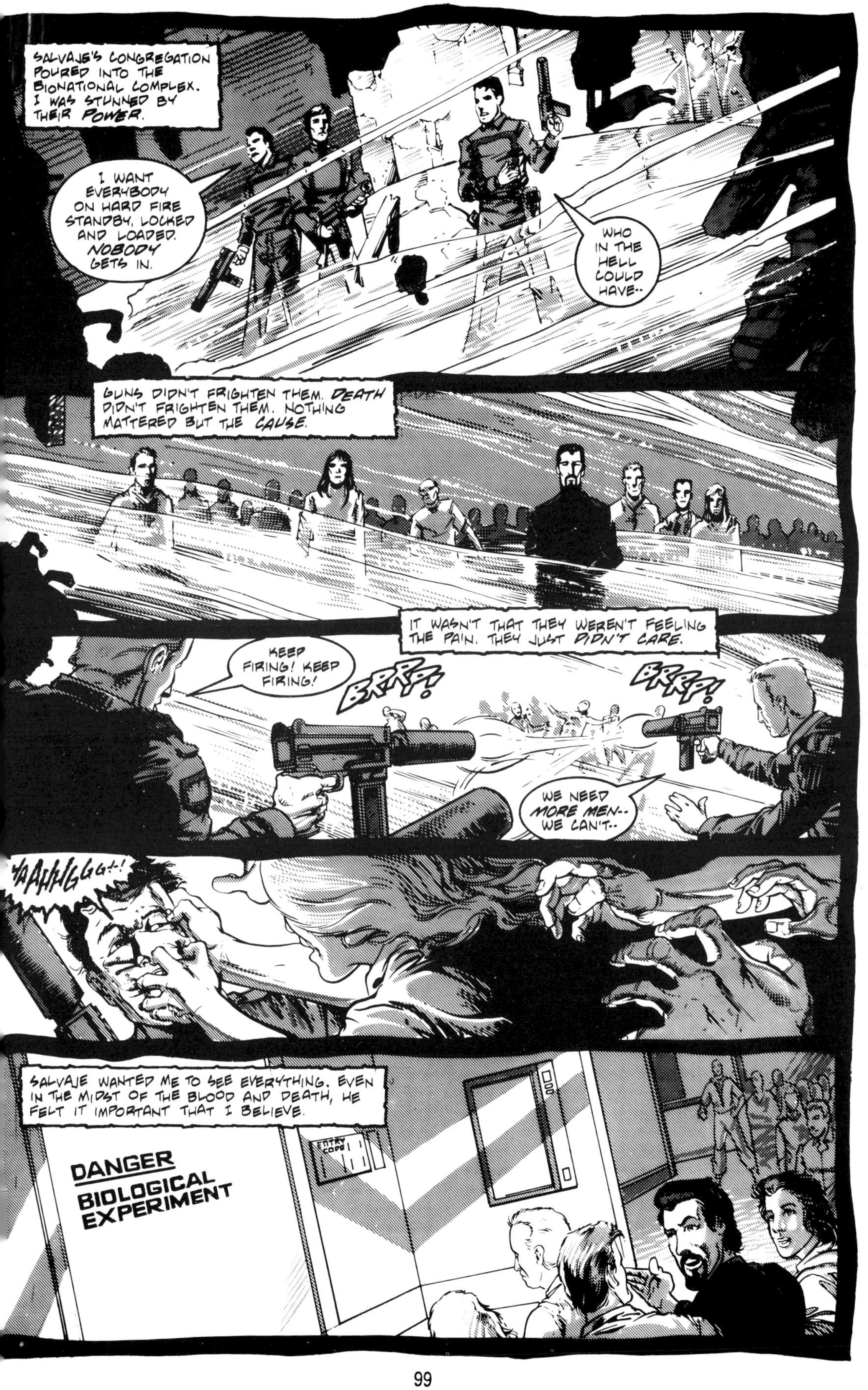
SALVAJE'S CONGREGATION POURED INTO THE BIONATIONAL COMPLEX. I WAS STUNNED BY THEIR *POWER*.
I WANT EVERYBODY ON HARD FIRE STANDBY, LOCKED AND LOADED. *NOBODY* GETS IN.
WHO IN THE HELL COULD HAVE--
GUNS DIDN'T FRIGHTEN THEM. *DEATH* DIDN'T FRIGHTEN THEM. NOTHING MATTERED BUT THE *CAUSE*.
IT WASN'T THAT THEY WEREN'T FEELING THE PAIN. THEY JUST *DIDN'T CARE*.
KEEP FIRING! KEEP FIRING!
BRRAP!
BRRAP!
WE NEED *MORE MEN*-- WE CAN'T--
YAAHHGGG!!
SALVAJE WANTED ME TO SEE EVERYTHING. EVEN IN THE MIDST OF THE BLOOD AND DEATH, HE FELT IT IMPORTANT THAT I BELIEVE.
ENTRY CODE
DANGER
BIOLOGICAL EXPERIMENT

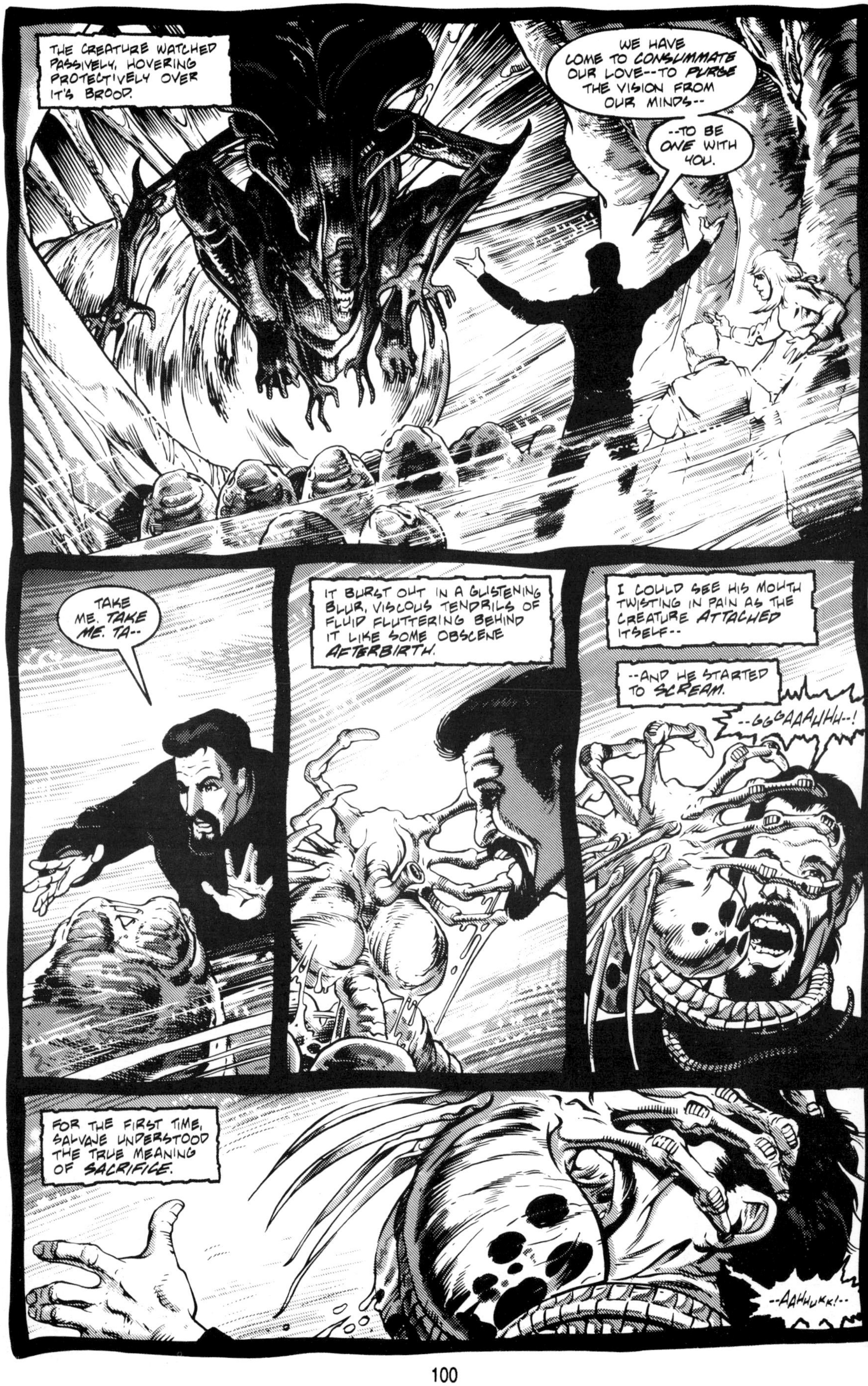
THE CREATURE WATCHED PASSIVELY, HOVERING PROTECTIVELY OVER IT'S BROOD.
WE HAVE COME TO CONSUMMATE OUR LOVE--TO PURGE THE VISION FROM OUR MINDS--
--TO BE ONE WITH YOU.
TAKE ME. TAKE ME. TA--
IT BURST OUT IN A GLISTENING BLUR, VISCOUS TENDRILS OF FLUID FLUTTERING BEHIND IT LIKE SOME OBSCENE AFTERBIRTH.
I COULD SEE HIS MOUTH TWISTING IN PAIN AS THE CREATURE ATTACHED ITSELF--
--AND HE STARTED TO SCREAM.
--GGGAAAUHH--!
FOR THE FIRST TIME, SALVANE UNDERSTOOD THE TRUE MEANING OF SACRIFICE.
--AAHHUKK!--

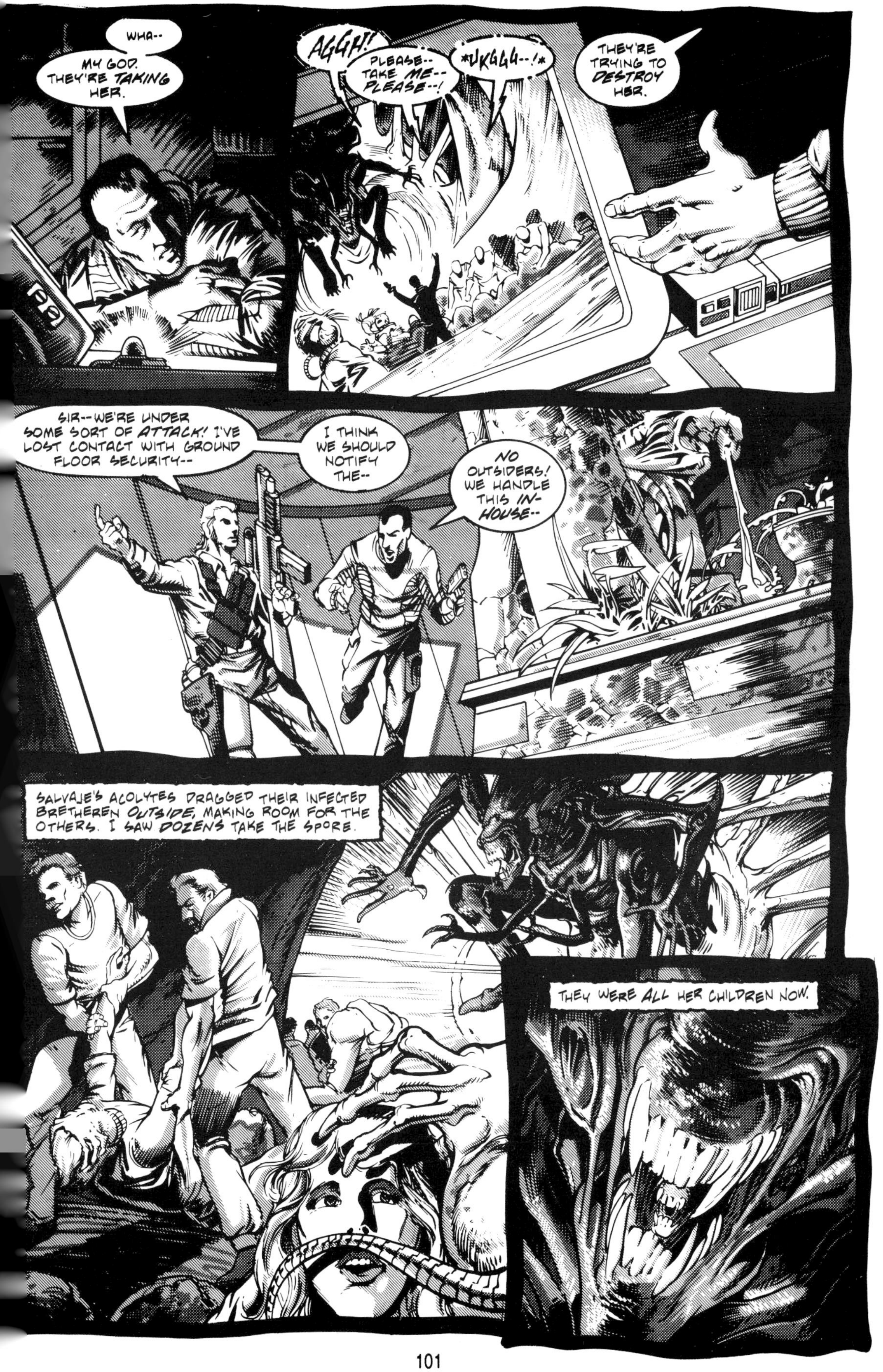
WHA--
MY GOD. THEY'RE TAKING HER.
AGGH!
PLEASE-- TAKE ME-- PLEASE--!
UKGGG--!
THEY'RE TRYING TO DESTROY HER.
SIR--WE'RE UNDER SOME SORT OF ATTACK! I'VE LOST CONTACT WITH GROUND FLOOR SECURITY--
I THINK WE SHOULD NOTIFY THE--
NO OUTSIDERS! WE HANDLE THIS IN-HOUSE--
SALVAJE'S ACOLYTES DRAGGED THEIR INFECTED BRETHEREN OUTSIDE, MAKING ROOM FOR THE OTHERS. I SAW DOZENS TAKE THE SPORE.
THEY WERE ALL HER CHILDREN NOW.

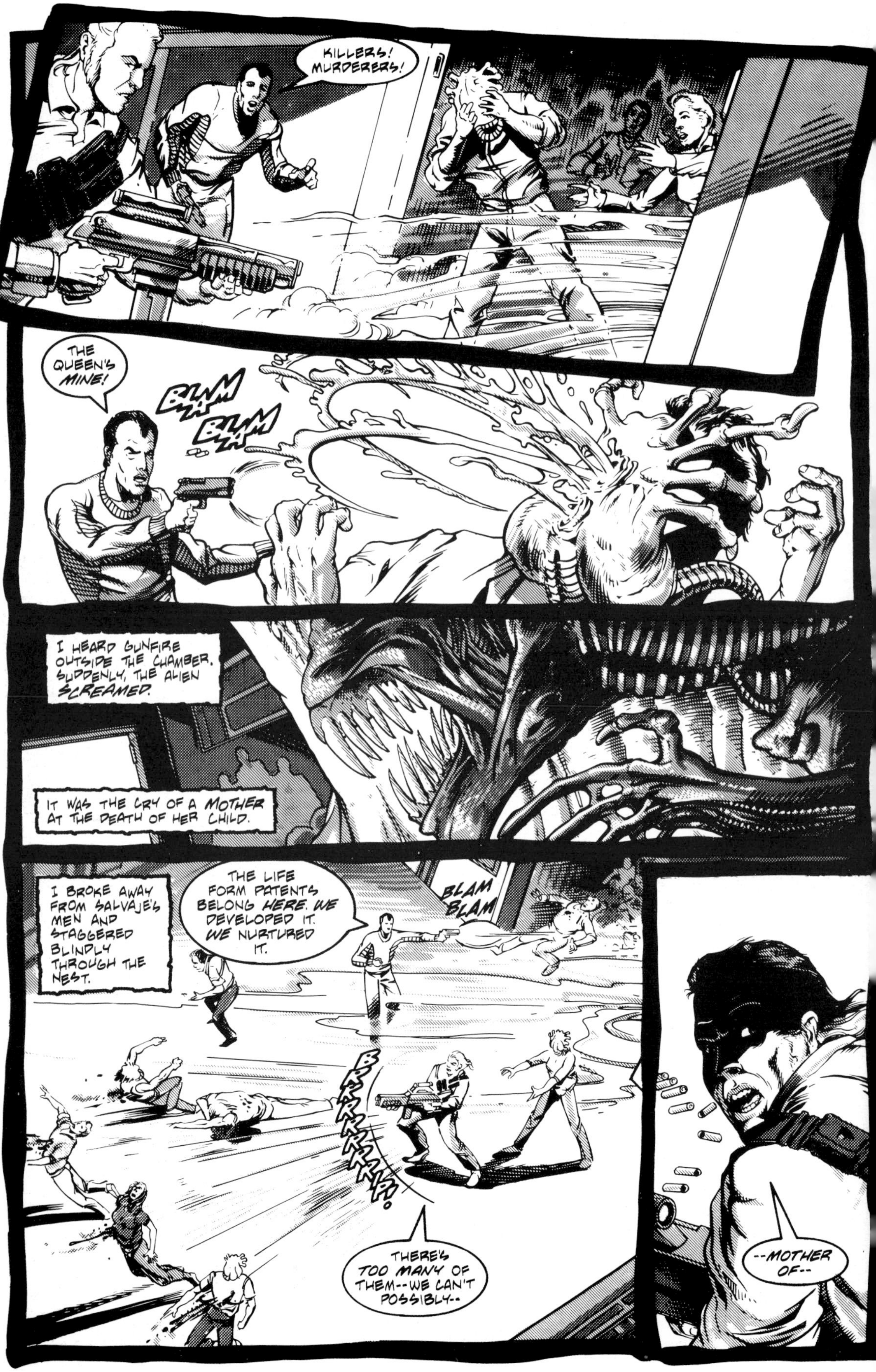

KILLERS! MURDERERS!
THE QUEEN'S MINE!
BLAM BLAM
I HEARD GUNFIRE OUTSIDE THE CHAMBER. SUDDENLY, THE ALIEN SCREAMED.
IT WAS THE CRY OF A MOTHER AT THE DEATH OF HER CHILD.
I BROKE AWAY FROM SALVAJE'S MEN AND STAGGERED BLINDLY THROUGH THE NEST.
THE LIFE FORM PATENTS BELONG HERE. WE DEVELOPED IT. WE NURTURED IT.
BLAM BLAM
BRRRRRRRIP!
THERE'S TOO MANY OF THEM--WE CAN'T POSSIBLY--
--MOTHER OF--

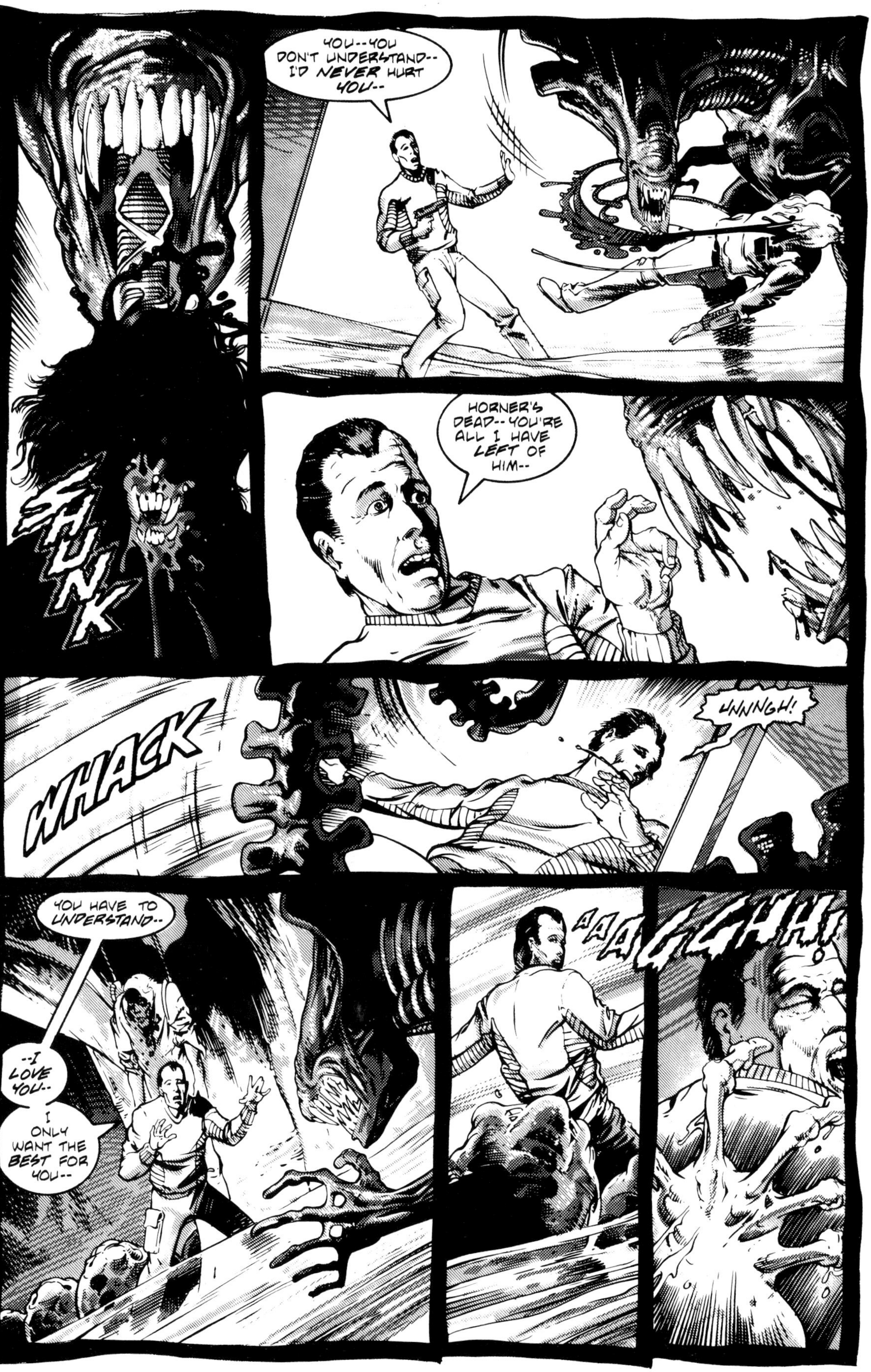
SHUNK
YOU--YOU DON'T UNDERSTAND--I'D NEVER HURT YOU--
HORNER'S DEAD--YOU'RE ALL I HAVE LEFT OF HIM--
WHACK
UNNGH!
YOU HAVE TO UNDERSTAND--
--I LOVE YOU--
I ONLY WANT THE BEST FOR YOU--
AAAAUGHH!

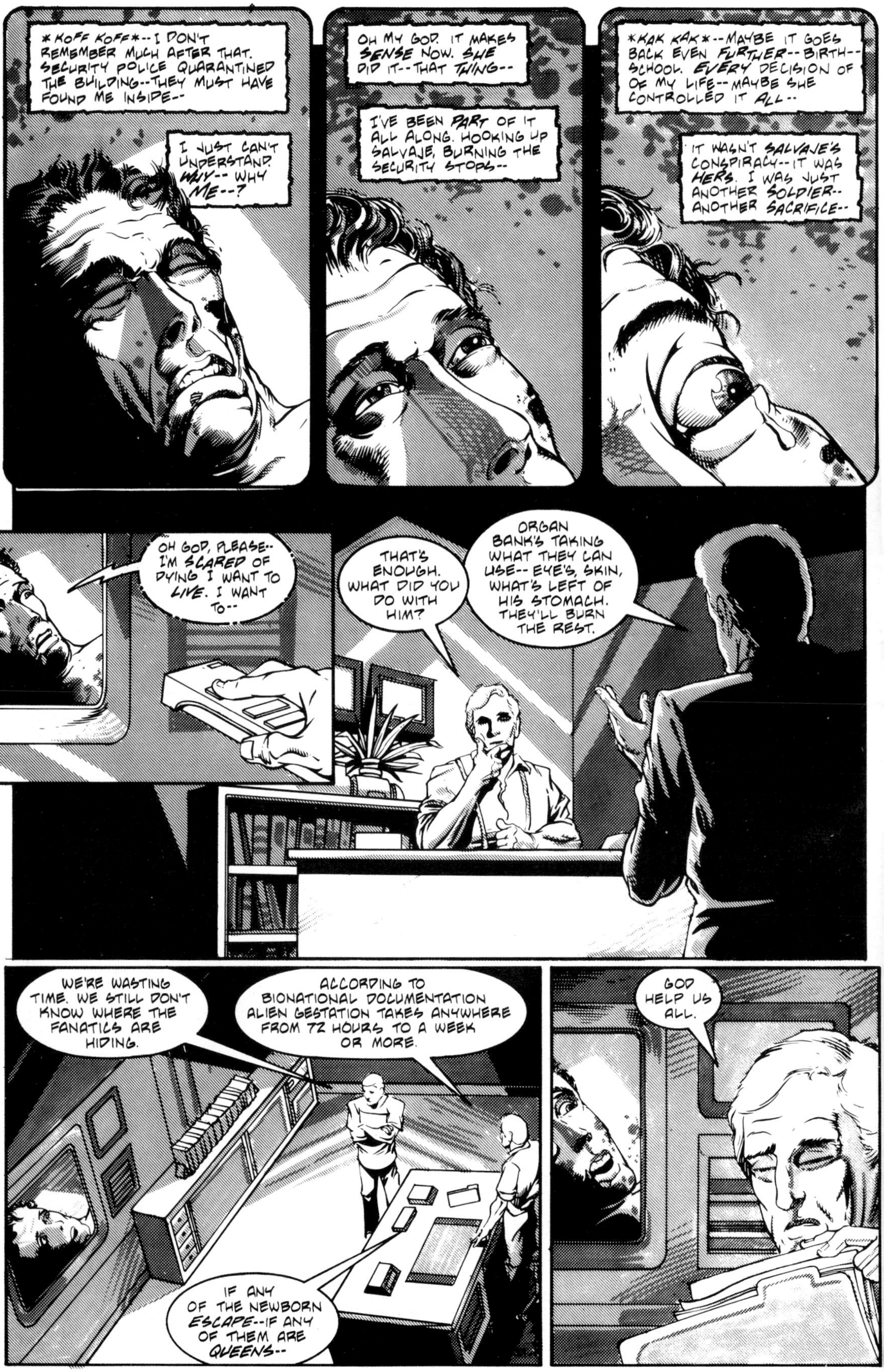
KOFF KOFF--I DON'T REMEMBER MUCH AFTER THAT. SECURITY POLICE QUARANTINED THE BUILDING--THEY MUST HAVE FOUND ME INSIDE--
I JUST CAN'T UNDERSTAND. WHY--WHY ME--?
OH MY GOD. IT MAKES SENSE NOW. SHE DID IT--THAT THING--
I'VE BEEN PART OF IT ALL ALONG. HOOKING UP SALVAJE, BURNING THE SECURITY STOPS--
KAK KAK--MAYBE IT GOES BACK EVEN FURTHER--BIRTH--SCHOOL. EVERY DECISION OF MY LIFE--MAYBE SHE CONTROLLED IT ALL--
IT WASN'T SALVAJE'S CONSPIRACY--IT WAS HERS. I WAS JUST ANOTHER SOLDIER--ANOTHER SACRIFICE--
OH GOD, PLEASE--I'M SCARED OF DYING I WANT TO LIVE. I WANT TO--
THAT'S ENOUGH. WHAT DID YOU DO WITH HIM?
ORGAN BANK'S TAKING WHAT THEY CAN USE--EYE'S, SKIN, WHAT'S LEFT OF HIS STOMACH. THEY'LL BURN THE REST.
WE'RE WASTING TIME. WE STILL DON'T KNOW WHERE THE FANATICS ARE HIDING.
ACCORDING TO BIONATIONAL DOCUMENTATION ALIEN GESTATION TAKES ANYWHERE FROM 72 HOURS TO A WEEK OR MORE.
IF ANY OF THE NEWBORN ESCAPE--IF ANY OF THEM ARE QUEENS--
GOD HELP US ALL.

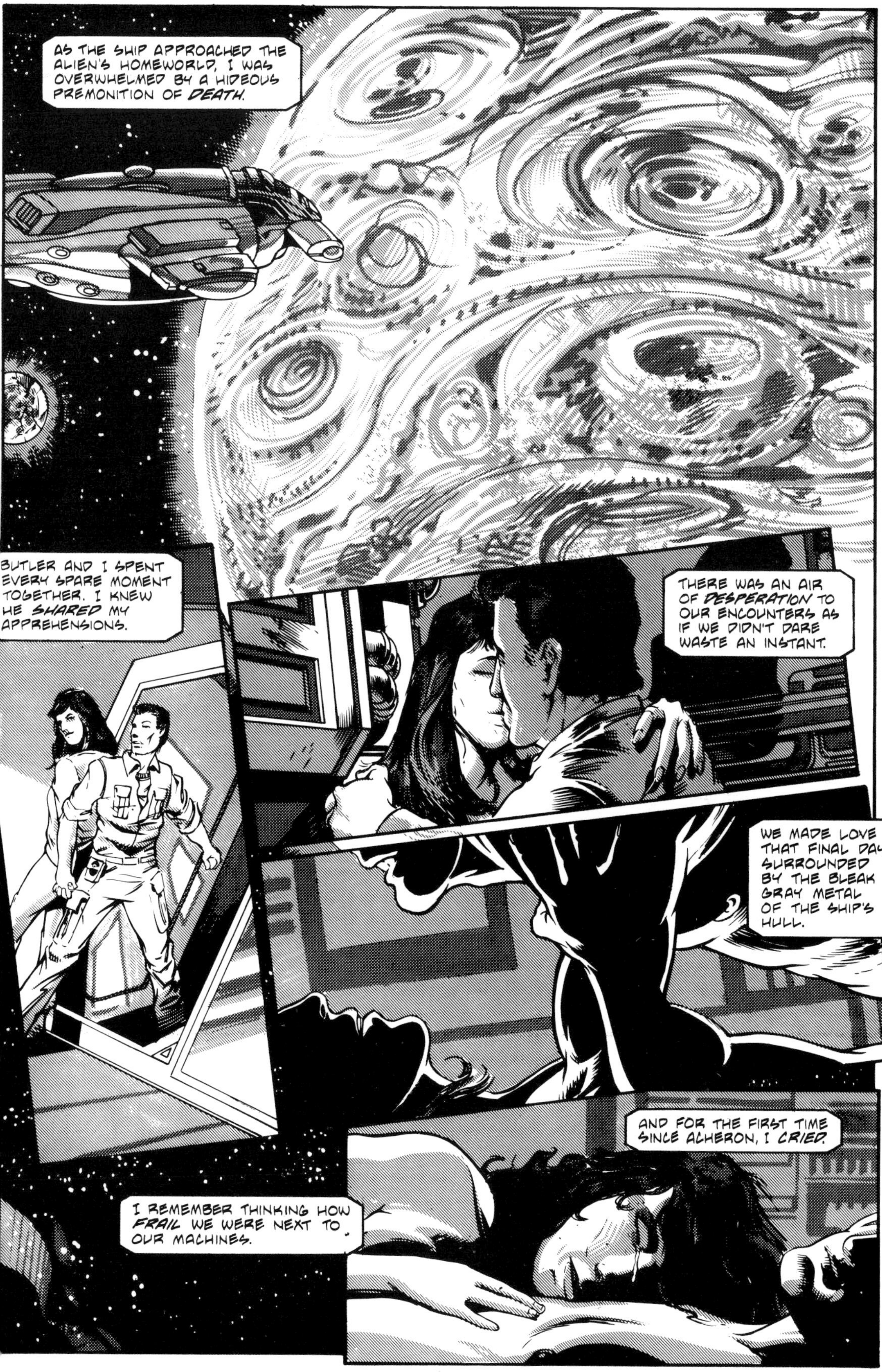

AS THE SHIP APPROACHED THE ALIEN'S HOMEWORLD, I WAS OVERWHELMED BY A HIDEOUS PREMONITION OF *DEATH*.
BUTLER AND I SPENT EVERY SPARE MOMENT TOGETHER. I KNEW HE *SHARED* MY APPREHENSIONS.
THERE WAS AN AIR OF *DESPERATION* TO OUR ENCOUNTERS AS IF WE DIDN'T DARE WASTE AN INSTANT.
WE MADE LOVE THAT FINAL DAY, SURROUNDED BY THE BLEAK GRAY METAL OF THE SHIP'S HULL.
I REMEMBER THINKING HOW *FRAIL* WE WERE NEXT TO OUR MACHINES.
AND FOR THE FIRST TIME SINCE ACHERON, I *CRIED*.

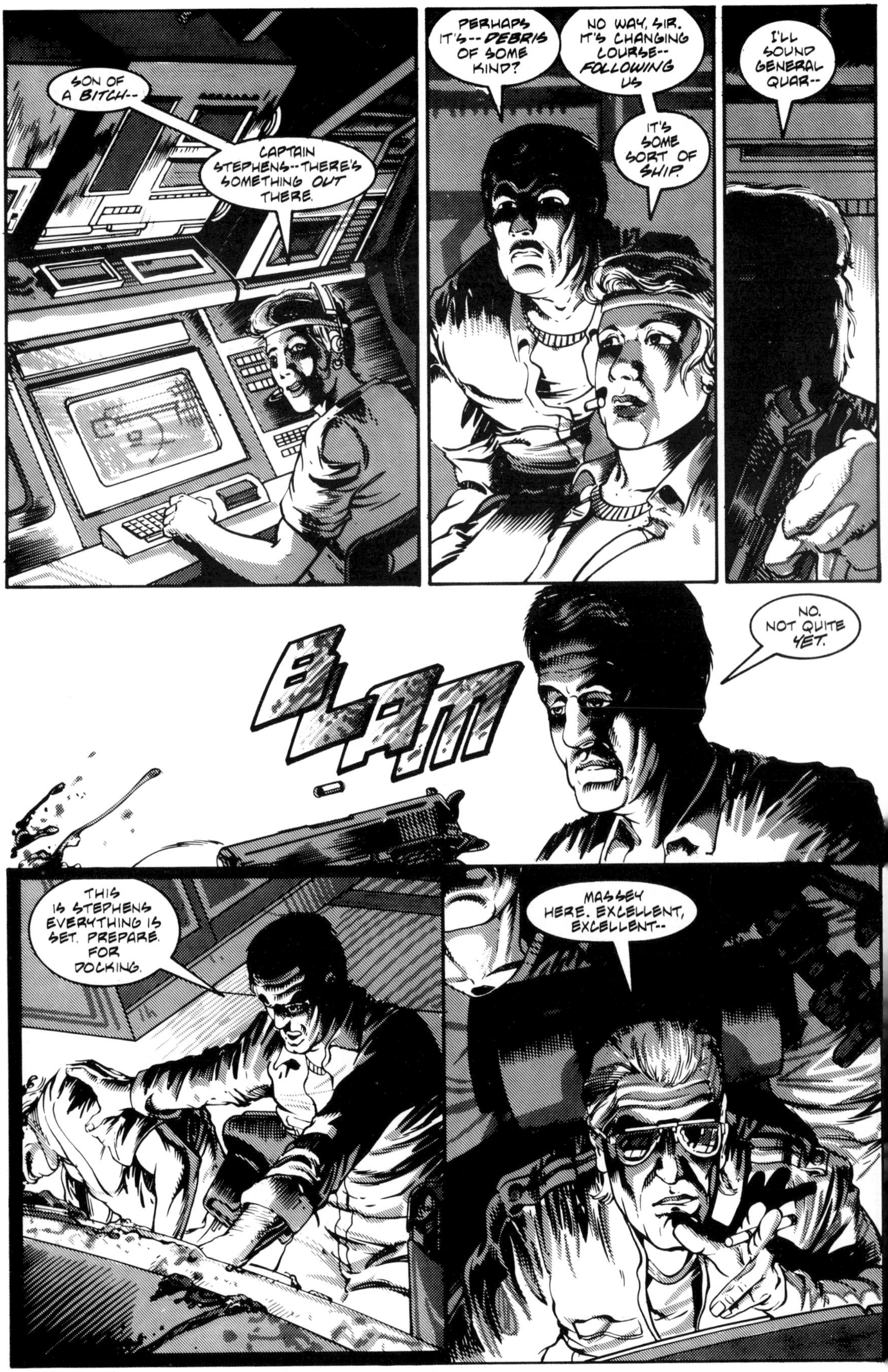

SON OF A BITCH--
CAPTAIN STEPHENS--THERE'S SOMETHING OUT THERE.
PERHAPS IT'S--DEBRIS OF SOME KIND?
NO WAY, SIR. IT'S CHANGING COURSE--FOLLOWING US
IT'S SOME SORT OF SHIP.
I'LL SOUND GENERAL QUAR--
BLAM
NO. NOT QUITE YET.
THIS IS STEPHENS EVERYTHING IS SET. PREPARE. FOR DOCKING.
MASSEY HERE. EXCELLENT, EXCELLENT--

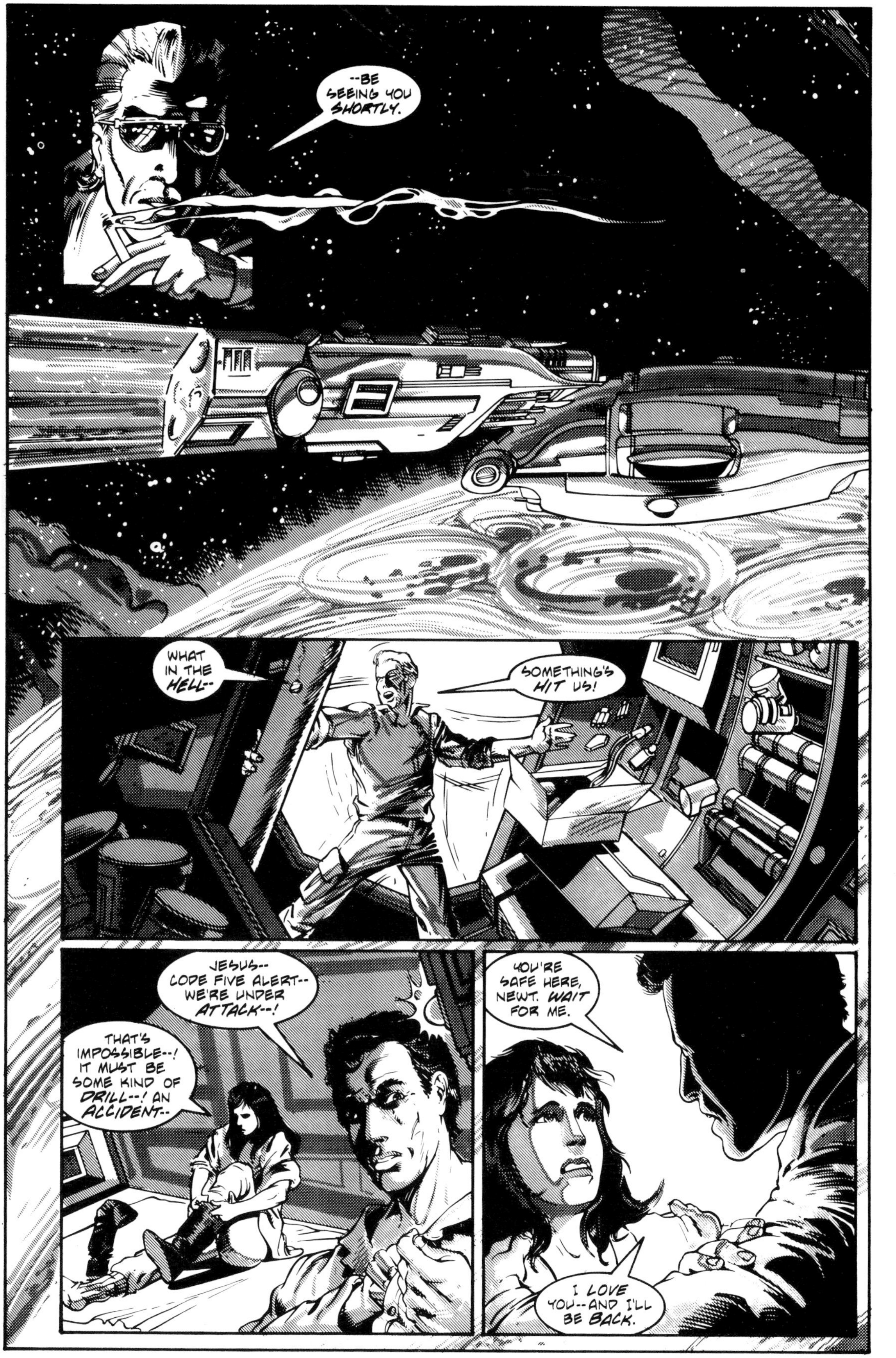
--BE SEEING YOU SHORTLY.
WHAT IN THE HELL--
SOMETHING'S HIT US!
JESUS-- CODE FIVE ALERT-- WE'RE UNDER ATTACK--!
THAT'S IMPOSSIBLE--! IT MUST BE SOME KIND OF DRILL--! AN ACCIDENT--
YOU'RE SAFE HERE, NEWT. WAIT FOR ME.
I LOVE YOU--AND I'LL BE BACK.

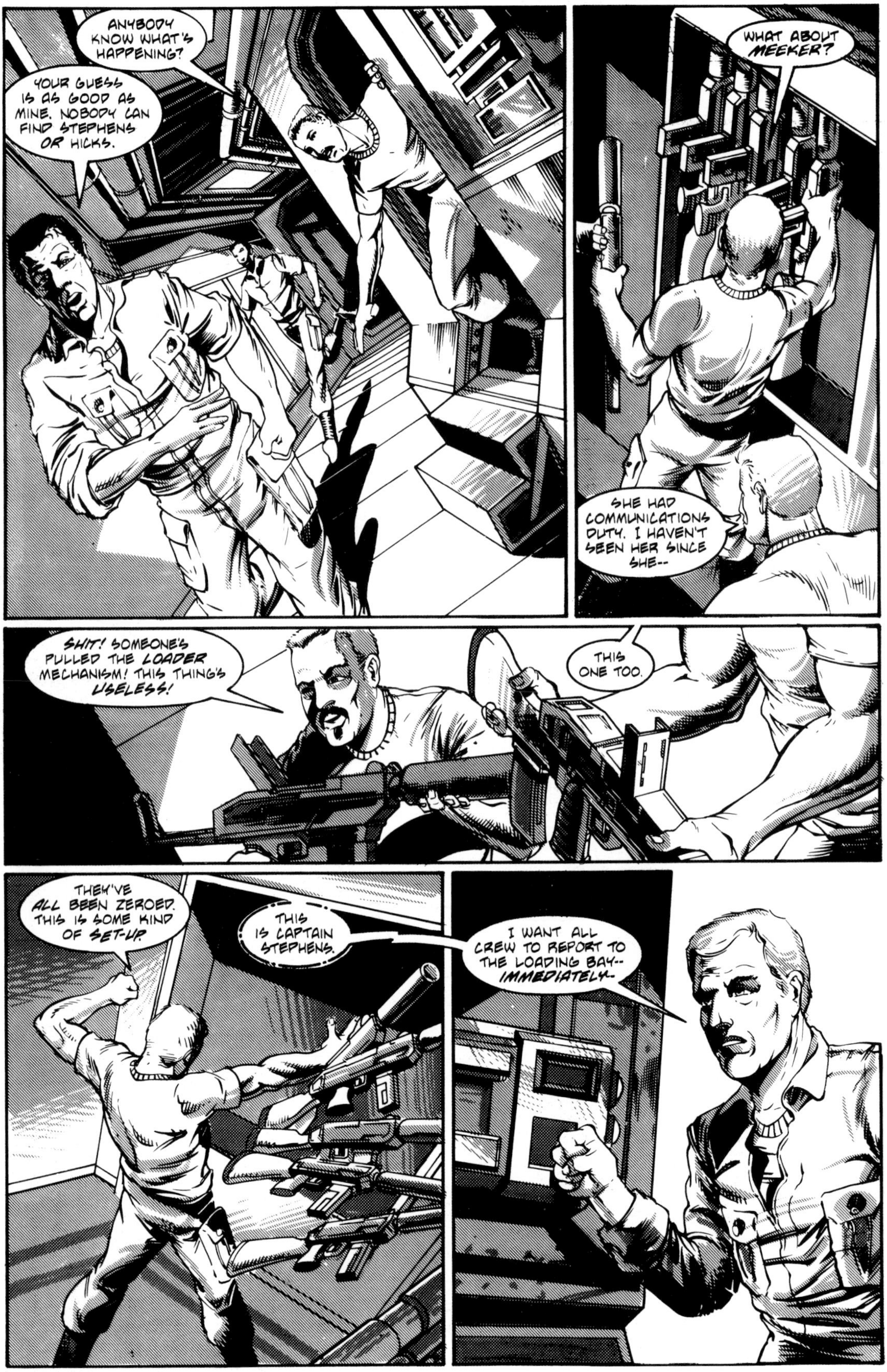
ANYBODY KNOW WHAT'S HAPPENING?
YOUR GUESS IS AS GOOD AS MINE. NOBODY CAN FIND STEPHENS OR HICKS.
WHAT ABOUT MEEKER?
SHE HAD COMMUNICATIONS DUTY. I HAVEN'T SEEN HER SINCE SHE--
SHIT! SOMEONE'S PULLED THE LOADER MECHANISM! THIS THING'S USELESS!
THIS ONE TOO.
THEY'VE ALL BEEN ZEROED. THIS IS SOME KIND OF SET-UP.
THIS IS CAPTAIN STEPHENS.
I WANT ALL CREW TO REPORT TO THE LOADING BAY-- IMMEDIATELY--

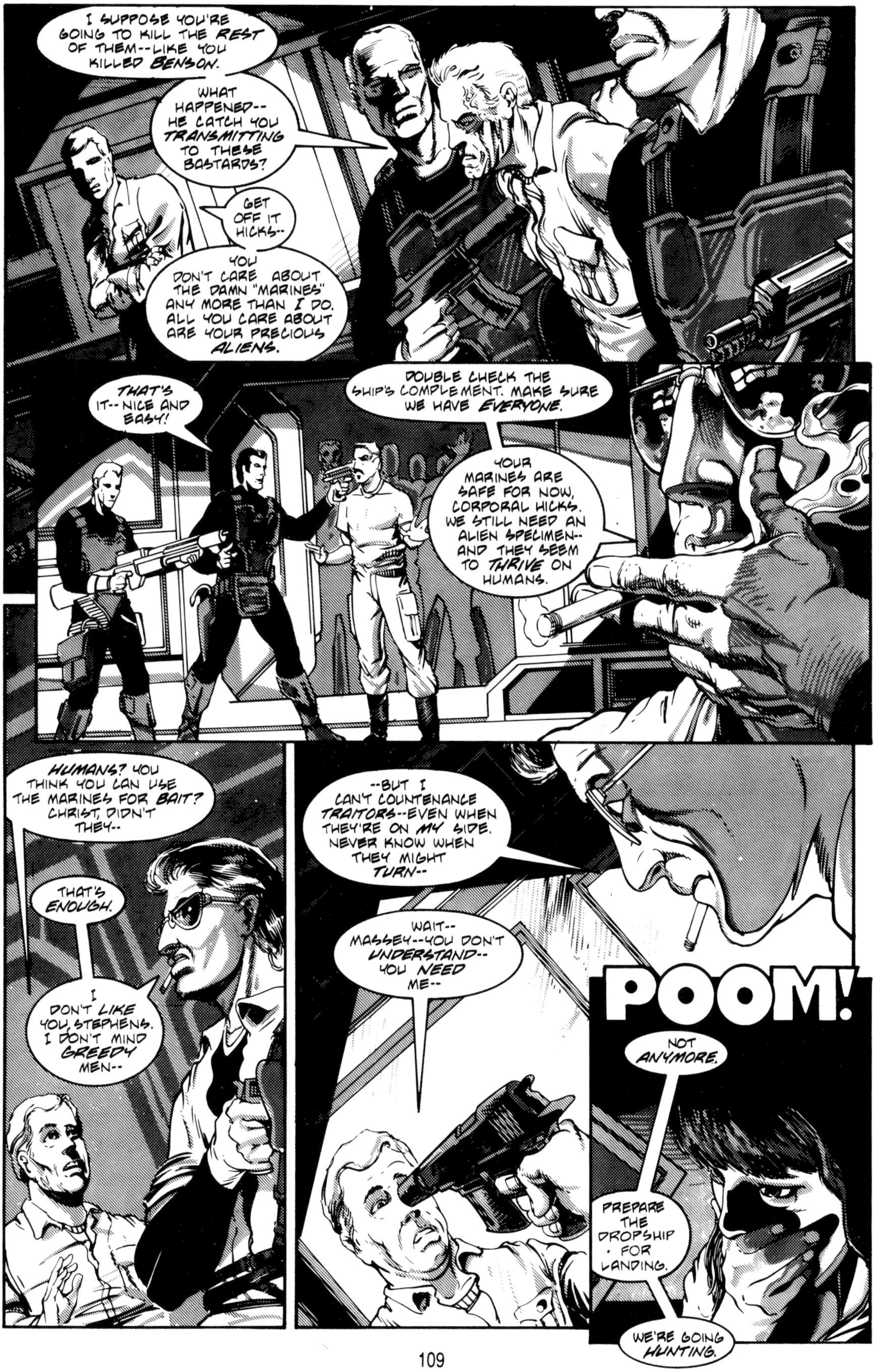
I SUPPOSE YOU'RE GOING TO KILL THE REST OF THEM--LIKE YOU KILLED BENSON.
WHAT HAPPENED--HE CATCH YOU TRANSMITTING TO THESE BASTARDS?
GET OFF IT HICKS--
YOU DON'T CARE ABOUT THE DAMN "MARINES" ANY MORE THAN I DO. ALL YOU CARE ABOUT ARE YOUR PRECIOUS ALIENS.
THAT'S IT--NICE AND EASY!
DOUBLE CHECK THE SHIP'S COMPLEMENT. MAKE SURE WE HAVE EVERYONE.
YOUR MARINES ARE SAFE FOR NOW, CORPORAL HICKS. WE STILL NEED AN ALIEN SPECIMEN--AND THEY SEEM TO THRIVE ON HUMANS.
HUMANS? YOU THINK YOU CAN USE THE MARINES FOR BAIT? CHRIST, DIDN'T THEY--
THAT'S ENOUGH.
I DON'T LIKE YOU, STEPHENS. I DON'T MIND GREEDY MEN--
--BUT I CAN'T COUNTENANCE TRAITORS--EVEN WHEN THEY'RE ON MY SIDE. NEVER KNOW WHEN THEY MIGHT TURN--
WAIT--MASSEY--YOU DON'T UNDERSTAND--YOU NEED ME--
POOM!
NOT ANYMORE.
PREPARE THE DROPSHIP FOR LANDING.
WE'RE GOING HUNTING.

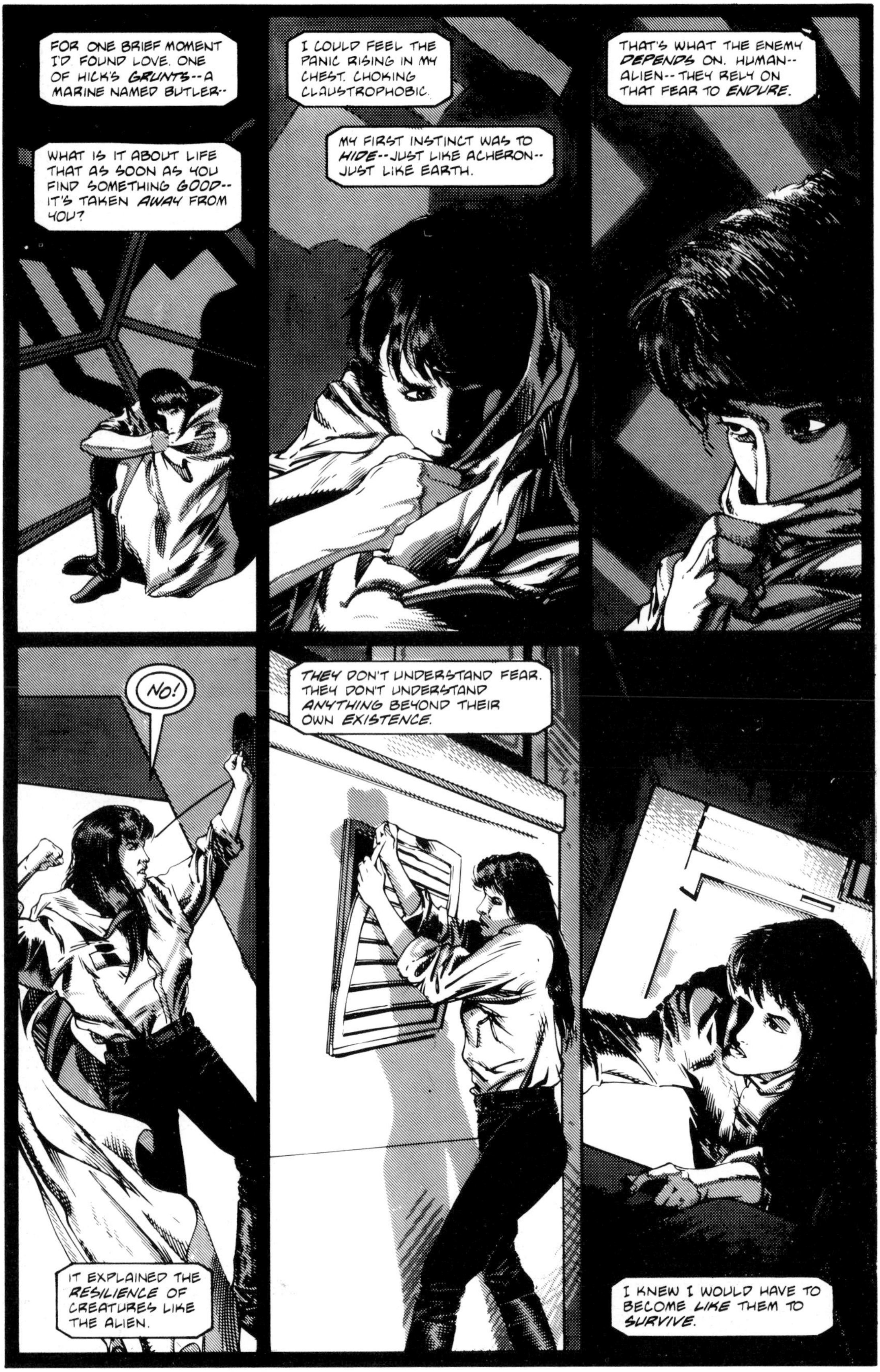
FOR ONE BRIEF MOMENT I'D FOUND LOVE. ONE OF HICK'S GRUNTS--A MARINE NAMED BUTLER--
WHAT IS IT ABOUT LIFE THAT AS SOON AS YOU FIND SOMETHING GOOD--IT'S TAKEN AWAY FROM YOU?
I COULD FEEL THE PANIC RISING IN MY CHEST. CHOKING CLAUSTROPHOBIC.
MY FIRST INSTINCT WAS TO HIDE--JUST LIKE ACHERON--JUST LIKE EARTH.
THAT'S WHAT THE ENEMY DEPENDS ON. HUMAN--ALIEN--THEY RELY ON THAT FEAR TO ENDURE.
NO!
IT EXPLAINED THE RESILIENCE OF CREATURES LIKE THE ALIEN.
THEY DON'T UNDERSTAND FEAR. THEY DON'T UNDERSTAND ANYTHING BEYOND THEIR OWN EXISTENCE.
I KNEW I WOULD HAVE TO BECOME LIKE THEM TO SURVIVE.

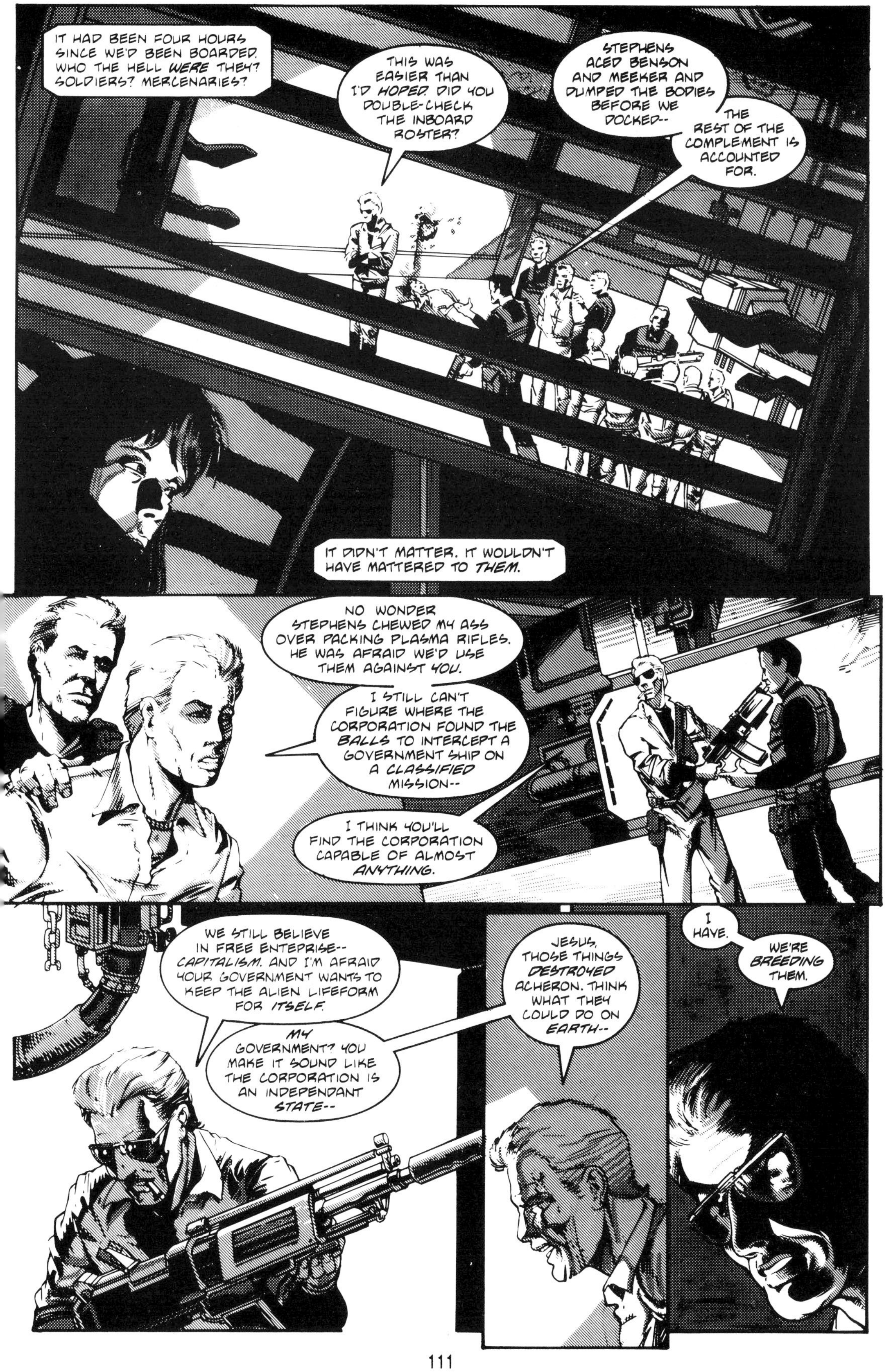
IT HAD BEEN FOUR HOURS SINCE WE'D BEEN BOARDED. WHO THE HELL *WERE* THEY? SOLDIERS? MERCENARIES?
THIS WAS EASIER THAN I'D *HOPED*. DID YOU DOUBLE-CHECK THE INBOARD ROSTER?
STEPHENS ACED BENSON AND MEEKER AND DUMPED THE BODIES BEFORE WE DOCKED--
THE REST OF THE COMPLEMENT IS ACCOUNTED FOR.
IT DIDN'T MATTER. IT WOULDN'T HAVE MATTERED TO *THEM*.
NO WONDER STEPHENS CHEWED MY ASS OVER PACKING PLASMA RIFLES. HE WAS AFRAID WE'D USE THEM AGAINST *YOU*.
I STILL CAN'T FIGURE WHERE THE CORPORATION FOUND THE *BALLS* TO INTERCEPT A GOVERNMENT SHIP ON A *CLASSIFIED* MISSION--
I THINK YOU'LL FIND THE CORPORATION CAPABLE OF ALMOST *ANYTHING*.
WE STILL BELIEVE IN FREE ENTEPRISE-- *CAPITALISM*. AND I'M AFRAID YOUR GOVERNMENT WANTS TO KEEP THE ALIEN LIFEFORM FOR *ITSELF*.
MY GOVERNMENT? YOU MAKE IT SOUND LIKE THE CORPORATION IS AN INDEPENDANT *STATE*--
JESUS, THOSE THINGS *DESTROYED* ACHERON. THINK WHAT THEY COULD DO ON *EARTH*--
I HAVE.
WE'RE *BREEDING* THEM.

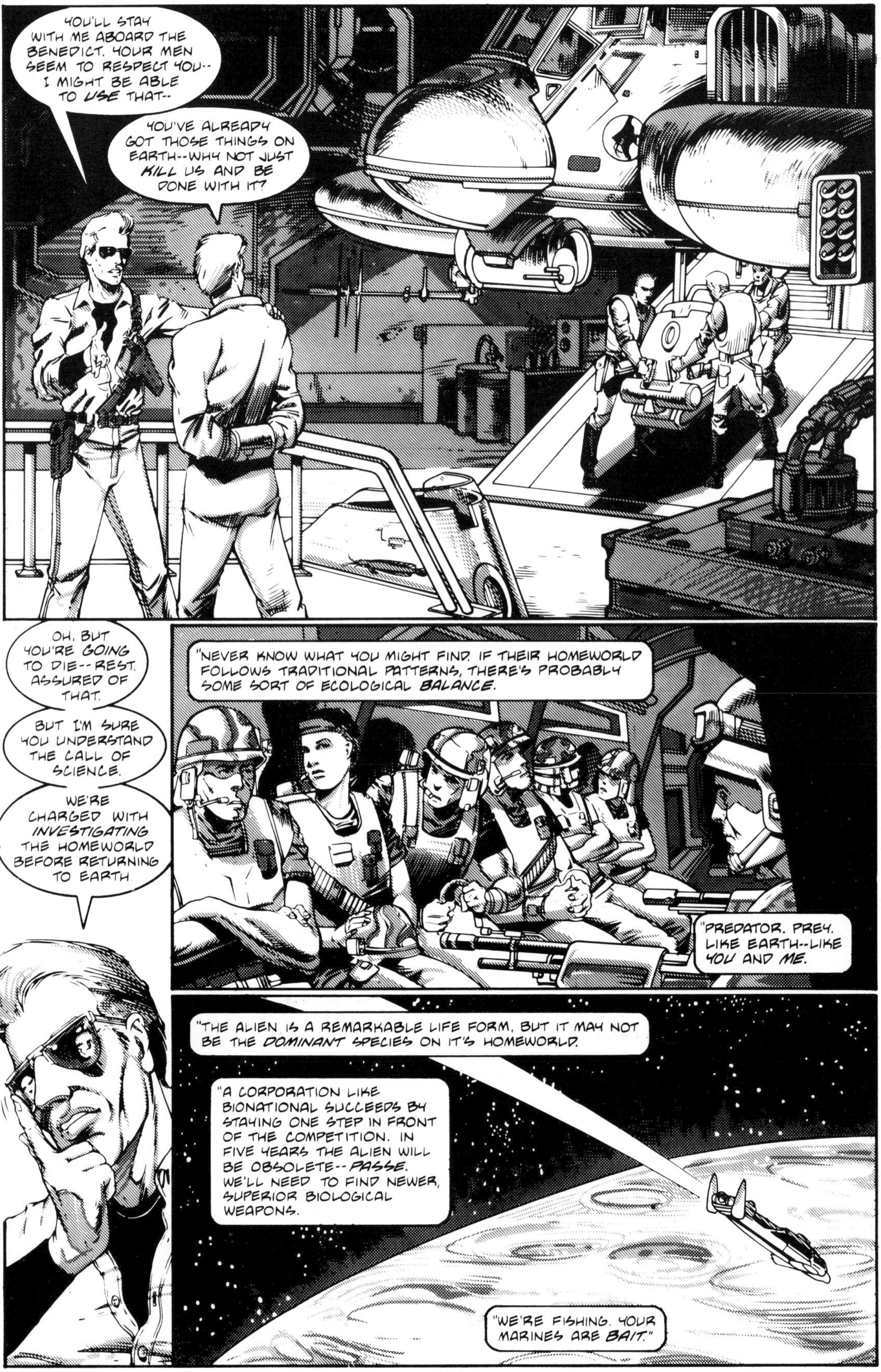
YOU'LL STAY WITH ME ABOARD THE BENEDICT. YOUR MEN SEEM TO RESPECT YOU-- I MIGHT BE ABLE TO USE THAT--
YOU'VE ALREADY GOT THOSE THINGS ON EARTH--WHY NOT JUST KILL US AND BE DONE WITH IT?
OH, BUT YOU'RE GOING TO DIE--REST ASSURED OF THAT.
BUT I'M SURE YOU UNDERSTAND THE CALL OF SCIENCE.
WE'RE CHARGED WITH INVESTIGATING THE HOMEWORLD BEFORE RETURNING TO EARTH.
"NEVER KNOW WHAT YOU MIGHT FIND. IF THEIR HOMEWORLD FOLLOWS TRADITIONAL PATTERNS, THERE'S PROBABLY SOME SORT OF ECOLOGICAL BALANCE.
"PREDATOR. PREY. LIKE EARTH--LIKE YOU AND ME.
"THE ALIEN IS A REMARKABLE LIFE FORM, BUT IT MAY NOT BE THE DOMINANT SPECIES ON IT'S HOMEWORLD.
"A CORPORATION LIKE BIONATIONAL SUCCEEDS BY STAYING ONE STEP IN FRONT OF THE COMPETITION. IN FIVE YEARS THE ALIEN WILL BE OBSOLETE--PASSE. WE'LL NEED TO FIND NEWER, SUPERIOR BIOLOGICAL WEAPONS.
"WE'RE FISHING. YOUR MARINES ARE BAIT."

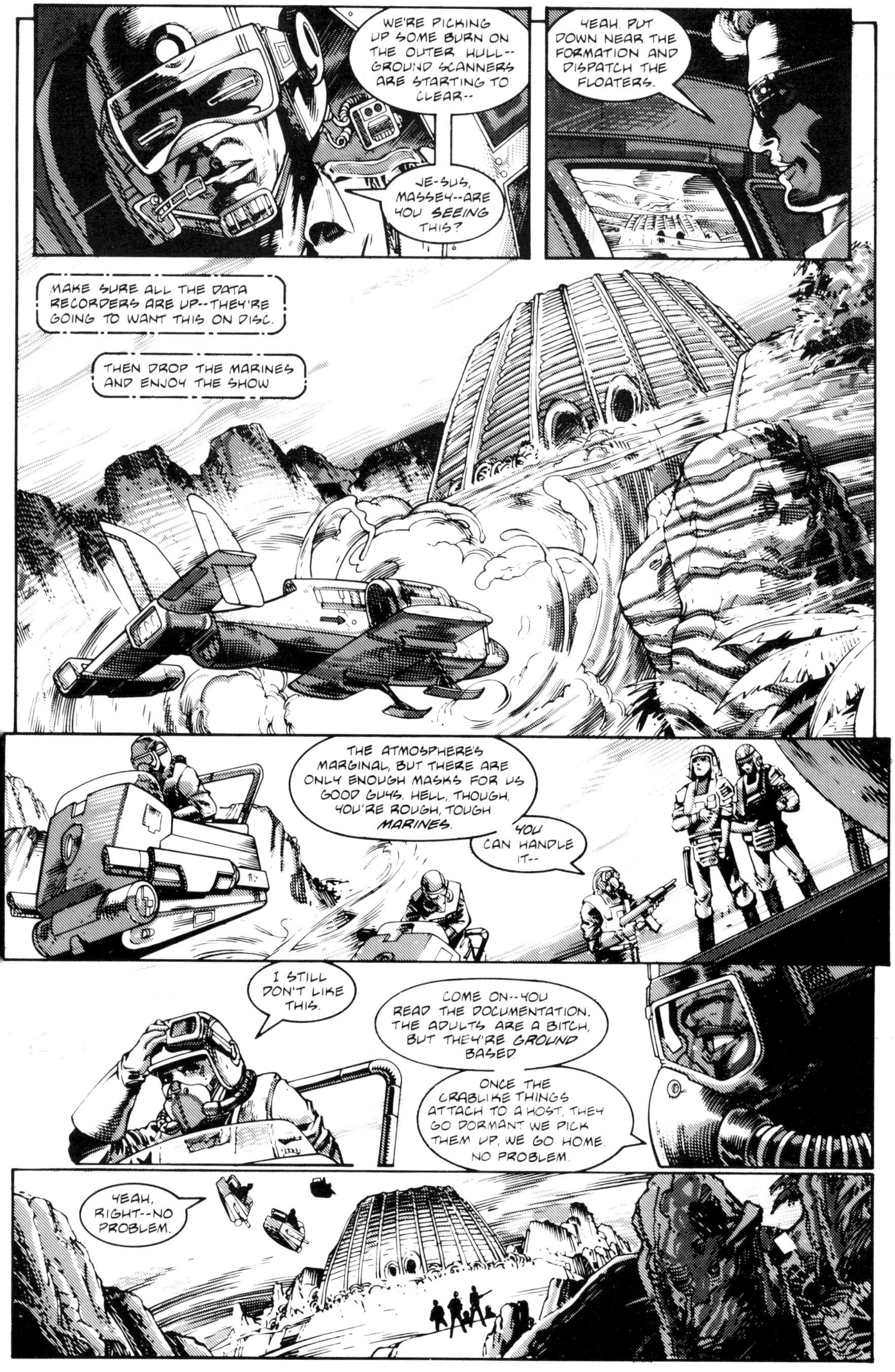
WE'RE PICKING UP SOME BURN ON THE OUTER HULL-- GROUND SCANNERS ARE STARTING TO CLEAR--
JE-SUS, MASSEY--ARE YOU SEEING THIS?
YEAH. PUT DOWN NEAR THE FORMATION AND DISPATCH THE FLOATERS.
MAKE SURE ALL THE DATA RECORDERS ARE UP--THEY'RE GOING TO WANT THIS ON DISC.
THEN DROP THE MARINES AND ENJOY THE SHOW.
THE ATMOSPHERE'S MARGINAL, BUT THERE ARE ONLY ENOUGH MASKS FOR US GOOD GUYS. HELL, THOUGH, YOU'RE ROUGH, TOUGH MARINES.
YOU CAN HANDLE IT--
I STILL DON'T LIKE THIS.
COME ON--YOU READ THE DOCUMENTATION. THE ADULTS ARE A BITCH, BUT THEY'RE GROUND BASED.
ONCE THE CRABLIKE THINGS ATTACH TO A HOST, THEY GO DORMANT. WE PICK THEM UP, WE GO HOME. NO PROBLEM.
YEAH, RIGHT--NO PROBLEM.

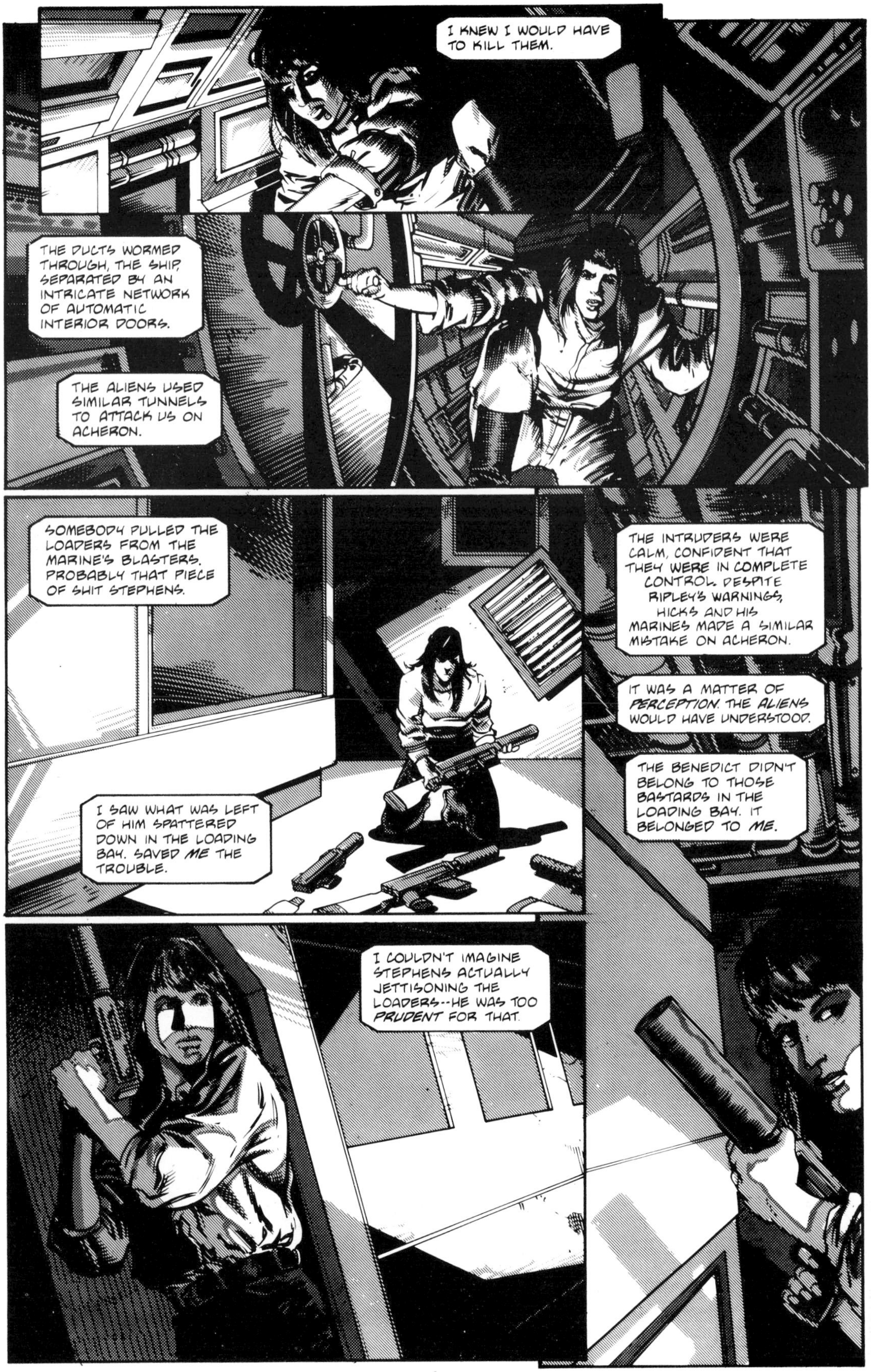
I KNEW I WOULD HAVE TO KILL THEM.
THE DUCTS WORMED THROUGH, THE SHIP, SEPARATED BY AN INTRICATE NETWORK OF AUTOMATIC INTERIOR DOORS.
THE ALIENS USED SIMILAR TUNNELS TO ATTACK US ON ACHERON.
SOMEBODY PULLED THE LOADERS FROM THE MARINE'S BLASTERS. PROBABLY THAT PIECE OF SHIT STEPHENS.
I SAW WHAT WAS LEFT OF HIM SPATTERED DOWN IN THE LOADING BAY. SAVED *ME* THE TROUBLE.
THE INTRUDERS WERE CALM, CONFIDENT THAT THEY WERE IN COMPLETE CONTROL. DESPITE RIPLEY'S WARNINGS, HICKS AND HIS MARINES MADE A SIMILAR MISTAKE ON ACHERON.
IT WAS A MATTER OF *PERCEPTION*. THE *ALIENS* WOULD HAVE UNDERSTOOD.
THE BENEDICT DIDN'T BELONG TO THOSE BASTARDS IN THE LOADING BAY. IT BELONGED TO *ME*.
I COULDN'T IMAGINE STEPHENS ACTUALLY JETTISONING THE LOADERS--HE WAS TOO *PRUDENT* FOR THAT.

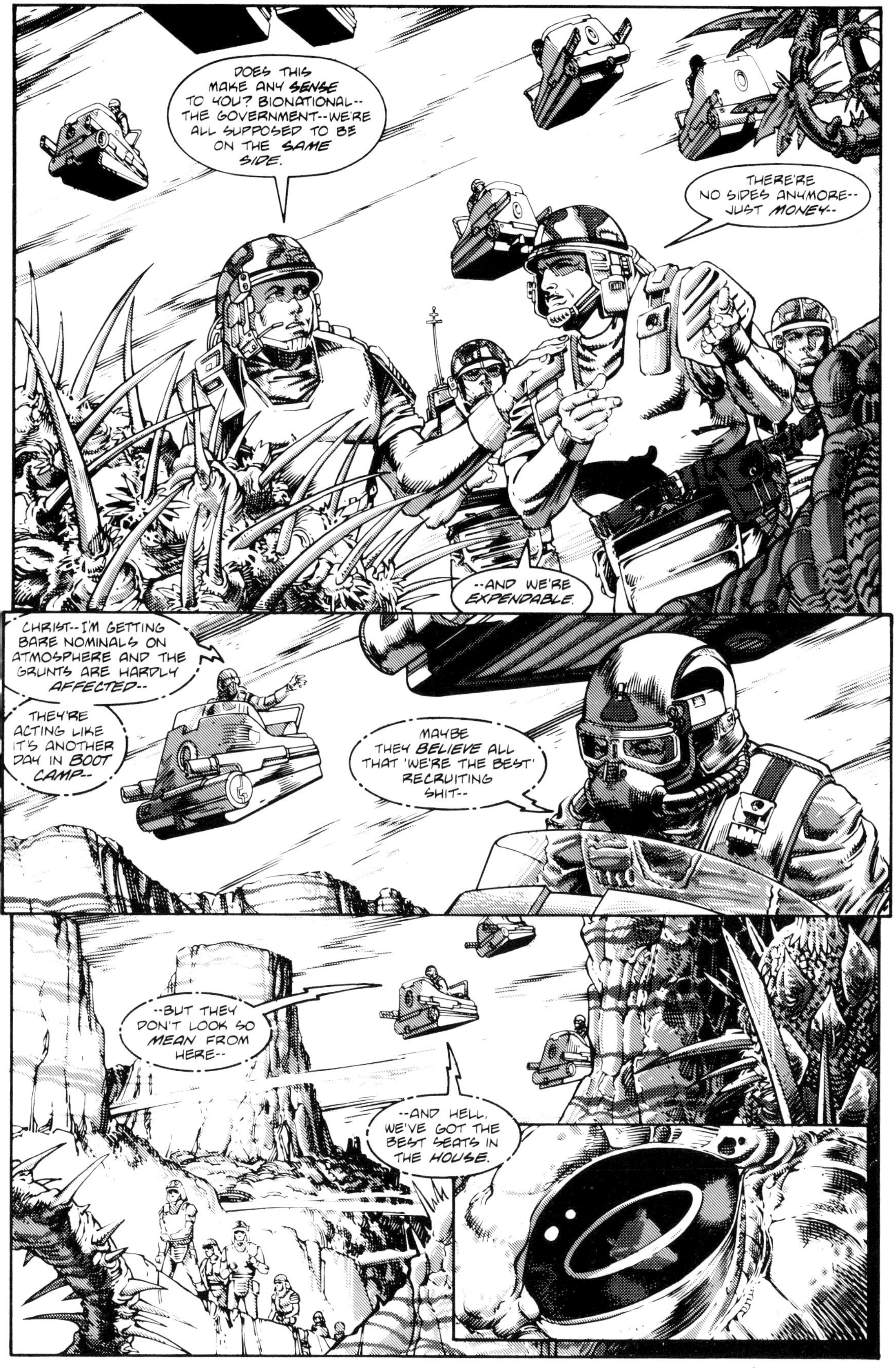
DOES THIS MAKE ANY SENSE TO YOU? BIONATIONAL-- THE GOVERNMENT--WE'RE ALL SUPPOSED TO BE ON THE SAME SIDE.
THERE'RE NO SIDES ANYMORE-- JUST MONEY--
--AND WE'RE EXPENDABLE.
CHRIST--I'M GETTING BARE NOMINALS ON ATMOSPHERE AND THE GRUNTS ARE HARDLY AFFECTED--
THEY'RE ACTING LIKE IT'S ANOTHER DAY IN BOOT CAMP--
MAYBE THEY BELIEVE ALL THAT 'WE'RE THE BEST' RECRUITING SHIT--
--BUT THEY DON'T LOOK SO MEAN FROM HERE--
--AND HELL, WE'VE GOT THE BEST SEATS IN THE HOUSE.

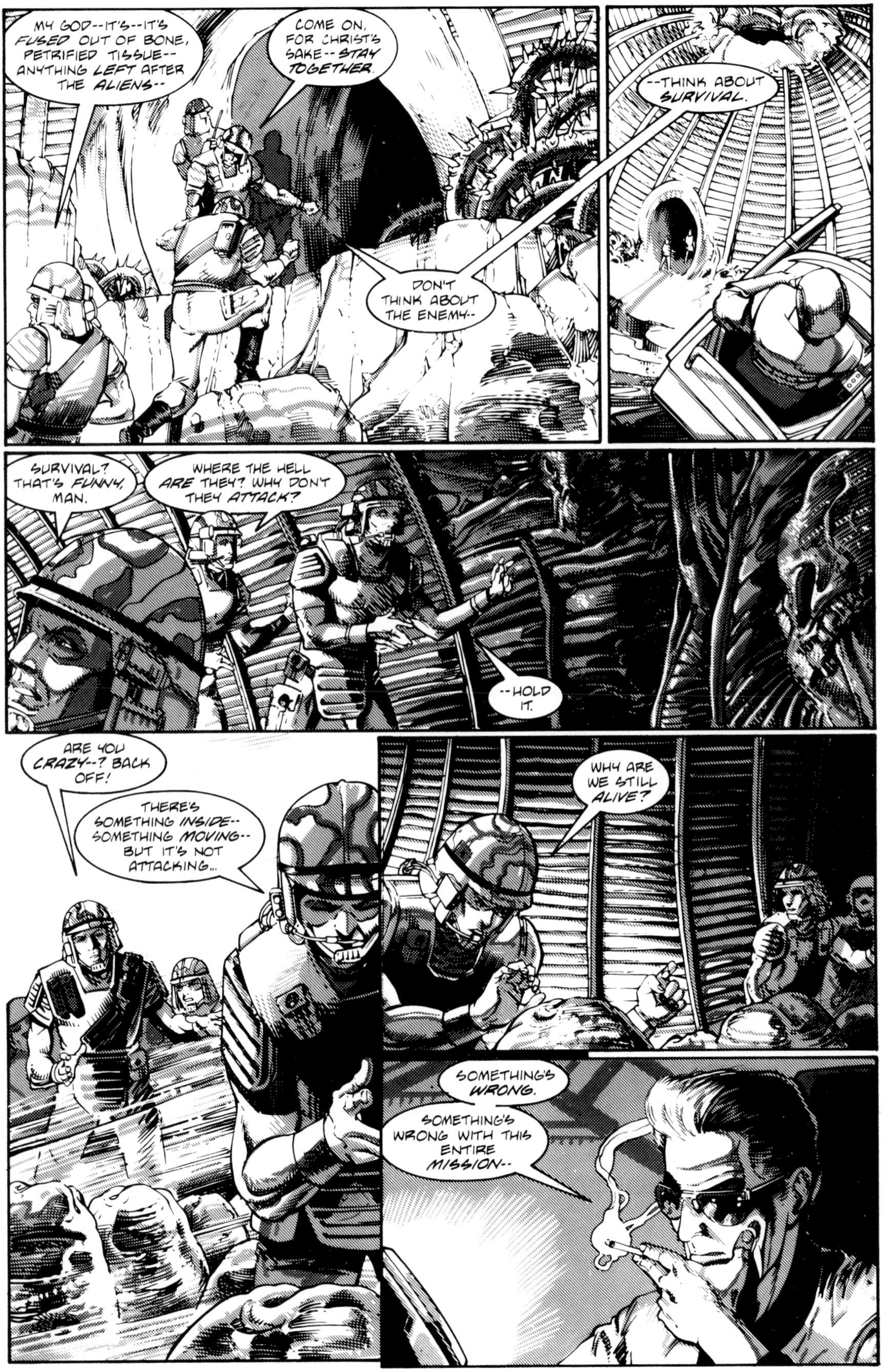
MY GOD--IT'S--IT'S FUSED OUT OF BONE, PETRIFIED TISSUE-- ANYTHING LEFT AFTER THE ALIENS--
COME ON, FOR CHRIST'S SAKE--STAY TOGETHER.
DON'T THINK ABOUT THE ENEMY--
--THINK ABOUT SURVIVAL.
SURVIVAL? THAT'S FUNNY, MAN.
WHERE THE HELL ARE THEY? WHY DON'T THEY ATTACK?
--HOLD IT.
ARE YOU CRAZY--? BACK OFF!
THERE'S SOMETHING INSIDE-- SOMETHING MOVING-- BUT IT'S NOT ATTACKING...
WHY ARE WE STILL ALIVE?
SOMETHING'S WRONG.
SOMETHING'S WRONG WITH THIS ENTIRE MISSION--

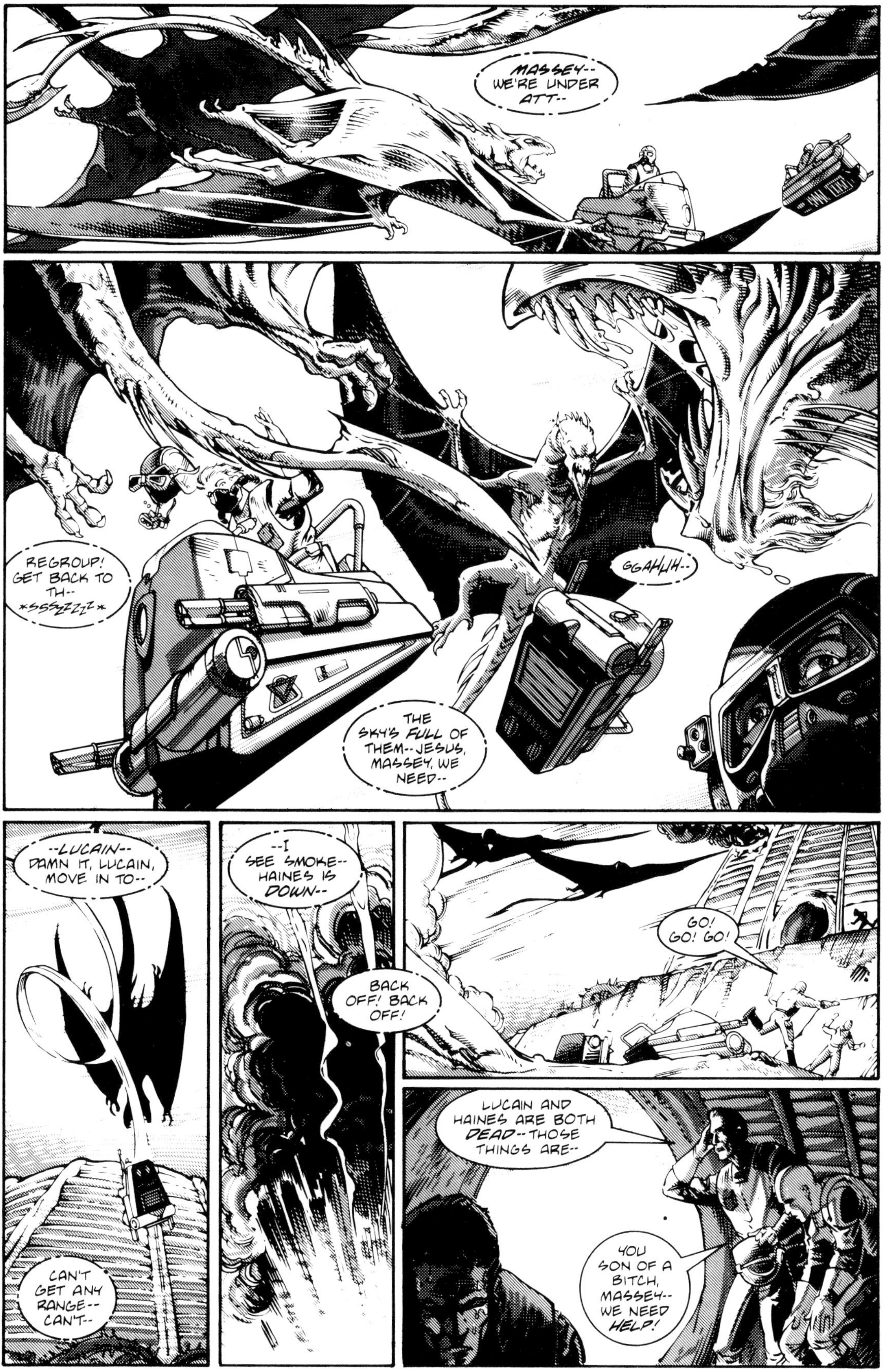
MASSEY-- WE'RE UNDER ATT--
REGROUP! GET BACK TO TH-- *SSSZZZZ*
GGAHHH--
THE SKY'S FULL OF THEM--JESUS, MASSEY, WE NEED--
--LUCAIN-- DAMN IT, LUCAIN, MOVE IN TO--
CAN'T GET ANY RANGE-- CAN'T--
--I SEE SMOKE-- HAINES IS DOWN--
BACK OFF! BACK OFF!
GO! GO! GO!
LUCAIN AND HAINES ARE BOTH DEAD--THOSE THINGS ARE--
YOU SON OF A BITCH, MASSEY-- WE NEED HELP!

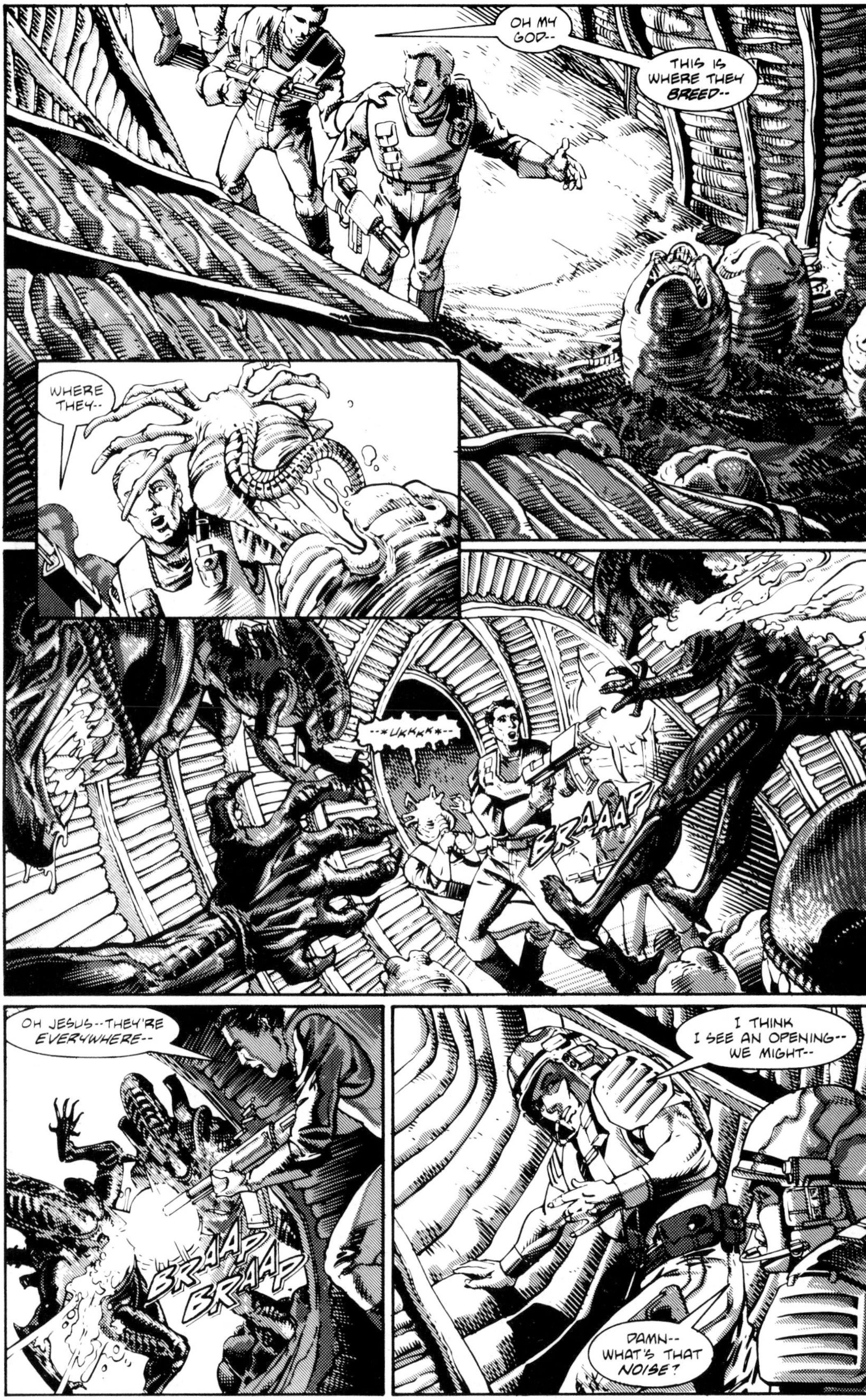
OH MY GOD--
THIS IS WHERE THEY BREED--
WHERE THEY--
--*UKKKK*--
BRAAAP
OH JESUS--THEY'RE EVERYWHERE--
BRAAAP BRAAAP
I THINK I SEE AN OPENING-- WE MIGHT--
DAMN-- WHAT'S THAT NOISE?

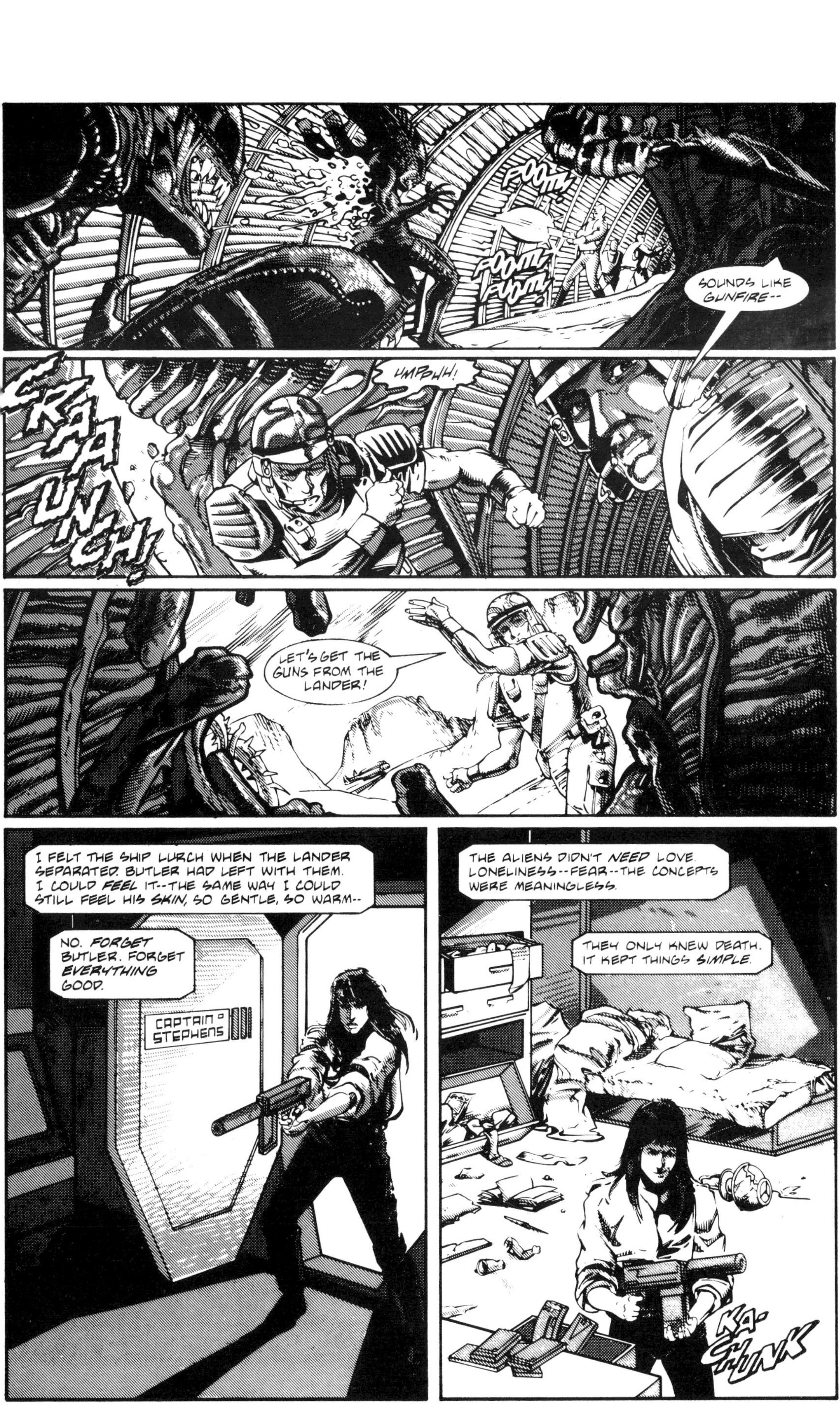
FOOM
FOOM
FOOM
SOUNDS LIKE GUNFIRE--
CRAAUNCH!
UMPHH!
LET'S GET THE GUNS FROM THE LANDER!
I FELT THE SHIP LURCH WHEN THE LANDER SEPARATED. BUTLER HAD LEFT WITH THEM. I COULD FEEL IT--THE SAME WAY I COULD STILL FEEL HIS SKIN, SO GENTLE, SO WARM--
NO. FORGET BUTLER. FORGET EVERYTHING GOOD.
CAPTAIN STEPHENS
THE ALIENS DIDN'T NEED LOVE. LONELINESS--FEAR--THE CONCEPTS WERE MEANINGLESS.
THEY ONLY KNEW DEATH. IT KEPT THINGS SIMPLE.
KA-CHUNK

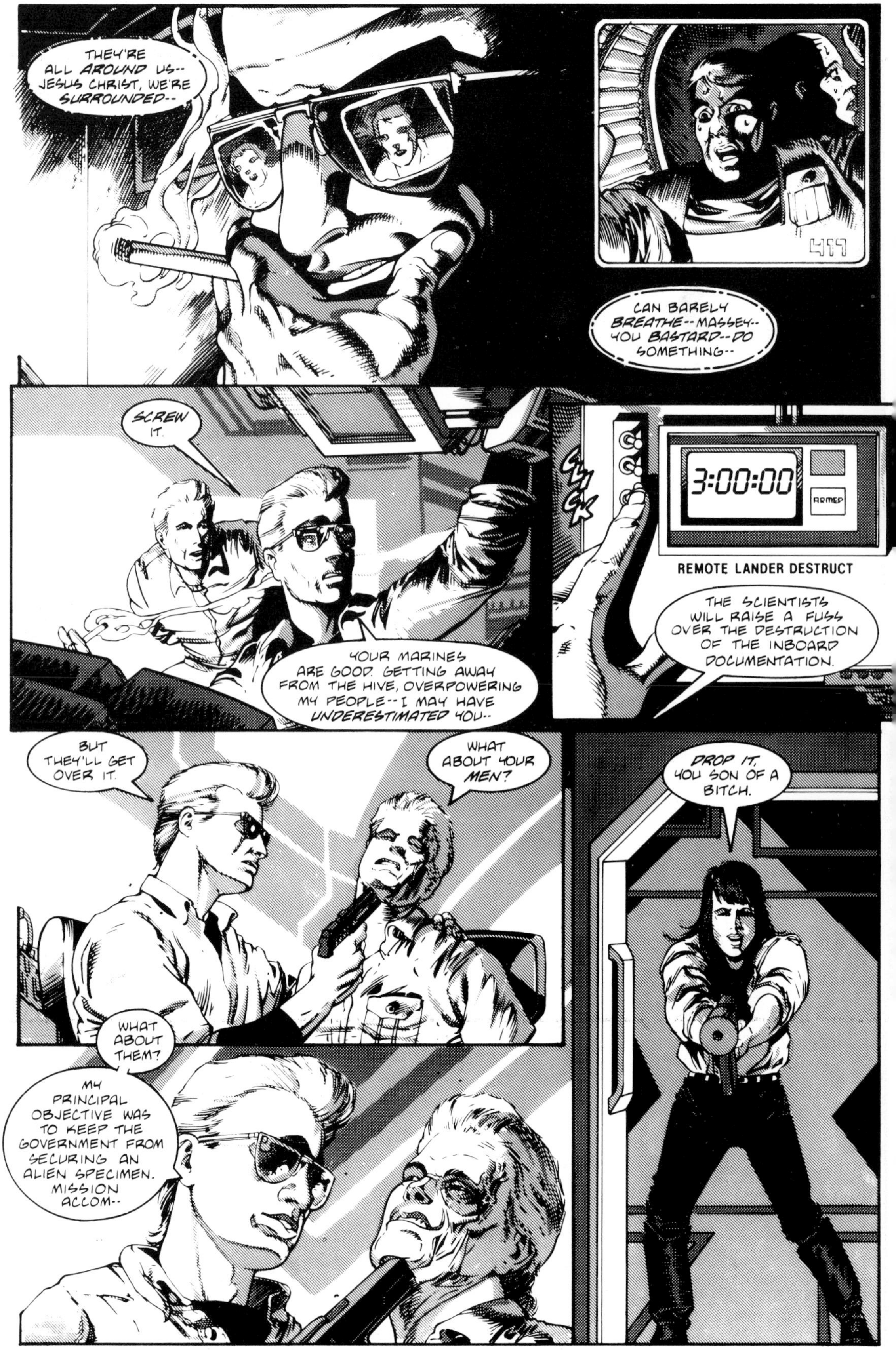
THEY'RE ALL AROUND US-- JESUS CHRIST, WE'RE SURROUNDED--
417
CAN BARELY BREATHE--MASSEY-- YOU BASTARD--DO SOMETHING--
SCREW IT.
CLICK
3:00:00
ARMED
REMOTE LANDER DESTRUCT
YOUR MARINES ARE GOOD. GETTING AWAY FROM THE HIVE, OVERPOWERING MY PEOPLE--I MAY HAVE UNDERESTIMATED YOU--
THE SCIENTISTS WILL RAISE A FUSS OVER THE DESTRUCTION OF THE INBOARD DOCUMENTATION.
BUT THEY'LL GET OVER IT.
WHAT ABOUT YOUR MEN?
DROP IT, YOU SON OF A BITCH.
WHAT ABOUT THEM?
MY PRINCIPAL OBJECTIVE WAS TO KEEP THE GOVERNMENT FROM SECURING AN ALIEN SPECIMEN. MISSION ACCOM--

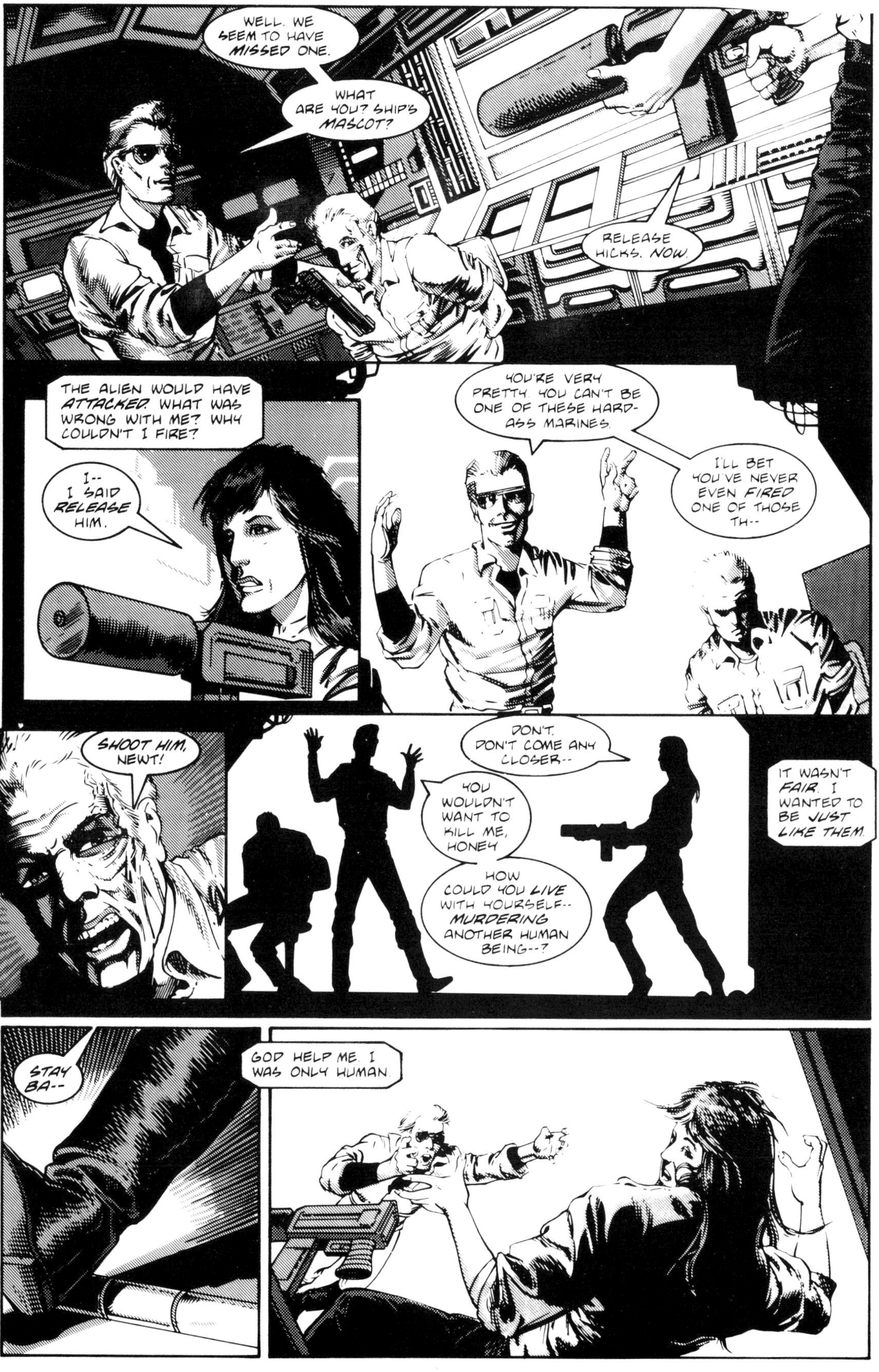

WELL. WE SEEM TO HAVE MISSED ONE.
WHAT ARE YOU? SHIP'S MASCOT?
RELEASE HICKS. NOW.
THE ALIEN WOULD HAVE ATTACKED. WHAT WAS WRONG WITH ME? WHY COULDN'T I FIRE?
I-- I SAID RELEASE HIM.
YOU'RE VERY PRETTY. YOU CAN'T BE ONE OF THESE HARD-ASS MARINES.
I'LL BET YOU'VE NEVER EVEN FIRED ONE OF THOSE TH--
SHOOT HIM, NEWT!
DON'T. DON'T COME ANY CLOSER--
YOU WOULDN'T WANT TO KILL ME, HONEY
HOW COULD YOU LIVE WITH YOURSELF-- MURDERING ANOTHER HUMAN BEING--?
IT WASN'T FAIR. I WANTED TO BE JUST LIKE THEM.
STAY BA--
GOD HELP ME. I WAS ONLY HUMAN.

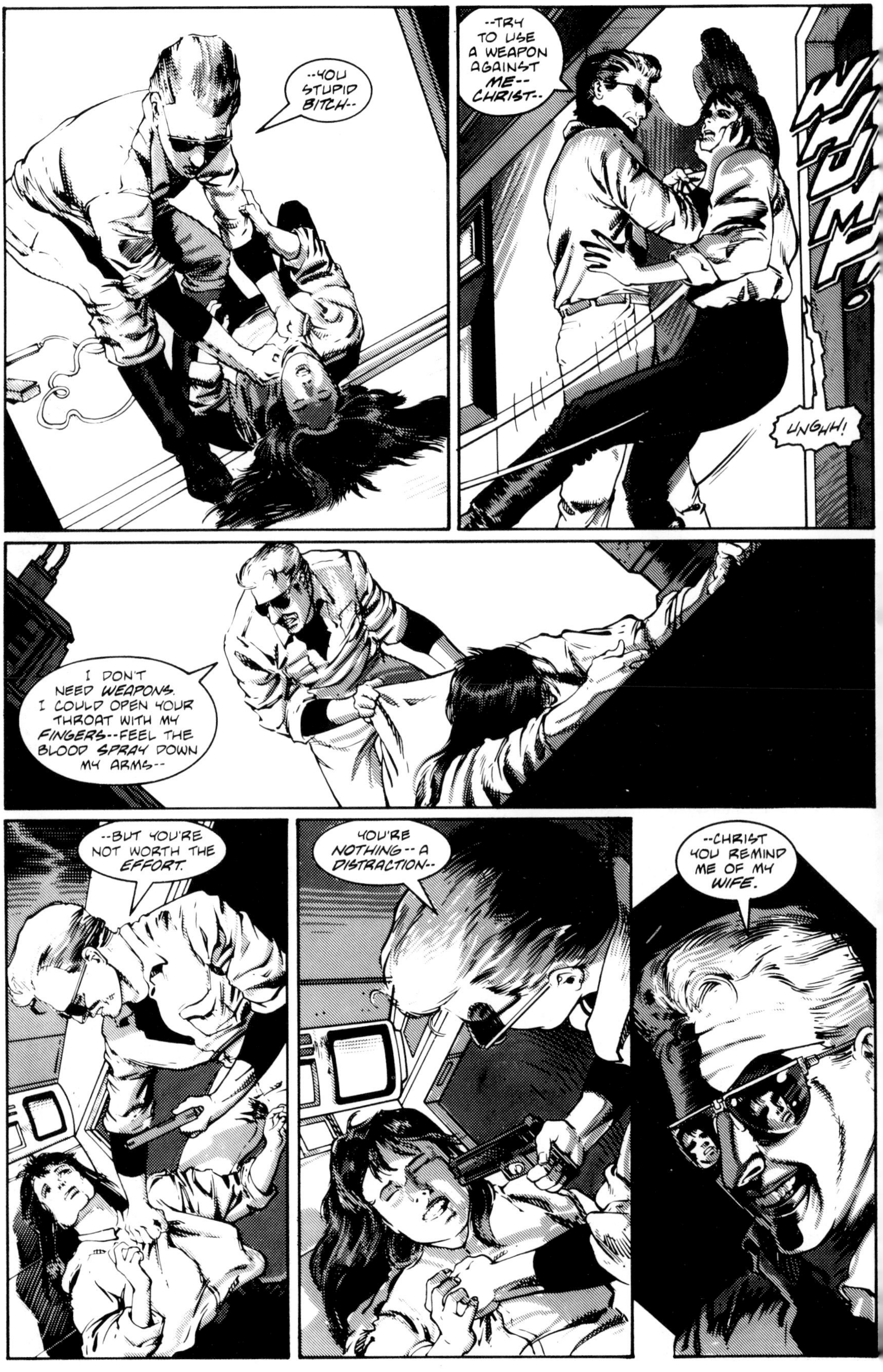
--YOU STUPID BITCH--
--TRY TO USE A WEAPON AGAINST ME--CHRIST--.
UNGHH!
I DON'T NEED WEAPONS. I COULD OPEN YOUR THROAT WITH MY FINGERS--FEEL THE BLOOD SPRAY DOWN MY ARMS--
--BUT YOU'RE NOT WORTH THE EFFORT.
YOU'RE NOTHING--A DISTRACTION--
--CHRIST YOU REMIND ME OF MY WIFE.

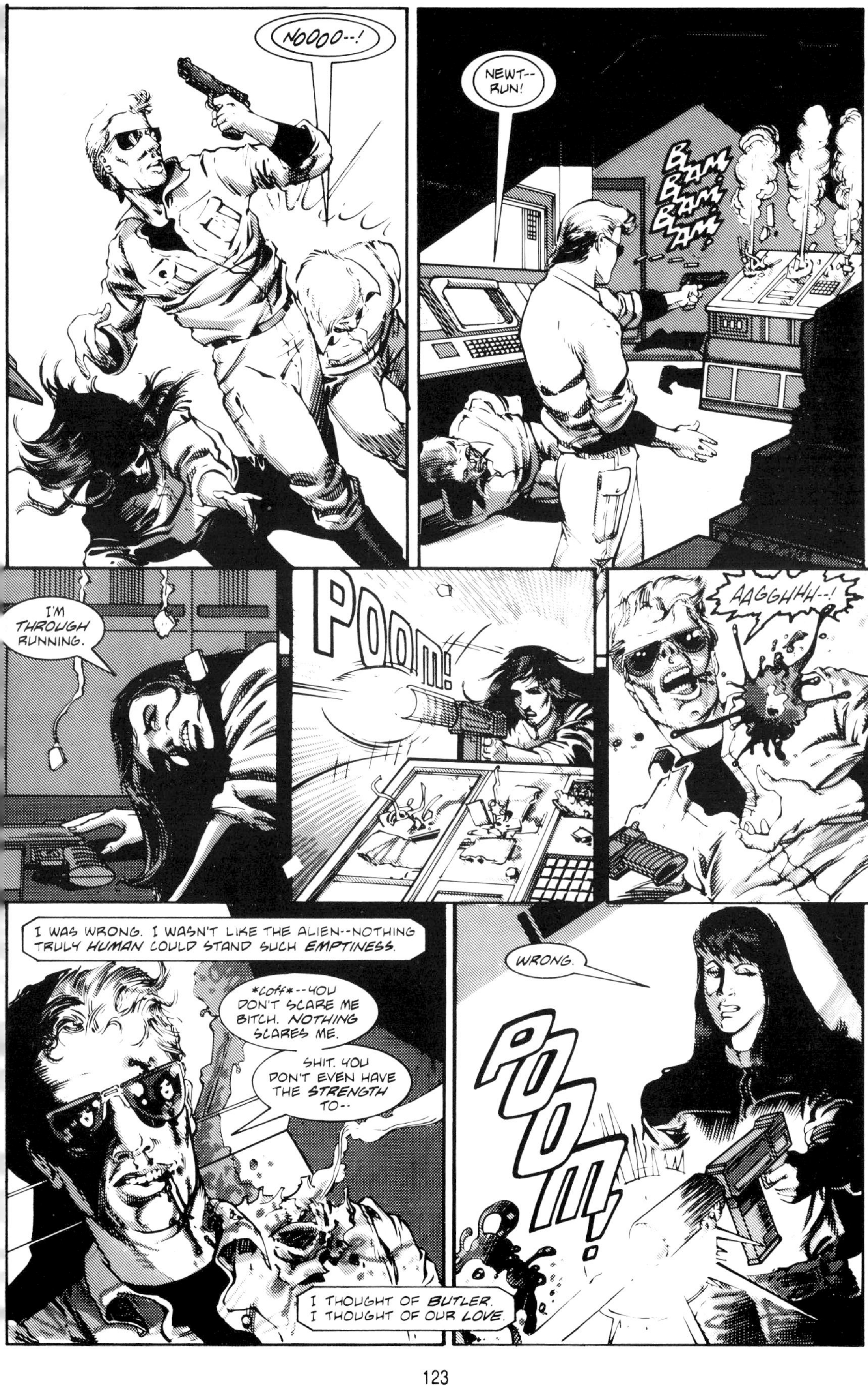
NOOOO--!
NEWT--RUN!
BLAM BLAM BLAM BLAM
I'M THROUGH RUNNING.
POOM!
AAGGHHH--!
I WAS WRONG. I WASN'T LIKE THE ALIEN--NOTHING TRULY HUMAN COULD STAND SUCH EMPTINESS.
COFF--YOU DON'T SCARE ME BITCH. NOTHING SCARES ME.
SHIT. YOU DON'T EVEN HAVE THE STRENGTH TO--
I THOUGHT OF BUTLER. I THOUGHT OF OUR LOVE.
WRONG.
POOM!

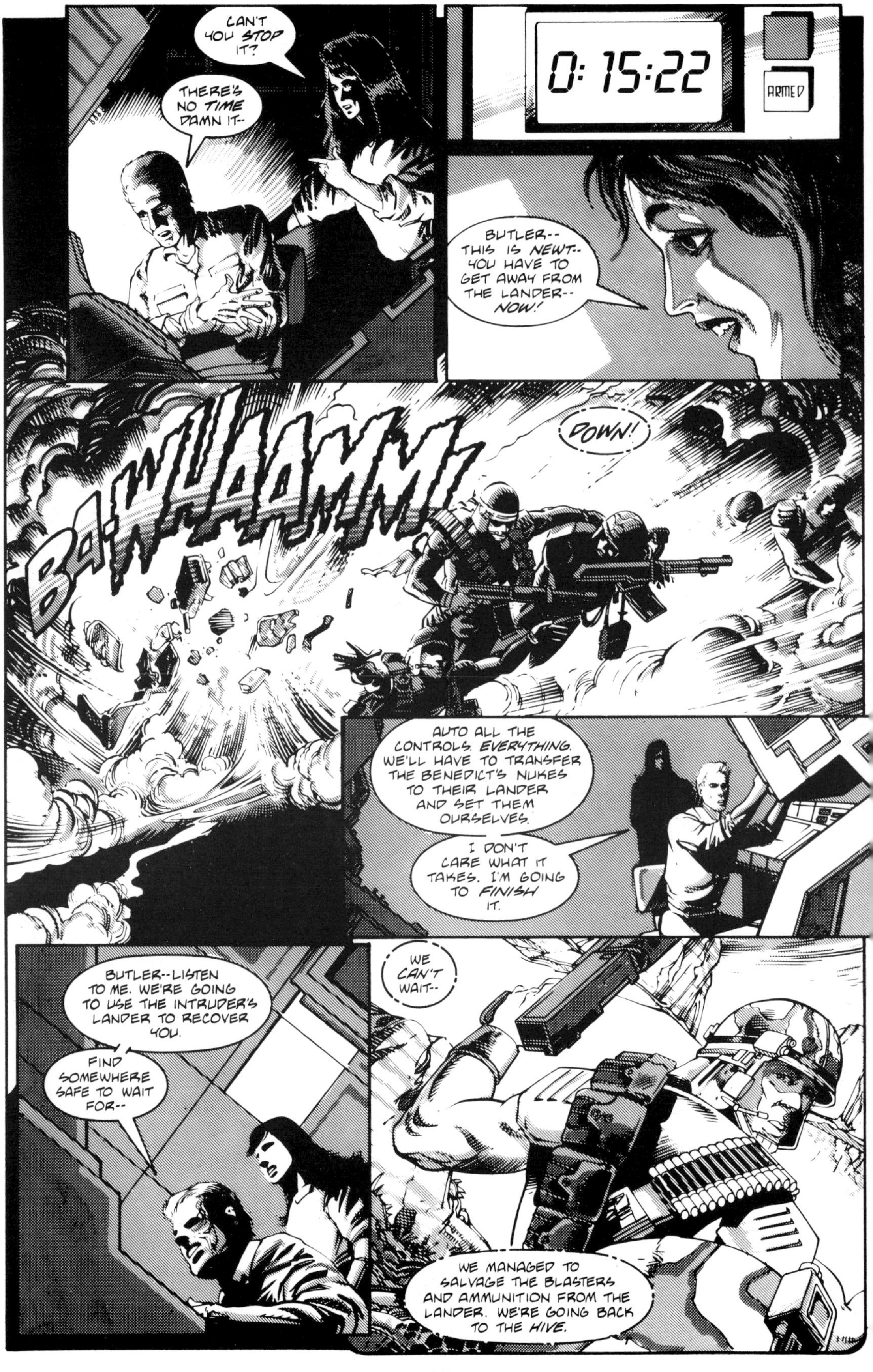

CAN'T YOU STOP IT?
THERE'S NO TIME DAMN IT--
0:15:22
ARMED
BUTLER-- THIS IS NEWT-- YOU HAVE TO GET AWAY FROM THE LANDER-- NOW!
BA-WHAAMM!
DOWN!
AUTO ALL THE CONTROLS. EVERYTHING. WE'LL HAVE TO TRANSFER THE BENEDICT'S NUKES TO THEIR LANDER AND SET THEM OURSELVES.
I DON'T CARE WHAT IT TAKES. I'M GOING TO FINISH IT.
BUTLER--LISTEN TO ME. WE'RE GOING TO USE THE INTRUDER'S LANDER TO RECOVER YOU.
FIND SOMEWHERE SAFE TO WAIT FOR--
WE CAN'T WAIT--
WE MANAGED TO SALVAGE THE BLASTERS AND AMMUNITION FROM THE LANDER. WE'RE GOING BACK TO THE HIVE.

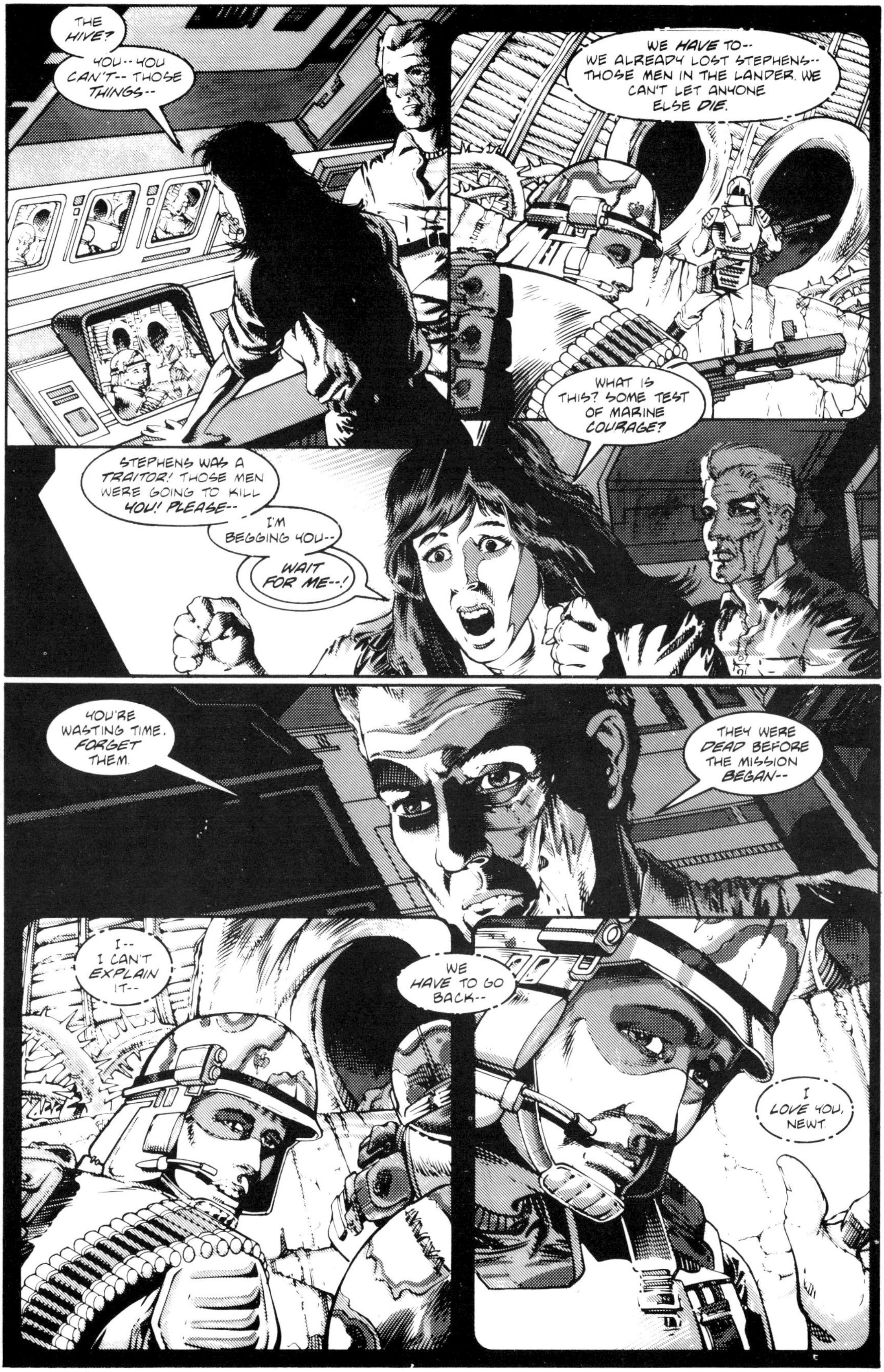
THE HIVE? YOU-- YOU CAN'T-- THOSE THINGS--
WE HAVE TO-- WE ALREADY LOST STEPHENS-- THOSE MEN IN THE LANDER. WE CAN'T LET ANYONE ELSE DIE.
WHAT IS THIS? SOME TEST OF MARINE COURAGE?
STEPHENS WAS A TRAITOR! THOSE MEN WERE GOING TO KILL YOU! PLEASE--
I'M BEGGING YOU--
WAIT FOR ME--!
YOU'RE WASTING TIME. FORGET THEM.
THEY WERE DEAD BEFORE THE MISSION BEGAN--
I-- I CAN'T EXPLAIN IT--
WE HAVE TO GO BACK--
I LOVE YOU, NEWT.

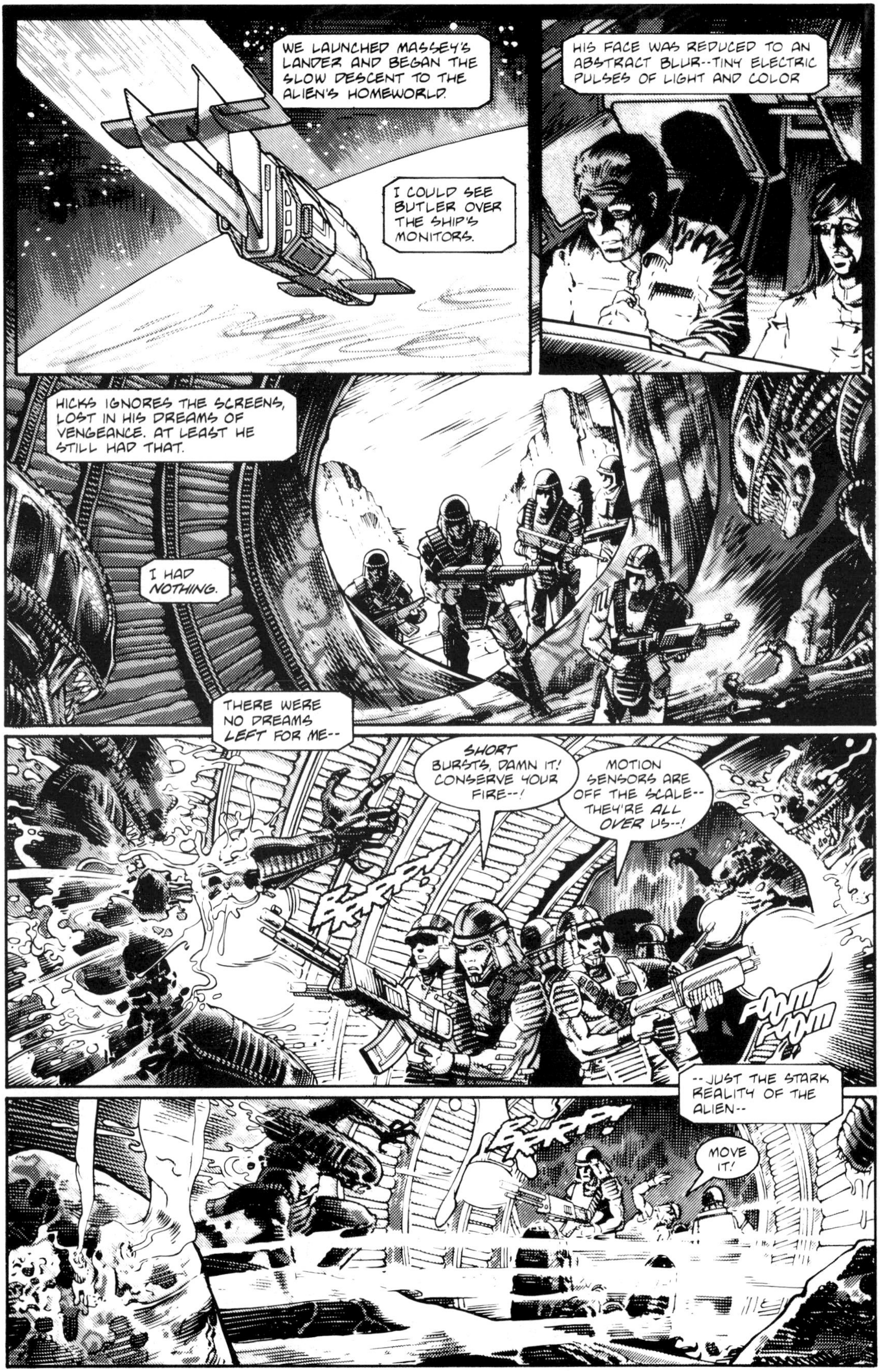
WE LAUNCHED MASSEY'S LANDER AND BEGAN THE SLOW DESCENT TO THE ALIEN'S HOMEWORLD.
I COULD SEE BUTLER OVER THE SHIP'S MONITORS.
HIS FACE WAS REDUCED TO AN ABSTRACT BLUR--TINY ELECTRIC PULSES OF LIGHT AND COLOR
HICKS IGNORES THE SCREENS, LOST IN HIS DREAMS OF VENGEANCE. AT LEAST HE STILL HAD THAT.
I HAD *NOTHING*.
THERE WERE NO DREAMS *LEFT* FOR ME--
SHORT BURSTS, DAMN IT! CONSERVE YOUR FIRE--!
MOTION SENSORS ARE OFF THE SCALE-- THEY'RE *ALL OVER* US--!
FOOM FOOM
--JUST THE STARK REALITY OF THE ALIEN--
MOVE IT!

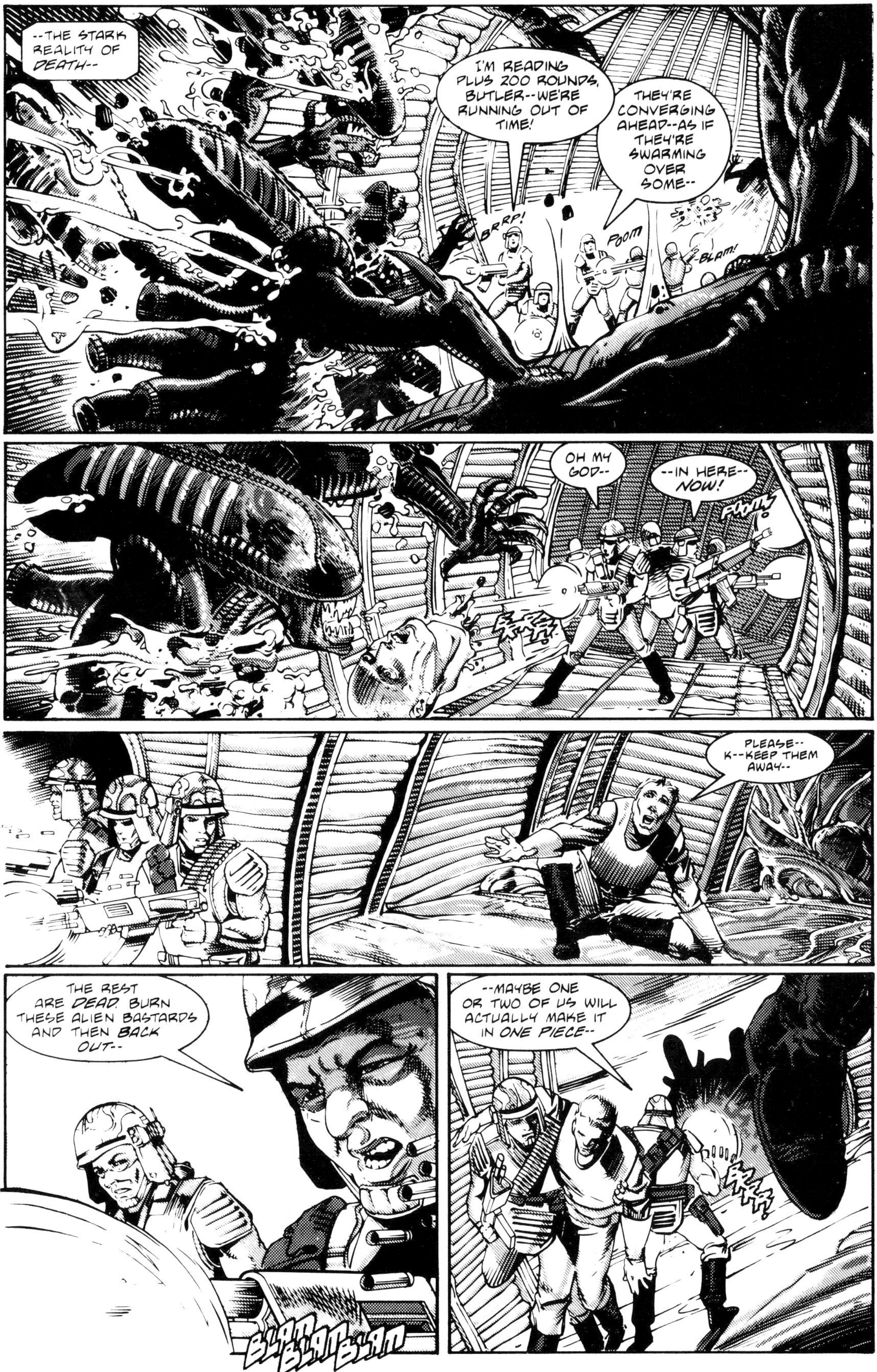
--THE STARK REALITY OF DEATH--
I'M READING PLUS 200 ROUNDS, BUTLER--WE'RE RUNNING OUT OF TIME!
THEY'RE CONVERGING AHEAD--AS IF THEY'RE SWARMING OVER SOME--
BRRP!
POOM
BLAM!
OH MY GOD--
--IN HERE-- NOW!
POOM!
PLEASE-- K--KEEP THEM AWAY--
THE REST ARE DEAD. BURN THESE ALIEN BASTARDS AND THEN BACK OUT--
--MAYBE ONE OR TWO OF US WILL ACTUALLY MAKE IT IN ONE PIECE--
BLAM BLAM BLAM

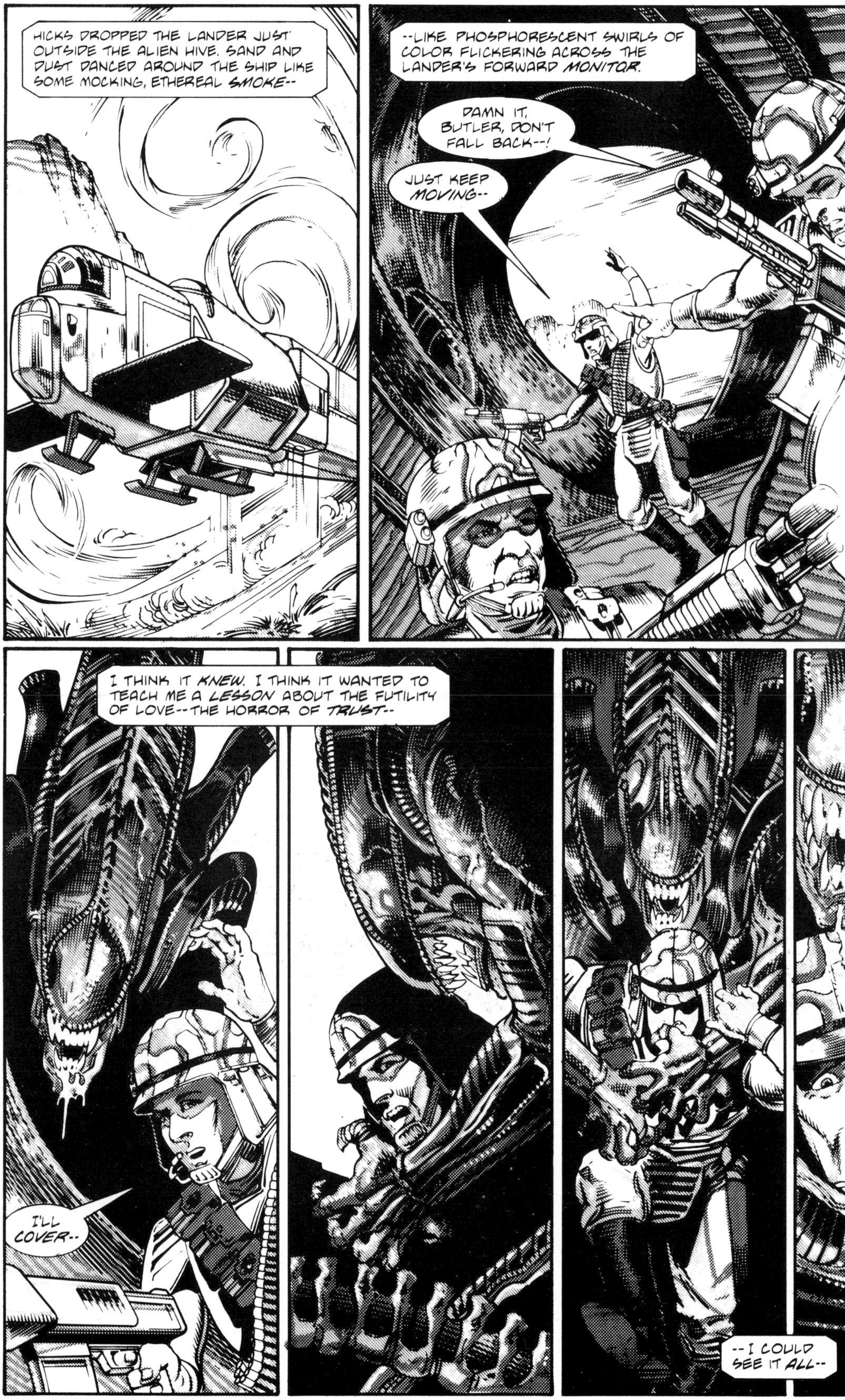
HICKS DROPPED THE LANDER JUST OUTSIDE THE ALIEN HIVE. SAND AND DUST DANCED AROUND THE SHIP LIKE SOME MOCKING, ETHEREAL SMOKE--
--LIKE PHOSPHORESCENT SWIRLS OF COLOR FLICKERING ACROSS THE LANDER'S FORWARD MONITOR.
DAMN IT, BUTLER, DON'T FALL BACK--!
JUST KEEP MOVING--
I THINK IT KNEW. I THINK IT WANTED TO TEACH ME A LESSON ABOUT THE FUTILITY OF LOVE--THE HORROR OF TRUST--
I'LL COVER--
--I COULD SEE IT ALL--

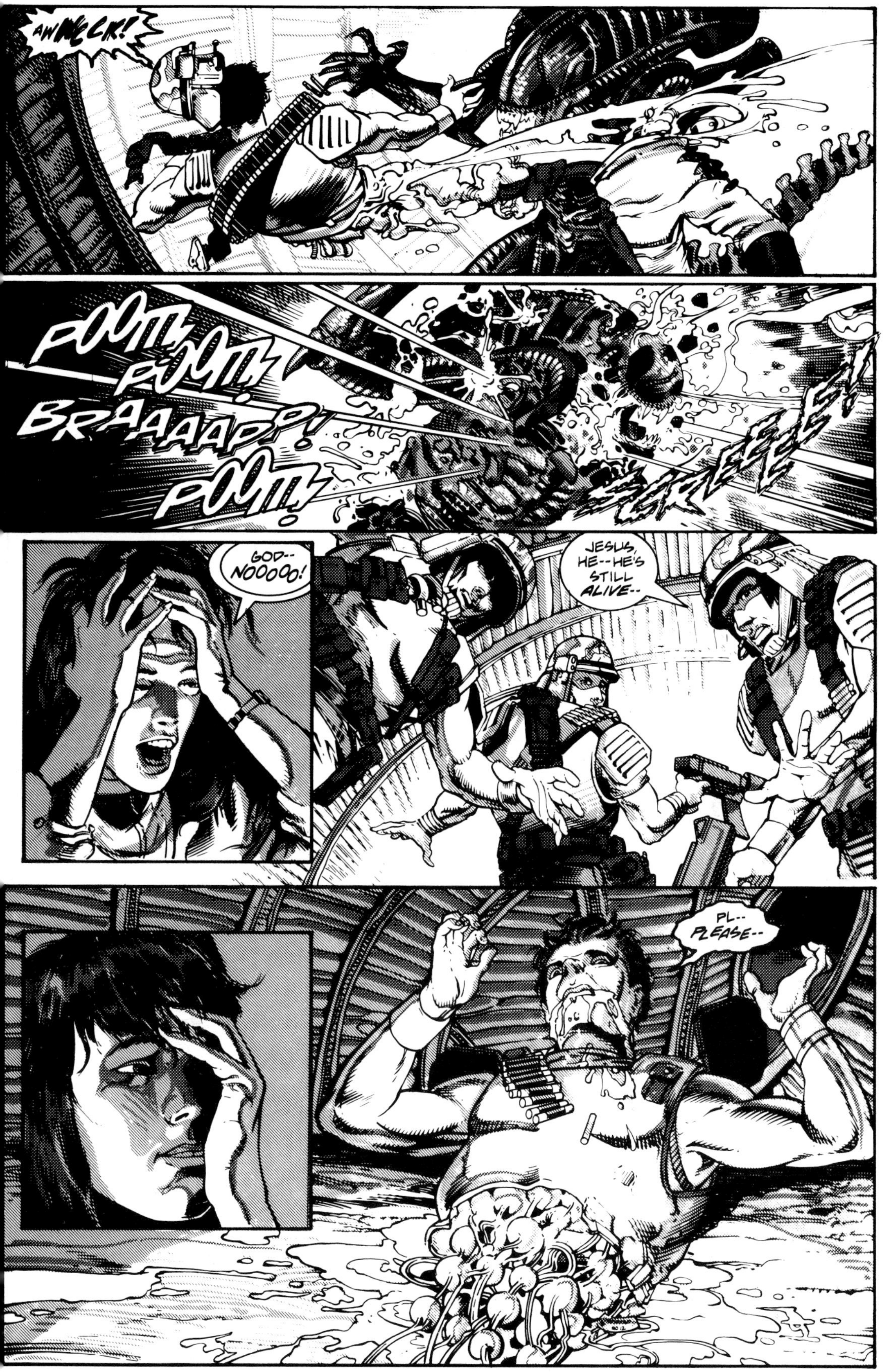
AWWECK!
POOM, POOM, POOM!
BRAAAAPP!
POOM!
GOD--
NOOOOO!
JESUS, HE--HE'S STILL ALIVE--
PL--
PLEASE--

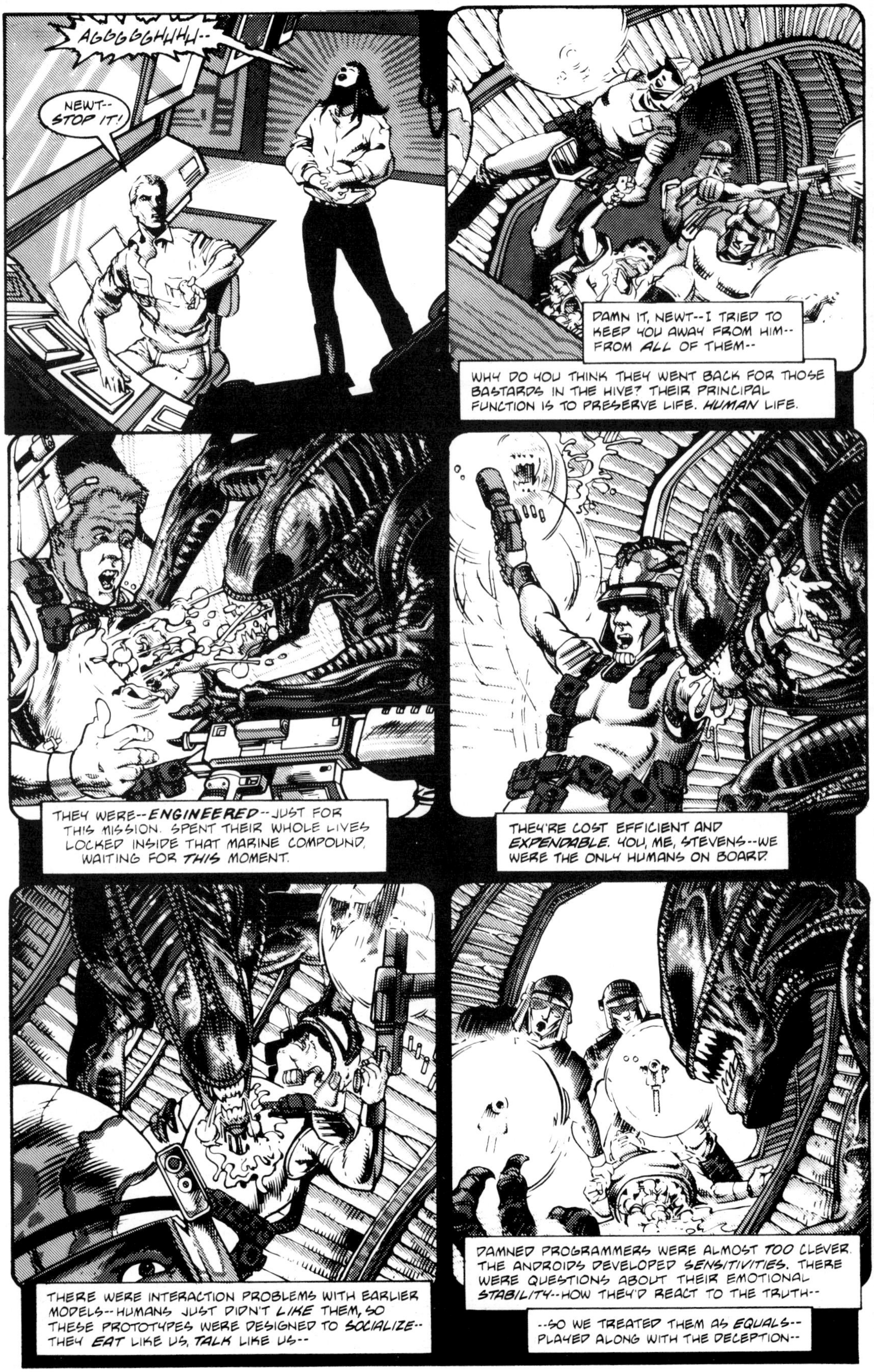
AGGGGGHHHH--
NEWT-- STOP IT!
DAMN IT, NEWT--I TRIED TO KEEP YOU AWAY FROM HIM-- FROM ALL OF THEM--
WHY DO YOU THINK THEY WENT BACK FOR THOSE BASTARDS IN THE HIVE? THEIR PRINCIPAL FUNCTION IS TO PRESERVE LIFE. HUMAN LIFE.
THEY WERE--ENGINEERED--JUST FOR THIS MISSION. SPENT THEIR WHOLE LIVES LOCKED INSIDE THAT MARINE COMPOUND, WAITING FOR THIS MOMENT.
THEY'RE COST EFFICIENT AND EXPENDABLE. YOU, ME, STEVENS--WE WERE THE ONLY HUMANS ON BOARD.
THERE WERE INTERACTION PROBLEMS WITH EARLIER MODELS--HUMANS JUST DIDN'T LIKE THEM, SO THESE PROTOTYPES WERE DESIGNED TO SOCIALIZE-- THEY EAT LIKE US, TALK LIKE US--
DAMNED PROGRAMMERS WERE ALMOST TOO CLEVER. THE ANDROIDS DEVELOPED SENSITIVITIES. THERE WERE QUESTIONS ABOUT THEIR EMOTIONAL STABILITY--HOW THEY'D REACT TO THE TRUTH--
--SO WE TREATED THEM AS EQUALS-- PLAYED ALONG WITH THE DECEPTION--

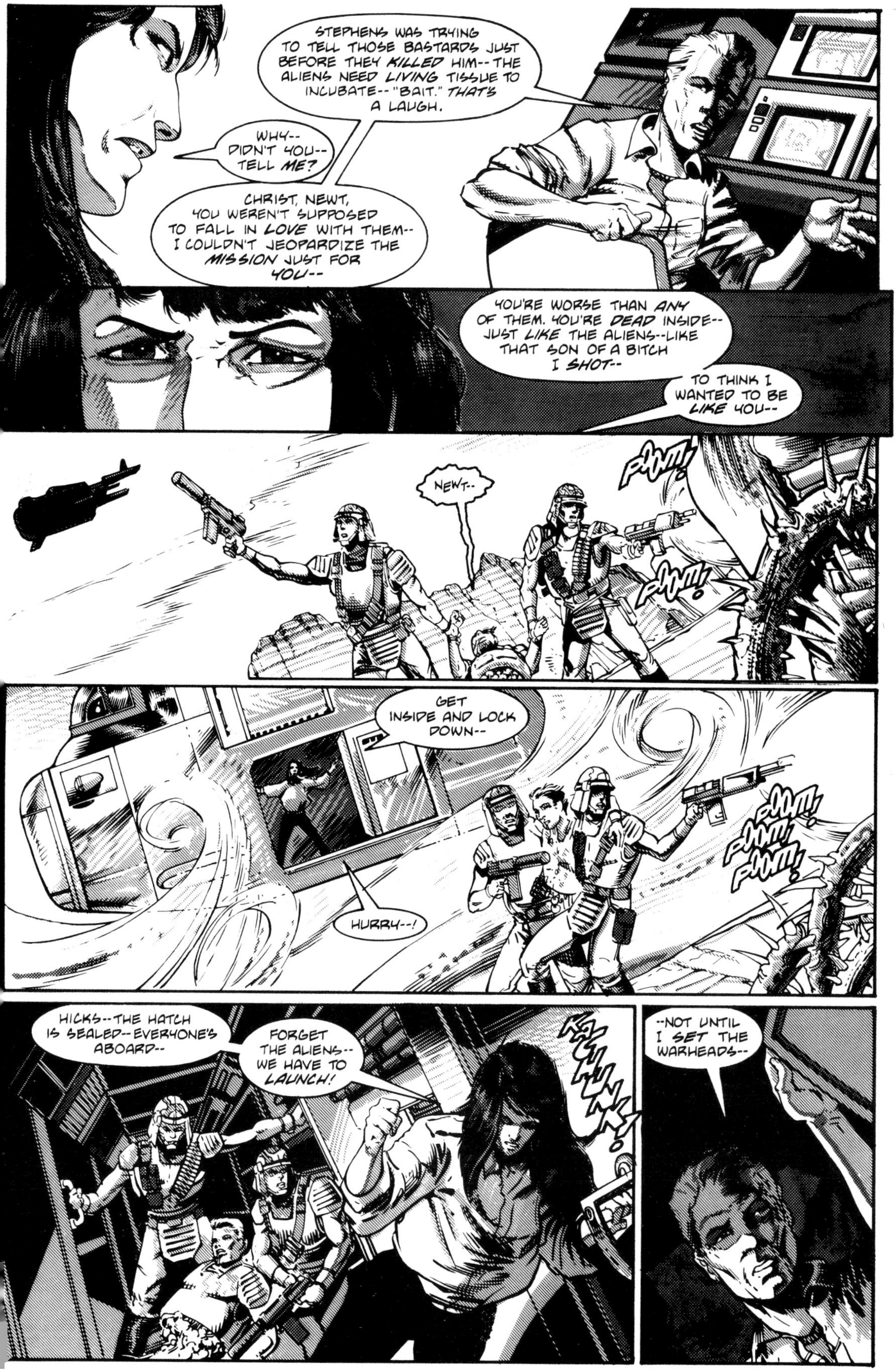
STEPHENS WAS TRYING TO TELL THOSE BASTARDS JUST BEFORE THEY *KILLED* HIM--THE ALIENS NEED *LIVING* TISSUE TO INCUBATE--"BAIT." *THAT'S* A LAUGH.
WHY--DIDN'T YOU--TELL *ME?*
CHRIST, NEWT, YOU WEREN'T SUPPOSED TO FALL IN *LOVE* WITH THEM--I COULDN'T JEOPARDIZE THE *MISSION* JUST FOR *YOU*--
YOU'RE WORSE THAN *ANY* OF THEM. YOU'RE *DEAD* INSIDE--JUST *LIKE* THE ALIENS--LIKE THAT SON OF A BITCH I *SHOT*--
TO THINK I WANTED TO BE *LIKE* YOU--
NEWT--
POOM!
POOM!
GET INSIDE AND LOCK DOWN--
HURRY--!
POOM! POOM! POOM!
HICKS--THE HATCH IS SEALED--EVERYONE'S ABOARD--
FORGET THE ALIENS--WE HAVE TO *LAUNCH!*
KA-CHUNK!
--NOT UNTIL I *SET* THE WARHEADS--

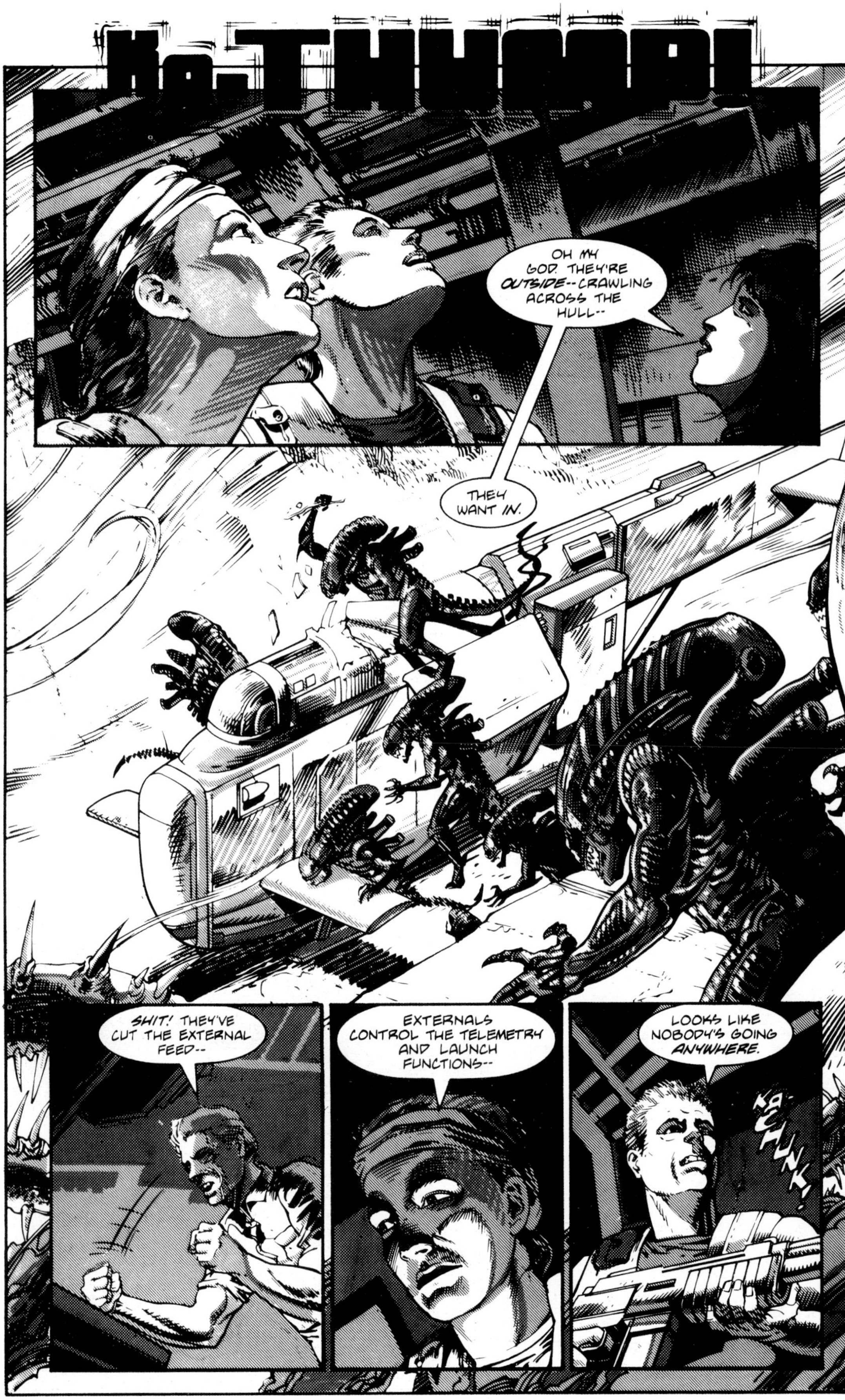
Ka-THUMP!
OH MY GOD. THEY'RE OUTSIDE--CRAWLING ACROSS THE HULL--
THEY WANT IN.
SHIT! THEY'VE CUT THE EXTERNAL FEED--
EXTERNALS CONTROL THE TELEMETRY AND LAUNCH FUNCTIONS--
LOOKS LIKE NOBODY'S GOING ANYWHERE.
Ka-CHUNK!

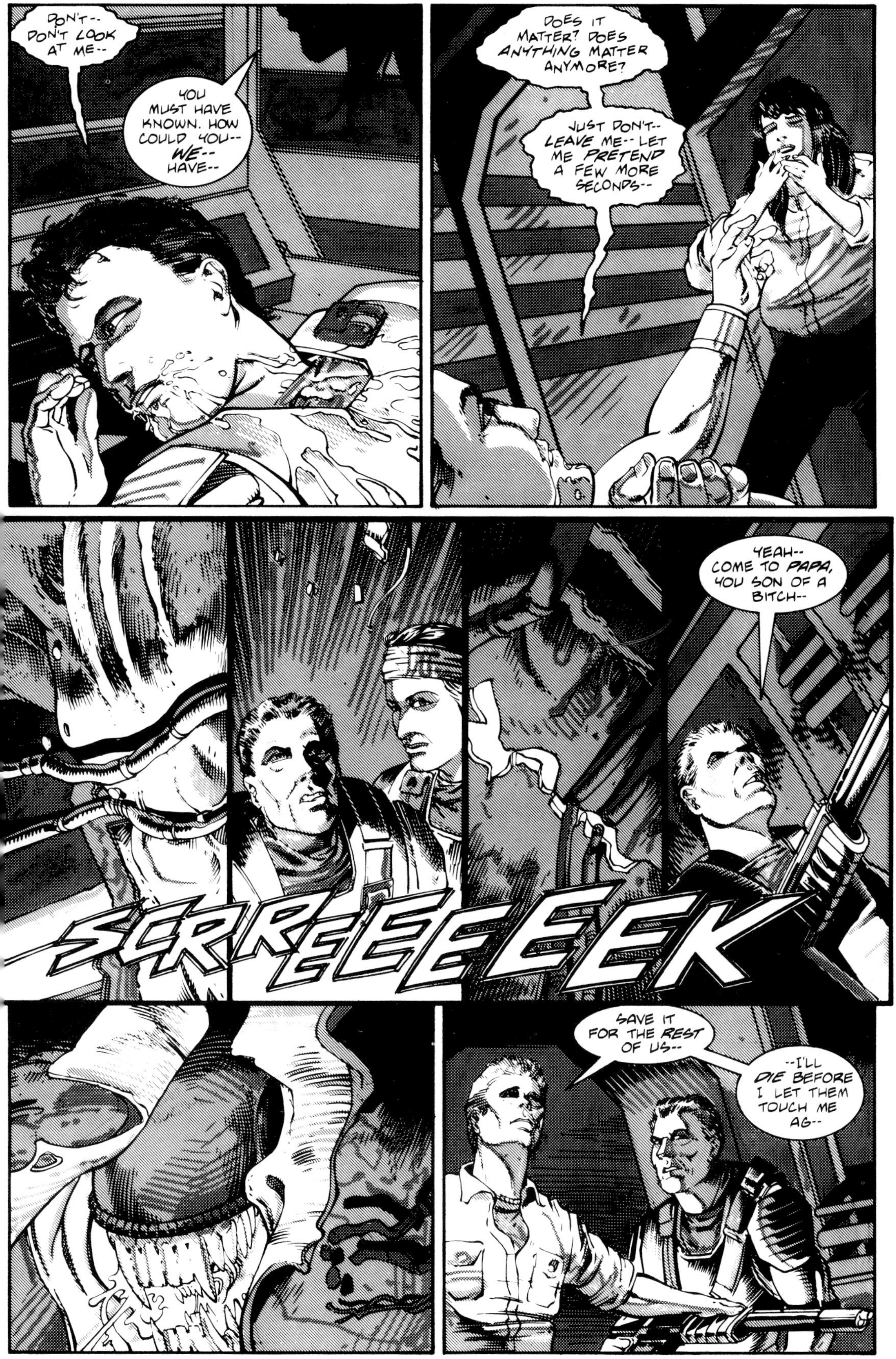
DON'T-- DON'T LOOK AT ME--
YOU MUST HAVE KNOWN. HOW COULD YOU-- WE-- HAVE--
DOES IT MATTER? DOES ANYTHING MATTER ANYMORE?
JUST DON'T-- LEAVE ME-- LET ME PRETEND A FEW MORE SECONDS--
YEAH-- COME TO PAPA, YOU SON OF A BITCH--
SCREEEEEEEK
SAVE IT FOR THE REST OF US--
--I'LL DIE BEFORE I LET THEM TOUCH ME AG--

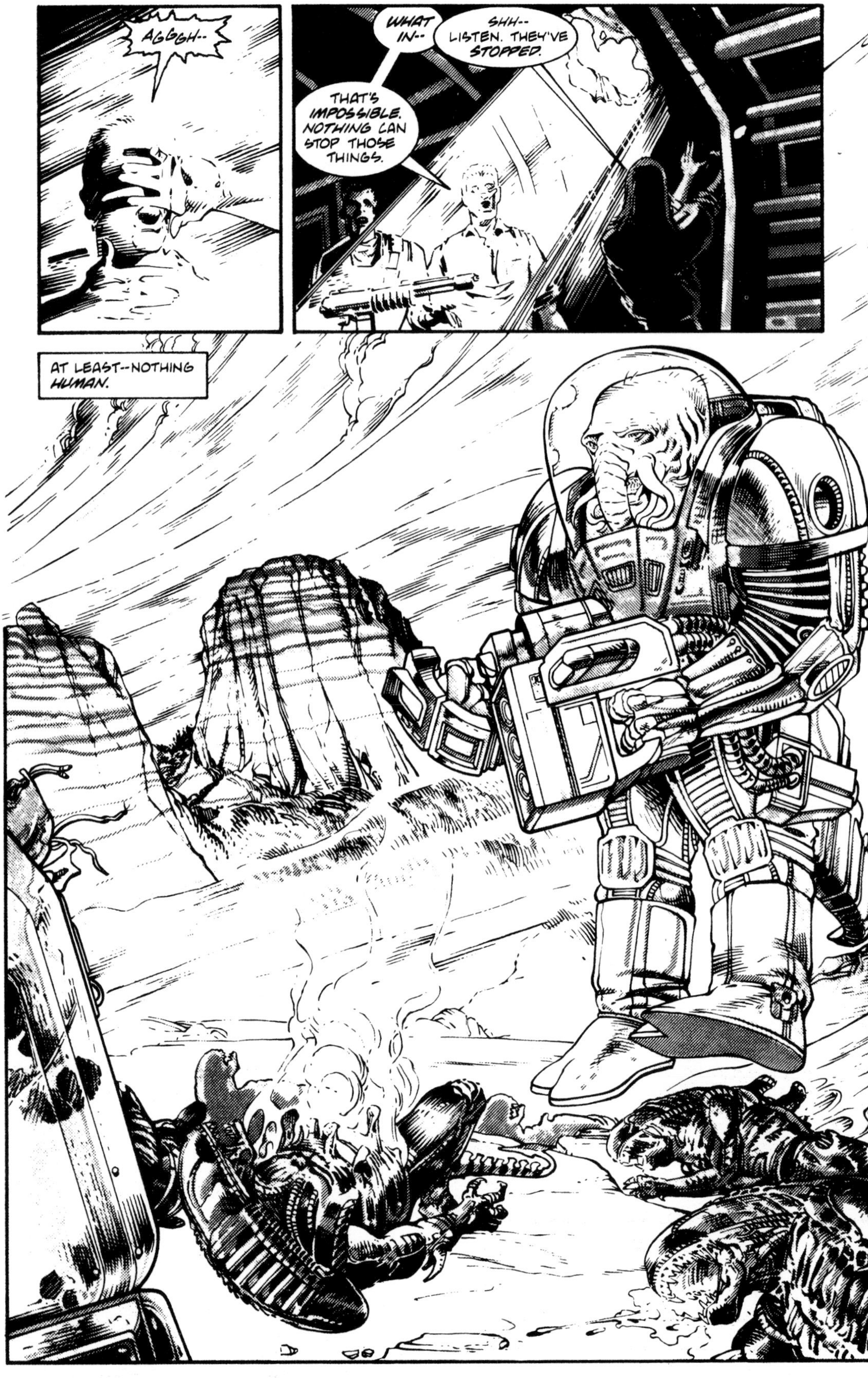
AGGGH--
WHAT IN--
SHH-- LISTEN. THEY'VE STOPPED.
THAT'S IMPOSSIBLE. NOTHING CAN STOP THOSE THINGS.
AT LEAST--NOTHING HUMAN.

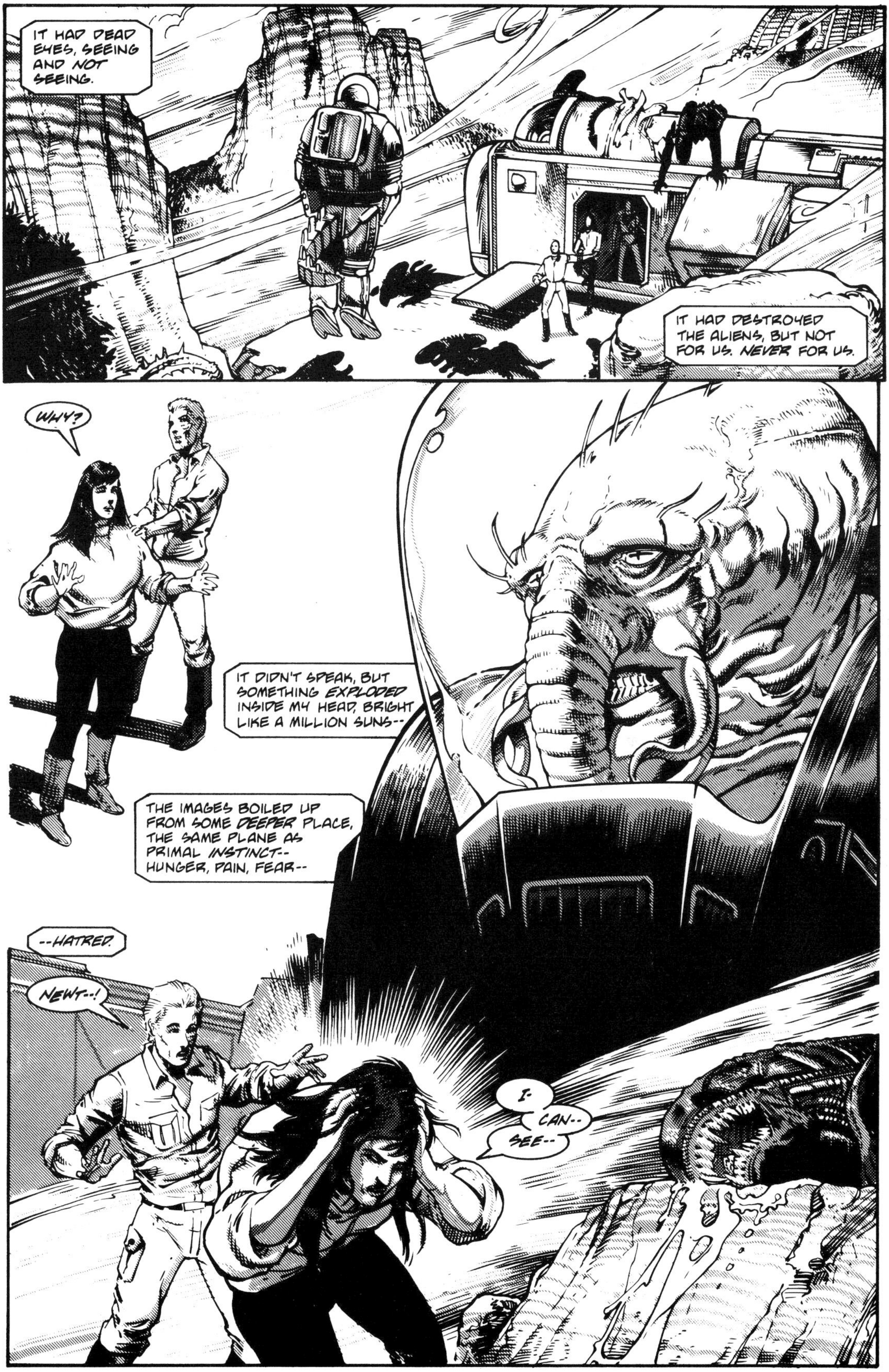
IT HAD DEAD EYES, SEEING AND NOT SEEING.
IT HAD DESTROYED THE ALIENS, BUT NOT FOR US. NEVER FOR US.
WHY?
IT DIDN'T SPEAK, BUT SOMETHING EXPLODED INSIDE MY HEAD, BRIGHT LIKE A MILLION SUNS--
THE IMAGES BOILED UP FROM SOME DEEPER PLACE, THE SAME PLANE AS PRIMAL INSTINCT-- HUNGER, PAIN, FEAR--
--HATRED.
NEWT--!
I-
CAN--
SEE--

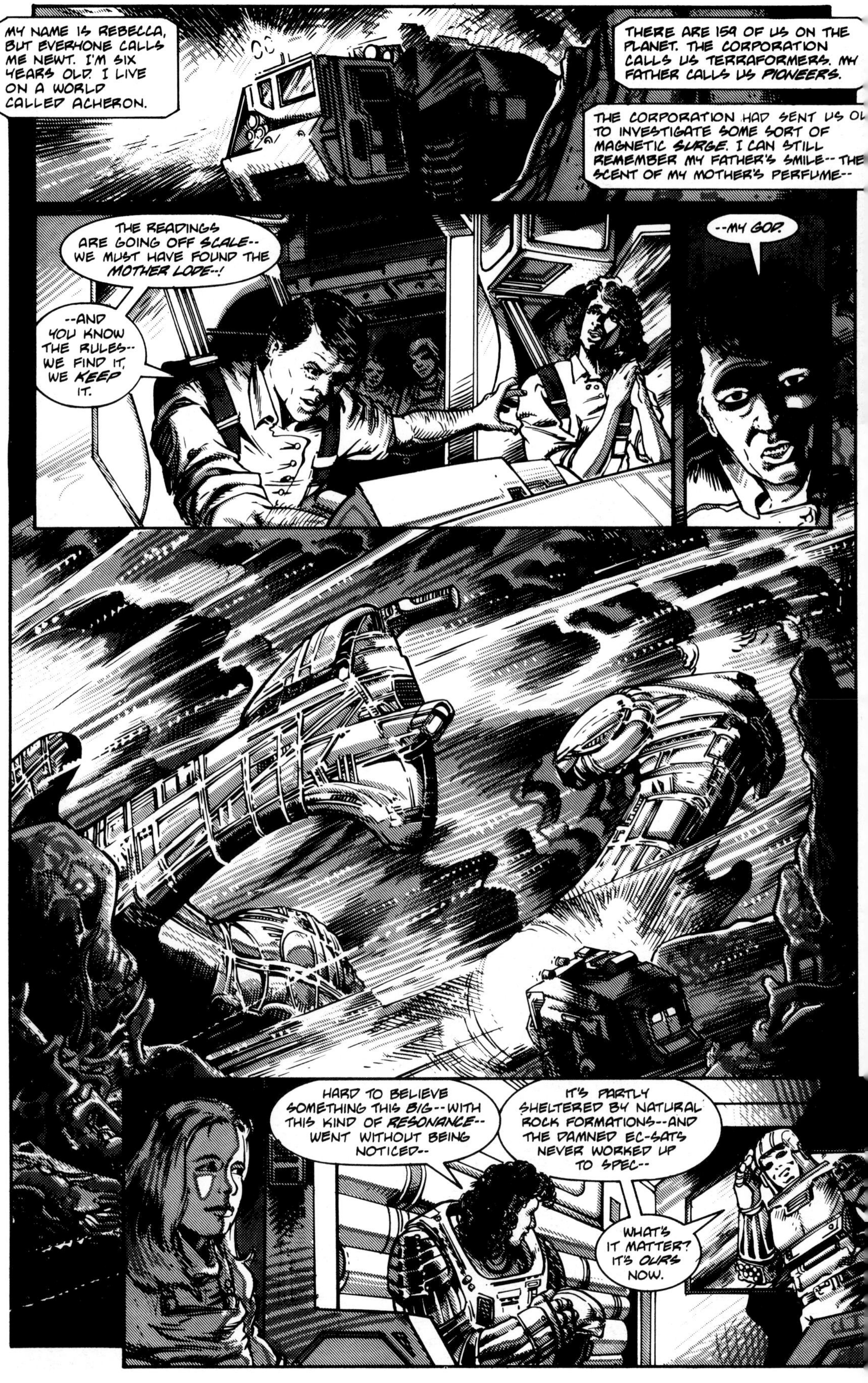

MY NAME IS REBECCA, BUT EVERYONE CALLS ME NEWT. I'M SIX YEARS OLD. I LIVE ON A WORLD CALLED ACHERON.
THERE ARE 159 OF US ON THE PLANET. THE CORPORATION CALLS US TERRAFORMERS. MY FATHER CALLS US PIONEERS.
THE CORPORATION HAD SENT US OU TO INVESTIGATE SOME SORT OF MAGNETIC SURGE. I CAN STILL REMEMBER MY FATHER'S SMILE-- THE SCENT OF MY MOTHER'S PERFUME--
THE READINGS ARE GOING OFF SCALE-- WE MUST HAVE FOUND THE MOTHER LODE--!
--AND YOU KNOW THE RULES-- WE FIND IT, WE KEEP IT.
--MY GOD.
HARD TO BELIEVE SOMETHING THIS BIG--WITH THIS KIND OF RESONANCE-- WENT WITHOUT BEING NOTICED--
IT'S PARTLY SHELTERED BY NATURAL ROCK FORMATIONS--AND THE DAMNED EC-SATS NEVER WORKED UP TO SPEC--
WHAT'S IT MATTER? IT'S OURS NOW.

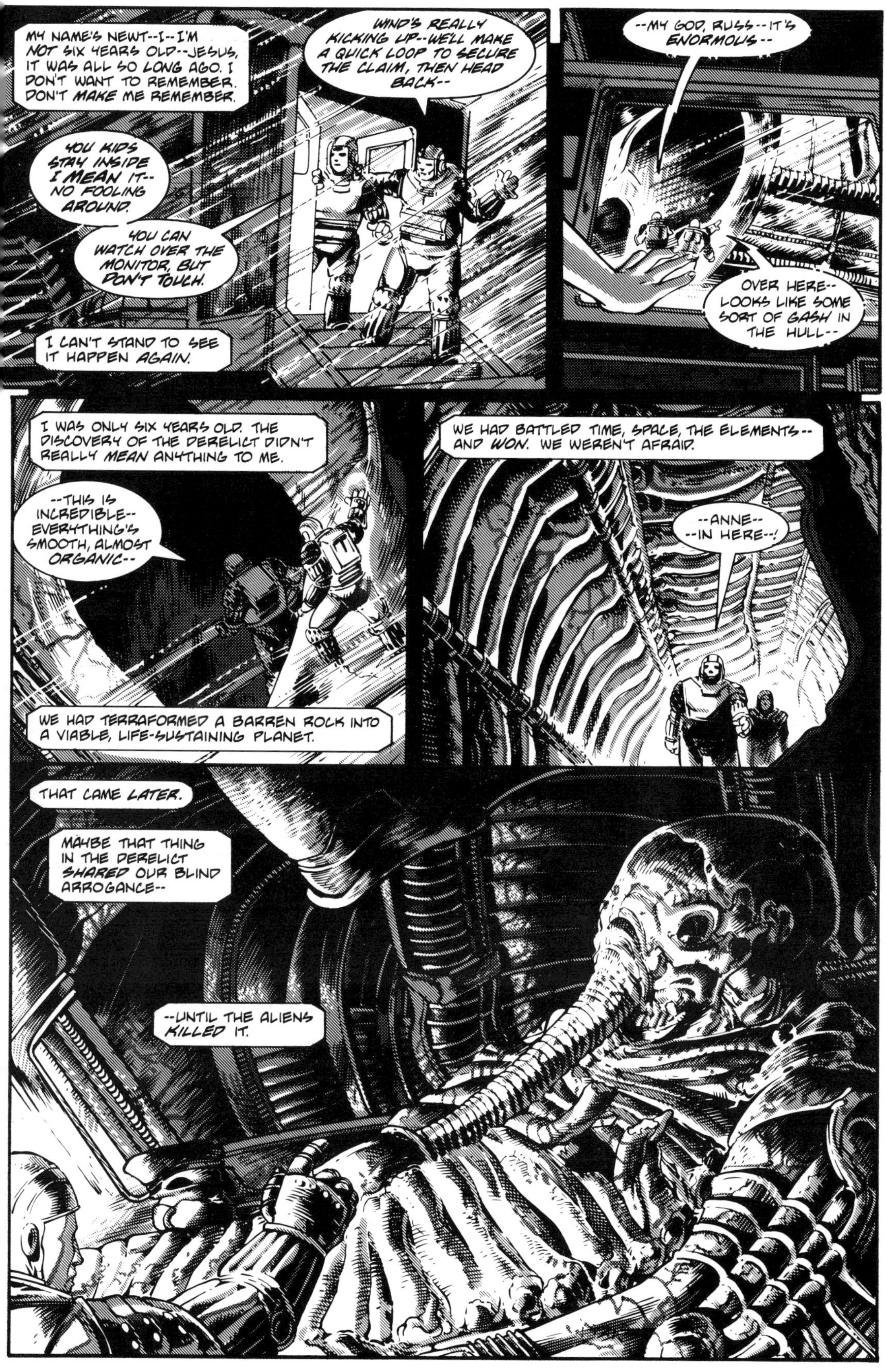
MY NAME'S NEWT--I--I'M NOT SIX YEARS OLD--JESUS, IT WAS ALL SO LONG AGO. I DON'T WANT TO REMEMBER. DON'T MAKE ME REMEMBER.
WIND'S REALLY KICKING UP--WE'LL MAKE A QUICK LOOP TO SECURE THE CLAIM, THEN HEAD BACK--
YOU KIDS STAY INSIDE I MEAN IT--NO FOOLING AROUND.
YOU CAN WATCH OVER THE MONITOR, BUT DON'T TOUCH.
I CAN'T STAND TO SEE IT HAPPEN AGAIN.
--MY GOD, RUSS--IT'S ENORMOUS--
OVER HERE--LOOKS LIKE SOME SORT OF GASH IN THE HULL--
I WAS ONLY SIX YEARS OLD. THE DISCOVERY OF THE DERELICT DIDN'T REALLY MEAN ANYTHING TO ME.
--THIS IS INCREDIBLE--EVERYTHING'S SMOOTH, ALMOST ORGANIC--
WE HAD TERRAFORMED A BARREN ROCK INTO A VIABLE, LIFE-SUSTAINING PLANET.
WE HAD BATTLED TIME, SPACE, THE ELEMENTS--AND WON. WE WEREN'T AFRAID.
--ANNE--
--IN HERE--!
THAT CAME LATER.
MAYBE THAT THING IN THE DERELICT SHARED OUR BLIND ARROGANCE--
--UNTIL THE ALIENS KILLED IT.

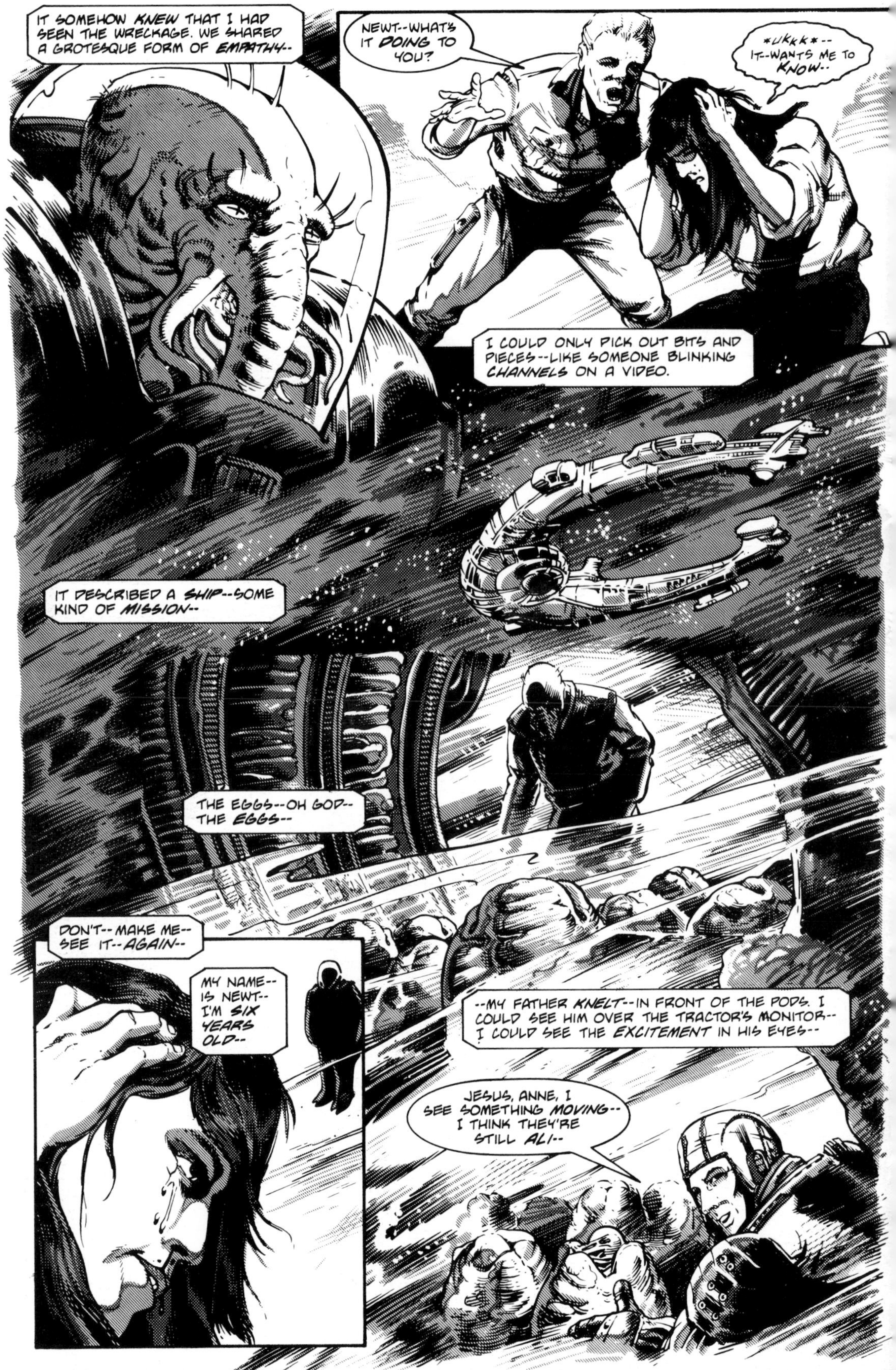
IT SOMEHOW KNEW THAT I HAD SEEN THE WRECKAGE. WE SHARED A GROTESQUE FORM OF EMPATHY--
NEWT--WHAT'S IT DOING TO YOU?
UKKK-- IT--WANTS ME TO KNOW--
I COULD ONLY PICK OUT BITS AND PIECES--LIKE SOMEONE BLINKING CHANNELS ON A VIDEO.
IT DESCRIBED A SHIP--SOME KIND OF MISSION--
THE EGGS--OH GOD-- THE EGGS--
DON'T--MAKE ME-- SEE IT--AGAIN--
MY NAME-- IS NEWT-- I'M SIX YEARS OLD--
--MY FATHER KNELT--IN FRONT OF THE PODS. I COULD SEE HIM OVER THE TRACTOR'S MONITOR-- I COULD SEE THE EXCITEMENT IN HIS EYES--
JESUS, ANNE, I SEE SOMETHING MOVING-- I THINK THEY'RE STILL ALI--

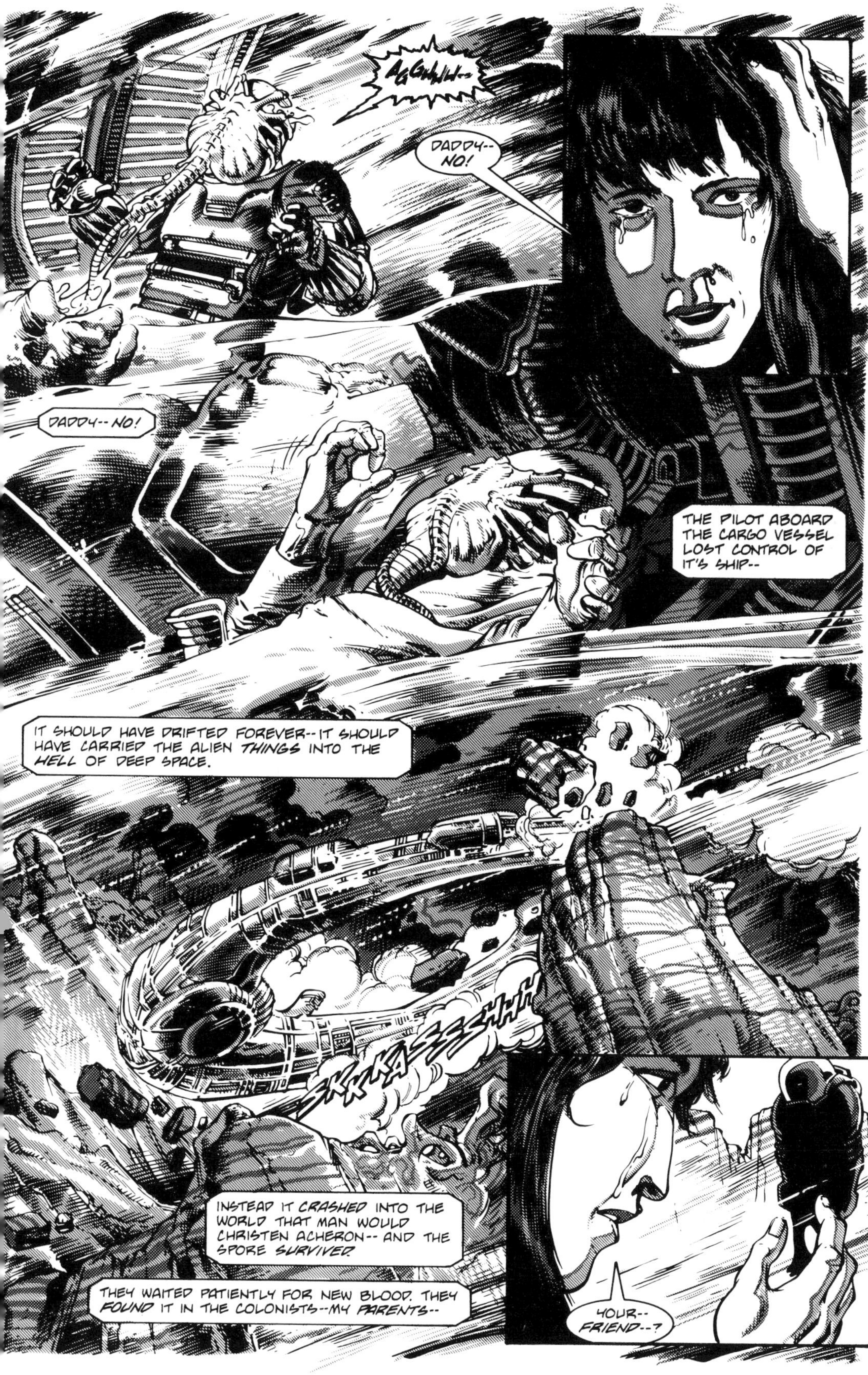
AAGHHHH--
DADDY-- NO!
DADDY-- NO!
THE PILOT ABOARD THE CARGO VESSEL LOST CONTROL OF IT'S SHIP--
IT SHOULD HAVE DRIFTED FOREVER-- IT SHOULD HAVE CARRIED THE ALIEN *THINGS* INTO THE *HELL* OF DEEP SPACE.
SKKKASSSHHH
INSTEAD IT *CRASHED* INTO THE WORLD THAT MAN WOULD CHRISTEN ACHERON-- AND THE SPORE *SURVIVED*.
THEY WAITED PATIENTLY FOR NEW BLOOD. THEY *FOUND* IT IN THE COLONISTS--MY *PARENTS*--
YOUR-- FRIEND--?

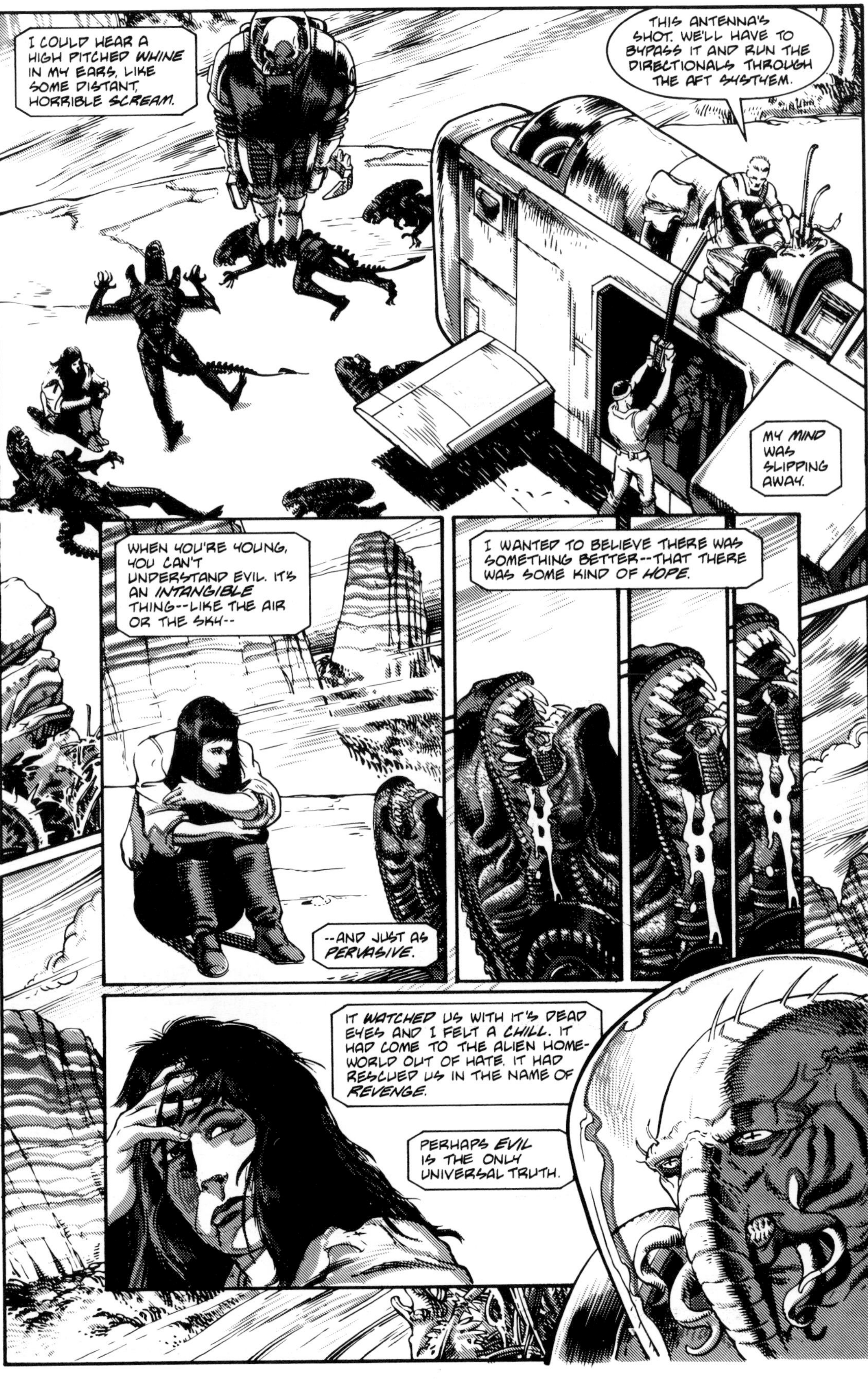
I COULD HEAR A HIGH PITCHED WHINE IN MY EARS, LIKE SOME DISTANT, HORRIBLE SCREAM.
THIS ANTENNA'S SHOT. WE'LL HAVE TO BYPASS IT AND RUN THE DIRECTIONALS THROUGH THE AFT SYSTYEM.
MY MIND WAS SLIPPING AWAY.
WHEN YOU'RE YOUNG, YOU CAN'T UNDERSTAND EVIL. IT'S AN INTANGIBLE THING--LIKE THE AIR OR THE SKY--
--AND JUST AS PERVASIVE.
I WANTED TO BELIEVE THERE WAS SOMETHING BETTER--THAT THERE WAS SOME KIND OF HOPE.
IT WATCHED US WITH IT'S DEAD EYES AND I FELT A CHILL. IT HAD COME TO THE ALIEN HOME-WORLD OUT OF HATE. IT HAD RESCUED US IN THE NAME OF REVENGE.
PERHAPS EVIL IS THE ONLY UNIVERSAL TRUTH.

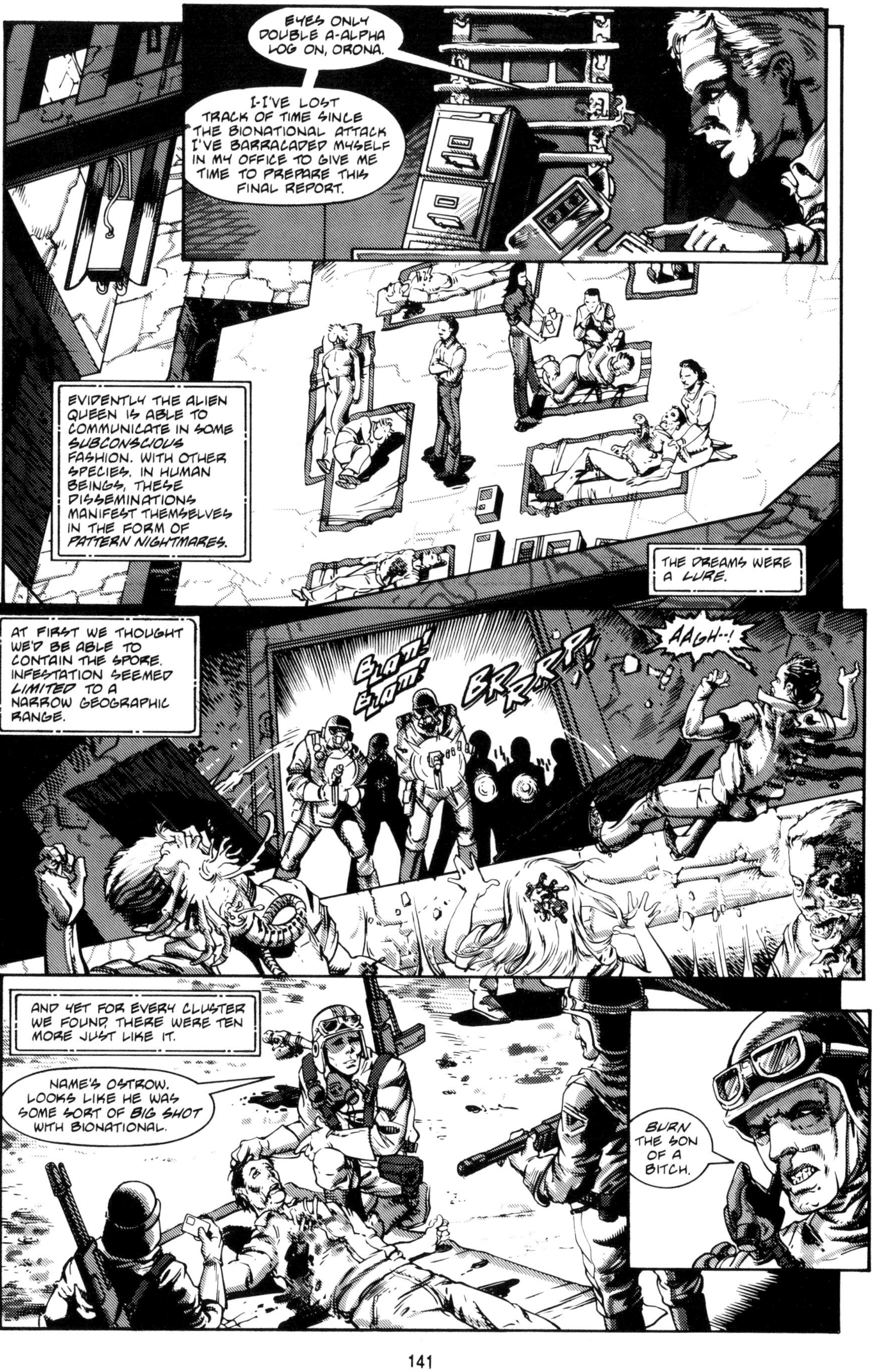
EYES ONLY DOUBLE A-ALPHA LOG ON, ORONA.
I-I'VE LOST TRACK OF TIME SINCE THE BIONATIONAL ATTACK I'VE BARRACADED MYSELF IN MY OFFICE TO GIVE ME TIME TO PREPARE THIS FINAL REPORT.
EVIDENTLY THE ALIEN QUEEN IS ABLE TO COMMUNICATE IN SOME SUBCONSCIOUS FASHION. WITH OTHER SPECIES. IN HUMAN BEINGS, THESE DISSEMINATIONS MANIFEST THEMSELVES IN THE FORM OF PATTERN NIGHTMARES.
THE DREAMS WERE A LURE.
AT FIRST WE THOUGHT WE'D BE ABLE TO CONTAIN THE SPORE. INFESTATION SEEMED LIMITED TO A NARROW GEOGRAPHIC RANGE.
BLAM! BLAM!
BRRRRP!
AAGH--!
AND YET FOR EVERY CLUSTER WE FOUND THERE WERE TEN MORE JUST LIKE IT.
NAME'S OSTROW. LOOKS LIKE HE WAS SOME SORT OF BIG SHOT WITH BIONATIONAL.
BURN THE SON OF A BITCH.

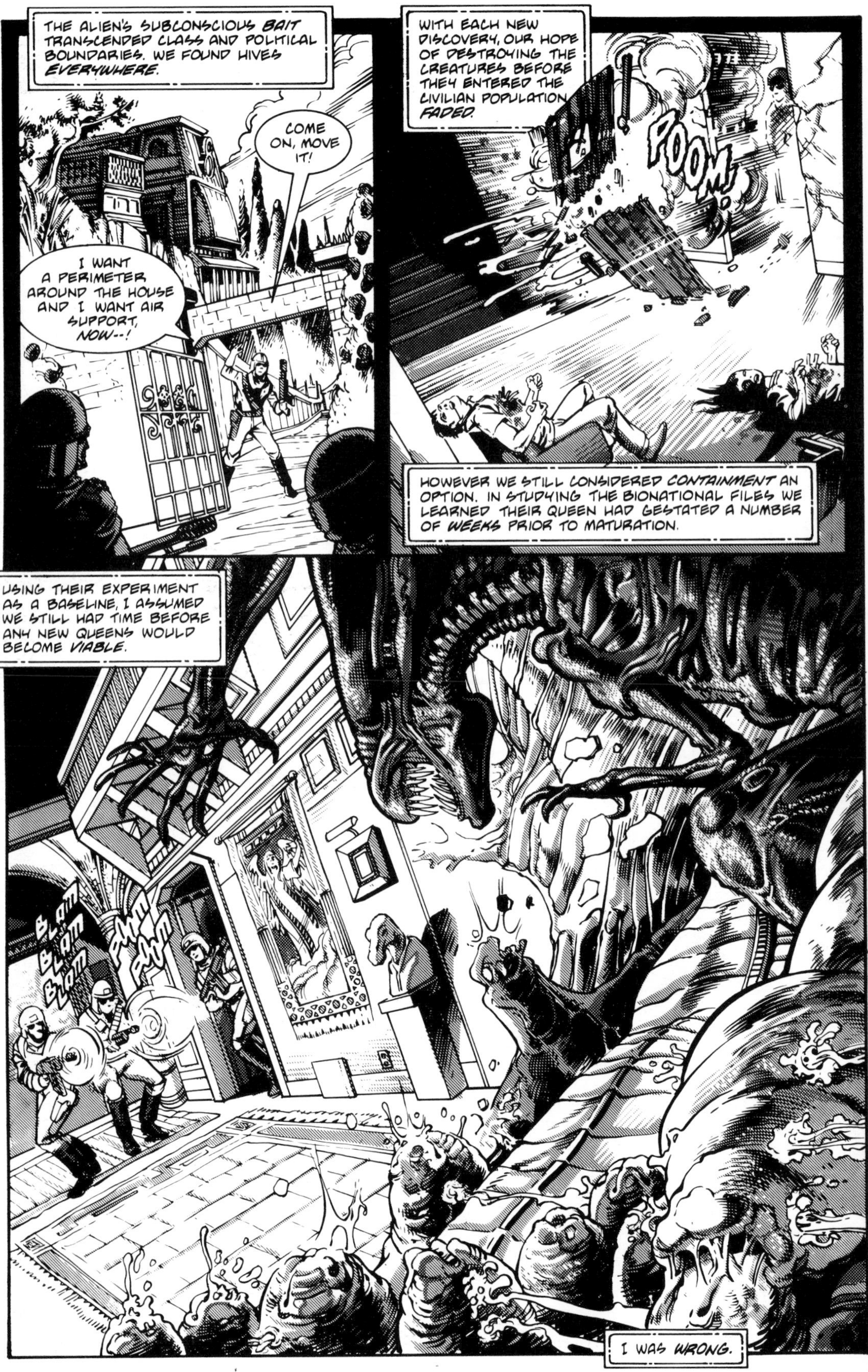
THE ALIEN'S SUBCONSCIOUS BAIT TRANSCENDED CLASS AND POLITICAL BOUNDARIES. WE FOUND HIVES EVERYWHERE.
COME ON, MOVE IT!
I WANT A PERIMETER AROUND THE HOUSE AND I WANT AIR SUPPORT, NOW--!
WITH EACH NEW DISCOVERY, OUR HOPE OF DESTROYING THE CREATURES BEFORE THEY ENTERED THE CIVILIAN POPULATION FADED.
POOM!
HOWEVER WE STILL CONSIDERED CONTAINMENT AN OPTION. IN STUDYING THE BIONATIONAL FILES WE LEARNED THEIR QUEEN HAD GESTATED A NUMBER OF WEEKS PRIOR TO MATURATION.
USING THEIR EXPERIMENT AS A BASELINE, I ASSUMED WE STILL HAD TIME BEFORE ANY NEW QUEENS WOULD BECOME VIABLE.
BLAM BLAM BLAM
I WAS WRONG.

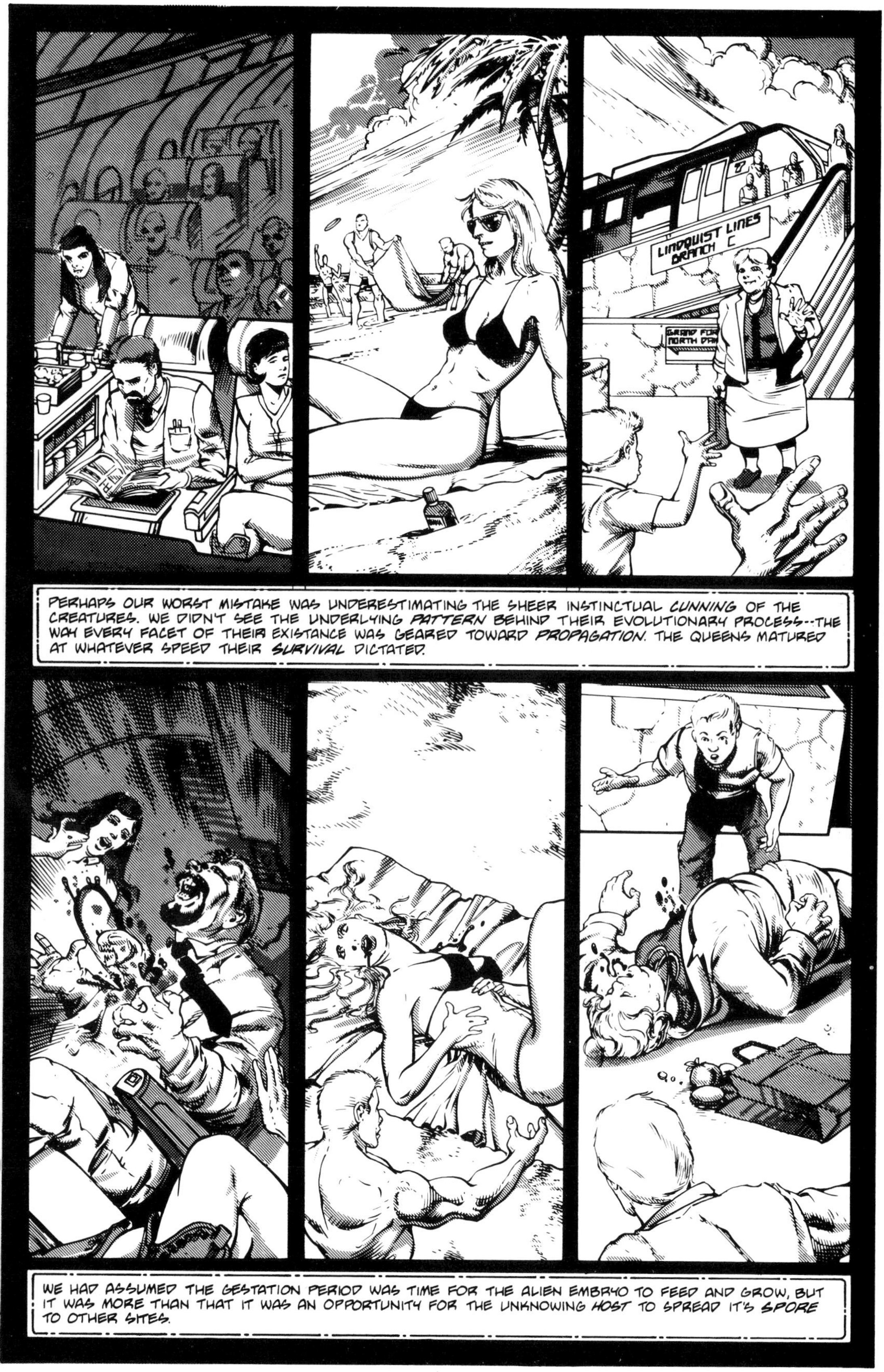
LINDQUIST LINES BRANCH C
PERHAPS OUR WORST MISTAKE WAS UNDERESTIMATING THE SHEER INSTINCTUAL *CUNNING* OF THE CREATURES. WE DIDN'T SEE THE UNDERLYING *PATTERN* BEHIND THEIR EVOLUTIONARY PROCESS--THE WAY EVERY FACET OF THEIR EXISTANCE WAS GEARED TOWARD *PROPAGATION*. THE QUEENS MATURED AT WHATEVER SPEED THEIR *SURVIVAL* DICTATED.
WE HAD ASSUMED THE GESTATION PERIOD WAS TIME FOR THE ALIEN EMBRYO TO FEED AND GROW, BUT IT WAS MORE THAN THAT IT WAS AN OPPORTUNITY FOR THE UNKNOWING *HOST* TO SPREAD IT'S *SPORE* TO OTHER SITES.

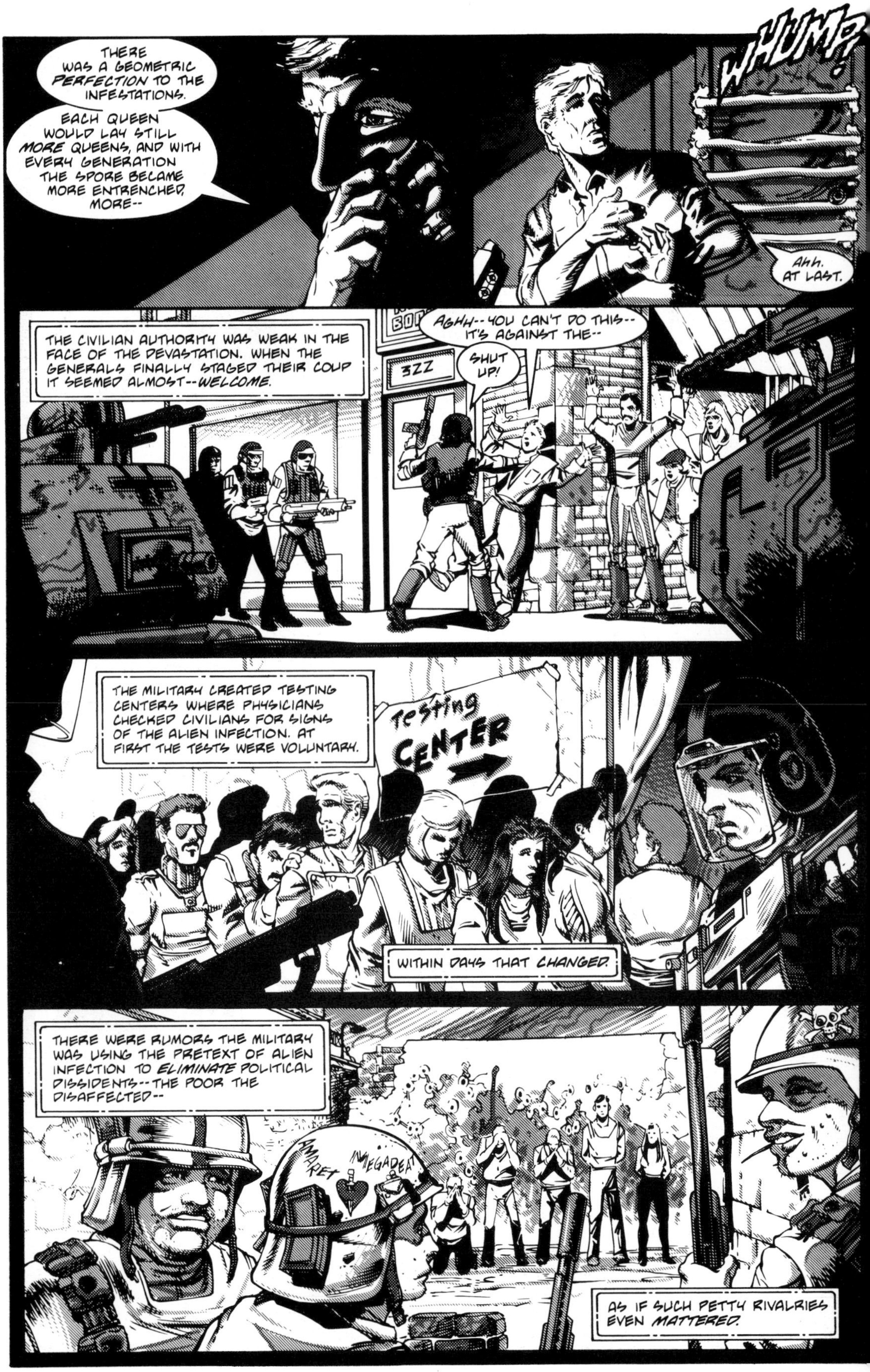
THERE WAS A GEOMETRIC PERFECTION TO THE INFESTATIONS.
EACH QUEEN WOULD LAY STILL MORE QUEENS, AND WITH EVERY GENERATION THE SPORE BECAME MORE ENTRENCHED, MORE--
WHUMP!
Ahh. AT LAST.
THE CIVILIAN AUTHORITY WAS WEAK IN THE FACE OF THE DEVASTATION. WHEN THE GENERALS FINALLY STAGED THEIR COUP IT SEEMED ALMOST--WELCOME.
AGHH--YOU CAN'T DO THIS--IT'S AGAINST THE--
SHUT UP!
3ZZ
THE MILITARY CREATED TESTING CENTERS WHERE PHYSICIANS CHECKED CIVILIANS FOR SIGNS OF THE ALIEN INFECTION. AT FIRST THE TESTS WERE VOLUNTARY.
Testing CENTER
WITHIN DAYS THAT CHANGED.
THERE WERE RUMORS THE MILITARY WAS USING THE PRETEXT OF ALIEN INFECTION TO ELIMINATE POLITICAL DISSIDENTS--THE POOR THE DISAFFECTED--
MEGADEATH
AS IF SUCH PETTY RIVALRIES EVEN MATTERED.

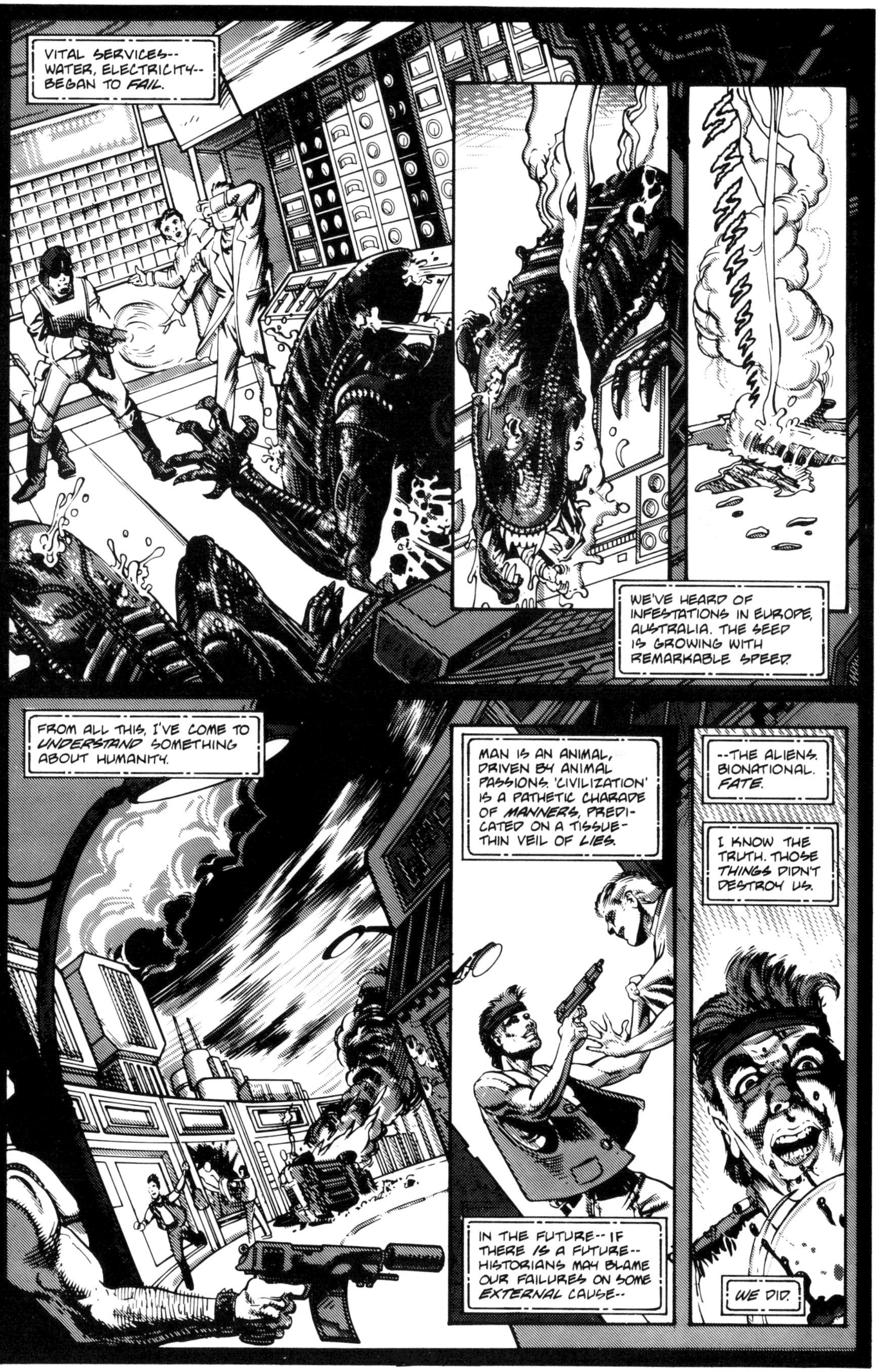
VITAL SERVICES-- WATER, ELECTRICITY-- BEGAN TO FAIL.
SHHHHHHHHHH
WE'VE HEARD OF INFESTATIONS IN EUROPE, AUSTRALIA. THE SEED IS GROWING WITH REMARKABLE SPEED.
FROM ALL THIS, I'VE COME TO UNDERSTAND SOMETHING ABOUT HUMANITY.
MAN IS AN ANIMAL, DRIVEN BY ANIMAL PASSIONS. 'CIVILIZATION' IS A PATHETIC CHARADE OF MANNERS, PREDI-CATED ON A TISSUE-THIN VEIL OF LIES.
IN THE FUTURE-- IF THERE IS A FUTURE-- HISTORIANS MAY BLAME OUR FAILURES ON SOME EXTERNAL CAUSE--
--THE ALIENS. BIONATIONAL. FATE.
I KNOW THE TRUTH. THOSE THINGS DIDN'T DESTROY US.
WE DID.

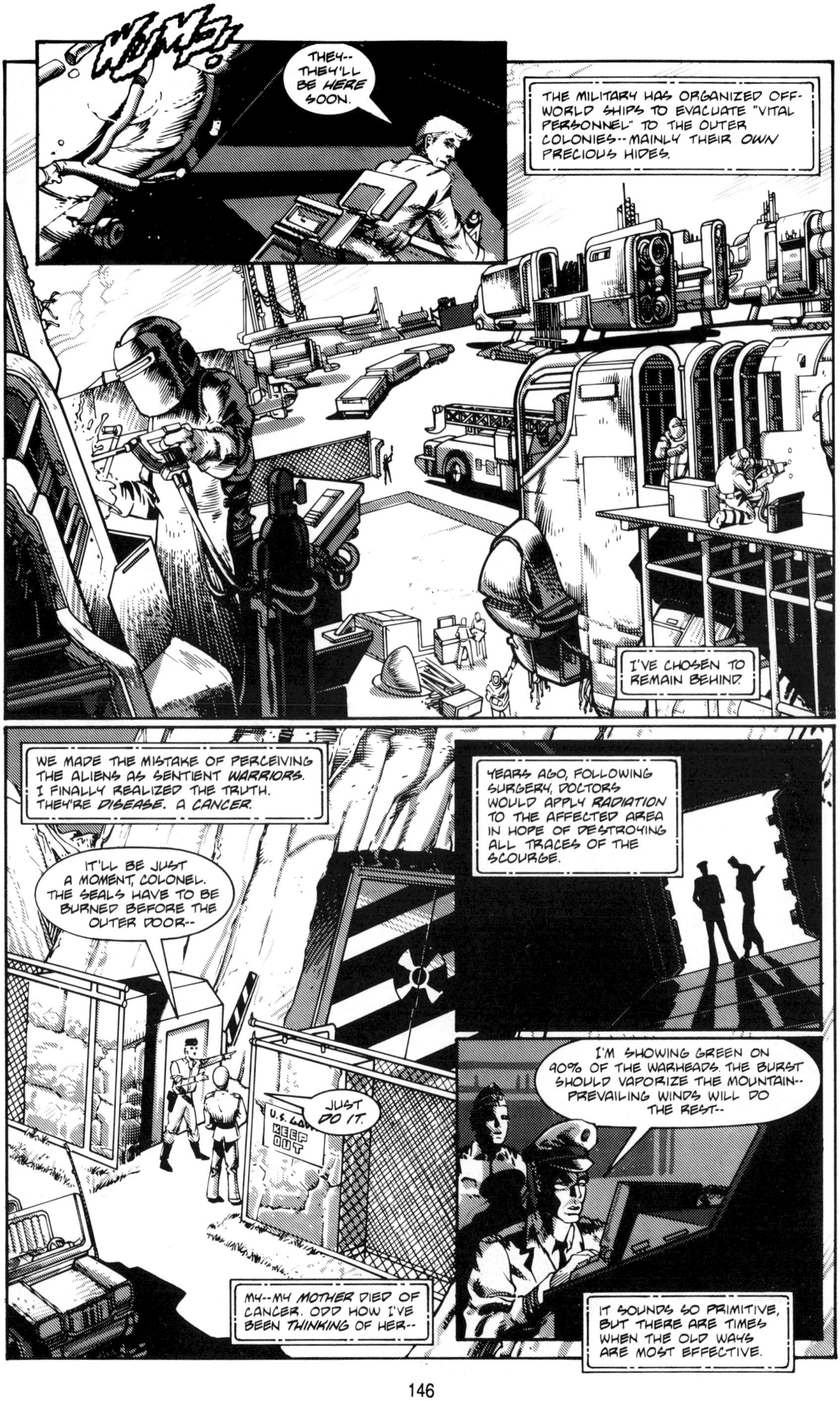
THEY-- THEY'LL BE *HERE* SOON.
THE MILITARY HAS ORGANIZED OFF-WORLD SHIPS TO EVACUATE "VITAL PERSONNEL" TO THE OUTER COLONIES--MAINLY THEIR *OWN* PRECIOUS HIDES.
I'VE CHOSEN TO REMAIN BEHIND.
WE MADE THE MISTAKE OF PERCEIVING THE ALIENS AS SENTIENT *WARRIORS*. I FINALLY REALIZED THE TRUTH. THEY'RE *DISEASE*. A *CANCER*.
IT'LL BE JUST A MOMENT, COLONEL. THE SEALS HAVE TO BE BURNED BEFORE THE OUTER DOOR--
JUST *DO IT*.
KEEP OUT
YEARS AGO, FOLLOWING SURGERY, DOCTORS WOULD APPLY *RADIATION* TO THE AFFECTED AREA IN HOPE OF DESTROYING ALL TRACES OF THE SCOURGE.
MY--MY *MOTHER* DIED OF CANCER. ODD HOW I'VE BEEN *THINKING* OF HER--
I'M SHOWING GREEN ON 90% OF THE WARHEADS. THE BURST SHOULD VAPORIZE THE MOUNTAIN-- PREVAILING WINDS WILL DO THE REST--
IT SOUNDS SO PRIMITIVE, BUT THERE ARE TIMES WHEN THE OLD WAYS ARE MOST EFFECTIVE.

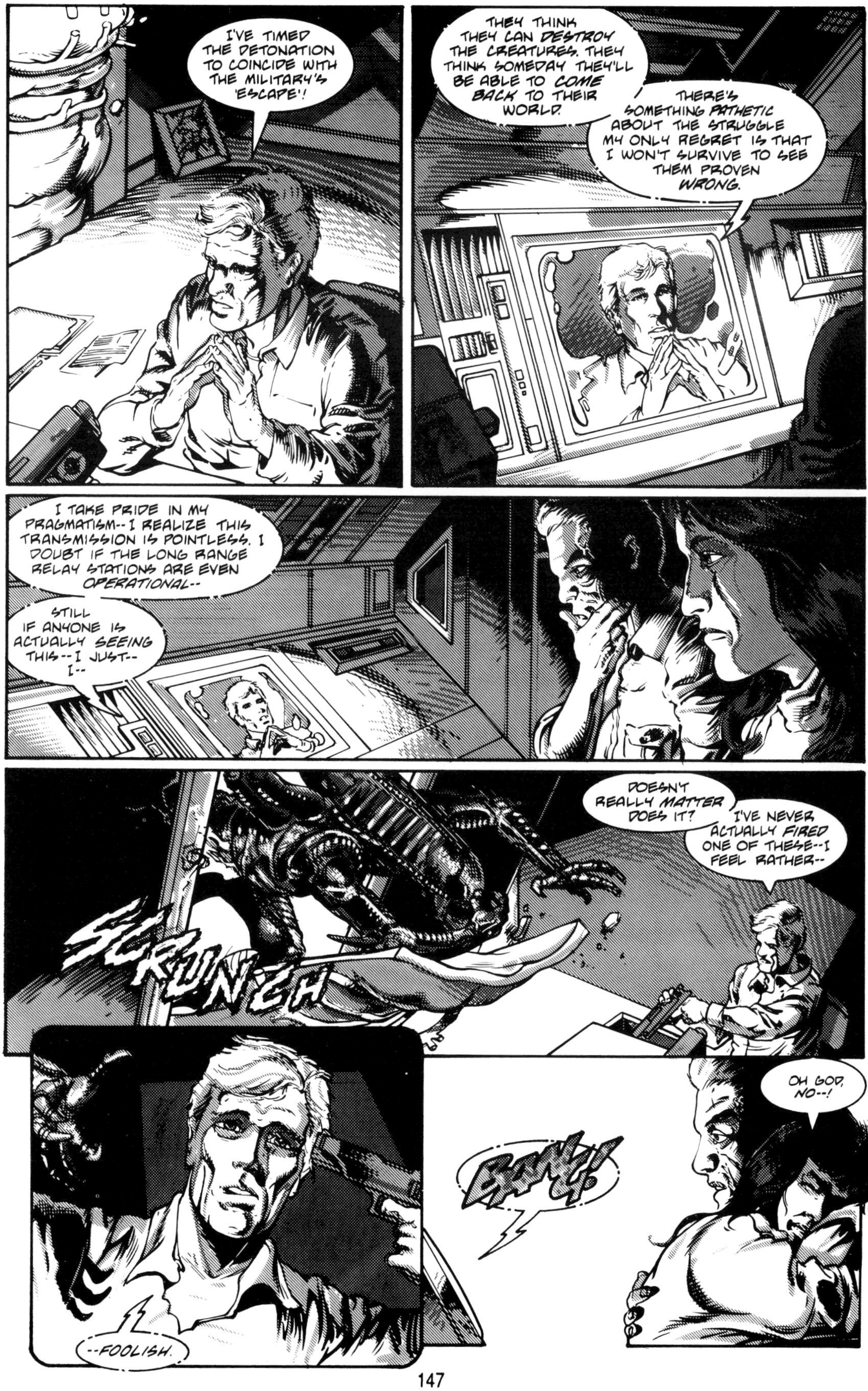

I'VE TIMED THE DETONATION TO COINCIDE WITH THE MILITARY'S 'ESCAPE'!
THEY THINK THEY CAN DESTROY THE CREATURES. THEY THINK SOMEDAY THEY'LL BE ABLE TO COME BACK TO THEIR WORLD.
THERE'S SOMETHING PATHETIC ABOUT THE STRUGGLE MY ONLY REGRET IS THAT I WON'T SURVIVE TO SEE THEM PROVEN WRONG.
I TAKE PRIDE IN MY PRAGMATISM--I REALIZE THIS TRANSMISSION IS POINTLESS. I DOUBT IF THE LONG RANGE RELAY STATIONS ARE EVEN OPERATIONAL--
STILL IF ANYONE IS ACTUALLY SEEING THIS--I JUST-- I--
SCRUNCH
DOESN'T REALLY MATTER DOES IT?
I'VE NEVER ACTUALLY FIRED ONE OF THESE--I FEEL RATHER--
--FOOLISH.
BANG!
OH GOD, NO--!

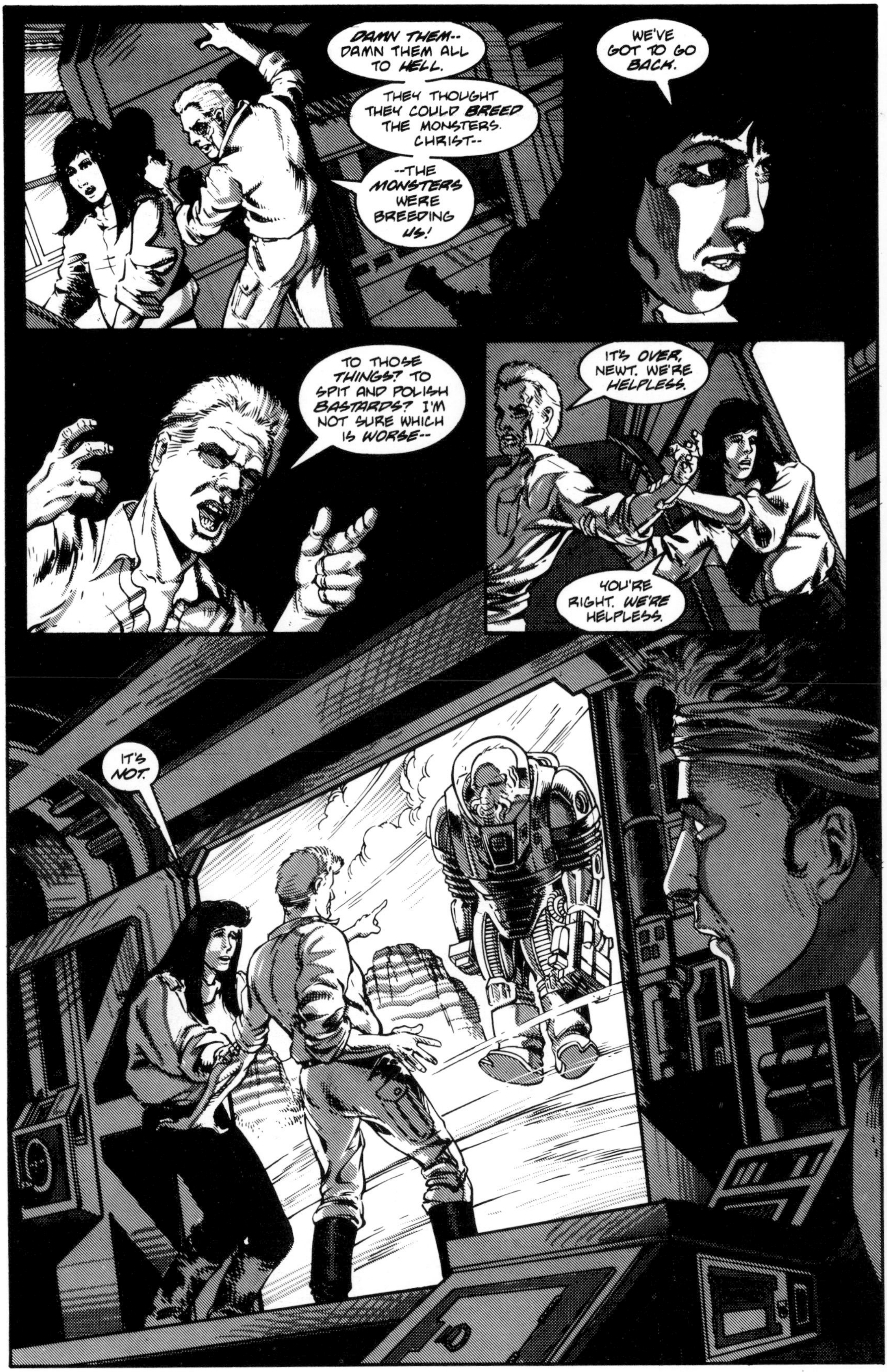
DAMN THEM-- DAMN THEM ALL TO HELL.
THEY THOUGHT THEY COULD BREED THE MONSTERS. CHRIST--
--THE MONSTERS WERE BREEDING US!
WE'VE GOT TO GO BACK.
TO THOSE THINGS? TO SPIT AND POLISH BASTARDS? I'M NOT SURE WHICH IS WORSE--
IT'S OVER, NEWT. WE'RE HELPLESS.
YOU'RE RIGHT. WE'RE HELPLESS.
IT'S NOT.

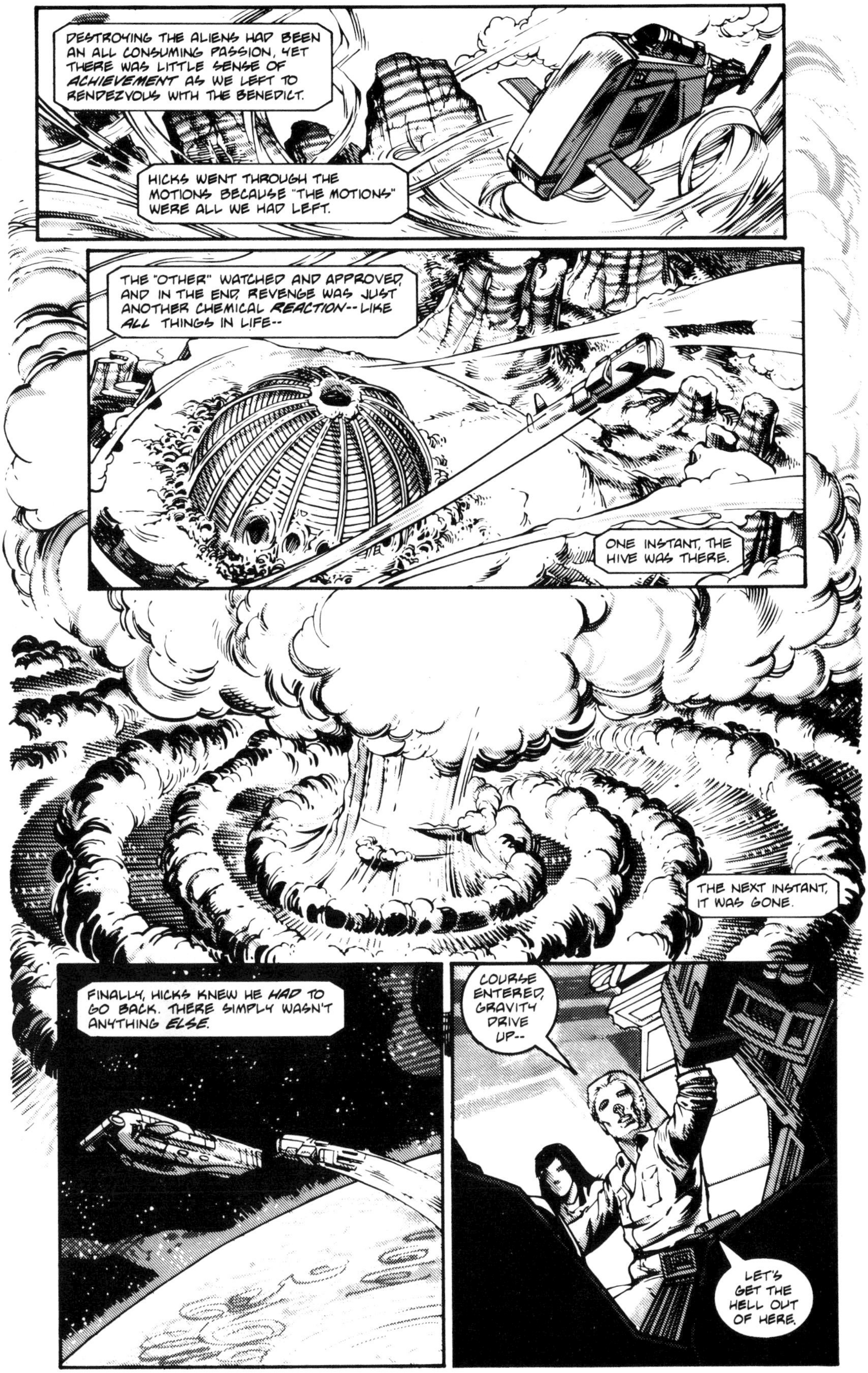
DESTROYING THE ALIENS HAD BEEN AN ALL CONSUMING PASSION, YET THERE WAS LITTLE SENSE OF *ACHIEVEMENT* AS WE LEFT TO RENDEZVOUS WITH THE BENEDICT.
HICKS WENT THROUGH THE MOTIONS BECAUSE "THE MOTIONS" WERE ALL WE HAD LEFT.
THE "OTHER" WATCHED AND APPROVED, AND IN THE END, REVENGE WAS JUST ANOTHER CHEMICAL *REACTION*--LIKE *ALL* THINGS IN LIFE--
ONE INSTANT, THE HIVE WAS THERE.
THE NEXT INSTANT, IT WAS GONE.
FINALLY, HICKS KNEW HE *HAD* TO GO BACK. THERE SIMPLY WASN'T ANYTHING *ELSE*.
COURSE ENTERED, GRAVITY DRIVE UP--
LET'S GET THE HELL OUT OF HERE.

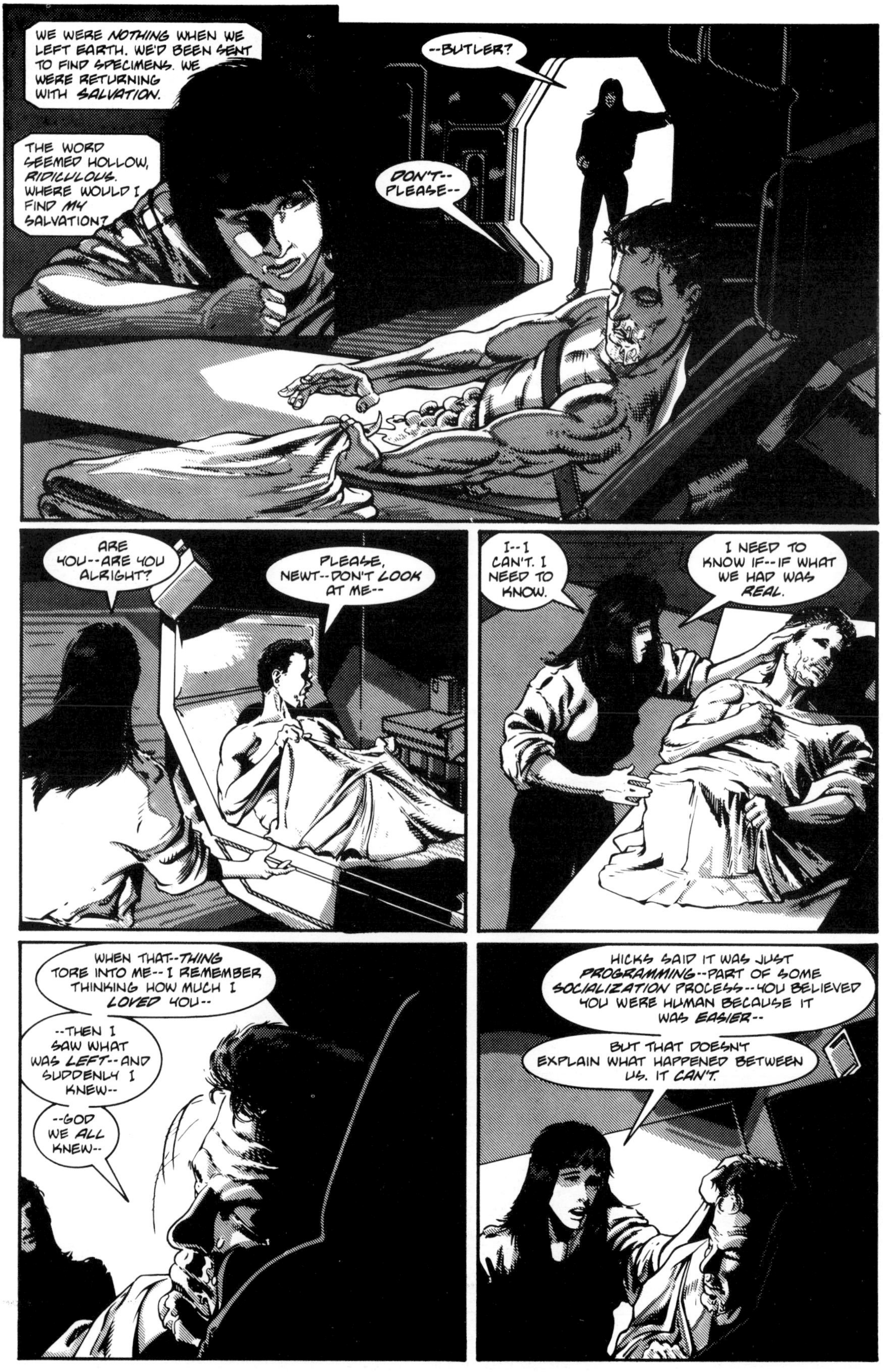
WE WERE NOTHING WHEN WE LEFT EARTH. WE'D BEEN SENT TO FIND SPECIMENS. WE WERE RETURNING WITH SALVATION.
THE WORD SEEMED HOLLOW, RIDICULOUS. WHERE WOULD I FIND MY SALVATION?
--BUTLER?
DON'T-- PLEASE--
ARE YOU--ARE YOU ALRIGHT?
PLEASE, NEWT--DON'T LOOK AT ME--
I--I CAN'T. I NEED TO KNOW.
I NEED TO KNOW IF--IF WHAT WE HAD WAS REAL.
WHEN THAT--THING TORE INTO ME--I REMEMBER THINKING HOW MUCH I LOVED YOU--
--THEN I SAW WHAT WAS LEFT--AND SUDDENLY I KNEW--
--GOD WE ALL KNEW--
HICKS SAID IT WAS JUST PROGRAMMING--PART OF SOME SOCIALIZATION PROCESS--YOU BELIEVED YOU WERE HUMAN BECAUSE IT WAS EASIER--
BUT THAT DOESN'T EXPLAIN WHAT HAPPENED BETWEEN US. IT CAN'T.

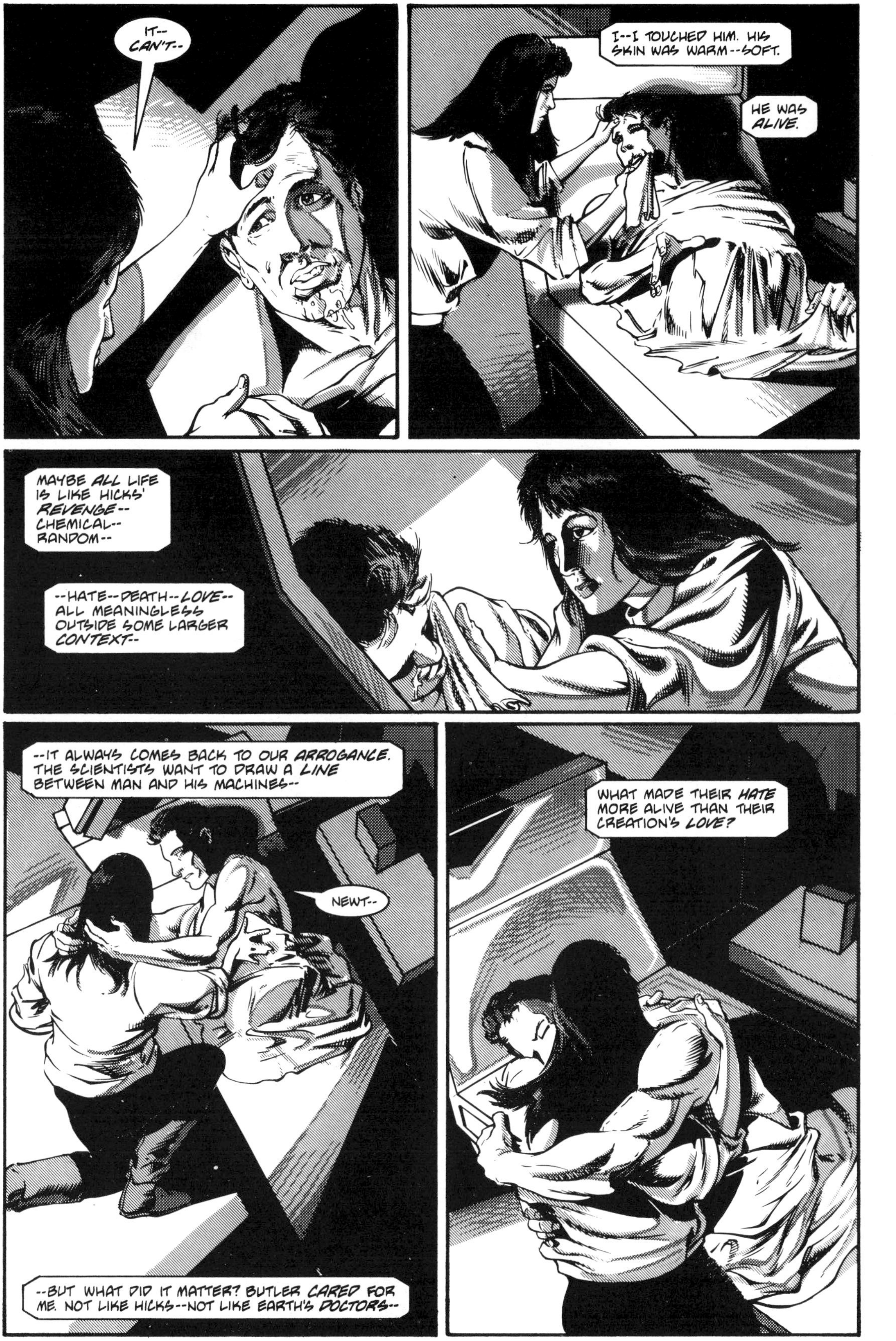

IT--
CAN'T--
I--I TOUCHED HIM. HIS SKIN WAS WARM--SOFT.
HE WAS ALIVE.
MAYBE ALL LIFE IS LIKE HICKS' REVENGE--CHEMICAL--RANDOM--
--HATE--DEATH--LOVE--ALL MEANINGLESS OUTSIDE SOME LARGER CONTEXT--
--IT ALWAYS COMES BACK TO OUR ARROGANCE. THE SCIENTISTS WANT TO DRAW A LINE BETWEEN MAN AND HIS MACHINES--
NEWT--
--BUT WHAT DID IT MATTER? BUTLER CARED FOR ME. NOT LIKE HICKS--NOT LIKE EARTH'S DOCTORS--
WHAT MADE THEIR HATE MORE ALIVE THAN THEIR CREATION'S LOVE?

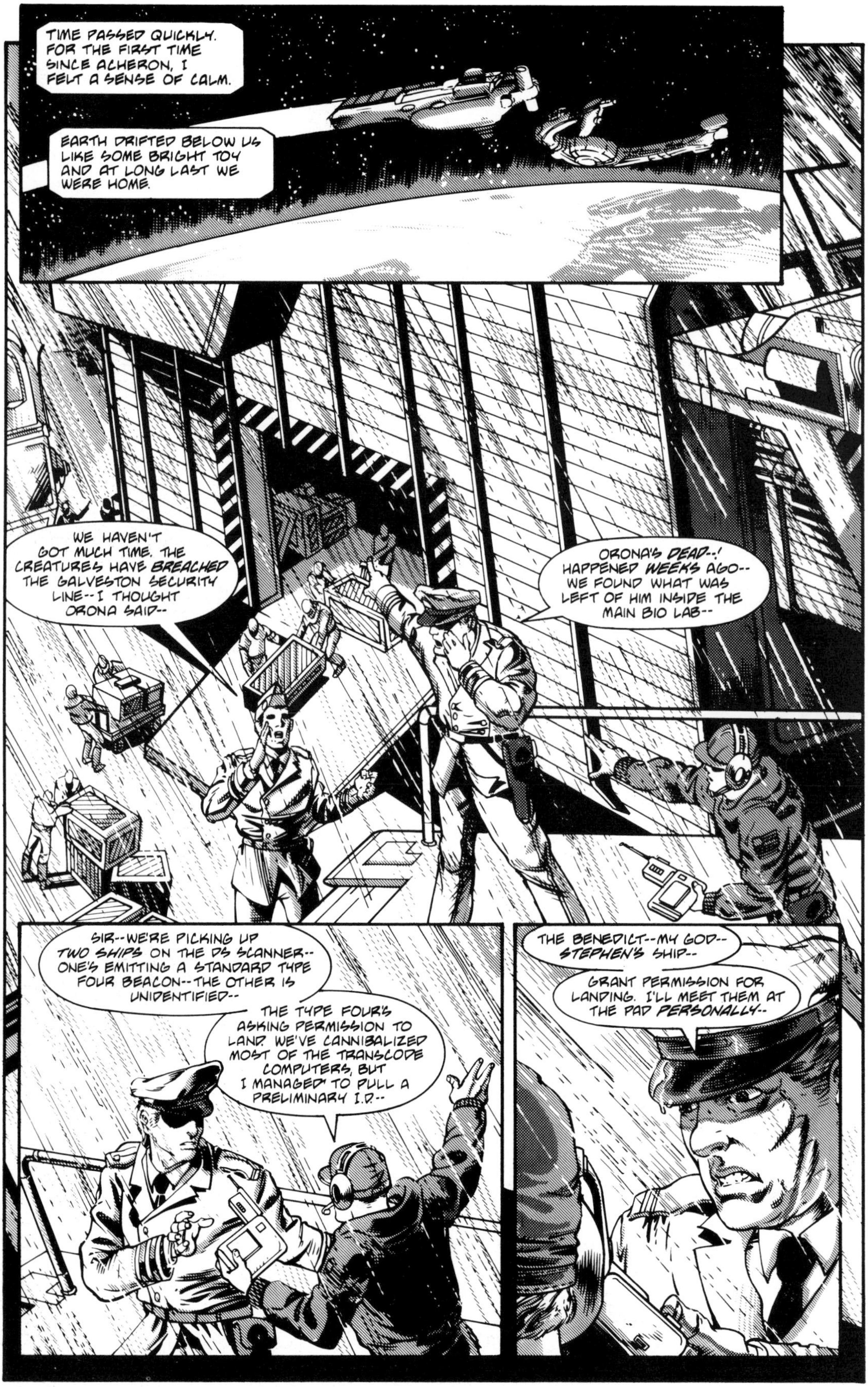
TIME PASSED QUICKLY. FOR THE FIRST TIME SINCE ACHERON, I FELT A SENSE OF CALM.
EARTH DRIFTED BELOW US LIKE SOME BRIGHT TOY AND AT LONG LAST WE WERE HOME.
WE HAVEN'T GOT MUCH TIME. THE CREATURES HAVE *BREACHED* THE GALVESTON SECURITY LINE--I THOUGHT ORONA SAID--
ORONA'S *DEAD*--! HAPPENED *WEEKS* AGO--WE FOUND WHAT WAS LEFT OF HIM INSIDE THE MAIN BIO LAB--
SIR--WE'RE PICKING UP *TWO SHIPS* ON THE DS SCANNER--ONE'S EMITTING A STANDARD TYPE FOUR BEACON--THE OTHER IS UNIDENTIFIED--
THE TYPE FOUR'S ASKING PERMISSION TO LAND. WE'VE CANNIBALIZED MOST OF THE TRANSCODE COMPUTERS, BUT I MANAGED TO PULL A PRELIMINARY I.D.--
THE BENEDICT--MY GOD--*STEPHEN'S* SHIP--
GRANT PERMISSION FOR LANDING. I'LL MEET THEM AT THE PAD *PERSONALLY*--

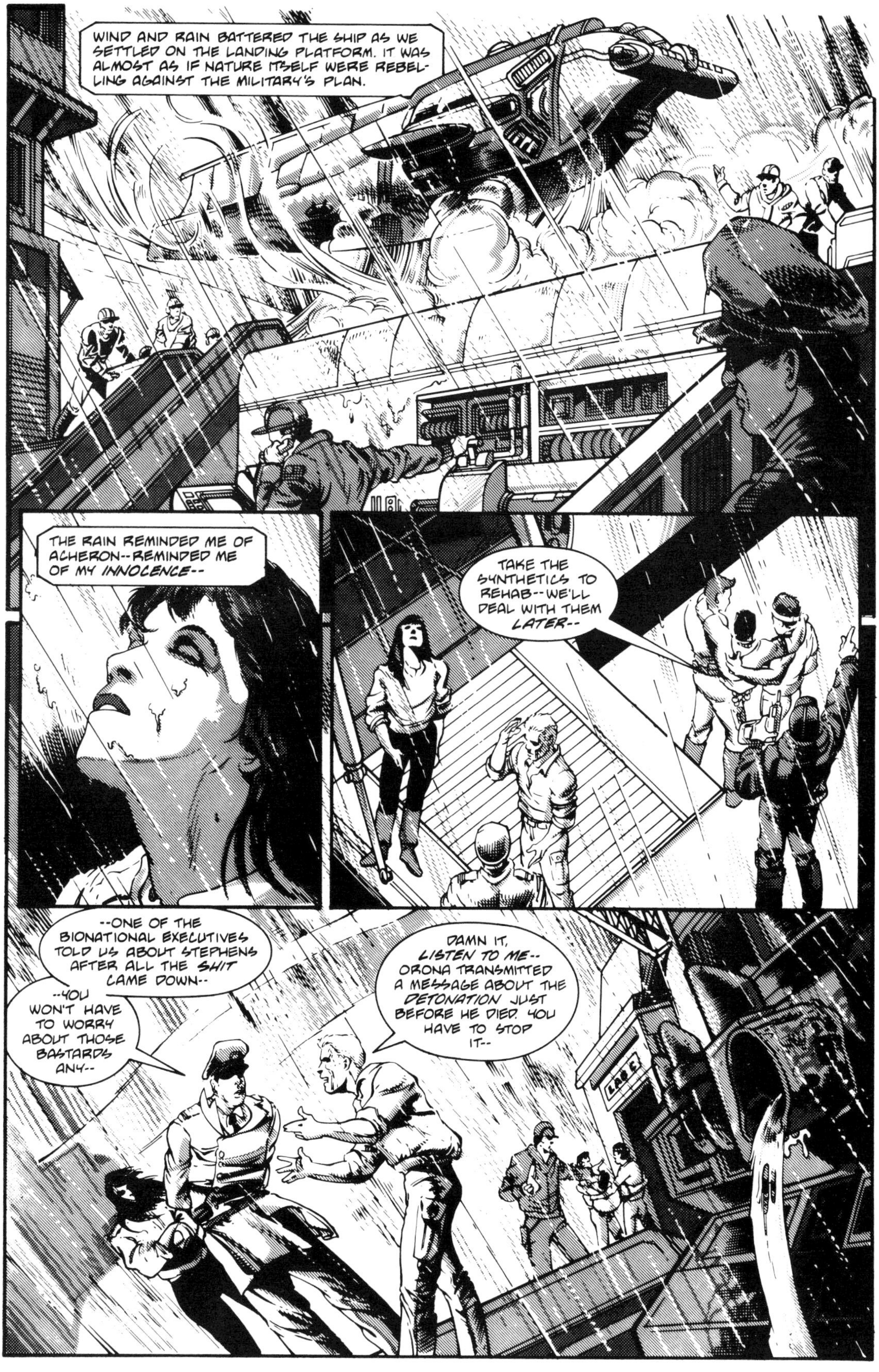

WIND AND RAIN BATTERED THE SHIP AS WE SETTLED ON THE LANDING PLATFORM. IT WAS ALMOST AS IF NATURE ITSELF WERE REBELLING AGAINST THE MILITARY'S PLAN.
THE RAIN REMINDED ME OF ACHERON--REMINDED ME OF MY *INNOCENCE*--
TAKE THE SYNTHETICS TO REHAB--WE'LL DEAL WITH THEM *LATER*--
--ONE OF THE BIONATIONAL EXECUTIVES TOLD US ABOUT STEPHENS AFTER ALL THE *SHIT* CAME DOWN--
--YOU WON'T HAVE TO WORRY ABOUT THOSE BASTARDS ANY--
DAMN IT, *LISTEN TO ME*--ORONA TRANSMITTED A MESSAGE ABOUT THE *DETONATION* JUST BEFORE HE DIED. YOU HAVE TO STOP IT--

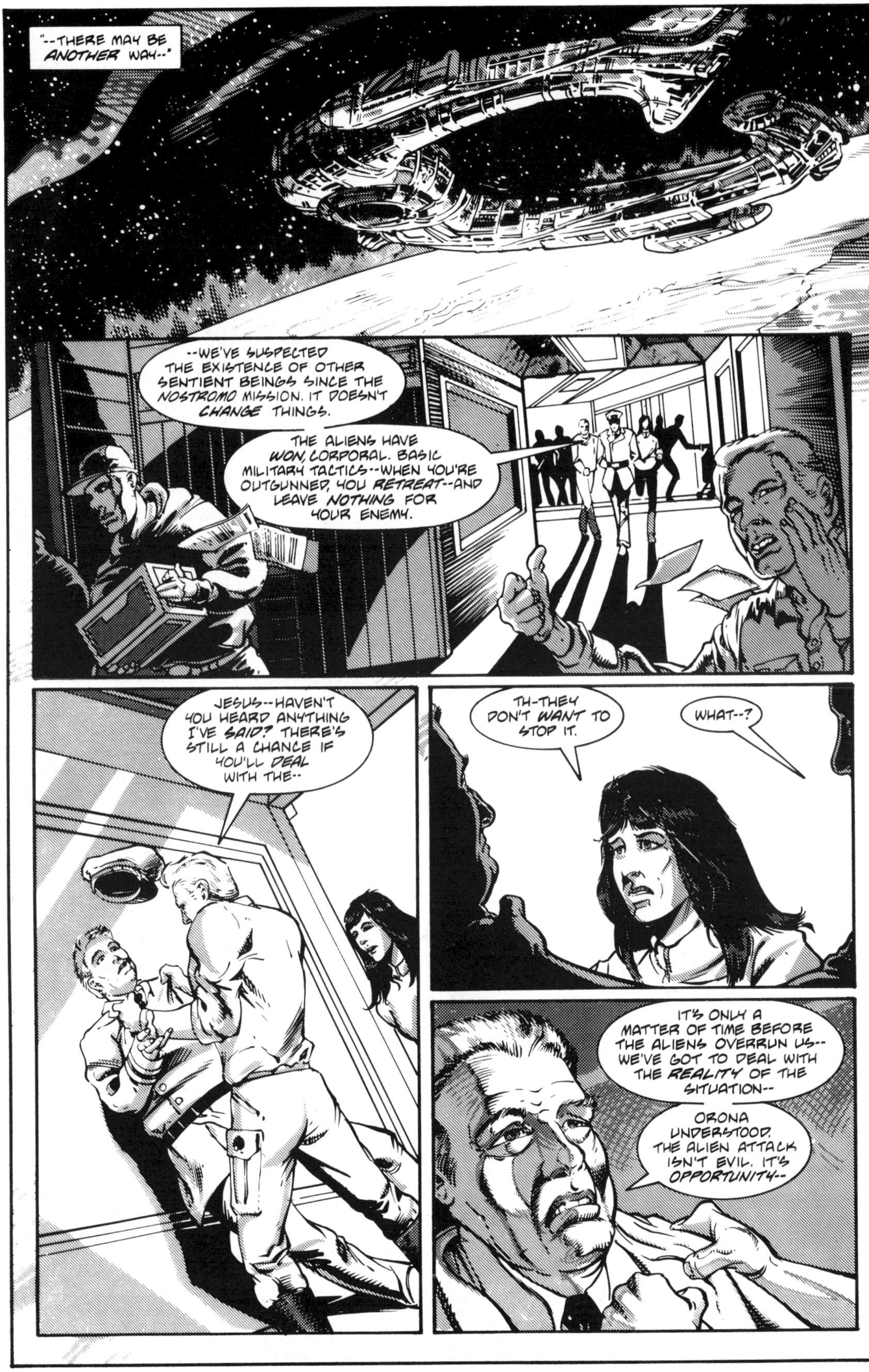
"--THERE MAY BE ANOTHER WAY--"
--WE'VE SUSPECTED THE EXISTENCE OF OTHER SENTIENT BEINGS SINCE THE NOSTROMO MISSION. IT DOESN'T CHANGE THINGS.
THE ALIENS HAVE WON, CORPORAL. BASIC MILITARY TACTICS--WHEN YOU'RE OUTGUNNED, YOU RETREAT--AND LEAVE NOTHING FOR YOUR ENEMY.
JESUS--HAVEN'T YOU HEARD ANYTHING I'VE SAID? THERE'S STILL A CHANCE IF YOU'LL DEAL WITH THE--
TH-THEY DON'T WANT TO STOP IT.
WHAT--?
IT'S ONLY A MATTER OF TIME BEFORE THE ALIENS OVERRUN US--WE'VE GOT TO DEAL WITH THE REALITY OF THE SITUATION--
ORONA UNDERSTOOD. THE ALIEN ATTACK ISN'T EVIL. IT'S OPPORTUNITY--

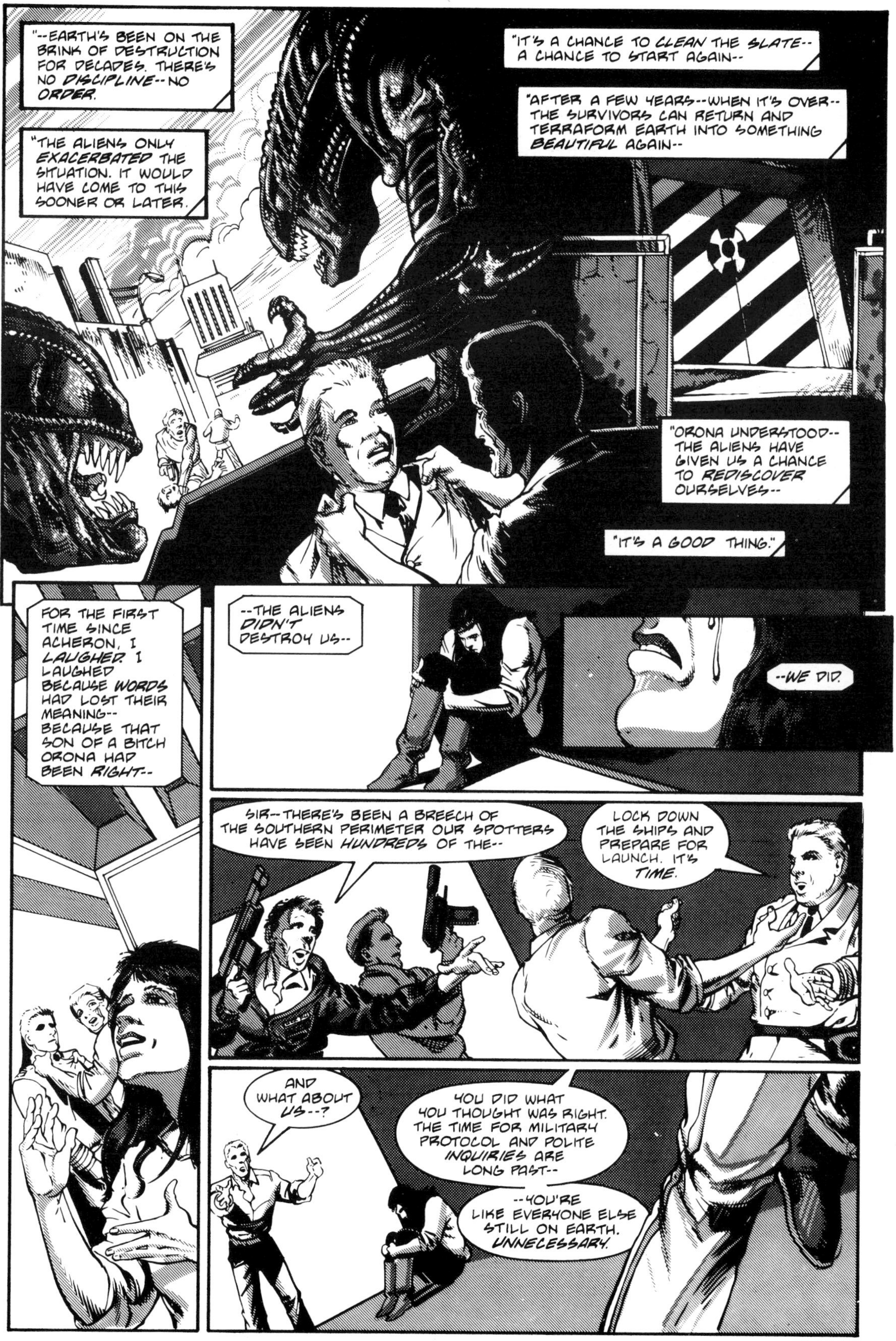
"--EARTH'S BEEN ON THE BRINK OF DESTRUCTION FOR DECADES. THERE'S NO DISCIPLINE--NO ORDER.
"THE ALIENS ONLY EXACERBATED THE SITUATION. IT WOULD HAVE COME TO THIS SOONER OR LATER.
"IT'S A CHANCE TO CLEAN THE SLATE--A CHANCE TO START AGAIN--
"AFTER A FEW YEARS--WHEN IT'S OVER--THE SURVIVORS CAN RETURN AND TERRAFORM EARTH INTO SOMETHING BEAUTIFUL AGAIN--
"ORONA UNDERSTOOD--THE ALIENS HAVE GIVEN US A CHANCE TO REDISCOVER OURSELVES--
"IT'S A GOOD THING."
FOR THE FIRST TIME SINCE ACHERON, I LAUGHED. I LAUGHED BECAUSE WORDS HAD LOST THEIR MEANING--BECAUSE THAT SON OF A BITCH ORONA HAD BEEN RIGHT--
--THE ALIENS DIDN'T DESTROY US--
--WE DID.
SIR--THERE'S BEEN A BREECH OF THE SOUTHERN PERIMETER OUR SPOTTERS HAVE SEEN HUNDREDS OF THE--
LOCK DOWN THE SHIPS AND PREPARE FOR LAUNCH. IT'S TIME.
AND WHAT ABOUT US--?
YOU DID WHAT YOU THOUGHT WAS RIGHT. THE TIME FOR MILITARY PROTOCOL AND POLITE INQUIRIES ARE LONG PAST--
--YOU'RE LIKE EVERYONE ELSE STILL ON EARTH. UNNECESSARY.

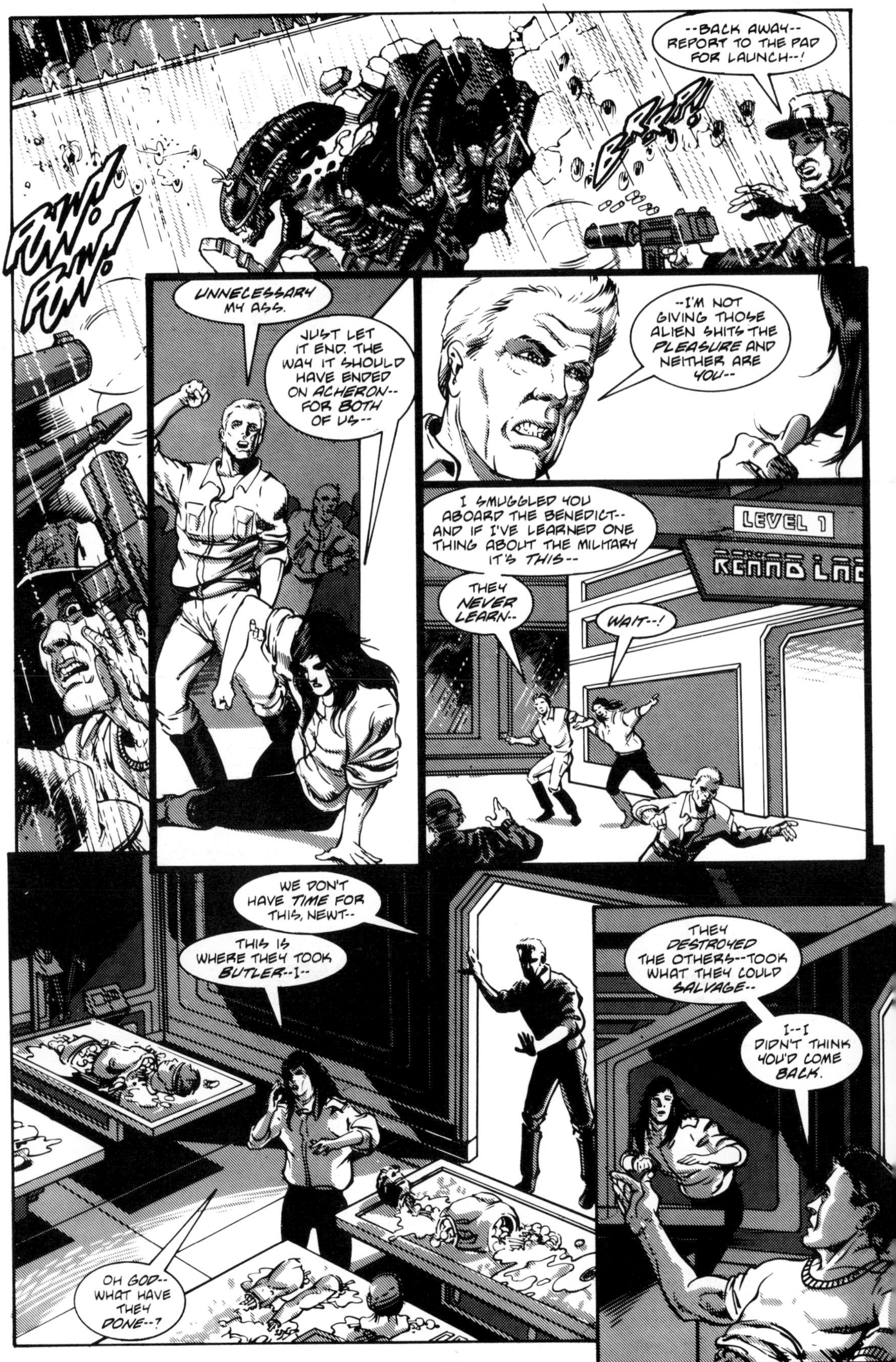
--BACK AWAY-- REPORT TO THE PAD FOR LAUNCH--!
BRRAP!
FUMP! FUMP! FUMP!
UNNECESSARY MY ASS.
JUST LET IT END. THE WAY IT SHOULD HAVE ENDED ON ACHERON-- FOR BOTH OF US--
--I'M NOT GIVING THOSE ALIEN SHITS THE PLEASURE AND NEITHER ARE YOU--
I SMUGGLED YOU ABOARD THE BENEDICT-- AND IF I'VE LEARNED ONE THING ABOUT THE MILITARY IT'S THIS--
LEVEL 1
THEY NEVER LEARN--
WAIT--!
WE DON'T HAVE TIME FOR THIS, NEWT--
THIS IS WHERE THEY TOOK BUTLER--I--
OH GOD-- WHAT HAVE THEY DONE--?
THEY DESTROYED THE OTHERS--TOOK WHAT THEY COULD SALVAGE--
I--I DIDN'T THINK YOU'D COME BACK.

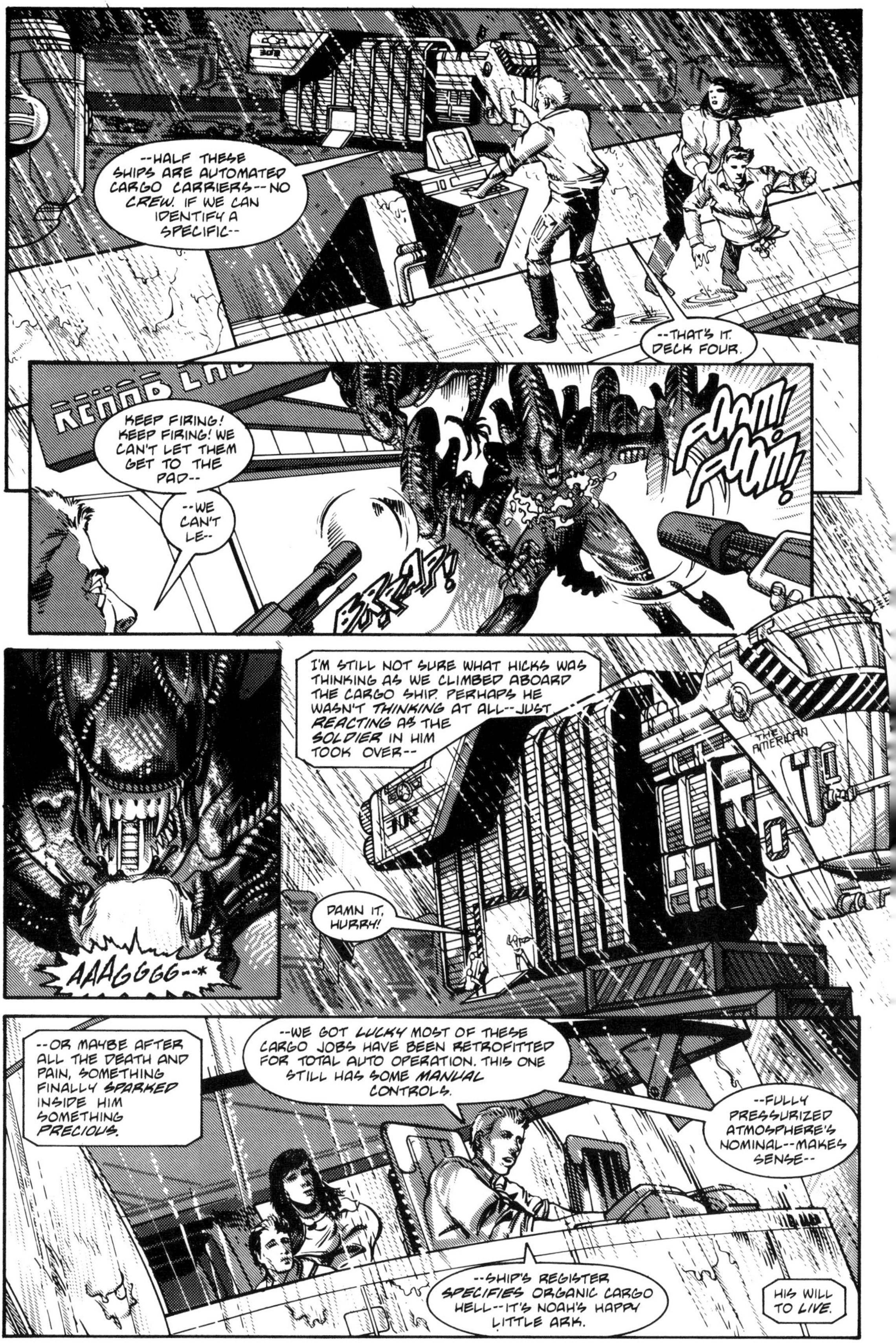
--HALF THESE SHIPS ARE AUTOMATED CARGO CARRIERS--NO CREW. IF WE CAN IDENTIFY A SPECIFIC--
--THAT'S IT. DECK FOUR.
KEEP FIRING! KEEP FIRING! WE CAN'T LET THEM GET TO THE PAD--
--WE CAN'T LE--
FOOM! FOOM!
BRRAP!
AAAGGGG--*
I'M STILL NOT SURE WHAT HICKS WAS THINKING AS WE CLIMBED ABOARD THE CARGO SHIP. PERHAPS HE WASN'T THINKING AT ALL--JUST REACTING AS THE SOLDIER IN HIM TOOK OVER--
THE AMERICAN
DAMN IT, HURRY!
--OR MAYBE AFTER ALL THE DEATH AND PAIN, SOMETHING FINALLY SPARKED INSIDE HIM SOMETHING PRECIOUS.
--WE GOT LUCKY MOST OF THESE CARGO JOBS HAVE BEEN RETROFITTED FOR TOTAL AUTO OPERATION. THIS ONE STILL HAS SOME MANUAL CONTROLS.
--FULLY PRESSURIZED ATMOSPHERE'S NOMINAL--MAKES SENSE--
--SHIP'S REGISTER SPECIFIES ORGANIC CARGO HELL--IT'S NOAH'S HAPPY LITTLE ARK.
HIS WILL TO LIVE.

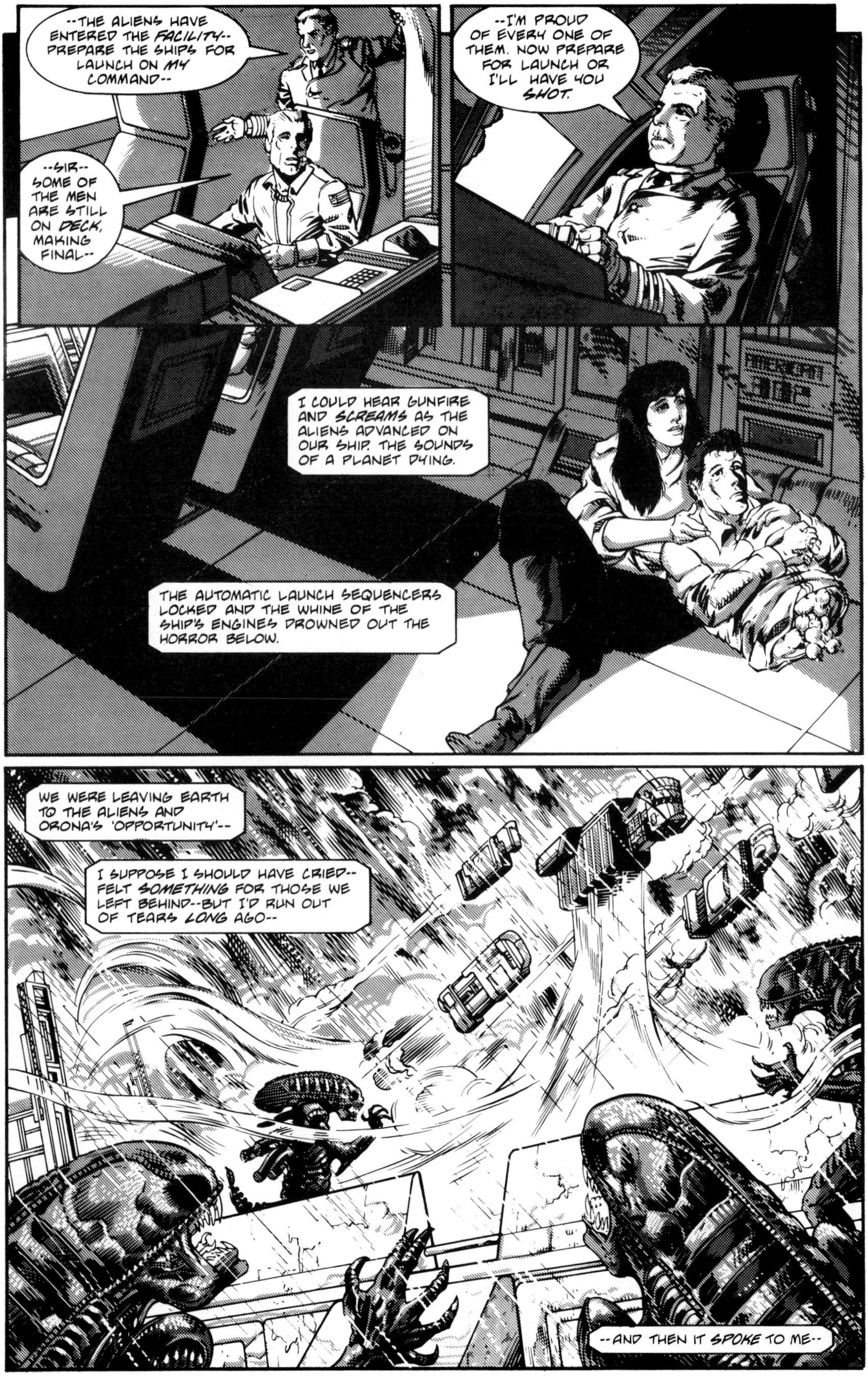
--THE ALIENS HAVE ENTERED THE FACILITY-- PREPARE THE SHIPS FOR LAUNCH ON MY COMMAND--
--SIR-- SOME OF THE MEN ARE STILL ON DECK, MAKING FINAL--
--I'M PROUD OF EVERY ONE OF THEM. NOW PREPARE FOR LAUNCH OR I'LL HAVE YOU SHOT.
I COULD HEAR GUNFIRE AND SCREAMS AS THE ALIENS ADVANCED ON OUR SHIP. THE SOUNDS OF A PLANET DYING.
THE AUTOMATIC LAUNCH SEQUENCERS LOCKED AND THE WHINE OF THE SHIP'S ENGINES DROWNED OUT THE HORROR BELOW.
WE WERE LEAVING EARTH TO THE ALIENS AND ORONA'S 'OPPORTUNITY'--
I SUPPOSE I SHOULD HAVE CRIED--FELT SOMETHING FOR THOSE WE LEFT BEHIND--BUT I'D RUN OUT OF TEARS LONG AGO--
--AND THEN IT SPOKE TO ME--

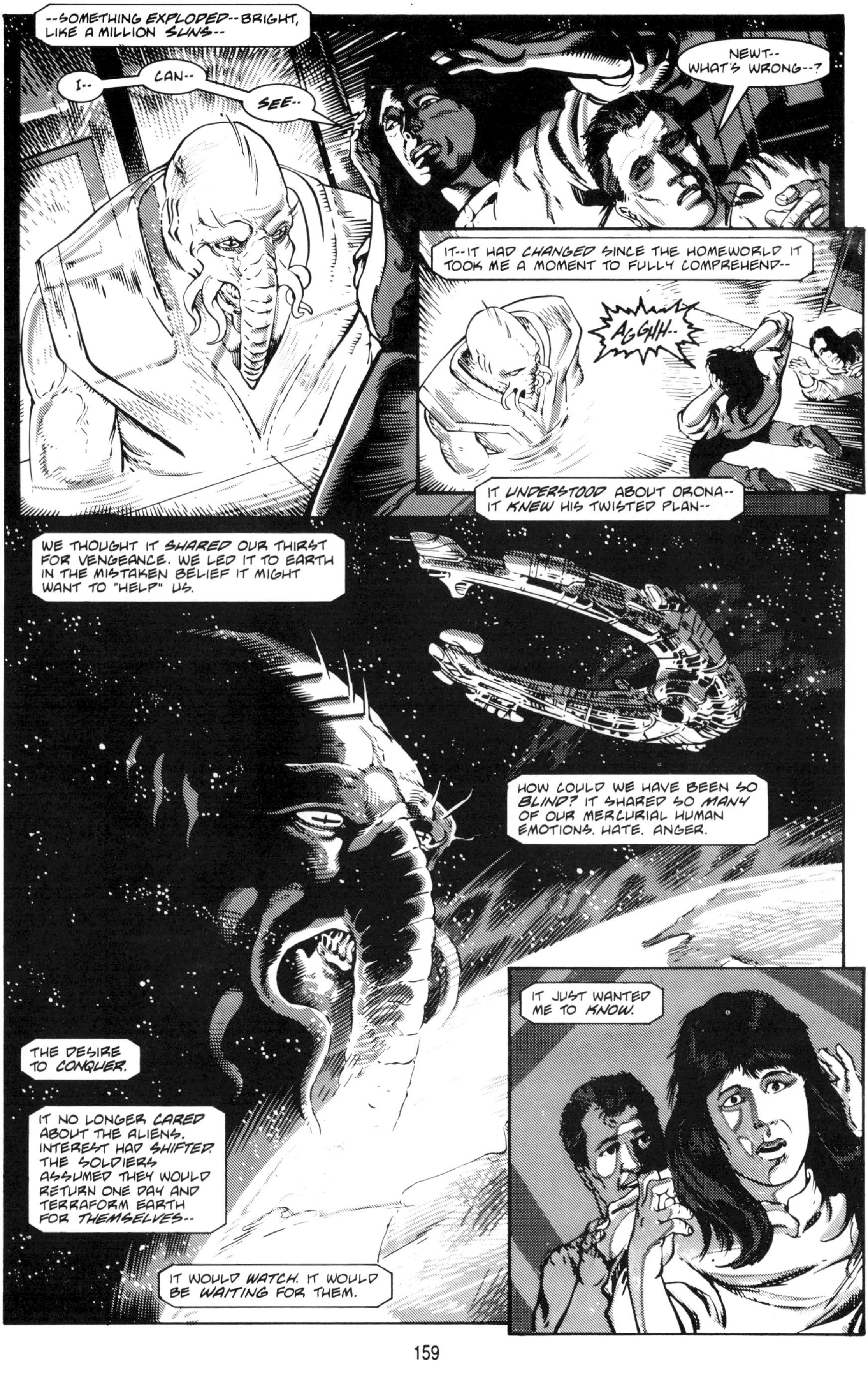

--SOMETHING EXPLODED--BRIGHT, LIKE A MILLION SUNS--
I--
CAN--
SEE--
NEWT-- WHAT'S WRONG--?
IT--IT HAD CHANGED SINCE THE HOMEWORLD IT TOOK ME A MOMENT TO FULLY COMPREHEND--
AGGHH--
IT UNDERSTOOD ABOUT ORONA-- IT KNEW HIS TWISTED PLAN--
WE THOUGHT IT SHARED OUR THIRST FOR VENGEANCE. WE LED IT TO EARTH IN THE MISTAKEN BELIEF IT MIGHT WANT TO "HELP" US.
HOW COULD WE HAVE BEEN SO BLIND? IT SHARED SO MANY OF OUR MERCURIAL HUMAN EMOTIONS. HATE. ANGER.
THE DESIRE TO CONQUER.
IT NO LONGER CARED ABOUT THE ALIENS. INTEREST HAD SHIFTED. THE SOLDIERS ASSUMED THEY WOULD RETURN ONE DAY AND TERRAFORM EARTH FOR THEMSELVES--
IT WOULD WATCH. IT WOULD BE WAITING FOR THEM.
IT JUST WANTED ME TO KNOW.

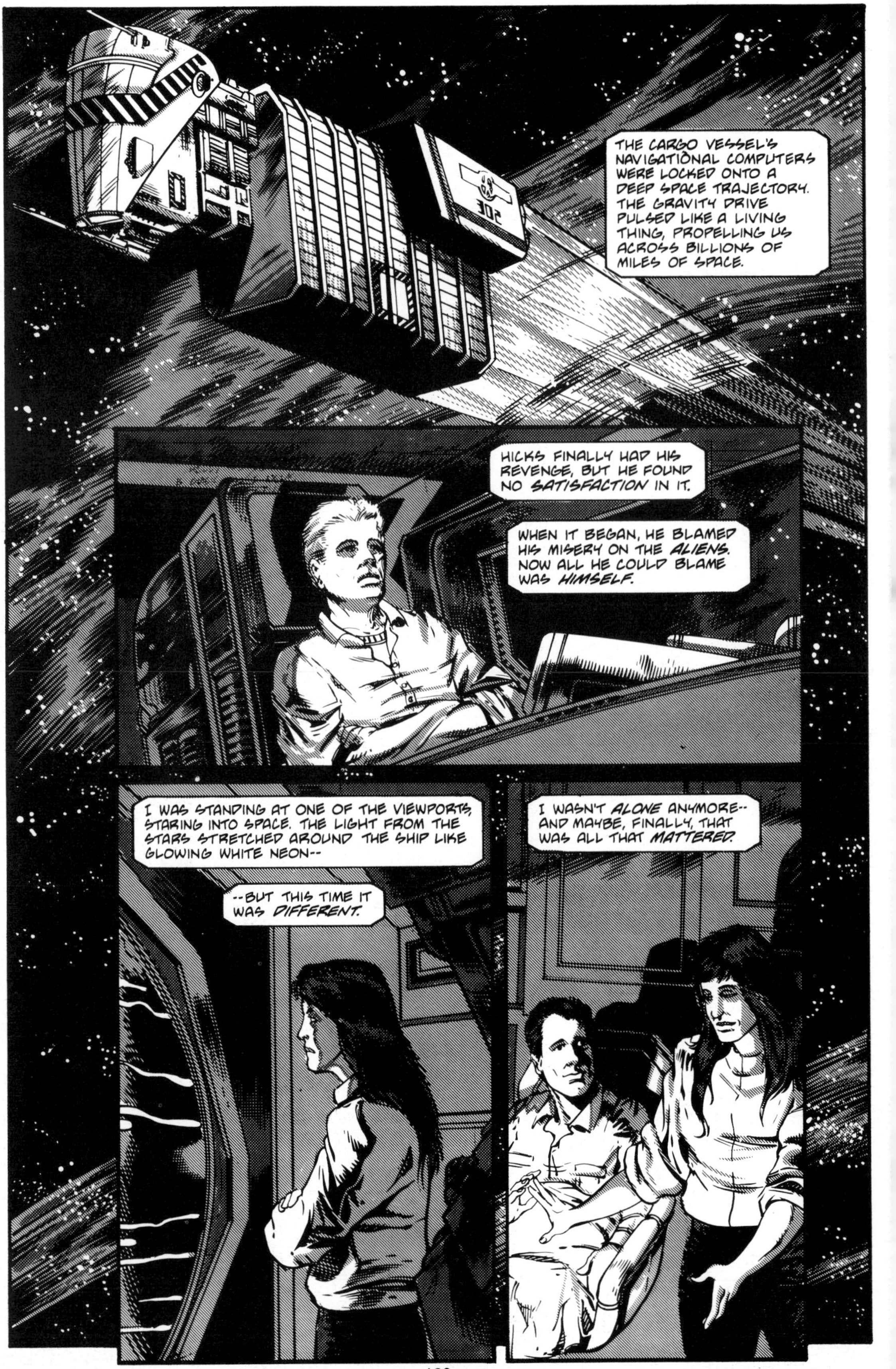
THE CARGO VESSEL'S NAVIGATIONAL COMPUTERS WERE LOCKED ONTO A DEEP SPACE TRAJECTORY. THE GRAVITY DRIVE PULSED LIKE A LIVING THING, PROPELLING US ACROSS BILLIONS OF MILES OF SPACE.
HICKS FINALLY HAD HIS REVENGE, BUT HE FOUND NO SATISFACTION IN IT.
WHEN IT BEGAN, HE BLAMED HIS MISERY ON THE ALIENS. NOW ALL HE COULD BLAME WAS HIMSELF.
I WAS STANDING AT ONE OF THE VIEWPORTS, STARING INTO SPACE. THE LIGHT FROM THE STARS STRETCHED AROUND THE SHIP LIKE GLOWING WHITE NEON--
--BUT THIS TIME IT WAS DIFFERENT.
I WASN'T ALONE ANYMORE-- AND MAYBE, FINALLY, THAT WAS ALL THAT MATTERED.

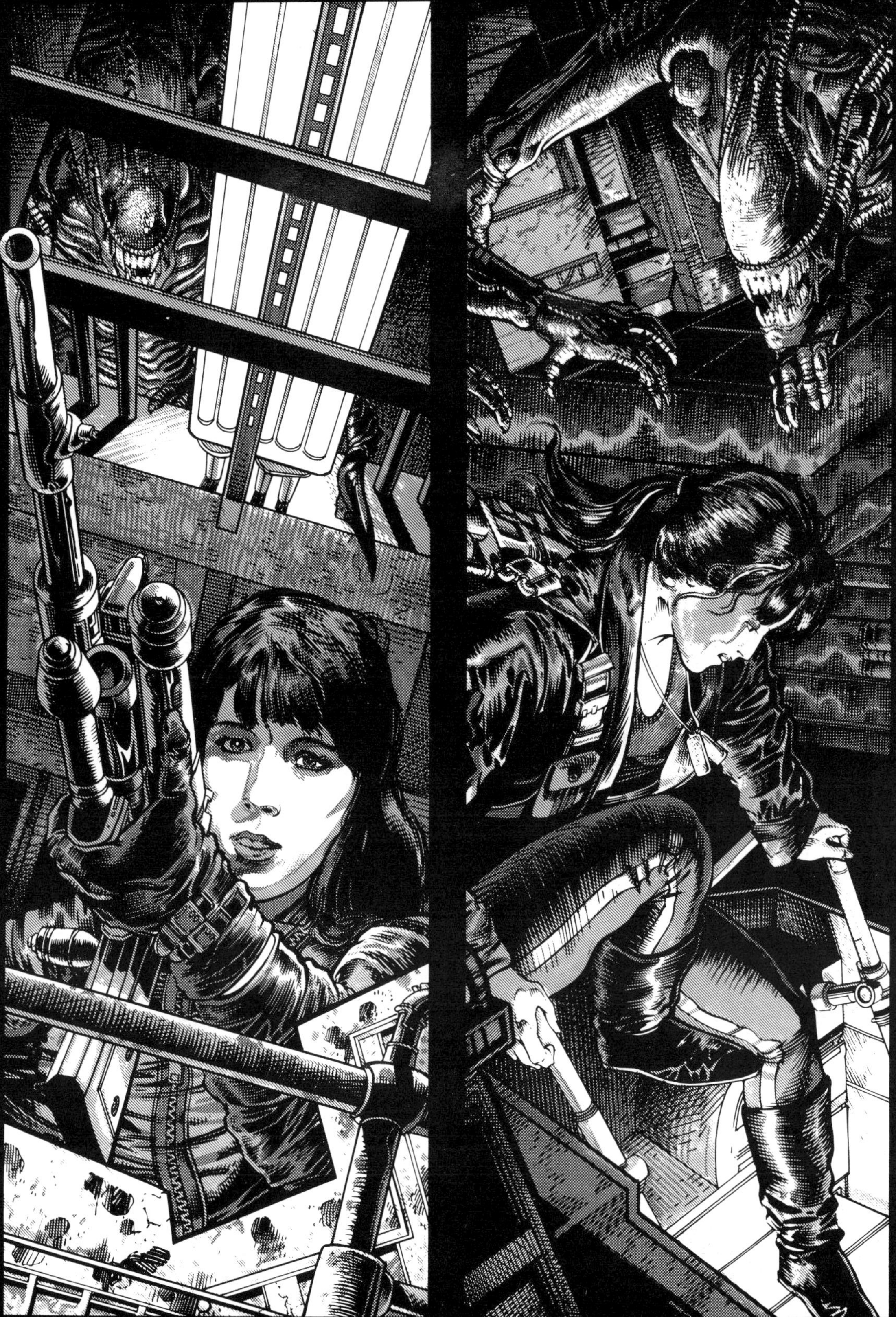

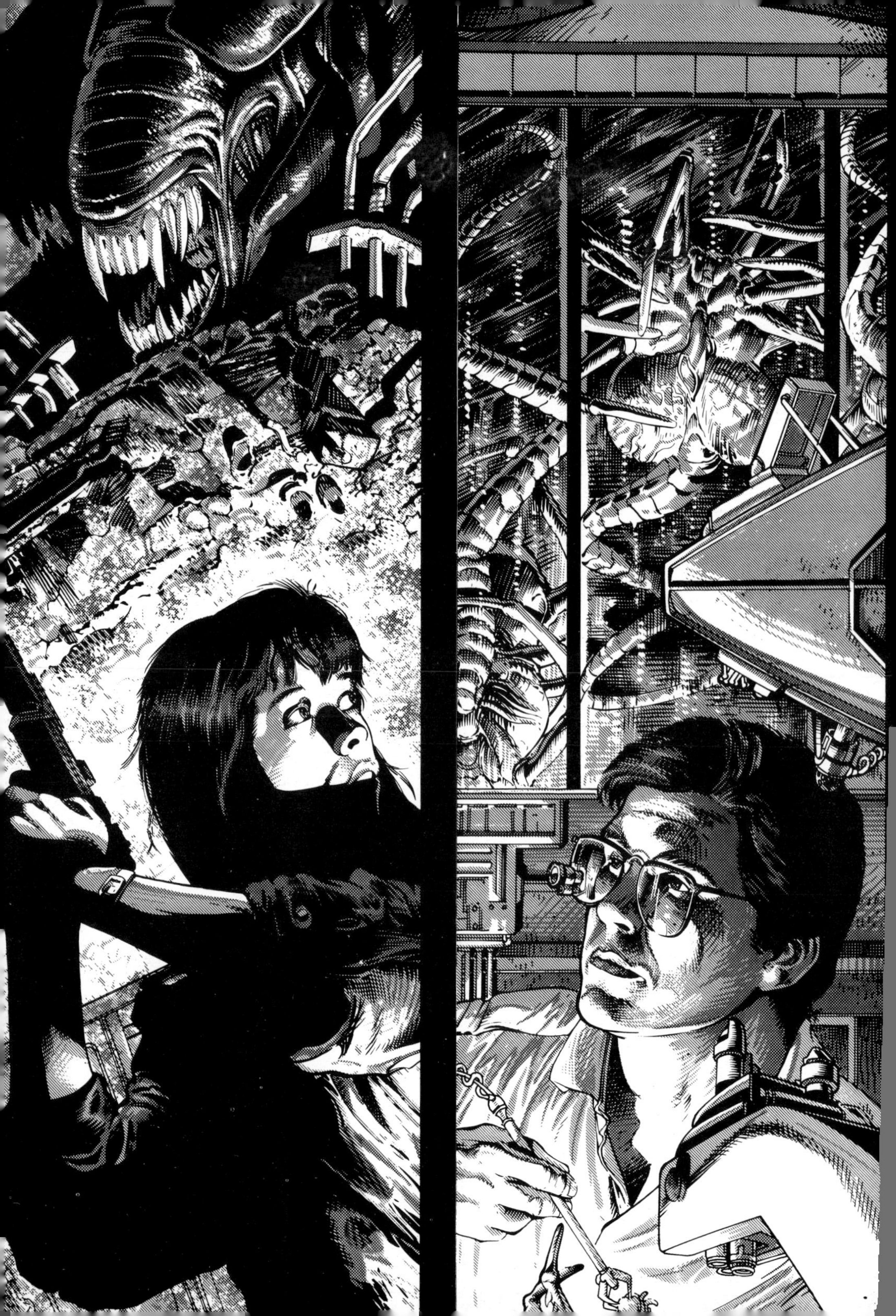

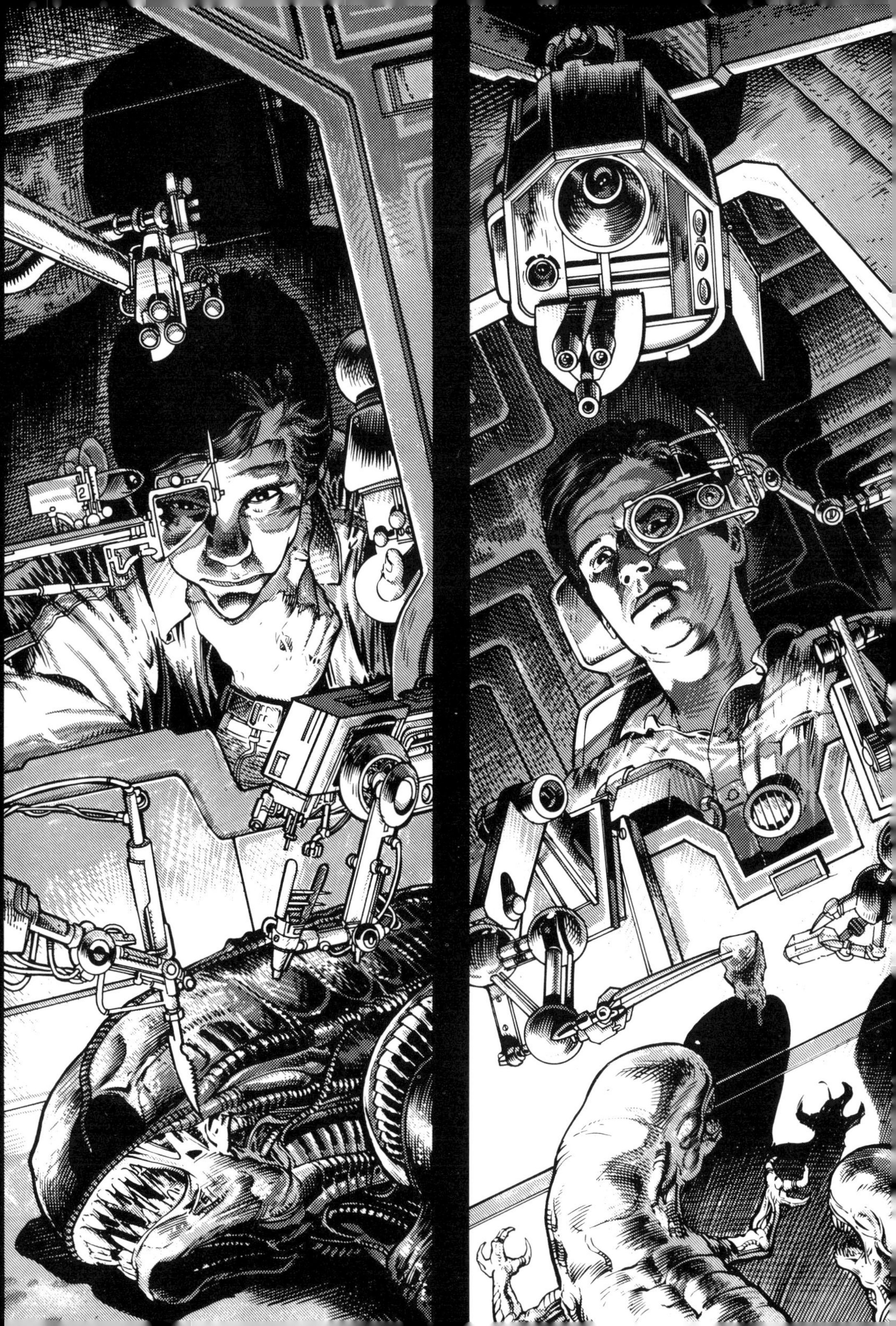

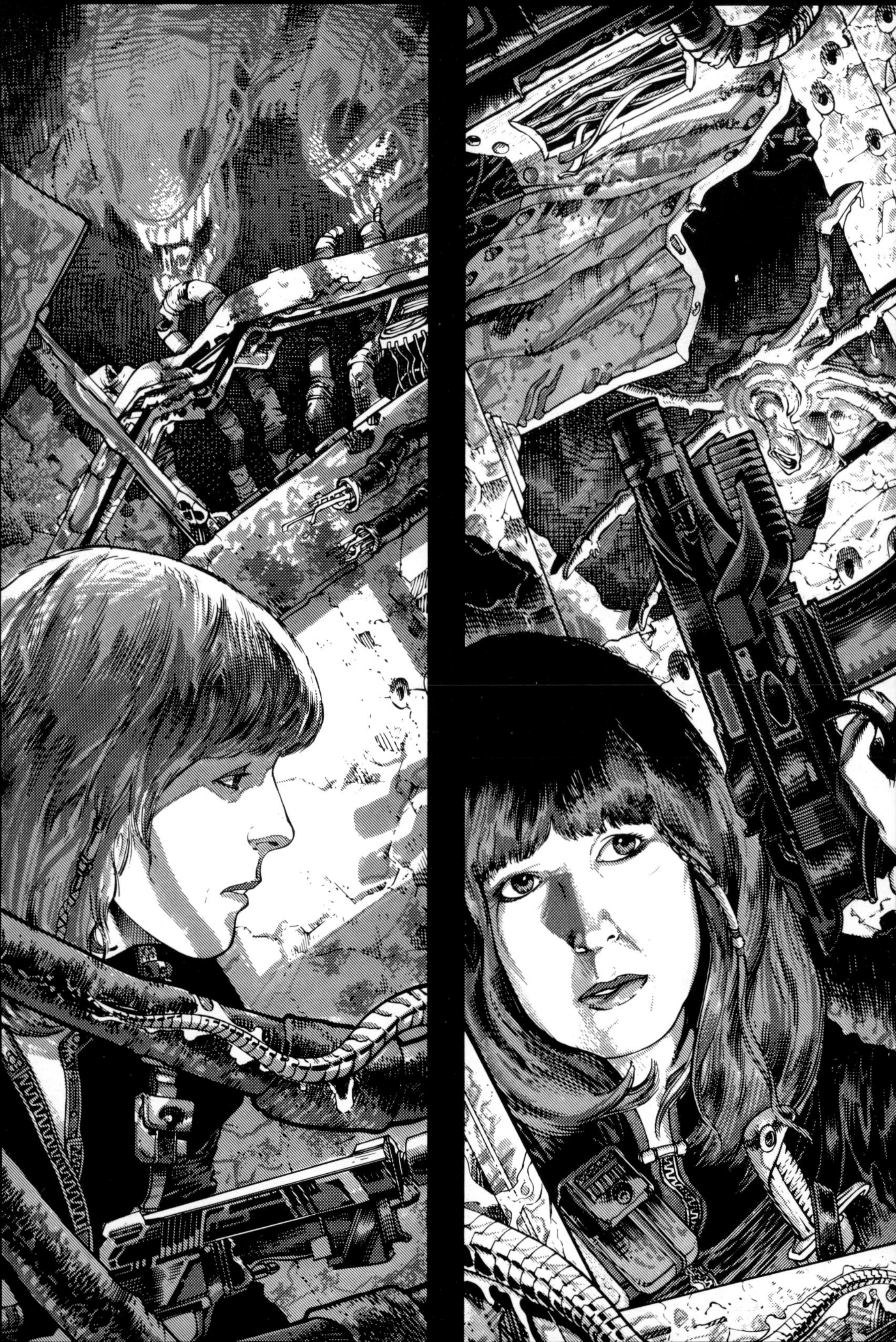

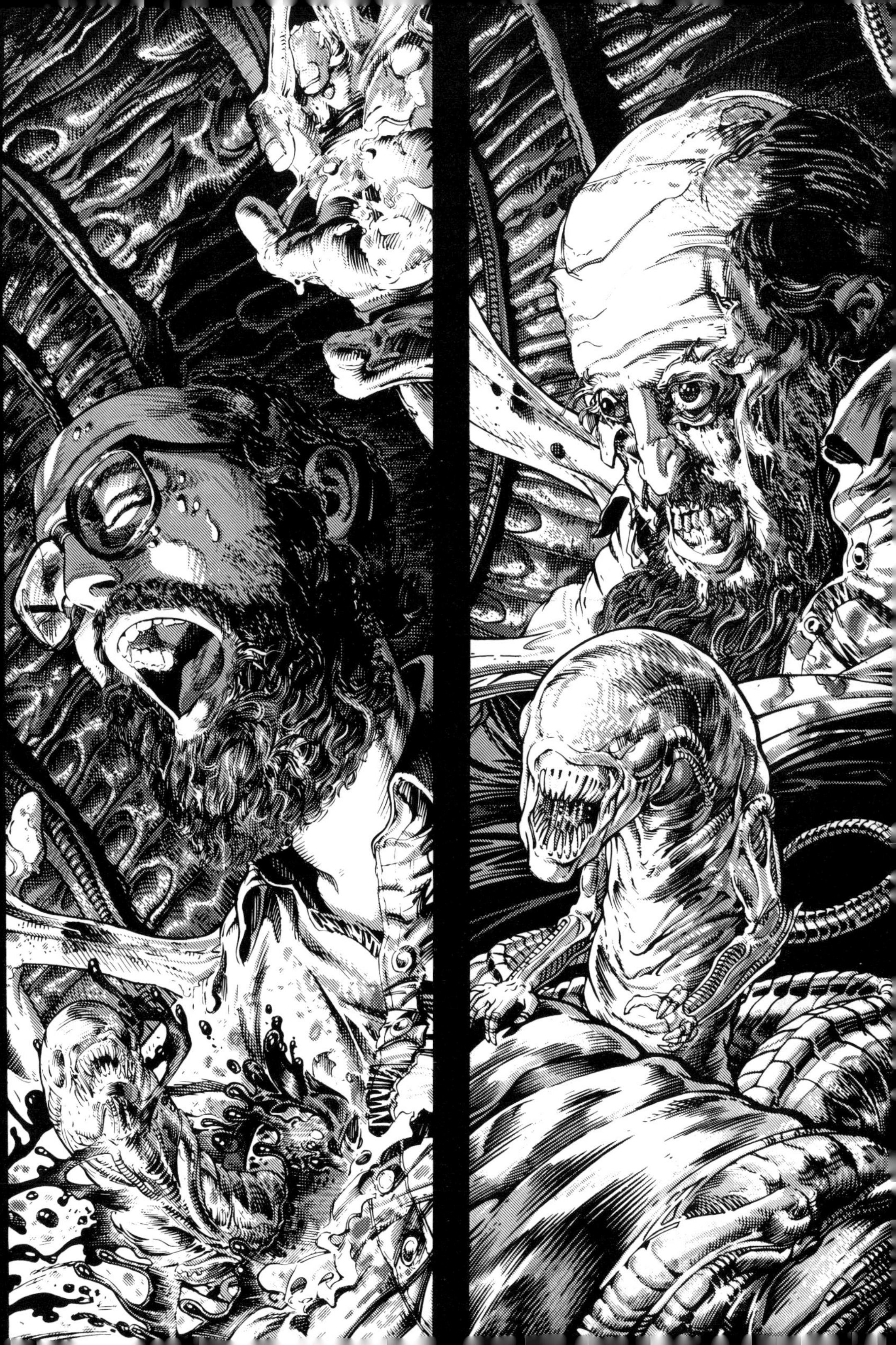

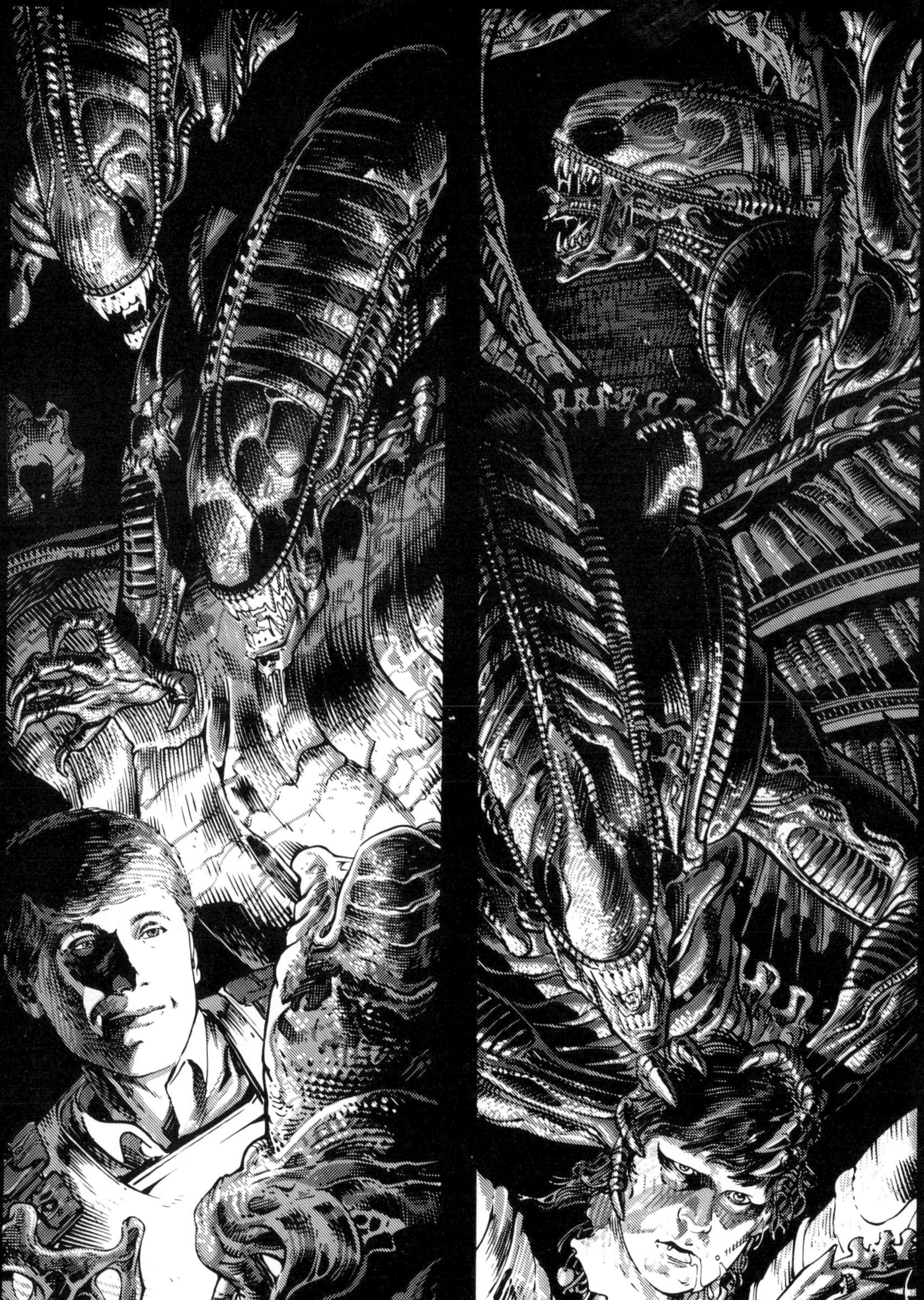

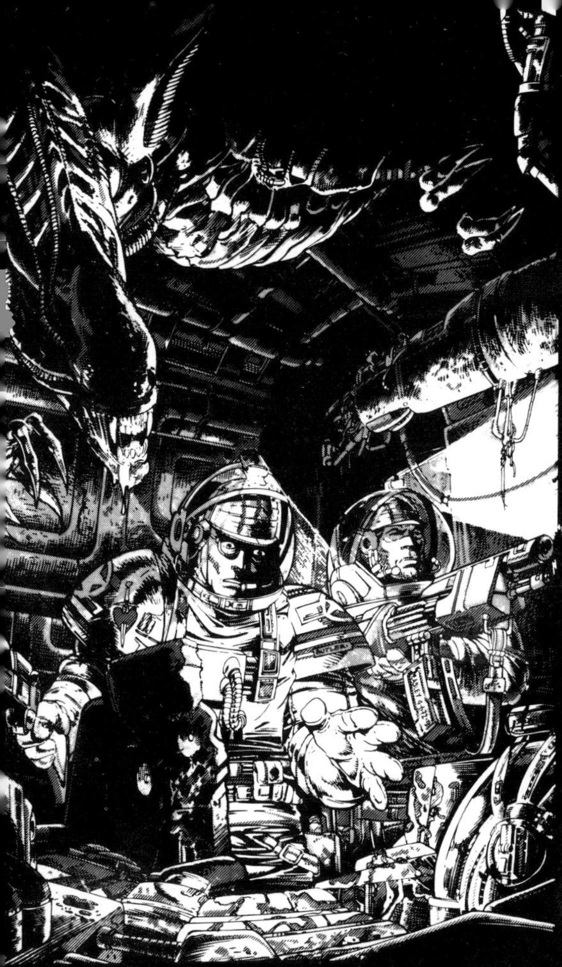

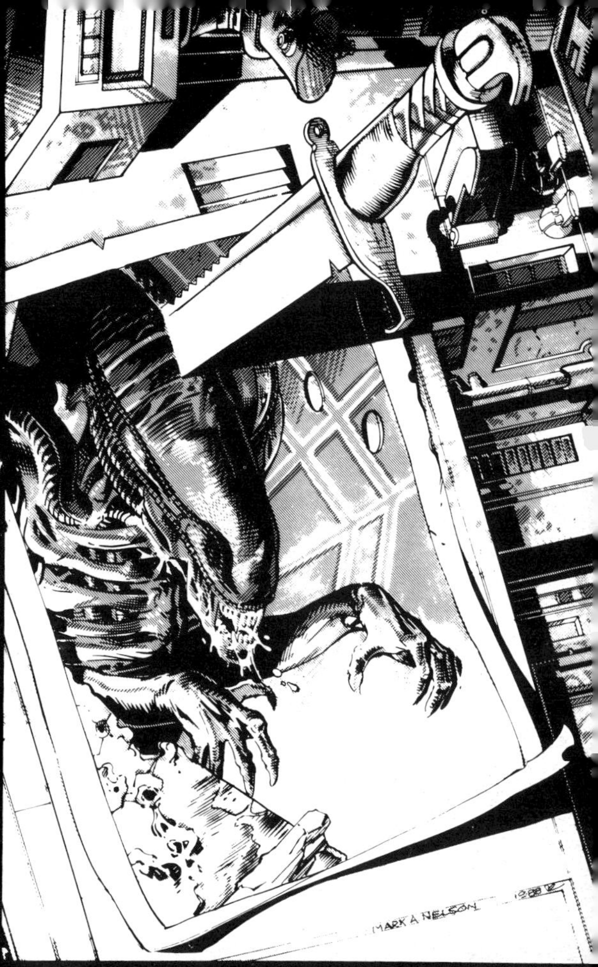
MARK A NELSON

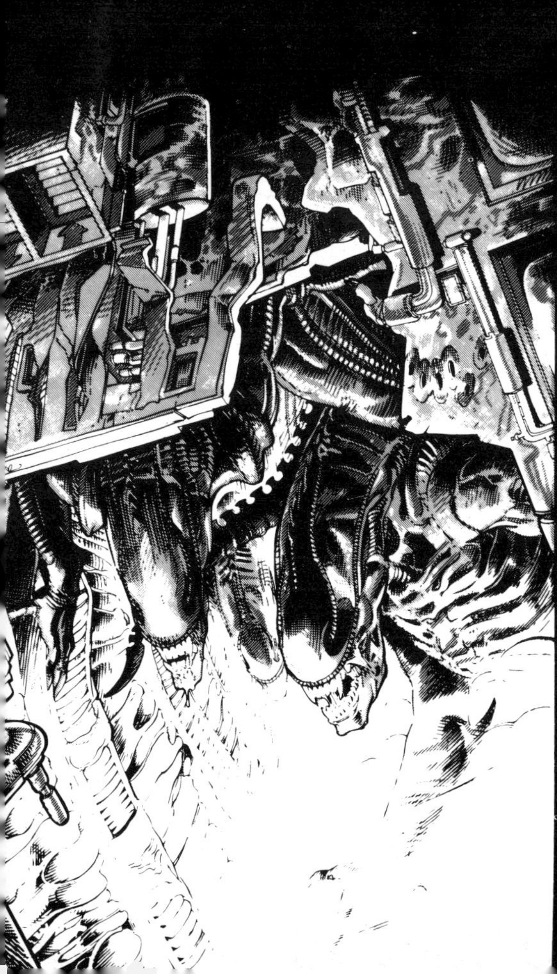

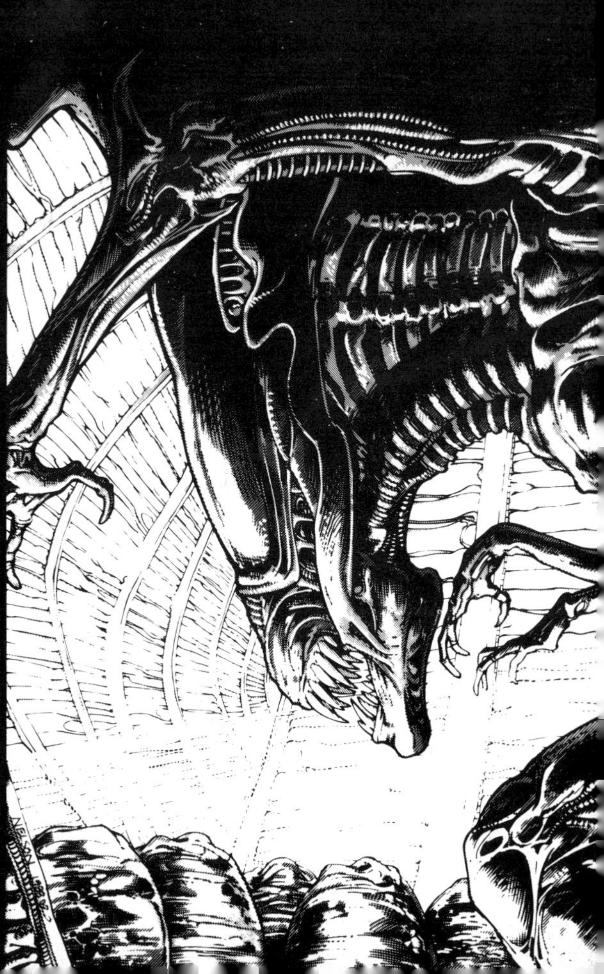

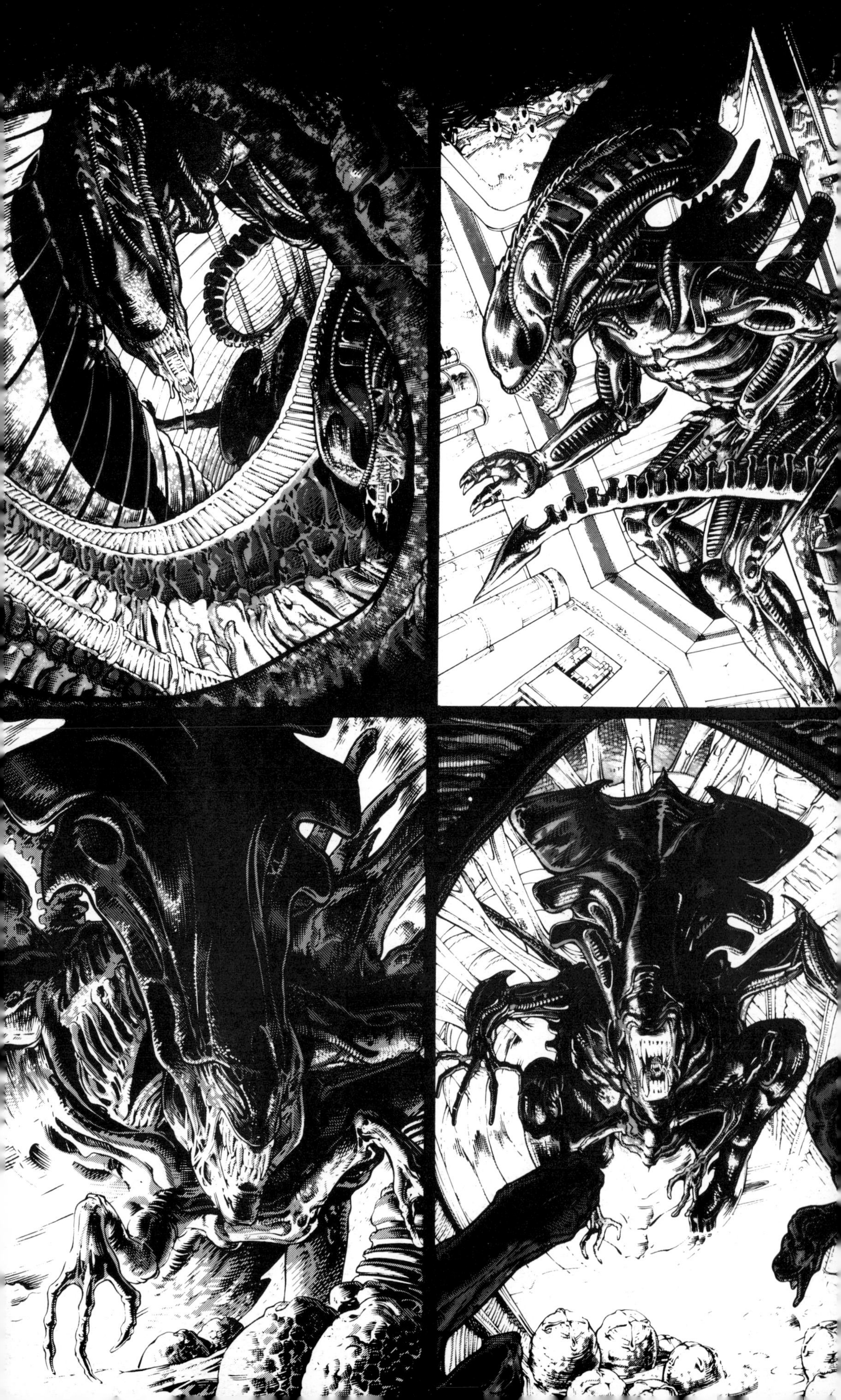